D1563440

THE CAMBRIDGE HISTORY OF
ENGLISH LITERATURE

VOLUME XI

THE PERIOD OF THE FRENCH REVOLUTION

THE
CAMBRIDGE HISTORY OF
ENGLISH LITERATURE

EDITED
BY
SIR A. W. WARD

AND

A. R. WALLER

VOLUME XI

THE PERIOD OF THE FRENCH REVOLUTION

CAMBRIDGE
AT THE UNIVERSITY PRESS
1970

Published by the Syndics of the Cambridge University Press
Bentley House, 200 Euston Road, London N.W. 1
American Branch: 32 East 57th Street, New York, N.Y. 10022

Standard Book Number: 521 04525 8

First edition 1914
New impression 1922
Cheap edition (text only) 1932
Reprinted 1934 1944 1953
1961 1964 1966 1970

Printed in Great Britain
at the University Printing House, Cambridge
(Brooke Crutchley, University Printer)

PREFATORY NOTE

The Cambridge History of English Literature was first published between the years 1907 and 1916. The General Index Volume was issued in 1927.

In the preface to Volume I the general editors explained their intentions. They proposed to give a connected account of the successive movements of English literature, to describe the work of writers both of primary and of secondary importance, and to discuss the interaction between English and foreign literatures. They included certain allied subjects such as oratory, scholarship, journalism and typography, and they did not neglect the literature of America and the British Dominions. The History was to unfold itself, "unfettered by any preconceived notions of artificial eras or controlling dates," and its judgments were not to be regarded as final.

This reprint of the text and general index of the *History* is issued in the hope that its low price may make it easily available to a wider circle of students and other readers who wish to have on their shelves the full story of English literature.

CAMBRIDGE
1932

CONTENTS

viii   *Contents*

CHAPTER I

EDMUND BURKE

EDMUND BURKE, the greatest of English orators, if we measure greatness not by immediate effect alone but by the durability and the diffusive power of that effect, and one of the profoundest, most suggestive and most illuminating of political thinkers, if we may not call a philosopher one who did not elaborate any system and who refrained on principle from the discussion of purely theoretical issues, was an Irishman of the usual blended native and English strain, born (1729) in a family which united the two creeds that divide Ireland more profoundly and fatefully than any distinction of race. His father, a small Dublin solicitor, was a protestant, his mother a catholic. Burke himself was educated in the protestant faith, but his sister adhered to the religion of her mother, and his wife was a catholic who conformed to the Anglican church after her marriage. Burke always professed his protestantism frankly and sincerely— 'We are protestants not from indifference but from zeal'—and the charges that were brought against him of having, at one time or other, been a catholic are without foundation, but his attitude towards the catholic church was at once tolerant and sympathetic. To him, she and every other church were allies in the defence of the religious conception of life which was the centre of all his thought about morals and politics, and of which atheistical Jacobinism was the antithesis. In the last years of his life, he fought for the cause of catholic emancipation in Ireland no less ardently than he opposed a 'regicide' peace with France. The 'directory of Ireland' which upheld protestant ascendancy at Dublin was hardly less odious to him than the Jacobin directory in Paris.

Burke's education was received at Ballitore, under a quaker, whose son, Richard Shackleton, became the chief friend of his early manhood, and at Trinity college, Dublin. Fox believed that Burke 'had not any very nice critical knowledge even of

Latin, still less of Greek,' but was well read in Latin authors, especially Cicero, Vergil, Ovid, Horace and Tacitus, and 'that he imitated the first mentioned of these authors most particularly, as well in his turn of thinking as in his manner of expression.' What survive of Burke's letters to Shackleton point to the same conclusion as Fox's observation, that Burke was a wide and curious reader rather than a minute scholar. Mathematics, logic, history were, each in turn, he tells Shackleton, in one letter, a passion, and all, for a time, yielded to poetry. The letter affords a vivid glimpse into the education of one to whom knowledge, knowledge varied and detailed, was always to be a passion, and who was seldom or never to pen a sentence that has not something in its form to arrest the attention or to give delight. But Burke was not a poet. He could do many things that were beyond the power of his less strenuous and less profound fellow student, Oliver Goldsmith, but he could never have written *The Deserted Village* or *The Vicar of Wakefield*. Nor, magnificent as Burke's prose was to be, picturesque, harmonious and full of cadence, is it ever the prose which affects us as poetry. It is always the prose of an orator, addressed to an audience and aiming at a practical effect. Beauty, as in the meditations of Browne or the oratory of Taylor, is never to Burke an end in itself.

The wide and varied reading which began at Trinity college was, apparently, the chief activity of the nine obscure years (1750—59) which Burke spent as a student of law in London, eating dinners at the Middle Temple, sojourning at country inns or rooms during the vacation with his namesake and, perhaps, kinsman William Burke, and making tentative excursions into letters with an ironical answer to Bolingbroke's posthumous writings in *A Vindication of Natural Society* (1756) and an essay in aesthetics after Addison in *A Philosophical Enquiry into the Origin of our Ideas of the Sublime and Beautiful* (1756). Fulness of mind was the quality of Burke's conversation which impressed Johnson and all who came to know him in these and later years—knowledge and the power of applying that knowledge, 'diversifying the matter infinitely in your own mind.' 'His stream of mind is perpetual,' was Johnson's comment; 'Burke is the only man whose common conversation corresponds with the general fame which he has in the world. Take up whatever topic you please, he is ready to meet you.' Burke owed his success in the House of Commons and its committees not more, perhaps, to his eloquence than to this fulness of mind, to the fact that, whatever topic he handled, America, India, Ireland, finance or trade, he spoke from a copious and close knowledge of the subject.

The works which Burke composed during these years are not of great importance. *A Philosophical Enquiry* is an unequal, and, in the main, rather jejune, treatise of which the fairest criticism is probably Lessing's, that it 'is uncommonly useful as a collection of all the occurrences and perceptions which the philosophers must assume as indisputable in inquiries of this kind.' Burke distinguishes the sublime so sharply from the beautiful that his description of the latter includes little which goes beyond the pretty. More interesting and suggestive is the analysis of the pleasure we take in terrible and painful spectacles—whether a tragedy in the theatre or an execution in the street. But, perhaps, most interesting of all is his discussion of the aesthetic and emotional qualities of words, which he finds to depend less on the images which they evoke than their other properties of sound and association. The business of poetry and rhetoric is 'to affect rather by sympathy than imitation ; to display rather the effect of things on the mind of the speaker, or of others, than to present a clear idea of the things themselves.' The germ of *Laocoon* is contained in these paragraphs.

A Vindication is a much more characteristic and significant document. In parodying the eloquence of Bolingbroke, Burke caught some of the first tones of his own more sonorous and varied harmonies. The conception of the essay, a defence of religion by the application of a *reductio ad absurdum* to Bolingbroke's method of attack, revealed the deep religious spirit in which all Burke's political and social speculation bottoms and roots itself. Bolingbroke had indicted revealed religions by pointing to some of the consequences which, in history, had flowed from dogmatic creeds, and Burke answers him by applying the same method to the criticism of political society.

> Shew me an absurdity in religion, and I will undertake to shew you an hundred for one in political laws and institutions.... If after all, you should confess all these things, yet plead the necessity of political institutions, weak and wicked as they are, I can argue with equal, perhaps superior, force concerning the necessity of artificial religion; and every step you advance in your argument, you add a strength to mine.

But, perhaps, the most interesting quality of the essay is the sidelight that it throws on Burke's temperament, the sensitive, brooding imagination which, coupled with a restless, speculative intellect, seeking ever to illuminate facts by principles, gives tone to Burke's speeches and pamphlets ; for it is this temperament which imparts vividness and colour to the dry details of historical and statistical knowledge, and it is this temperament which at once directs, keeps in check and prescribes its limits to, that speculative, enquiring intellect. In the sentences in which Burke paints the lot of those who bear the burden of political society, the unhappy wretches employed in lead, tin, iron, copper and coal mines, who scarce ever see the light of the sun, the *enfans perdus* of the army of civil society ; in these vivid paragraphs, and not less in his failure to draw from them any but an ironical conclusion, a *reductio ad absurdum* of Bolingbroke's paradoxes, we get an insight into one of the most radical characteristics of Burke's mind. In his later works, he did not often touch directly on the subject of the poor and their lot, though it was a theme, he says, on which he had 'often reflected and never reflected without feeling from it'; but his sensibility was not more acute than his conviction was profound that legislation and political adjustment could do little or nothing to alleviate their lot. Burke's whole life was a prolonged warfare against the folly and injustice of statesmen ; but there was no admixture in his nature of what the old physiologists called the sanguine temperament. His political life was inspired by no gleam of the confidence which animated a statesman like Gladstone. The connection between revealed religion and political society was, to him, a deeper one than the superficial irony of *A Vindication* might suggest. If we confine our view to this life, the lot of humanity must always seem a dubious one. Wise government may lighten the lot of men, it can never make it more than tolerable for the great majority. The effect of this cast of mind on Burke's attitude towards the French revolution, and the interval which it creates between him and the great poets of the romantic revival, with whom he has otherwise much in common, will appear later.

In closing *Reflections on the Revolution in France* (1790), Burke declares that

they come from one, almost the whole of whose public exertion has been a struggle for the liberty of others; from one in whose breast no anger durable or vehement has ever been kindled, but by what he considered as tyranny.

In all those struggles, he declared in 1795, when his hopes for catholic emancipation in Ireland were shattered by the dismissal of Lord Fitzwilliam, he had been unsuccessful.

My sanguine hopes are blasted, and I must consign my feelings on that terrible disappointment to the same patience in which I have been obliged to bury the vexation I suffered on the defeat of the other great, just, and honourable causes in which I have had some share, and which have given more of dignity than of peace to a long laborious life.

A brief enumeration of these 'great, just, and honourable causes' will indicate sufficiently for the purposes of this *History* the outlines of Burke's public career.

After a brief time as secretary to William Gerard Hamilton, then chief secretary for Ireland, Burke entered public life as member for Wendover (1765), to which he was presented by Lord Verney, the friend and fellow-speculator of Burke's kinsman and namesake mentioned above. At the same time, he became secretary to Lord Rockingham, then in power and engaged in repealing Grenville's unfortunate Stamp act. Thenceforth, through the life of that short administration and in the sixteen years of opposition which followed, Burke was the animating spirit of the Rockingham section of the whigs, the germ of the subsequent liberal party. The two chief causes for which he fought during these years were those of the freedom of the House of Commons against the designs of George III and the 'king's friends,' and of the American colonies against the claim of the home government to tax them directly. The writings in which Burke's views in these conflicts are most fully preserved are *Observations on a late publication entitled 'The Present State of the Nation'* (1769), *Thoughts on the Cause of the Present Discontents* (1770), the speech *On American Taxation* (1774), that *On moving his Resolutions for Conciliation with the Colonies* (1775) and *A Letter...to...[the] Sheriffs of...Bristol* (1777)[1]. These, of course, are only those utterances which Burke thought fit to issue to the public. Of his innumerable speeches on these and other subjects, including the great speech against employing Indians in the war, we have only the scantiest records.

Two other topics interested Burke during these years: Ireland and India, and, as the American war drew to an end, they became his chief preoccupation. He had early reflected and written on the iniquity of the penal laws—though the draft which he prepared about 1760—5 was not issued till much later—and he supported and watched with sympathy the policy or revolution which emancipated Irish trade and secured the independence

---

[1] To these may be added the posthumously published *An Address to the King*, drawn up when a secession of the whigs from parliament was contemplated in 1777 and an *Address to the British Colonists in North America*.

of the Irish parliament (1778—82). By reason of his support of
Irish trade, he lost, in 1780, the representation of Bristol, which
his opposition to the American war had gained for him in
1774 ; and *Two Letters...to Gentlemen in the City of Bristol*
(1778), with the *Speech at the Guildhall, in Bristol, previous to
the late Election* (1780), are the noble record of his courage, independence and wisdom in this hour of defeat. In the years following
the outbreak of the French revolution, Burke advocated, with
unabated ardour, the cause of catholics, his views being expressed,
not in speeches, but in long letters to Sir Hercules Langrishe,
Thomas Burgh, his son Richard Burke, Dr Hussey and others.

In the government of our East Indian dominions, Burke was
early interested. It is usual now to affirm dogmatically that he
participated in the speculations of his brother Richard, his
kinsman William and Lord Verney, in East India stock. It may
be so, but is not proved; and Burke himself declared, in 1772,
'I have never had any concern in the funds of the East India company, nor have taken any part whatsoever in its affairs, except when
they came before me in the course of parliamentary proceedings.'
During the attempts made by Lord North's government to regulate
the East India company, Burke was the warm supporter and
diligent adviser of the company (1766—74). It was after 1780
that he became an active member of the committees which
investigated the affairs of India, and, in consequence of what was
revealed, the relentless foe of Warren Hastings and of the privileges
and powers of the company. In the East India bill of 1783, he
flung to the winds that fear of increasing the influence of the
crown which had dictated his earlier support of the company, and
proposed to transfer to parliament and the crown the whole
administration and patronage of India. In 1785, he entered upon
the attack upon Hastings which was to occupy him for ten years.
In the same year, he delivered the famous *Speech on the...Nabob of
Arcot's Private Debts*. The articles of indictment against Hastings,
with the speeches delivered by Burke, fill some six volumes of the
collected works. With the speeches of 1783 and 1785, they are
the record of his labours in this cause, in conducting which he
exhibited at once all the vast range of his knowledge, the varied
powers of his eloquence and the worst errors of taste and judgment of which his great and increasing sensibility of mind made
him guilty in the years from 1780 onwards.

The last great cause in which Burke fought his usual splendid
but losing battle was that of resistance to the French revolution

and the philosophy and spirit of atheistical Jacobinism. Beginning with a speech on the army estimates (9 February 1790), the crusade was continued with ever increasing indignation through the famous *Reflections on the Revolution in France* (1790), *A Letter ... to a Member of the National Assembly* (1791), *An Appeal from the New to the Old Whigs* (1791), *Thoughts on French Affairs* (1791), *Remarks on the Policy of the Allies* (1793), *A Letter ... to a Noble Lord* (1795) and *Letters ... on the Proposals for Peace with the Regicide Directory of France* (1795—7). Burke died in 1797 with his last hopes for justice to Irish catholics shattered, and believing that his country was on the eve of a peace which could be no peace but only a humiliating truce while the enemy made ready to pursue their destructive crusade.

These, in outline, are the campaigns of Burke. Whatever be now our judgment on the questions of a bygone age with which he was concerned, the importance of the principles to which his mind always gravitated, his preoccupation at every juncture with the fundamental issues of wise government, and the splendour of the eloquence in which he set forth these principles, an eloquence in which the wisdom of his thought and the felicity of his language and imagery seem inseparable from one another, an eloquence that is wisdom (not 'seeming wisdom' as Hobbes defined eloquence), have made his speeches and pamphlets a source of perennial freshness and interest.

The first of the pamphlets on public affairs was a brief statement of what had been achieved by the Rockingham administration to restore order and good government at home and in the colonies. The *Observations* are a more detailed defence of that administration against the attack of an anonymous pamphlet, attributed to George Grenville. Grenville, in this pamphlet, defended his own government, which was responsible for the peace of Paris and the first proposal to tax the colonies, and criticised the repeal of the Stamp act. Both the peace and the resolution to tax America were the consequence, he argued, of the charges incurred by the great wars. Burke's reply consists in showing that Grenville had underestimated the power of England and her expanding trade to support these increased charges, and especially had exaggerated the sufferings of this country when compared with those of France, the condition of whose lower classes, and the 'straitness and distraction of whose finances,' seemed, to Burke, at this period, to forbode 'some extraordinary convulsion ... the effect of which on France, and

even on all Europe, it is difficult to conjecture.' But much of
the ground that is covered in this first controversial pamphlet
was again traversed with a more confident step, with a wider
outlook and a loftier eloquence, in the writings which followed
it. Less hampered by the necessity of controverting an opponent,
Burke addresses himself to the fundamental constitutional and
imperial questions at issue in a spirit of elevated political wisdom.

The position which Burke adopts in *Present Discontents*
(1770) is eloquent of the temper in which he ever approached
questions affecting the constitution. The conflict which raged
round Wilkes and the Middlesex election was, he saw clearly,
a conflict between the crown and the constituencies, 'the crown
acting by an instrumental house of commons.' He admitted
the ultimate authority of the people. 'Although government
certainly is an institution of divine authority, yet its forms, and
the persons who administer it, all originate from the people.'
But he shrank from the inference that, if government were
emancipating itself from the control of the people, if the crown
were threatening to deprive the House of Commons of its peculiar
'virtue, spirit and essence,' namely, to be 'the express image of
the feelings of the nation,' it was because the constituencies
themselves had ceased to represent the people. The proposals
to enlarge the number of constituents, coupled, as they were,
with the expedient of triennial parliaments, he always resisted. To Burke, a constitutional state was one in which, in
some degree, a balance had been secured between the various
powers which, in the state, represent the complex nature of man,
and, in the British constitution, as it had taken shape in history ;
and especially with the revolution, he saw, if not an ideal, yet,
the weak and imperfect nature of man considered, a wonderful
balance of powers, aristocracy (the power which springs from
man's natural regard for inherited distinction and privilege) and
property exerting in a healthy and not sinister fashion their
natural and inevitable influence, while the popular will made
itself felt directly and indirectly, by actual and by 'virtual'
representation, as a controlling and, at times, an inspiring influence. He would not do anything to disturb this balance.
'Our constitution stands on a nice equipoise with steep precipices
and deep waters upon all sides of it. In removing it from a
dangerous leaning towards one side there may be a risk of over-
setting it on the other.' He would rather 'by lessening the number
add to the weight and independency of our voters.'

Unable, therefore, to acquiesce in the only practical means by which the people were to recover the control of parliament, and enforce loyalty to principle and party, Burke could only indicate the chief symptom of the disease, the disintegration of party, and elaborate a philosophic defence of party-government, which, since Bolingbroke, it had become the fashion, and was now the interest, of many to decry.

Characteristically, Burke defends party as an indispensable instrument of practicable statesmanship, and as an institution which has its roots in some of the profoundest and most beautiful instincts of the heart; for utility, but utility rooted—if one may so speak—in man's moral constitution, is Burke's court of appeal in all questions of practical politics. Bolingbroke's condemnation of party as identical with faction, and his dream of a patriot king who should govern without reference to party, must have seemed to Burke the result of a view of human nature that was at once too cynical and too sanguine. Party-loyalty might degenerate into self-seeking factiousness, but, in its idea, party is 'a body of men united for promoting by their joint endeavours the national interest upon some particular principle in which they are all agreed'; and the feelings which cement a party are not purely selfish, but include and 'bring into the service and conduct of the common-wealth' 'the dispositions that are lovely in private life.' To be unable to act in loyal concert with others is to condemn ourselves to ineffectiveness, and 'all virtue which is impracticable is spurious,' for 'public life is a situation of power and energy : he trespasses against his duty who sleeps upon his watch, as well as he that goes over to the enemy.' 'In the way which they call party,' he declared, when, at a later juncture, he was charged with factiousness, 'I worship the constitution of your fathers ; and I shall never blush for my political company.'

Though not one of the best, and certainly the most inconclusive, of all Burke's political writings, *Present Discontents* reveals the chief characteristics of his thought and style—the tendency to go at once to the root of the matter, to illuminate facts by principles, and to clothe these in felicitous images and phrases which seem to shed a new light, to 'pour resistless day,' on the moral and political constitution of man. In these things, Burke is without a rival. His aphorisms crowd upon one another and rise out of one another (as was noted by one who heard his first speech in the House of Commons) until the reader can hardly go forward, so many vistas of fresh thought are opened before him.

And Burke's political aphorisms are so pregnant that they distend the mind with the same sense of fulness with which Shakespeare's lines affect the student of the passions and movements of the human heart.

But Burke's oratory was not here illumined by the vision of a large concrete issue in which the future of an empire and the fate of peoples depended on the wisdom or unwisdom of the policy chosen and pursued. That came with the American controversy. It may be clear to the student of history that the causes of that conflict, and of the ultimate separation of the colonies from the mother country, lay deeper than in the schemes of taxation by which Grenville, Townshend and North precipitated matters. It is yet equally certain that, at a great juncture, English statesmanship was found wanting in the wisdom, imagination and sympathy requisite to solve the problem of governing a growing overseas empire. It was his gifts of sympathy and imagination, combined with a wise spirit of practicable statesmanship which distinguishes Burke among all who discussed the colonial question on one side or the other, and have caused his words to bear fruit in the long run, fruitless as, at the moment, they seemed to be.

Two or three principles underlie all that Burke said or wrote on the question. The first of these is that, in practical politics, the guiding star of statesmanship is expediency, not legal or abstract right. Our arguments on political questions may often be

'conclusive as to right, but the very reverse as to policy and practice.' 'Politics ought to be adjusted not to human reasonings but to human nature; of which the reason is but a part and by no means the greatest part.' 'The opinion of my having some abstract right in my favour would not put me much at my ease in passing sentence; unless I could be sure that there were no rights which in their exercise were not the most odious of all wrongs, and the most vexatious of all injustice.'

Such quotations could be multiplied. It is the principle which dictated the coupling of the Declaratory act with the repeal of the Stamp act in 1766, the assertion of a legal right which, in some conceivable emergency, it might be necessary to assert, but the general exercise of which was to be regulated by an entire regard for liberty and the spirit of the British constitution. When the word 'expediency' is given its full moral significance, this principle may be said to be the foundation-stone of Burke's political philosophy.

The second position reiterated in these speeches is that, in the search for what is expedient and, therefore, right, the statesman must be guided by circumstances, of which the most important is the temper and character of the people for whom he is legislating. The statesman, like Bacon's natural philosopher, rules by obeying. The principle is obvious, but its application requires sympathy and imagination, and George III, with his entire lack of both, was a better representative of the average Englishman than either Burke or Chatham. Burke's imagination was filled with the greatness of the American people, the wild, irregular greatness of a people who had grown up to manhood nurtured by a 'wise and salutary neglect.' 'Nothing in history is parallel to it,' he declares in his earliest reply to Grenville. 'All the reasonings about it that are likely to be at all solid must be drawn from its actual circumstances.' And such reasoning will include the all-important consideration that these people are Englishmen with the inherited tradition of political liberty and self-government. The magnificent paragraphs, in the speech *On Conciliation*, devoted to the Americans, their numbers, their enterprise, their spirit and the sources from which it is sustained, are not a purple patch of diffuse, descriptive oratory alone. Like the similar paragraphs on the peoples and civilisation of India, in a later speech, they are an appeal to the imagination of the speaker's audience, that, realising the magnitude of the issue at stake, they may rise above a narrow legalism to the contemplation of what is greater even than America, namely an empire which shall include free peoples, and different civilisations.

But, to discover what is expedient in the complexity of circumstances, which include the tempers of people, is no easy task, and, hence, Burke's third principle, that our safest guide is experience. The past illumines the future, it may be but a few feet in advance, yet sufficiently to walk by.

Again and again and again revert to your own principles—leave America, if she has taxable matter in her, to tax herself.... Leave the Americans as they anciently stood, and these distinctions born of our unhappy contest will die along with it.... Be content to bind America by laws of trade; you have always done it. Let this be your reason for binding their trade. Do not burthen them with taxes; you were not used to do so from the beginning. Let this be your reason for not taxing. These are arguments for states and kingdoms. Leave the rest to the schools; for there only they may be discussed with safety.

Such are the principles which guided Burke in adumbrating in these speeches the lines to be followed in solving the problem the character and complexity of which he alone seems to have grasped, the problem of governing and maintaining the great

empire which Chatham's successful wars had called into existence,

of reconciling the strong presiding power that is so useful towards the con-
servation of a vast, disconnected, infinitely diversified empire, with that
liberty and safety of the provinces, which they must enjoy (in opinion and
practice at least) or they will not be provinces.

He was provided with no theoretical plan that would suit all
circumstances, 'the natives of Hindustan and those of Virginia
alike, the Cutchery court and the grand jury of Salem.' His
appeal was to the wisdom of experience, the spirit of the English
constitution and the magnanimity of statesmen.

Of the American speeches, the greatest, as it is the most
elaborate, is, doubtless, the second, *On Conciliation*; but the first,
On American Taxation, which has more the character of being,
as, indeed, it was, the spontaneous product of debate, combines,
in a wonderful manner, simplicity and directness of reasoning with
ardour and splendour of eloquence. There is something of Rubens
or Rembrandt in the easy, broad, bold strokes with which Burke
paints the history of English policy in America ; the rich, diffused,
warm colouring of the whole ; the concentration of the high lights
and more brilliant tints on the chief episodes and figures—the
upright but narrow-minded Grenville ; Conway, whose face in the
hour of victory was as the face of an angel; the tessellated ministry
of Chatham ; the passing of that great and theatrical figure, and
the dazzling advent of Townshend. Such 'characters' had been a
feature of earlier oratory and history like that of Bolingbroke and
Clarendon—both of them writers with whose work Burke was intimately acquainted—but these, again, are, in Burke's speeches, no
mere rhetorical device or literary ornament. They illustrate his conviction that politics have their roots in human character ; that, to
understand policies, we must study personalities, whether individuals or corporate bodies like the House of Commons and the
National Assembly.

The speech *On Conciliation* is the most greatly builded of all
Burke's speeches, not excepting those on India, which belong rather
to forensic than deliberative oratory. Perhaps its structure is too
elaborate for its immediate purpose. The sonorous parade of the
parallel cases of Wales, Chester and Ireland was not likely to have
much weight with the House of Commons. It is rather a great
concio ad populum et regem, a last impassioned, elevated and
conciliatory appeal to the government and the nation ; and, if
delivered under the conditions of a later period, when it would

have been read in every household on the day following, could not but have reacted with power on both House and government. As it is, it remains some compensation to English literature for the dismemberment of the British empire. Whether we reflect on the art with which it is constructed, the skill with which the speaker winds into the heart of his subject[1] and draws from it the material of his splendid peroration on 'the spirit of the English constitution' and its power to unite, invigorate and vivify the British empire in all its diverse members ; or reflect on the temper, passionate and moving yet restrained and conciliatory, in which the argument is conducted ; or recall simply the greater flights of picturesque eloquence, the description of American industry and enterprise, the imagery in which the speaker clothes his conception of the spirit of the English constitution and the sovereign authority of parliament— the speech takes its own place beside the greatest masterpieces of our literature, the plays of Shakespeare and the poems of Milton. It produces the same impression of supremacy in its own kind ; it abounds, like these, in phrases which seem to enrich our language with a new felicity and dignity : 'enjoyments which deceive the burthen of life,' 'a wise and salutary neglect,' 'I do not know the method of drawing up an indictment against a whole people,' 'man acts from adequate motives relative to his interest, and not on metaphysical speculations,' 'magnanimity in politics is not seldom the truest wisdom ; and a great empire and little minds go ill together.'

In these speeches, Burke is the orator following consciously the ancient tradition of oratory; combining all the styles, the plain, the ornate, the impassioned, each used as the theme requires, in the manner which Cicero, in the *Orator*, describes as constituting the authentic Attic and Demosthenic eloquence. In Burke's *Letter to the Sheriffs of Bristol*, the style is more uniform and unadorned, a vigorous and straight hitting polemic. He sweeps aside with the scorn of which he was a master the cant charges which, in time of war, are levelled at those who question either the foolish policy or arbitrary tyranny of the government, and defines, more clearly than ever, what had always been his conception of the nature of the problem presented by the government of a complex and scattered empire, and the entire competence in the matter of 'prudence, constituted as the god of this lower world,' and prudence only.

What Burke deplored in the American policy of George III

[1] See Boswell's *Life of Johnson* (ed. Hill, G. B., vol. ii, p. 260).

and his ministers was the entire absence of this prudence. He did not take any side in the battle of 'rights,' natural and legal, but stood firmly upon the basis of experience and expediency. In the cases of Ireland and India, he showed that, by a policy based on expediency he understood something very different from opportunism ; that, if he disdained discussion of metaphysical rights, it was not that he did not believe in the existence of rights prior to and above all human conventions and laws, but because he deemed that their abstract definition was either an impossible or a useless labour, apt to hinder, rather than to promote, their practical realisation. But that there is an eternal law of which human law is, at its best, but declaratory is the assumption and the express affirmation underlying his attacks on the tyranny of the penal laws in Ireland and on the claim to arbitrary power in India put forward by Warren Hastings, as the vindication of his treatment of the rajah of Benares. There is a law which neither despot nor people may violate ; any law in contradiction of it not only may, but must, be resisted,

because made against the principle of a superior law, which it is not in the power of any community, or of the whole race of men to alter—I mean the will of Him who gave us our nature, and in giving impressed an invariable law upon it. It would be hard to point out any error more truly subversive of all the wonder and beauty, of all the peace and happiness of human society, than the position—that any body of men have a right to make what laws they please, or that laws can derive any authority from their institution merely and independent of the quality of the subject-matter. No argument of policy, reason of state, or *preservation of the constitution* can be pleaded in favour of such a practice.

So he wrote between 1760 and 1765 in *Tracts relative to the Laws against Popery* in Ireland and his position is unchanged in 1788 when he denounces Warren Hastings.

Arbitrary power is a thing which neither any man can hold nor any man can give.... We are all born in subjection...to one great, immutable, preexistent Law, prior to all our devices, and prior to all our contrivances, paramount to all our ideas, and all our sensations, antecedent to our very existence, by which we are knit and connected in the eternal frame of the Universe, out of which we cannot stir.... Those who give and those who receive arbitrary power are alike criminal, and there is no man but is bound to resist it to the best of his power whenever it shall show its face in the world.

It is in view of this fundamental doctrine that we must interpret Burke's appeals to experience and expediency. In the last resort, Burke's politics are religious, and rest on the conviction that human authority and laws derive from an ultimate Divine authority and law. The bearing of this conviction on Burke's attitude to the incidents and doctrines of the French revolution will appear later. It accounts for the deeper note of passion audible in the speeches and pamphlets on Irish and Indian questions when these are compared with the more persuasive and conciliatory defence of the Americans and the cause of prudence and her great teacher experience.

Ireland, indeed, though perhaps closer to Burke's heart than any other country, fills a comparatively small part of his collected works, though, to a student of his mind and thought, not the least interesting part. He had studied Irish history, and knew from what a tissue of falsehoods the prevalent English view of the rebellion in 1641 and other episodes in that history was woven. He knew the working of the penal laws from within, and for the ancient church whose worship and creed were barred and penalised he had an understanding and sincere respect. None of his writings is less touched with the faults of Burke's great qualities, occasional rhetorical parade, an extravagant sensibility, a tendency to factious exaggeration, than are the letters *To a Peer of Ireland on the Penal Laws* (1782), *To Sir Hercules Langrishe* (1792) and to others which Matthew Arnold collected and republished in 1881, including, with these, the *Speech at the Guildhall, in Bristol* (1780) when Burke closed his connection with that great mercantile constituency. No better and more triumphant *apologia* was ever written. Burke had his back to the wall and, in the end, declined the election. But he was fighting, also, with the consciousness that what he foretold had come true. America was lost. England had sown the wind and was reaping the whirlwind. And part of that harvest was Ireland. The refusal to grant those concessions, for supporting which Burke forfeited the confidence of his constituents (despite *Two Letters* (1778) in defence of his vote), had resulted in a practical revolution in Ireland and 'a universal surrender of all that had been thought the peculiar, reserved, uncommunicable rights of England....We were taught wisdom by humiliation.' And from the same source had flowed the other cause of complaint in Bristol, the repeal of the penal laws. When Burke turns from the justice of the policy of repeal to vindicate its expedience, his argument is summarised in an aposiopesis, 'Gentlemen, America—. He does not spare his critics nor disguise the humiliation of England any the more that he approves of the measures of justice which that humiliation has exacted from an unwilling country. And he is equally fearless in his defence of his conduct as regards the defeated bill for the relief of debtors, and the amendment of the 'gross and cruel facts in our law.' The only purple patch in the speech is the brief panegyric upon Howard, the reformer of prisons. Otherwise, the style is as simple and nervous as the prose of Swift, but fired with a nobler passion and illumined by a wider vision of general principles.

If Ireland were a subordinate though a very real interest to Burke, India was the centre of his activity from 1780 until the French revolution came, not to supersede India but to share with it and Ireland his thoughts and labours. From the problem of the government of colonies peopled by Englishmen, habituated to freedom and jealous of authority, he turned to the other problem with which Chatham's wars had also embarrassed England, the problem of governing a great empire of peoples who had never known any other rule than an absolute despotism, a despotism which, through an era of anarchy, was passing, or had passed, to a trading company and its ill-controlled and ill-remunerated servants. 'The proud day of Asia is passed.' The relaxation and dissolution of the Mogul government had made the Indian company what the Roman law had supposed 'irreconcilable to reason and property— *eundem Negotiatorem et Dominum*; the same power became the general trader, the same power became the supreme lord.'

The Indian speeches are distinguished from the American not alone by the greater passion that inspires them but by partaking more of the nature of forensic and, occasionally, epideictic or panegyric, than of deliberative oratory[1]. Each of them is an indictment—that *On Mr Fox's East-India Bill* (1783) of the East India company and its administration; that *On the Nabob of Arcot's Debts* (1785) of Dundas's India board for its protection of the nabob's creditors; and the series of speeches with which Burke opened and closed the trial of Warren Hastings, an impeachment which, for variety and vehemence of oratory, has no parallel except in Cicero's *Verrines*. And they are not only indictments—like the speech on the employment of Indians in the American war—but legal indictments, in which proof is interwoven with narrative and exposition.

The distinction is of importance, because it explains the fact that these speeches, despite the occasional splendour of their eloquence, are of less vital interest than the American, Irish, or French revolution speeches and pamphlets; and because, in oratory of this description, the faults of Burke's judgment and temperament made themselves, at times, only too apparent. It is impossible to read the most eloquent of indictments, especially of

---

[1] Adopting Aristotle's classification in *Rhetoric*.

individuals, based on alleged facts, without the wish to hear the other side. The force of the indictment, we feel, depends on the strength of the evidence advanced in support of the speaker's charges, and these, in Aristotle's phrase, are ἄτεχνοι πίστεις, proofs which depend neither on the arguments nor the eloquence of the orator but on the credibility of witnesses, and the authenticity and interpretation of documents. And the more vehement, the less judicial in tone, the orator, the more insistent becomes the thoughtful reader's demand for relative evidence. But, in the Indian speeches, Burke's tone is never judicial ; when Hastings is in question, it is never either temperate or fair. The Verrine orations of Cicero are not more fiercely vituperative than the speeches of Burke before the House of Lords. But, from what we know otherwise of Verres, he was all that Cicero tells us. The history of Warren Hastings's government has been the subject of careful investigation, and, whatever we may think of his faults, he was certainly no Verres. Burke's whole treatment of that great case was vitiated by his determination to find the sole motive of every crime with which Hastings was charged in a base, selfish, corrupt cupidity,—'Money is the beginning, the middle, and the end of every kind of act done by Mr Hastings—pretendedly for the Company, but really for himself.' But, of all charges, this is the least true. Hastings was not scrupulous in his choice of means, and he was responsible for acts both of extortion and cruelty, but the motives which actuated them were public not private, the service of the company and the preservation of British rule in India at a season of the utmost peril. The fury with which Burke assailed Hastings's character was, therefore, misdirected. He fledged the arrows of his eloquence with the vindictive malice of Francis, and, in so doing, obscured and weakened what is the main burden and justification of his indictment, and of all his labours in the cause of India—the distinction, which he places in the forefront of his opening addresses to the House of Lords, and recurs to in his final replies, between absolute authority and arbitrary power. In so far as he meets Hastings's claim to arbitrary power by an appeal to the authority of law as formulated in the codes of the Hindoos, the Mohammedans and the Tartars, the argument is more interesting ('there never was such food for the curiosity of the human mind as is found in the manners of this people' *i.e.* the Gentûs or Hindoos) than relevant, for, at the time when Warren Hastings was struggling with the Mahrattas and Hyder Ali, all law in India was in suspension. If, in the anarchy which prevailed, Hastings had fettered himself by the ideal prescripts of Timur or Mohammed, the British power in India would, indeed, have been Swift's 'single man in his shirt' contending with eleven armed men. But, in his appeal to the eternal laws which no human power may abrogate any more than it may dispense with physical laws, Burke (as has been already indicated) was stating the fundamental principle of his political philosophy, and, at the same time, helping, almost as effectively as Hastings himself, to lay the foundation of British rule in India. In the American and Indian speeches of Burke is contained, one might say without exaggeration and making full allowance for the faults of the Indian series, the grammar of British empire—the free self-government of white communities, the just rule of peoples for whom representative government is impracticable, the qualification of absolute government by an entire regard for the welfare and the prejudices of the governed.

The great instrument of Burke's oratory in the Indian, as in the American, speeches is the philosophical imagination. The same faculty that evoked a vivid and instructive picture of the spirit and enterprise of a people 'yet in the gristle' elaborates, in the speech on Fox's East India bill, a sublimer and more moving vision of the ancient civilisation of India,

princes once of great dignity, authority, and opulence...an ancient and venerable priesthood, the depository of their laws, learning and history, the guides of the people while living and their consolation in death...millions of ingenious manufacturers and mechanics; millions of the most diligent and not the least intelligent, tillers of the earth...almost all the religions professed by men, the Braminical, the Mussulman, the Eastern and the Western Christian.

And, over against this picture, he places that of English rule, the rule of merchants intent only on profits and corrupt gain. The sentences seem to ring for ever in the ear, in which the orator describes the young men who ruled India, with all the avarice of age and all the impetuosity of youth, rolling in wave after wave, birds of prey and passage who leave no trace that England has been represented in India 'by any thing better than the ourang-outang or the tyger,' for 'their prey is lodged in England; and the cries of India are given to seas and winds, to be blown about at every breaking up of the monsoon over a remote and unhearing ocean.' But the most terrible and the most faithful picture of British misrule which Burke painted, and of what that misrule meant for the wretched natives, is that in the speech *On the Nabob of Arcot's Debts*; and nothing in Burke's speeches is more Miltonic in its sublimity and gloom than the description of the vengeance taken by Hyder Ali

on the 'abused, insulted, racked and ruined' Carnatic. Of the
epideictic or panegyric oratory with which Burke occasionally
illumines his tenebrous and fiery denunciations of waste and
oppression, the Indian speeches afford the most sustained and
elaborate example in the eulogy of Fox which closes the speech
on the East India bill, 'a studied panegyric; the fruit of much
meditation ; the result of the observation of nearly twenty years.'

These words were spoken in 1783. In 1791, that friendship was
formally terminated, and Burke and Fox met as strangers in the
conduct of the long impeachment. It was not a private quarrel
which alienated them. It was the French revolution. That great
upheaval agitated Burke's sensitive and passionate imagination
certainly no less than the misgovernment of India, but it did so in
a way that has left a more interesting record in his work, for it
quickened and intensified the activity of his speculation. In
judging of events and persons, his mind was, perhaps, not less
prejudiced ; but, in the main, the controversy which he waged was
not forensic but deliberative, a discussion not of facts and proofs
but of principles and the spirit that inspires or is inspired by
principles. He was at war with the philosophy and with the
temper of the revolution. He was driven back on first principles ;
and the flame which was kindled in his imagination served to
irradiate and illumine every vein and nerve in the complex and
profound philosophy of human nature and political society which
had underlain and directed all that, since he entered public life
and earlier, he had done or written as statesman and thinker.

It is a mistake to represent Burke as by philosophical principle
and temperament necessarily hostile to revolution or rebellion.
Politically, he was the child of the revolution of 1688, and an
ardent champion of the principles of that revolution. He condoned
and approved the revolution (for as such he regarded it) by
which Ireland, in 1781, secured freedom of trade and legislative
independence. He believed that the Americans had done right in
resisting by arms the attempt to tax them directly. Moreover,
the fundamental principle of Burke's political philosophy, his
conviction that behind all human law was a divine law which
human authority could never override, carried with it, as the
same principle did for the Calvinists of Holland or for the
puritans of England in the sixteenth and seventeenth centuries,
the possibility that it might be a duty to rebel. Burke and
Rousseau are agreed on one point, that force is not right,
that no *force majeure* can justify a man in renouncing his

liberty, or, what is the same thing, his responsibility to God. It was not a revolt against legitimate authority, it was not even any radical reconstruction of the machinery of the state (though Burke always distrusted the wisdom and, even, the possibility of radical reformation), which made him the enemy of the revolution. He admits, in his *Reflections,* that such reconstruction was required, and would have had the Assembly set to work with an eye upon their old constitution to guide them, and, where that failed them, on the British constitution. What roused Burke's passionate antagonism was the philosophy of the revolution and the spirit of the revolution, an abstract philosophy which seemed to him false to the fundamental facts of man's moral and political nature, a spirit which he detested as the relentless enemy alike of liberty and religion—of that religion which alone can teach men to subordinate power to duty, to accept the mysterious dispensation which assigns to each of us his place in society, which alone can guide us in life and console us in death. His foe was the same in this as in all his previous conflicts,—arbitrary power, not claiming legal right for its justification, as the British parliament had claimed it in the case of America, nor inherited absolute authority, as Hastings had in the case of Cheyte Sing and the begums, but asserting the indisputable authority of the people, of democracy. Compared with such a tyranny, every other seemed less deplorable.

Under a cruel prince men have the balmy consolation of mankind to assuage the smart of their wounds; they have the plaudits of the people to animate their generous constancy under suffering; but those who are subjected to wrong under multitudes are deprived of all external consolations. They seem deserted by mankind; overpowered by a conspiracy of their whole species.

Reflections on the Revolution in France (1790) is the most important manifesto of Burke's anti-revolutionary crusade. A critic has remarked, with some justice, that the writings on the revolution 'are perhaps the worse written for not being speeches... they did not call out Burke's architectonic faculty[1].' But Burke was not less a master of disposition than of invention, and there is an art in the loosely ordered sequence of his *Reflections.* Such an elaborate architecture as that of the speech *On Conciliation* would have been out of place in dealing with what was still fluid. None of the fatal issues of the revolution had yet emerged, but, studying its principles and its temper, the trend of its shifting and agitated currents, Burke foresees them all, down to the advent of the popular general as the saviour of society. Beginning with Price's

[1] Oliver Elton, *A Survey of English Literature* (1912), vol. I.

sermon, the occasion of his pamphlet, he endeavours to show that the revolution of 1688 did not involve any breach of the hereditary principle, or invalidate the inherited right of the king to govern independent of the choice of the people. He recurred at great length to this in the later *Appeal from the New to the Old Whigs*. The argument is necessarily inconclusive[1], yet not without importance as establishing the fact that the success of the revolution was due to the skill with which its managers had succeeded in transferring unimpaired to the new government the authority of the old. This was just what the assembly had failed to do; and, hence, the necessity for the authority of the guillotine and the sword. A brief contrast of the English revolution with the French leads, naturally, to just such a sketch of the personal factor in the Assembly—the classes from which it was drawn —as, at an earlier date, in the speech *On American Taxation*, when discussing the source of colonial discontent, he had given of English statesmen and the House of Commons. Recurring to Price's eulogy of the French revolution, he is led rapidly on to what was the distinctive character of that revolution, the subject of Price's approval and Burke's condemnation. It lay in the fact that, unlike all other revolutions, the French started from no mere desire for the redress of grievances or shifting of the centre of gravity of government, but promulgated a new philosophy, a new gospel, judged by which all governments are usurpations, and that its watchword was 'the rights of man.'

Against these there can be no prescription; against these no argument is binding: these admit no temperament and no compromise: anything withheld from their full demand is so much of fraud and injustice.

The paragraphs on the abstract rights of man and the inevitable tendency of such a doctrine to identify right with power leads Burke back again to Price and his exultation over the leading in triumph of the king and queen from Versailles. And, thence, he passes to an impassioned outburst on the spirit of the revolution, the temper of those in whom the religion of the 'rights of man' has 'vanquished all the mean superstitions of the heart,' has cast out all the sentiments of loyalty and reverence which constitute 'the decent drapery of life,' serving 'to cover the defects of our naked shivering nature, and to raise it to dignity in our own estimation.' From these two sections, on 'the rights of man' and the spirit of their devotees,

---

[1] Burke had himself declared, in 1777, that 'to the free choice therefore of the people, without either king or parliament, we owe that happy establishment, out of which both king and parliament were regenerated.' *An Address to the King*. This was not published till after Burke's death.

s all that follows—the vindication of prejudice, the
f religion in the state and defence of an established
view of the progress of democratic tyranny in France
in the abolition of nobility and confiscation of the church and the
examination of the constitution set up by the Assembly—the
legislature, executive, judicature and army, their consistence with
the doctrine of 'the rights of man' and their probable doom.

To the charge of inconsistency which the publication of
Reflections and his speeches in the House brought upon him,
Burke replied in *An Appeal from the New to the Old Whigs*
(1791), published anonymously and written in the third person.
From a general defence of the consistency of his denunciation of
the French revolution with his defence of the American colonies
and proposals for economic reform, Burke proceeds to elaborate
his defence of the view he had put forward in *Reflections* of
the revolution of 1688, as preserving, not destroying, inherited,
prescriptive rights ; and closes with an elaboration of his views on
the prescriptive, inherited character of all the institutions and
rights which constitute a state ; the involuntary, inherited nature
of all our most sacred ties and duties.　Taken together, these two
pamphlets form the most complete statement of Burke's anti-
revolutionary philosophy, which his other writings on the subject
serve only to amplify and adorn.

It is in his attack on the abstract and individualistic doctrine of
the 'rights of man' that Burke develops most fully this philosophy
of society, and breaks most decisively with the mechanical and
atomic political theory which, inherited from Locke, had dominated
the thought of the eighteenth century.　Over against the view of
the state as the product of a 'contract' among individuals, whose
'rights' exist prior to that contract, and constitute the standard
by which at every stage the just claim of society on the individual
is to be tested, he develops the conception of the individual as
himself the product of society, born to an inheritance of rights
(which are 'all the advantages' for which civil society is made)
and of reciprocal duties, and, in the last resort, owing these concrete rights (actual rights which fall short in perfection of those
ideal rights 'whose abstract perfection is their practical defect')
to convention and prescription.　Society originates not in a free
contract but in necessity, and the shaping factor in its institutions
has not been the consideration of any code of abstract preexistent
rights ('the inherent rights of the people') but 'convenience.'
And, of these conveniences or rights, two are supreme, government

and prescription, the existence of 'a power out of themselves by which the will of individuals may be controlled,' and the recognition of the sacred character of prescription. In whatever way a particular society may have originated—conquest, usurpation, revolution ('there is a sacred veil to be drawn over the beginnings of all government')—in process of time, its institutions and rights come to rest upon prescription. In any ancient community such as that of France or Britain, every constituent factor, including what we choose to call the people, is the product of convention. The privileges of every order, the rights of every individual, rest upon prescription embodied in law or established by usage. This is the 'compact or agreement which gives its corporate form and capacity to a state,' and, if it is once broken, the people are

a number of vague, loose individuals and nothing more. Alas! they little know how many a weary step is to be taken before they can form themselves into a mass which has a true politic personality [1].

There is, therefore, no right of revolution, or rebellion at will. The 'civil, social man' never *may* rebel except when he *must* rebel. Revolution is always the annulment of some rights. It will be judged in the last resort by the degree in which it preserves as well as destroys, and by what it substitutes for what it takes away. At its best, revolution is 'the extreme medicine of the constitution,' and Burke's quarrel with the Assembly is that they have made it 'its daily bread'; that, when the whole constitution of France was in their hands to preserve and to reform, they elected only to destroy.

Burke's denunciation of the spirit or temper of the revolution follows as naturally from his philosophy of the state as that from the doctrine of the revolutionists. 'The rights of man' was a religion, a fanaticism expelling every other sentiment, and Burke meets it with a philosophy which is also a religion, no mere theory of the state but a passionate conviction. He and the revolutionists were at one in holding that there is a law, a principle superior to positive law, by which positive law must be tested. Had he not declared that there were positive rights which, in their exercise, were 'the most odious of all wrongs, and the most vexatious of all injustice'? But, whereas they sought this law in abstract rights prior to, and independent of, the state, for Burke, the essential condition of every 'right' is the state itself. There can be no right which is incompatible with the very existence of the state. Justice is not to be sought in or by the destruction of

[1] *An Appeal from the New to the Old Whigs.*

that which has given us the idea of justice, has made us the moral
beings we are, for it is the privilege of 'that wonderful structure
Man' 'to be in a great degree the creature of his own making,'
and 'He who gave our nature to be perfected by our virtue willed
also the necessary means of its perfection; He willed therefore the
state[1].' The state is no mere prudential contract for material ends,
security of property and life (though these are its primary ends
and fundamental conditions); it is the partnership between men
from which has sprung science and art and virtue—all human
perfection; a partnership which links one generation to another,
the living to the dead and the unborn. It is more; 'each contract
of each particular state is but a clause in the great primeval
contract of eternal society,' which is the law of God and 'holds all
physical and all moral natures, each in their appointed place.' To
the religion of the natural man, Burke thus opposes the religion
of the state, of man as civilisation has made him, for 'Art is man's
nature.' The established church is the recognition of the sacred
character of the state. The prejudices and sentiments which
attach us to the community are not to be abolished by the 'con-
quering light of reason,' but cherished as the very substance of the
moral reason. It is this thought which underlies Burke's defence
of prejudice. Following, as it does, the highly coloured threnody
on the fate of the queen of France and the decay of the sentiments of loyalty and chivalry, Burke has exposed himself to the
charge of identifying moral feeling with fleeting and artificial
sentiments. But this is only partly just. Burke does not really
confound the sentiments which adorn life with those which sustain
life, the draperies of the moral life with its flesh and blood. His
defence of prejudice against the claims of a fanatical abstract
reason is just such a recognition of the nature of moral reason as
that which turned Wordsworth from Godwin's 'political justice'
to the emotions and prejudices of the peasant.

To Burke, thus encountering the philosophy and fanaticism of
the French revolution with a deeper philosophy and an equal zeal,
war with France was a crusade ; and he pressed for it passionately

[1] It must be admitted, too, that, at this stage, Burke is more disposed than when
he wrote the *Tracts relative to the Laws against Popery* (see the first quotation at p. 14),
or defended the American rebellion or the Irish 'revolution,' to identify the state with
the particular constitution of a concrete state, Britain or France ; to refuse to consider
any claim of 'right' which is incompatible with this—a position which comes near to
denying any right of reform at all. It is against this view that Wordsworth protested
in his early *Apology for the French Revolution*. But it is a mistake to take this rejection
of reform as the cardinal article of Burke's political creed. His thought, in its whole
drift and content, has a deeper significance.

before Pitt's hand was forced by the invasion of Holland.
The rest of Burke's life was mainly devoted to the crusade
against Jacobinism at home and abroad, and it is well to
understand what he understood by the term. It is not republicanism, nor even democracy, though it is, he seems to think, that
to which a pure democracy inevitably tends. Burke did not
believe that this country was at war with the French people, for
there was no French public. 'The country is composed but of
two descriptions ; audacious tyrants and trembling slaves.' By
Jacobinism, he understood the tyranny of unprincipled and irresponsible ability or talent[1]—talent divorced from religious awe and
all regard for individual liberty and property, supporting itself
by appealing to the passions and ignorance of the poor. This was
the character of the government of France as one set of rulers
succeeded another in what he calls 'the tontine of infamy,' and
the war which it waged was a war of conquest essential to its own
existence. Peace with such a power could only be made on the
same conditions as it was to be made with the Saracens in the full
tide of conquest. This is the burden of the impassioned and lurid
Letters on a Regicide Peace (1797), which, like the denunciations
of Warren Hastings, tend to weary us, by the reiteration of shrill
vituperation, the want of coolness and balance of judgment. Burke
was, in himself, 'the counter-revolution,' and, as in the sixteenth
and seventeenth centuries, excess begat excess.

This is not the place for a full discussion of Burke's treatment
of the French revolution. He died before any final issue was even
in sight. It might be urged, with some justice, that he was so
moved by the furious symptoms of the disease that he never
thoroughly gauged its deeper sources or foresaw the course it
must ultimately run, clearly as he did foresee its immediate issues.
It might be contended that, fleeing from one abstraction, he drew
near to another, and consecrated prescription, inherited right, when
judged and condemned by that expediency which is the sanction
of prescription. In a history of literature, it is more interesting
to note that he had not enough faith in his own principles ; for
the deficiency reveals the writer's temperament. Believing, as he
did, that society and the particular form which society has taken
is of divine origin, that in the history of a nation was revealed
the working of providence shaping the moral and spiritual being
of those who composed it, he is singularly fearful of the issue.

---

[1] *Letter to William Smith* (1795) and the first of the *Letters on a Regicide Peace*
(1797).

Was the British constitution which the political wisdom of generations had shaped so wanting in elasticity that it could endure no change, adapt itself to no new conditions? Could the folly of the Assembly, the madness of the Terror, the cynical corruption of the Directory undo, in a few years, the work of centuries and permanently alter the character of the French people? The France which emerged from the revolution was, in all essential respects, De Tocqueville has argued, the France of the *ancien régime.* What disappeared was already dead. In the *Code Napoléon,* which embodied the legal outcome of the revolution, law became 'the expression of settled national character, not of every passionate and casual mood.'

We touch here on a trait of Burke's character which is evident in his earliest pamphlet, the ironical reply to Bolingbroke, the want of any sanguine strain in his mental constitution, or, if one cares to put it so, of faith. Despite all that he had said of the wisdom latent in prejudice ; despite the wonder and admiration with which, in the speech *On Conciliation,* he contemplated a people governing themselves when the machinery of government had been withdrawn; the advent of democracy inspired him with anxiety qualified neither by faith in the inherent good sense and rectitude of human nature, nor by any confidence in the durability of inherited sentiment and prejudice. Nothing, it seemed to him, but the overruling providence of God could have evolved from the weak and selfish natures of men the miracle of a free state with all its checks and balances and adjustments to the complex character and manifold wants of the physical and spiritual nature of man ; and, in a moment, the work of ages might be undone, the 'nice equipoise' overset, the sentiments and prejudices of ages destroyed, and 'philosophy' and 'Jacobinism' be among us, bringing with them anarchy and the 'end of all things.' Nothing marks so clearly the interval between Burke's temperament and that of the romantic revival as it is revealed in Wordsworth. What Burke has of the deeper spirit of that movement is seen not so much in the poetic imagery of his finest prose as in the philosophical imagination which informs his conception of the state, in virtue of which he transcends the rationalism of the century. His vision of the growth of society, his sense of something mysterious and divine at work in human institutions and prejudices, of something at once sacred and beautiful in the sentiments of chivalrous loyalty and honour, in the stately edifice of the British constitution with all its orders, in the ancient civilisation

of India—all these have in them more than Sir Walter Scott's love
of a romantic and picturesque past. There is in them the same
mood of mind as is manifest in Wordsworth's sense of something
mysterious and divine in the life of nature and the emotions of
simple men, which links the eternal process of the stars to the
moral admonitions of the human heart. But there is a difference.
The illusion or faith, call it what one will, which made lyrical the
prose of Rousseau and inspired the youthful Wordsworth when he
hailed the French revolution as a new era in the history of the race,

> Bliss was it in that dawn to be alive,
> But to be young was very heaven,

was a stranger to Burke's mind; nor has the stoicism with
which he contemplates the successive defeat of all his undertakings anything in common with the soberer optimism, the
cultivation of a steadfast hopefulness, which, in Wordsworth's mind,
succeeded to disillusionment, and rested on his faith in the invinci-
bility of the moral reason. Wordsworth the stamp-distributor
did not remain a democrat, but Wordsworth the poet derived from
his early experiences of the peasantry a faith in human nature, in
those who go to make the people, which Burke's experience of
'the swinish multitude' at contested elections, and in Gordon riots,
never permitted to his reflective mind and sensitive temperament.
In his crusade against Jacobinism and a regicide peace, Burke
appealed to kings and nobles and the duty of a government to
guide the people; in continuing the crusade against Napoleon,
Wordsworth delighted to note that the firmest opposition came
from the peasantry of Spain and the Tyrol: 'In the conduct of
this argument,' he writes, in *The Convention of Cintra*, 'I am not
speaking to the humbler ranks of society: it is unnecessary: they
trust in nature and are safe.'

This temper of Burke's mind is reflected in his prose. In
essential respects, in idiom, structure and diction, the prose of
Burke is that of his period, the second half of the eighteenth
century. To the direct, conversational prose of Dryden and Swift,
changed social circumstances and the influence of Johnson had
given a more oratorical cast, more dignity and weight, but, also,
more of heaviness and conventional elegance. From the latter faults,
Burke is saved by his passionate temperament, his ardent imagination and the fact that he was a speaker conscious always of his
audience. Burke loves a generalisation as much as Johnson, and his
generalisations are profounder, more philosophic, if, like Johnson's,

they begin in common sense. But Burke never fails to illuminate his
generalisations by concrete and glowing imagery. And the splendour of his imagery, the nervous vigour of his style, its pregnancy,
connect his prose with that of the great sixteenth and seventeenth
century writers, Hooker and Milton and Browne and Clarendon.
Though he does not abuse quotation, like some of the seventeenth
century writers, he employs it with great effect, weaving the
quotation with consummate skill into the texture of his own prose :

'Old religious factions,' he says, speaking of the unitarians, 'are volcanoes
burnt out. But when a new fire breaks out...when men come before us, and
rise up like an exhalation from the ground, they come in a questionable shape,
and we must exorcise them, and try whether their intents be wicked or
charitable; whether they bring airs from Heaven or blasts from Hell.

What Burke's prose has not is the lyrical note of the, not
more imaginative, but more romantic, prose of Wordsworth and
Coleridge, of Carlyle and Ruskin ; the note, not of exaltation,
which was often Burke's mood, but of exultation, a mood with
which he never was acquainted.

A rapid review of the main causes which engaged Burke's
oratory has necessitated the omission in their proper places of one
or two speeches and writings which deserve notice in even a short
sketch. The quietest, the lightest in tone—if Burke's oratory can
ever be so described—is the speech on economical reform of
February 1780. It forms a point of rest between the earlier and
the later storms. In no other speech is Burke so content to be
simply persuasive, at times genial and amusing ; and the philosophical colour of his mind, the tendency to elevate the discussion
of every point by large generalisations, the fruit of long study
and deep insight, gains a new interest from the absence of the
passion with which his wisdom is usually coloured or set aglow.
The exordium, after stating the end of his reforms to be not
merely economy but the reduction of corrupt influence, winds its
way into the subject by a skilful suggestion of the odium which
such proposals must excite and of the necessity which alone has
induced him to incur that odium—a necessity arising at once from
the dire straits in which the war has involved the nation's finances
and from the imperative demand of the people. The first consideration is skilfully heightened by a reference to the reform of
French finances under Louis XVI and Necker—'The French have
imitated us ; let us, through them, imitate ourselves ; ourselves
in our better and happier days.' The second is used to point the
difference in characteristic fashion between a timely and temperate,

and a late and violent, reform. The principles which have shaped
his proposals are then enunciated and the details elaborated with
a knowledge of the expedients and methods of finance which
justifies Burke's claim that he had made political economy an
object of his studies before 'it had employed the thoughts of
speculative men in other parts of Europe.'   And, at every turn, the
dry details of economy are illuminated by broad generalisations,
on not the economic only, but the moral, aspects of the question—
'Kings are naturally lovers of low company'—and by the colours
of a rich imagination, as in the description of the last relics of
feudal institutions :

> Our palaces are vast inhospitable halls. There the bleak winds, there 'Boreas
> and Eurus and Caurus and Argestes loud,' howling through the vacant
> lobbies,and clattering the doors of deserted guard-rooms, appal the imagination
> and conjure up the grim spectres of departed tyrants—the Saxon, the Norman,
> and the Dane; the stern Edwards and fierce Henries—who stalk from deso-
> lation to desolation, through the dreary vacuity and melancholy succession
> of chill and comfortless chambers.

Burke's humour, when not barbed and winged with scorn, is somewhat elephantine. The paragraph on the difficulties which beset
Lord Talbot's attempts to reform the Household from the fact that
'the turnspit in the king's kitchen was a member of Parliament'
is a good example of his over-elaborate, somewhat turgid art.
The peroration, on the other hand, on the will of the people
and the responsibility of the House to its constituents, with a
covert reference to the corrupt influence of the court, illustrates the
power of this diffuseness, this elaboration of the details of a figure,
to adorn a sentiment which comes warm from the speaker's heart :

> Let us cast away from us, with a generous scorn, all the love-tokens and
> symbols that we have been vain and light enough to accept;—all the bracelets
> and snuff-boxes and miniature pictures, and hair devices, and all the other
> adulterous trinkets that are the pledges of our alienation, and monuments of
> our shame. Let us return to our legitimate home and all jars and quarrels
> will be lost in embraces.... Let us identify, let us incorporate ourselves with the
> people. Let us cut all the cables and snap the chains which tie us to an un-
> faithful shore, and enter the friendly harbour that shoots far out into the
> main its moles and jettees to receive us.

Fifteen years after this speech, the government of Pitt was
attacked for granting a pension to Burke, and, in accepting it, he
was said to have been false to the principles laid down by himself
on the subject of economy. The chief critics of the pension in
the House of Lords were the duke of Bedford and the earl of
Lauderdale. Burke replied in *A Letter to a Noble Lord*, the
finest example of his blended irony, philosophy, feeling and

imagination. As a master of pure irony, Burke is surpassed by Swift, who is at once more unscrupulous and less elaborate, more inventive and venomous. Except when he had to deal with those whom he regarded as the enemies of the human race, the professors of 'the cannibal philosophy of France,' Burke could never have attacked anyone with the venom with which Swift assailed Wharton. It is the truth which gives such deadly force to Burke's ironical description of the duke of Bedford, this noble champion of the rights of man, as himself the creature, the Leviathan, of royal favour and prescriptive right. Burke has but to elaborate the fact with the art of the rhetorician, and to point the contrast between the merits which earned these favours in the ancestor of the house of Russell and the services which he himself has rendered to his country and to the constitution on whose preservation depends the security of all the duke of Bedford's inherited property and privileges. The pamphlet is a masterpiece of its kind, but is not untouched with the overelaboration of Burke's later rhetoric when the perils of Jacobinism had become something in the nature of a fixed idea.

Of the three chief means by which Cicero, following the Greeks, declares that the orator achieves his end of winning over men's minds, *docendo, conciliando, permovendo*, tradition and the evidence of his works point to Burke's having failed chiefly in the second. He could delight, astound and convince an audience. He did not easily conciliate and win them over. He lacked the first essential and index of the conciliatory speaker, *lenitas vocis*; his voice was harsh and unmusical, his gesture ungainly. The high qualities, artistic and intellectual, of his speeches are better appreciated by readers and students than by 'even the most illustrious of those who watched that tall gaunt figure with its whirling arms, and listened to the Niagara of words bursting and shrieking from those impetuous lips[1].' And, even in the text of his speeches there is a strain of irony and scorn which is not well fitted to conciliate. The most persuasive of all his speeches are the American; yet, in these too, there is comparatively little effort to start from the point of view of his audience, to soothe and flatter them, to win them over by any artifice other than an appeal to the rare qualities of wisdom and magnanimity. And, when he speaks at Bristol on the eve of his rejection, the tone is the same, not egotistic or arrogant, but quite unyielding in his defence of principles, quite unsparing in his exposure of error and folly.

[1] Johnson, Lionel, *Postliminium*, p. 261.

Of Burke's power *permovendi animos*, of the passionate quality of his eloquence, there can be no question, yet here, too, it is necessary to distinguish. We have evidence that he could do both things on which Cicero lays stress—move his audience to tears and delight them by his wit. In the famous speech on the employment of Indian auxiliaries, he did both, the first by the manner in which he told the story of the murder of a Scottish girl on the eve of her marriage, the second by his parody of Burgoyne's address to the Indians. Yet, neither pathos nor humour is Burke's *forte*. His style wants the penetrating simplicity which is requisite to the highest effects in pathos. His tendency in the Indian speeches is to overelaboration ; his sensibility carries him away. There is more of sublime pathos alike in the image, and in the simplicity of the language in which it is conveyed, in Bright's famous sentence on the Angel of Death than in all that Burke ever wrote. Of irony and scorn, again, there is abundance in Burke ; of the *cavillatio*, the raillery which is diffused through the speech, there are examples in all the chief speeches ; but, of pure wit, which conciliates an audience by delighting it, there is little or none in the speeches as we know them, and Johnson would never admit that, in conversation, Burke's wit was felicitous.

Burke's unique power as an orator lies in the peculiar interpenetration of thought and passion. Like the poet and the prophet, he thinks most profoundly when he thinks most passionately. When he is not deeply moved, his oratory verges towards the turgid ; when he indulges feeling for its own sake, as in parts of *Letters on a Regicide Peace*, it becomes hysterical. But, in his greatest speeches and pamphlets, the passion of Burke's mind shows itself in the luminous thoughts which it emits, in the imagery which at once moves *and* teaches, throwing a flood of light not only on the point in question but on the whole neighbouring sphere of man's moral and political nature. Such oratory is not likely to be immediately effective. ' One always came away from Burke with one's mind full,' Wordsworth declared ; but it was necessary first to have a mind. The young men who jeered at Burke and interrupted him did so because they could not understand him ; and Pitt and Dundas found it unnecessary to reply to the speech *On the Nabob of Arcot's Debts*. The successful orator moves most safely among the topics familiar to his audience, trusting for success to the art with which he adapts and adorns them. But Burke combined the qualities of the orator with

those of the seer, the logical architecture of western oratory
with qualities which we find in the Hebrew prophets—moral
exaltation, the union of dignity with trenchancy of language,
vehemence, imagery that ranges from the sublime to the de-
grading. As the accidents of his political career recede into
the distance we perceive more and more clearly for what he
stood. He is the enemy of the spirit of Macchiavelli and Hobbes,
which would exempt politics from the control of morality, and,
in so far, is at one with Rousseau and the revolutionists. But,
he is equally opposed to the new puritanism of the revolutionists,
which claimed in the eighteenth century, as the puritans claimed
in the sixteenth and seventeenth, to break in pieces the state
or church that they might reconstruct it after an abstract and
ideal pattern. His attitude to the doctrinaires of the 'rights
of man' is very similar to that of Hooker towards the followers
of Cartwright. Yet, the first opposition is the more fundamental of the two. He is the great champion of the control of
politics, domestic and foreign, by moral considerations. Philosophy was not so much the foe of his latter days as Jacobinism ;
and Jacobinism was simply Macchiavellism come back to fill the
void which the failure of philosophy had created. It may be that,
in his defence of moral prejudices and inherited institutions, he
sometimes mistook the unessential for the vital ; that his too
passionate sensibility rendered his conduct at times factious,
unjust and unwise. He brought into politics the faults as well as
the genius of a man of letters and a prophet. When all is said,
his is one of the greatest minds which have concerned themselves
with political topics, and, alike, the substance and the form of his
works have made him the only orator whose speeches have secured
for themselves a permanent place in English literature beside
what is greatest in our drama, our poetry and our prose. Of his
many literary and artist friends, Johnson, Goldsmith, Reynolds and
others, the foremost is Johnson. They differed radically in party
politics, but they were knit together by a practical philosophy
rooted in common sense and religious feeling.

CHAPTER II

POLITICAL WRITERS AND SPEAKERS

THE growth and improvement of the daily newspaper, in itself not a strictly literary event, had a natural and marked effect on political literature. In some ways, that effect was merely temporary. The supersession of the weekly essay, of *The North Briton* type, by the effusions of the letter-writers of 1760—75 in a genuine newspaper[1] was soon cancelled; for the newspapers introduced a daily essay, the leading article, and letter-writers sank into the subordinate *rôle* they have held ever since. But, in political verse, a more permanent effect of the new conditions is noticeable. In 1760, we have still the pamphlet-poem and the decadent ballad. Some twenty years later, beside these there flourishes an almost new form, that of light, short, satiric verse, altogether slighter in immediate purpose and more playfully teasing in its objects and manner than its predecessors. It has flourished in the nineteenth century and has been marked by an ever-increasing attention to form, ending in a lyric precision surpassing, in some cases, that of serious poetry. For long, however, this new kind of verse was barely aware of its own existence, and wavered tentatively in methods and in choice of models; and, as often happens, in its careless youth it possessed a virility and fire not to be found in the perfected elegance of a later day.

Its rise seems traceable to the year 1784. At that time, the whigs were smarting under their utter rout in the recent general election. The king, their enemy, was victorious: the youthful Pitt was triumphant master of parliament; and revenge, though trifling and ephemeral, was sweet. The whig lampooners, indeed, were not without a serious object. The nation had ratified the king's choice of an administration. The whigs were concerned to show that the choice was wrong; and, in default of evidence derived from the acts of Pitt's ministry, they were reduced to

[1] See vol. x, chap. XVII.

merely personal mockery of him and his followers. Ministers were to be discredited by whig satire, if not by their own actions. And a number of brilliant devotees of Fox formed themselves into a club, *Esto Perpetua*, with the intent to mar the king's success.

Someone hit on the happy idea of a mock review of a mock epic, and thus *Criticisms of the Rolliad* began. The successive numbers of this production appeared, from time to time, in *The Morning Herald*, and won instantaneous popularity; when collected in book-form, they ran through twenty-two editions. Each number professed to be a commentary on a new epic that had just appeared. This mythical composition, *The Rolliad*, took its name from one of the chief butts of its wit, John Rolle, M.P. for Devonshire, whose stolid toryism had latterly found vent in an attempt to cough down Burke. He was provided with an ancestor, the Norman duke Rollo, whose adventures were a burlesque version of the *Aeneid*, and who, in due course (in the sixth book), is shown his descendant by Merlin in the House of Commons amid his party friends. The contemporary House of Lords, on the other hand, is revealed to Rollo by the dying Saxon drummer whom he has mortally wounded at Hastings. With the advent of fresh matter for ridicule, fresh editions of the epic were feigned to appear, and the topical insertions its author was supposed to make were quoted in prompt reviews, till, at last, even the dying drummer is allowed to die :

> Ha! ha!—this soothes me in severest woe;
> Ho! ho!—ah! ah!—oh! oh!—ha! ah!—ho!—oh!!!

Although their vivacity and wit, very different from Churchill's solemn tirades and the steely passion of Junius, had captivated the public, the authors of *The Rolliad* were too wise to overdo a happy invention. After a while, they transferred their efforts to another style of railing. This took the form of *Political Eclogues*, where prominent ministerialists lament or strive in rime after the fashion of the outspoken, yet literary, shepherds of Vergil. The new vein, in its turn, was worked out, and was succeeded by a series of *Probationary Odes* for the laureateship, vacant by the death of Whitehead in 1785, and filled by the appointment of Thomas Warton. The victims thus made to submit specimen odes to the lord chamberlain were by no means chosen from purely literary circles. Politicians and divines are burlesqued together with poets of lesser rank. To be a supporter of Pitt was a sufficient ground for the fathership of an ode, in which

the peculiarities of 'the author' were gaily ridiculed. All these
compositions had to submit to some sort of plan, epic, or collection
of eclogues and odes; but, naturally, were accompanied by a
number of scattered *jeux d'esprit* which had no such bond of connection between them.   They were afterwards republished as
Political Miscellanies, and, never very amusing, grew duller and
feebler as the zeal of *The Rolliad* clique declined.

Not many of the members of the *Esto Perpetua* club, who took
part in this baiting, were of the first rank of politicians. Two
of them, and two only, were ex-ministers: general Richard
Fitzpatrick, man of fashion and intimate of Fox, whose 'cheerful
countenance' and 'gay voice' are curiously apparent in his
printed page, and Lord John Townshend, less jovial but quite as
witty.   Of higher literary eminence was the antiquary George
Ellis, a harbinger, in his way, of the so-called romantic movement.
Other members were journalists, of whom Joseph Richardson was
the chief; while French Laurence was professor of civil law at
Oxford, and Richard Tickell a librettist of repute. The names
now appeal to few; the importance of *The Rolliad's* creators,
in spite of their ability, was as fugitive as their verses; but,
working in unison, they obtained a collective interest otherwise
denied them.

Nice respects and goodnature were not to be expected and
not called for in the rough and tumble of political battle; but
the vindictive feelings of the ousted whigs spurred them on, sometimes, to venomous railing and, sometimes, to scurrility, and it
is characteristic of *The Rolliad* that personalities and barbed
gossip not only abound but form nearly the whole of its matter.
One and all of its authors are irresistibly diverted from the
public demerits of their quarry to his mannerisms, his oddities
and his private life. Pitt's continence and the dissoluteness of
Dundas, the piety of one minister, the profanity of another, anything personal, in fact, form the staple of the jokes. Yet it is
impossible not to relish the humorous satire of Ellis's critique
on Pitt's style of eloquence or the similar squib by Laurence:

> crisply nice
> The muffin-toast, or bread and butter slice,
> Thin as his arguments, that mock the mind,
> Gone, ere you taste,—no relish left behind.

A whole gallery of caricatured portraits comes before us, each
touched with party malice and etched with cynical knowledge.

On one occasion, for instance, Richardson explored the kitchen of the parsimonious duke of Richmond:

> Whether thou go'st while summer suns prevail,
> To enjoy the freshness of thy kitchen's gale,
> Where, unpolluted by luxurious heat,
> Its large expanse affords a cool retreat[1].

It is one of the merits of *The Rolliad* to have abandoned the tragedy airs and desperate wrath of the political satire that immediately preceded it. Severe and rasping as are its flouts, they seldom lose the tone of club-room pleasantry, and its rimed heroics recall Gay's *Eclogues* rather than the polished verse of Pope. Being so much concerned with the personal foibles of forgotten men, its lines, for the most part, fall flat on a later generation, since they lack the finish which would make them interesting. The exceptions, like Fitzpatrick's couplets on the bishops,

> Who, still obedient to their Maker's nod,
> Adore their Sov'reign, and respect their God—

are few and far between. Very seldom is any squib complete in the verse alone; they are supported by a less epigrammatic raillery in the prose comment; which, however, for humour and sly fun, not infrequently surpasses the satire it is supposed to criticise.

To nothing more, perhaps, was *The Rolliad* indebted for its success than to the high spirits of its authors. They were gay; they seem to accompany their jokes with an infectious laugh. In consequence, the longer we read them, the more we fall into their humour; and their thin voices seem to gather volume as one after another takes up the theme and adds his quota to the burlesque. This may be one reason why the five *Political Eclogues*, in continuous verse and isolated in subject, have lost their savour, with the exception of Fitzpatrick's immortal *Lyars*, where two of Pitt's henchmen strive for the prize of mendacity. But, in *The Probationary Odes*, all ringing changes on the same caricature, they regain audience, whether it is George Ellis scoffing:

> Oh! deep unfathomable Pitt!
> To thee Ierne owes her happiest days!
> Wait a bit,
> And all her sons shall loudly sing thy praise!
> Ierne, happy, happy Maid!
> Mistress of the Poplin trade!

[1] Probably suggested by Dryden's line : " Cool were his kitchens though his brain were hot." *Absalom and Achitophel*, i, l. 621.

or another of the club penning an Ossianic duan :

> A song shall rise!
> Every soul shall depart at the sound!!!
> The wither'd thistle shall crown my head!!!
> I behold thee, O King!
> I behold thee sitting on mist!!!
> Thy form is like a watery cloud,
> Singing in the deep like an oyster!!!!

This admirable fooling was succeeded by the still more amusing drolleries of a clerical black sheep, whose real talent, allied with certain respectable qualities, is obscured by his sordid life and offensive compositions. Peter Pindar was the pseudonym of John Wolcot, a country surgeon's son, who hovered during a long life on the dubious confines of society and Bohemia. He began his career as a physician, but, while well employed in Jamaica, was ordained in the hope of a living. Later, when practising as a doctor in his native county Cornwall, he discovered the painter Opie, helped to train him and came with him to London in 1781. He was to receive half Opie's profits, and they soon quarrelled. Wolcot's good judgment in art and his skill in minor verse, however, enabled him to make an income by a series of severe squibs on the royal academicians. Thus, he was led to satirise their patron, the king, and *The Rolliad* gave him the cue for further achievements in the same style. In 1785, he scored considerable success in his mock-heroic poem, *The Lousiad*, which now, at least, reads very tediously. He followed this up, in 1787, by his profitable *Ode upon Ode*; it had an enormous, and, in a way, deserved, vogue. The absurdities of the yearly official ode-writing and the painful vagaries, together with some real faults, of George III were well known ; and Wolcot, hampered by few convictions and fewer scruples, found a ready market among indignant whigs for his small scandal. What with legal threats and negotiations for a pension, which broke down, he decided, in two or three years, to choose less potent objects of attack ; but he found his profits dwindle, and returned to the king and Pitt in 1792. His powers, of no uncommon vigour at best, were, however, waning; he was worsted by the surly Gifford, both in fisticuffs and in abusive verse. His later satire and his serious rimes were not of any merit, and he subsisted on a fortunate sale of his copyrights. When blindness overtook him, he displayed a stoical good humour, which makes us regret that a musical, artistic man, of a 'kind and hearty disposition,' played so scurvy a literary *rôle*.

Peter Pindar's verse is not of the kind that appears in anthologies, from which the immense length of his rambling drollery tends to bar him out. Still, the nature of his talent is the chief reason for his exclusion. He lacks altogether elect phrase, musical rhythm and any charm of imagination or thought. He sins constantly in baseness and vulgarity. As an imitator of La Fontaine, whose irregular verse was his chief model, and as a precursor of *The Ingoldsby Legends*, he takes a position of hopeless inferiority. None the less, one cannot but admire his positive ability. A mixture of good sense and mischievousness transpires successfully through his elaborately roguish airs. His shrewd hits at the king's stinginess and obtuseness went home. He is, perhaps, the very best of English caricaturists in verse, reaching his highest level in his account of the royal visit to Whitbread's brewery[1]. In its kind, it was delicate work; the lines of his drawing are very little out of their natural position; but the whole forms a glaring comic exaggeration. *Bozzy and Piozzi*, the amoebean strife of the two worshippers of Dr Johnson in rimed quotations from their books, is another masterpiece in this style. Each absurdity of his two victims is emphasised with an adroit legerdemain of words, and Wolcot, for once, suppresses his irritating snigger. The pair are left to tell their own tale. Bozzy, for instance, says:

> But to return unto my charming child—
> About our Doctor JOHNSON she was *wild*;
> And when he left off speaking, she would flutter,
> Squall for him to begin again, and sputter!
> And to be *near* him a strong wish express'd,
> Which proves he was not such a horrid beast.

As appears in this instance, Peter Pindar's strength lies in his power of realising for his reader a comic situation; polished epigram and the keener arrows of wit are not in his quiver. He loves to slip one or two sly colloquialisms into verses written in the formal eighteenth century style, and, thus, brings out the broad fun of his conceptions. But his tricky method could only secure a temporary success; and, since his humour was not many-sided and depended on one or two foibles in his subject, he lost his hold on the public, when his lucky pocket of ore was exhausted. Nor could the scolding, dull invective, to which he then resorted, restore his popularity in an age that, after 1789, became engrossed in greater matters than the tattle of the servants' hall at Windsor.

---

[1] *Instructions to a celebrated Laureat.*

The French revolution was essentially a proselytising move
ment. Republicanism, liberty, equality and fraternity, became a
kind of creed, which was zealously propagated by pen and sword.
Thus, the opposition to it in England was, at the same time, an
effort to maintain the ancient social order, with its ideals and
institutions, and a struggle to preserve national independence from
the universal aggressions of the new France. And the champion
of both endeavours was the younger Pitt. The times seemed to
grow more and more dangerous. In 1797, cash payments were suspended at the Bank of England; seamen were mutinying at the
Nore; Ireland was seething with discontent; the French arms were
victorious against their continental foes; while, in England itself,
a violent revolutionary propaganda was being carried on, which,
if it were more potent in appearance than in real significance, might
still decoy the younger generation. It was to combat this propaganda and to hearten the national resistance that George Canning,
Pitt's ablest lieutenant, founded his periodical, *The Anti-Jacobin*.
The new journal, in addition to the customary contents of a newspaper, was to contradict systematically the statements of the
other side, to ridicule any prominent person well-disposed towards
the revolution, and to hold up to honour the old ideals of English
polity. These objects it fulfilled. In contrast to its trivial predecessors, *The Anti-Jacobin* breathed a proud conviction and a
religious fervour which lift it above mere party polemics. It is,
indeed, bigoted in tone; for was it not fighting in the cause of
righteousness and human happiness? To its authors, the favourers
of the revolution are miscreants whom it is necessary to pillory and
deride, and thus to render harmless. They themselves are confessors
of the true political faith.

The men who wrote this fiery periodical may surprise us by
their mundane character. There was the many-sided, brilliant
Canning, then in the heyday of his youth; George Ellis, the
amiable antiquary, by this time, a fervent tory and repentant of
The Rolliad; and John Hookham Frere, the ideal of a cultivated
country gentleman, whose striking literary achievement it was to
introduce the satiric Italian epic into English. The editor was
a man of literary mark, William Gifford. No one, perhaps, of
the tribe of poor authors has gone through a more bitter struggle
than his with the obstacles and misfortunes in his way, although
they were not spread over a long term of years. He was the son
of a ne'er-do-well, whose main occupation was that of a glazier at
Ashburton in Devonshire. After a miserable boyhood, obsessed

by a passionate and seemingly hopeless desire for learning amid the handicraft work to which he was forced, he was befriended by William Cookesley, a surgeon, and sent to Oxford by subscription. While there, he came to the notice of earl Grosvenor, and was appointed travelling tutor to his son. He was able to make something of a name, in 1794 and 1795, by his mediocre satires, *The Baviad* and *The Maeviad,* directed against the ridiculous Della Cruscan school[1] of poets and the small dramatic fry of the day. Although their merit was not great, his ample quotations from his victims made his conquest easy. When *The Anti-Jacobin* was set on foot, his sledge-hammer style and industry made him a fit editor for it; but he was mainly concerned with its prose. He did his task well, and, when *The Quarterly Review* was started in 1809, he was selected as its editor, a post he occupied for fifteen years, in despotic fashion, even finding it in his heart to mutilate an essay by Lamb. Meanwhile, he did yeoman service to literature by his translation of Juvenal in 1802 and by some editions of older English dramatists. Sound common-sense redeems his commonplace ability, while his sour, fierce criticisms find an explanation in his early hardships and constant ill-health. He seems to have written verse because it was, then, a regular accomplishment of literary men.

Even in its own day, *The Anti-Jacobin* was chiefly notable for its poets' corner, which contained the best political satire since the age of Dryden. The greater part of these compositions developed their wit in some form or another of parody. Jacobins were supposed to write them—Jacobins, who always preferred the most blatant version of extreme opinions. As usual, the idea was not quite new. *The Rolliad* had feigned to be the work of a ministerialist, and there was an element of parody in *Political Eclogues* and in *Probationary Odes,* although the veil was exceedingly conventional. Now, in *The Anti-Jacobin,* caustic parody was the essence of the satire. Among the earliest victims was the later tory poet laureate, Southey, who was just recovering from a severe attack of revolutionary fever. His conversion did not influence Canning and Frere, if they knew of it, and to their hostility we owe the verses among which *The Needy Knife-grinder* stands chief. Southey's sentimentalism and his halting accentual sapphics and dactylics were mercilessly imitated and surpassed. It was not only parody and ridicule of a particular victim, but humorous mockery of a type of

[1] See *post,* chap. VIII.

thought, and, as such, has continued to live by reason of its admirable combination of inventive power, metre, phrase and artful contrast:

> Weary Knife-grinder! Little think the proud ones,
> Who in their coaches roll along the turnpike-
> road, what hard work 'tis crying all day 'Knives and
>   Scissars to grind O!'

The scholarly *négligé* of the form, the whimsical plight of the unlucky knife-grinder and the comedy of his 'hard work' make us indifferent to the temporary politics which inspired this immortal skit.

More body, if less *bouquet*, is to be found in two longer contributions. It was a time when the genuine muse had retired to her 'interlunar cave,' and massive didactic poems enjoyed a transitory reign. Two authors of note took the lead, Richard Payne Knight and Erasmus Darwin[1]. Both were *philosophes* in their opinions and broached a variety of doctrines most obnoxious to *The Anti-Jacobin.* And, however invulnerable to attack they might be in their serious work, they were mortal in their verse. Knight's *Progress of Civil Society* was pompous and humourless; Darwin's machine-turned couplets glittered with a profusion of inappropriate poetical trappings. Knight's turn came first. *The Progress of Man* traced, with mischievous assurance, the decline of the human race from the days of the blameless savage, who fed 'on hips and haws.'

> Man only,—rash, refined, presumptuous man,
> Starts from his rank, and mars creation's plan.
> Born the free heir of nature's wide domain,
> To art's strict limits bounds his narrow'd reign;
> Resigns his native rights for meaner things,
> For faith and fetters—laws, and priests, and kings.

Darwin's *Loves of the Plants* was taken off as *The Loves of the Triangles.* The merit of both these parodies consists, not only in their sparkling wit, but in their genuine exaggeration of the original authors' foibles. They are not a forced, ridiculous echo; only the real traits are accentuated to caricature.

Burlesque of the same high rank appears in *The Rovers.* This delicious mock-play parodies certain productions of the German drama, then only beginning to be known in England by translations. Like its fellow-satires, it derived assistance from the extravagances to be found in some of the works it derided. These extravagances differed from one another in kind as well as in degree;

---

[1] See *post*, chap. VIII.

but Goethe, Schiller and Kotzebue seemed alike fair game to the
satirist, and the result was a spirited farce, which has remained
amusing long after the close of the literary controversy which
was its occasion.

The series of parodies surpass the other poetry of *The Anti-
Jacobin* in that they were perfect in their kind. None the less,
in absolute merit, they fall behind its most serious piece, *The
New Morality.* In 1798, *The Anti-Jacobin* had done its office of
cheapening and discrediting the revolutionary propagandists, and
its gall and licence of satire were in danger of alienating less
fervent supporters. So it was decided to cease its publication.
Canning gathered together all his power for a final, crushing blow.
With but little assistance from his friends, he composed a formal
satire in the manner of Churchill; and, although *The New
Morality* is hardly the work of a great poet, yet its sincerity
of passionate conviction, no less than its admirable rhetoric and
skilful versification, raises it above the ill-formed genius of its
model. Canning was not a cosmopolitan philosopher; he was
full of insular patriotism, and produced his best when giving full-
hearted expression to it. From his sneering contempt of sympa-
thisers with France and of halfhearted—perhaps impartial—
'candid friends' of the ministry, he rises, through fierce denun-
ciatory scorn of the French publicists, to an appeal to maintain
the older England of law and right. Burke is his prophet:

> Led by thy light, and by thy wisdom wise;

he urges the claims of the native past—

> Guard we but our own hearts; with constant view
> To ancient morals, ancient manners true;
> True to the manlier virtues, such as nerv'd
> Our fathers' breasts, and this proud isle preserv'd
> For many a rugged age: and scorn the while
> Each philosophic atheist's specious guile;
> The soft seductions, the refinements nice,
> Of gay Morality, and easy Vice;
> So shall we brave the storm; our 'stablish'd pow'r
> Thy refuge, EUROPE, in some happier hour.

Thus, *The Anti-Jacobin*, at its close, bade farewell to the burlesque spirit which had guided political satire since the days of
The Rolliad. The utmost in that style of writing—after all, not
a lofty style, not an important species of literature—had been
achieved, and the exhausted wave drew back again. Canning's
own subsequent political verse, scanty in quantity as it was, never

attained the excellence of his contributions to his famous news-paper; and the successors to *The Anti-Jacobin*, which borrowed its title, were unable to supply verse of real merit.

One of the butts of *The Anti-Jacobin*, who was treated with a tolerant good-humour which he well deserved, was 'Mr. Higgins of St. Mary Axe.' In real life, he was the most extreme of the English revolutionary philosophers, William Godwin. This amiable commonplace man, who, however, possessed a marvellous capacity for reasoning without regard to experience, was born in 1756, a younger son of a dissenting minister. He obtained his education, first at a Norfolk grammar school, and then at Hoxton academy in London. In 1778, he became, in his turn, a minister, but he never stayed long at one place and soon adopted the more congenial profession of authorship. Much conscientious, ephemeral work was done by him in history and literature; but he was brought into sudden prominence by a book of startling opinions, *Political Justice*, published in 1793. The influence of this book was great among the younger generation, which, indeed, Godwin was naturally able to attract and advise in private life as well as by political speculation. His kindly sympathy and almost boyish optimism were never better applied than in his friendships with young men. Bred a Calvinist, he had become a believer in materialism and necessity, passing, in 1792, to atheism, and re-nouncing it somewhere about 1800. He was, above all things, a system-maker; philosophy and politics were, for him, indistinguish-able; and, of his views on both, he was an eager advocate in public and private, whenever he had the opportunity. Meanwhile, he was obliged to earn a living besides propagating his opinions. So, we find him writing proselytising novels, *Caleb Williams* and *St Leon*, which he hoped would insinuate his views in the public mind. During these years, he met and married another writer of innovating beliefs. Mary Wollstonecraft, to use her maiden name, is a far more attractive person than her placid husband. She was of Irish extraction, and had the misfortune to be one of the children of a ne'er-do-well. In 1780, at the age of twenty, Mary Wollstonecraft took up the teaching profession, as schoolmistress and governess. She was almost too successful, for, in 1788, she lost her post as governess for Lady Kingsborough, in consequence of her pupils becoming too fond of her. The next four years she passed as a publisher's hack, till, at last, her *Vindication of the Rights of Woman* made her name known in 1792. Shortly after its publication, she made the mistake of her life by accepting the 'protection' of Gilbert Imlay, an American, during a residence in France. Marriage, in her eyes, was a superfluous ceremony, and it was not celebrated between her and Imlay, who, in the end, became unfaithful beyond endurance. Thus, in 1796, she began single life again in London with a daughter to support. She had written, in 1794, a successful account of the earlier period of the French revolution, and her literary reputation was increased by letters written to Imlay during a Scandinavian tour. Very quickly, she and Godwin formed an attachment, which, in accordance with their principles, only led to marriage in 1797 in order to safeguard the interests of their children. But the birth of a child, the future wife of Shelley, was fatal to the mother, in September 1797. She had been a generous, impulsive woman, always affectionate and kind. Godwin's second choice of a wife was less fortunate and conduced to the unhappy experiences of his later years, which fill much space in the life of Shelley. Pursued by debt, borrowing, begging, yet doing his best to earn a living by a small publishing business, and by the production of children's books, novels, an impossible play and divers works in literature, history and economics, he at last obtained a small sinecure, which freed his later years from pecuniary anxiety. He died in 1836.

While both Godwin and Mary Wollstonecraft were rebels against the established order, and contemned the traditional usages of mankind, not only as obsolete and calling for improvement, but as, in themselves, of no account, Godwin was, by far, the greater visionary of the two. Mary Wollstonecraft, in spite of the pompous energy of her expressions in her *Vindication of the Rights of Woman*, was essentially an educational reformer, urging schemes all of which were, possibly, practicable, if not necessarily advisable. Girls should be educated in much the same way as boys, and the two sexes should be taught together. Thus, she says, women would become genuine companions of men, and would be fitted to share in the rights, both civil and political, of which they were deprived. The opposition which the book aroused, however, was not only due to its definite proposals, but, also, to the slashing attack on her own sex, as she conceived it to be, and to the coarseness with which she described certain social evils. But it reveals an amiable spirit, characteristic of the writer, and its fire and somewhat shrill enthusiasm make some amends for the lack of exact reasoning and the excess of unrestrained, glittering rhetoric. As a landmark in the evolution of social ideas, and a sign of revolt against a then prevailing sexual cant, it has an importance which it cannot be said to possess in literature or, perhaps, as a statement of historical facts : there was, at the time, much more education of women, both separate and in conjunction with the male sex, than she was willing to allow. As a governess, she had had too vivid an experience of the fine lady and the conventional miss of the eighteenth century.

The visions of Godwin, however, were visions indeed. He dreamed of a new-made world, of perfect or nearly perfected beings with no government, scarcely any cooperation, no laws, no diseases, no marriage, no trade, only perfect peace secured by a vigilant, and, in truth, perpetually meddling, public opinion. This programme, in Godwin's eyes, was rendered practicable by his views on human nature. Men's actions were due to a process of reasoning, founded on their opinions, which, in turn, were formed by a process of reasoning.

'When' a murderer 'ultimately works up his mind to the perpetration, he is then most strongly impressed with the superior recommendations of the conduct he pursues.'

Free-will, he denied : thus, if a man's reason were really convinced, no doubt remained as to his actions. The reformer, in consequence, was not to be a revolutionary; since, by means of revolution, he would only introduce measures to which he had been unable to convert his fellow-countrymen. The real way to change the world for the better was a continuance of peaceful argument, wherein truth, naturally having stronger reasons in its favour than error, would prevail. Incessant discussion would gradually alter the general opinions of men. Then, the changes he desired would be made. The obvious counter-argument, that, by his own theory, error had won in the contest with truth up to his time and that the actual course of human politics had been a mistake, did not occur to him ; and the attractiveness of his optimistic outlook combined with the rigidity of his deductive logic, much incidental shrewdness and a singular force of conviction to gain him a numerous following. His style, too, deserved some success. He was always clear and forcible ; his sentences convey his exact meaning without effort, and display a kind of composed oratorical effect. In curious contrast to Mary Wollstonecraft, who advocated what might be described as a practical, if novel, scheme of education with the enthusiasm of a revolutionary, her husband outlined the complete wreck of existing institutions, with a Utopia of the simple life to follow, in a calm philosophising manner, which

ignored even the lukewarm emotions felt by himself. The passion
he lacked was to be supplied, later, by his son-in-law, Shelley.

Godwin's *Political Justice* escaped suppression owing to the
small number of readers whom a costly book[1], even one which
passed through several editions, could reach. He gained a larger
audience for his novels, which were intended to lead to the same
convictions. The only one of these which still finds readers is *The
Adventures of Caleb Williams, or, Things as They Are*, published
in 1794. Here, Godwin is concerned with two aspects of the
same thesis ; first, the oppression which a poor man could suffer
under the existing institutions, and, secondly, the perversion of
character in a member of the ruling class through his acceptance
of the ideals of chivalry. With these ingredients, the tale, as a
whole, is most bizarre. Its personages act in a very unlikely way.
Falkland, the virtuous villain, who, because of a chivalric regard
for his reputation, has allowed two innocent men to be executed
for a murder he himself committed, shows a persistent ingenuity in
harassing his attached dependent, Williams, who has guessed his
secret, into accusing him ; a brigand band, led by a philanthropic
outlaw, establishes its headquarters close to a county town ; Williams
surpasses the average hero in prodigies of resource and endurance ;
Falkland, in the end, confesses his guilt in consequence of the
energy with which his victim expresses the remorse he feels at
making the true accusation. Yet, with all this, the story is put
together with great skill. In spite of its artificial rhetoric and
their own inherent improbability, there is a human quality in the
characters, and Williams's helplessness in his attempt to escape
from his persecutor gives us the impression, not so much of the
forced situations of a novel, as of unavoidable necessity. In fact,
Godwin's talent as a novelist lay in his remarkable powers of
invention, which were heightened by his matter of fact way of
relating improbabilities. He was partly aware of it, perhaps,
and his other important novel, *St Leon*, attempted the same
feat with impossibilities. But, in spite of a temporary vogue,
it is now only remembered for its portrait of Mary Wollstonecraft,
and the retractation of his theoretic abolition of 'the charities of
private life.'

From Godwin, who, in his worst days, kept round him a tattered
cloak of magnanimity, it is an abrupt change to his fellow-
revolutionary, the coarse-grained, shrewd Thomas Paine. Yet,

---

[1] Its price was three guineas.

the latter had virtues which were missing in his contemporary. His public spirit led him to disregard all profit from political works which had a large sale; he was not a beggar, and the rewards he was forced to ask from the American governments were the barest payments on account of admitted services to the United States. In fact, he was a born pamphleteer, never happy unless he was divulging his opinions for the welfare of the human race as he conceived it. Dogmatic and narrow-minded, he was not a man to be troubled by doubts: the meaning of history, the best form of government, right and wrong, falsehood and truth, all seemed quite plain to him, and he had no more hesitation than Godwin in making a working model of the universe, as he did of the iron bridge by him invented. It was not till he was well advanced in middle life that he obtained an opportunity of showing his great talents. He was the son of a poor Norfolk quaker, and spent all his earlier years in the struggle to make a decent livelihood. In turn, a staymaker, a seaman, a school-usher, a tobacconist and an exciseman, he moved from place to place, until he was finally dismissed from the excise in 1774, and, in the same year, emigrated to Philadelphia. There, he almost immediately edited *The Pennsylvania Magazine* and proved at once his literary talent and the advanced character of his opinions by attacking slavery and advocating American independence. In 1776, he became famous by his pamphlet, *Common-Sense*, which he, at least, looked on as the principal instrument in consolidating American opinion in favour of war. Having gained the public ear, he continued the work of encouraging resistance to English rule by two series of effective pamphlets, called *The Crisis*, and was soon recognised as the leading writer of his new country, while, with characteristic versatility, he also served as a soldier, as secretary to the congress's foreign committee and as clerk to the Pennsylvania assembly. Peace brought him moderate rewards and a retirement which he could not endure. He returned to England to prosecute his mechanical inventions, the fruit of his leisure hours, and soon became involved anew in politics. The French revolution proved a fresh turning-point in his career. In 1791—2, he took up the cudgels against Burke in the two parts of *The Rights of Man*. The ability, and, still more, the wide circulation, of these tracts brought him in danger of arrest, and he fled to France, where he became a member of Convention, and, after all but falling a victim to the guillotine, was a founder of the new sect of theophilanthropists. Then he dropped into obscurity and, in

1802, went once more to America, only to find that his *Age of Reason*, published in 1794—5, had alienated from him almost all his friends. A thick crop of slanders grew up round him, without, apparently, any foundation save the fact that he was occasionally drunk. Still, he kept a bold front to the world, and continued to write pamphlets almost till his death in 1809.

Paine was a prince of pamphleteers and all his literary talent seems confined to that end. His general ideas were of the simplest, not to say the shallowest; but he grasped them firmly and worked them out with a clear and ready logic. His immense ignorance of history and literature was by no means ill compensated by an intimate knowledge of actual affairs; and his shrewdness made him a formidable critic even of Burke. His style was always clear, and, a little rhetoric apart, unaffected. Quite without charm as it was, his warmth and force and command of appropriate words made it more than passable. Every now and then, he falls into sheer vulgarity, which is most noticeable in his theological writings; but, more usually, he can alternate a mediocre eloquence with trenchant argumentative composition. So far as copying the written word was concerned, Paine was quite original; but, doubtless, he owed much to the debates and casual conversations in which he took part. In *The Rights of Man*, he appears as a narrow doctrinaire; he takes over the theory of the social contract as the basis for his constructive views, and justifies revolution, partly on the ground that no generation can bind its successors, and partly by the argument that the social contract must be embodied in a formal constitution : where such did not exist, a mere tyranny prevailed, which had no basis in right. He was thus, like Godwin, entirely opposed to Burke's doctrine of prescription. To criticise the faults of the existing state of things was easy and obvious; but Paine expounded, also, a radical constructive policy, including parliamentary reform, old age pensions and a progressive income-tax. With these and other changes, he looked forward to a broadcloth millennium. *The Age of Reason* showed all Paine's qualities and an unusual abundance of his defects. His want of taste and the almost complete absence in him of any sense of beauty or grandeur are as conspicuous as his narrow self-complacency. But his reasoning, however limited in scope, was shrewd enough. Generally speaking, he combined a rough historical criticism of the Bible with the argument that the Jewish and Christian conceptions of the Deity were incompatible with the deism revealed to man by external nature and by his own conscience. In this way, the truculent pamphleteer seems to stand near one of the sources of modern theology.

The heir to the pamphleteering eminence of Paine was a man oddly like, and, again, oddly unlike, his predecessor. William Cobbett, too, rose by his own efforts from the poorer classes. His father was a small farmer and innkeeper in Hampshire, and he educated himself with indomitable pluck while he was serving as a soldier. Owing to his accomplishments, he rose to the rank of sergeant-major and became a kind of clerk-factotum to his regiment; but, in 1791, he suddenly obtained his discharge and attempted to convict several of his former officers of peculation. No facilities for proof were allowed him and he did not appear at the court-martial. Instead, he went to France, and, after a short residence there, occupied in acquiring the language, he emigrated, like Paine, to Philadelphia. Still following Paine's precedent, he had not been settled long in America before he took up the pamphlet-writing trade. Under the apt pseudonym of Peter Porcupine, he conducted a pro-British and anti-French campaign, until he was ruined by libel cases and obliged to return to England, in 1800. He was well received, as was natural, in government circles, and soon started work as a tory freelance. His first venture, *The Porcupine*, failed ; but his second, *Cobbett's Political Register*, a weekly newspaper with long leaders, which he began in 1802, gained the public ear. At first tory, then independent, at last strongly radical, he maintained, till his death, an influence of which no persecution and no folly could deprive him. He appealed to the farmer and small trader as no one else could. The composition of his weekly *Register* was not his only occupation. Besides other publishing ventures, including *Parliamentary Debates*, later undertaken by Hansard, and *State Trials*, he combined business and enthusiastic pleasure as a model farmer. All went well until, in 1810, he received a sentence of two years' imprisonment on account of an invective against military flogging. He could keep up writing his *Register* ; but his farm went to wrack, and he came out heavily in debt. Still, however, his hold on the public increased, and, when, in 1816, he succeeded in reducing the price to twopence, the circulation of his paper rose to over 40,000 copies. A temporary retreat to America did little to impair the extent of his audience, and, all through the reign of George IV, he was a leader of political opinion. Books from his pen, egotistic in character, on farming, on politics, on the

conduct of life by the young, appeared one after another, had
their temporary use and still provide specimens of his character
and his literary style. By 1830, his fortunes were reestablished;
the Reform act opened the doors of parliament to him, and he sat
in the Commons till his death in 1835.

Personal ambition and public spirit had nearly equal shares
in the indomitable Cobbett. Enormously and incorrigibly vain,
'pragmatic, busy, bustling, bold,' he loved to be, or to think
himself, the centre of the stage, to lay down the law on everything, to direct, praise or censure everybody, to point out how
things ought to be done, and, best of all, to spar furiously with
those who held opposite opinions. General principles were beyond the limit of his faculties; hence, he completely veered
round in his politics with hardly a suspicion of the fact. His
explanations of the state of things that he saw round him were
hasty guesses, rapidly matured into unreasoning prejudices. It
was all due to the funded debt and paper money, aggravated by
progressive depopulation (in 1820 !)[1], tithes and the tardy adoption
of his improvements in farming. Yet, he was a shrewd and
accurate observer, and an expert and fair judge of the state
of agriculture and the condition of tillers of the soil. True,
he had much good sense and critical faculty to apply to other
political matters; but, regarding the land, he was always at his
best. Peasant-bred, with a passion for farming, and a most
genuine, if quite unpoetic, love of the open country and all that
it could offer eye or ear, he depicted, with Dutch honesty, the
rural England that he knew how to see, its fertility and beauty,
the misery that had descended on many of its inhabitants, the
decent prosperity remaining to others. And he was master of
a style in which to express his knowledge. It is not one of those
great styles which embalm their authors' memory; but it was
serviceable. He is vigorous, plain and absolutely unaffected. The
aptest words come to him with most perfect ease. His eloquence
springs from vivid insight into the heart of his theme, and from
a native fervour and energy that do not need art to blow them
into flame. Apart from his plebeian virulence, he shows a natural
good taste in writing. The flaccid elegance and pompous rotund
verbiage then in vogue are, by him, left on one side. If he cannot
frame a period, every sentence has its work to do, and every

---

[1] Cobbett's determination, in spite of the census returns, to consider the population
as decreasing, is a remarkable instance of the strength of his prejudices. It is true that
he acknowledged the growth of the great towns.

sentence tells. What mars his farmer's Odyssey, *Rural Rides*, is, perhaps, the excess of this very disregard for fine writing. They are notes of what he saw, and notes must often be brief, formless and disconnected. Imagination and the charm it gives are, indeed, absent throughout; but his sympathetic realism has an attraction of its own. He scans the look and manners of the labourers; he calculates whether they have bacon to eat; he descants on the capabilities of the soil; and he is able to impress upon his readers the strength of his interest in these things and of his enjoyment of field and woods and streams and the palatable salmon that inhabit the latter. He seems to give an unconscious demonstration how excellent a tongue English could be for a man, who saw and felt keenly, to express the facts as he saw them, and the emotions which possessed him.

The forms of political literature which have been described— verse and prose, solemn treatise, pamphlet or weekly essay—all possess one advantage over oratory. We can judge of their effectiveness from themselves, as well as from what we are told about them. Something we may miss in atmosphere which the contemporary reader enjoyed; but, in all things else, we are under the same conditions as his. In oratory, however, the case is different. We have to piece together scattered reminiscences of those who heard the speaker, and to imagine, as well as we can, the effective delivery, the charm of voice and gesture, and, still more, the momentary appropriateness of argument, phrase and manner which gave life and force to what is now dead or semi- animate matter. It is hardly possible, in fact, to do justice, long after, in cold blood, to debating points, for, unlike the hearers, unlike the speaker himself, we are not strung up, waiting for the retort to an argument or invective. The necessary medium of interest and excitement is not to be conjured up. These con- siderations, however, represent the least of the disadvantages we are under in estimating English oratory at the close of the eighteenth century. We do not even possess the great speeches of that day in anything like completeness. The merest frag- ments remain of the elder Pitt, perhaps the first among all English orators. And we do not, apparently, find lengthy reports till about the year 1800, while even these are, possibly, somewhat curtailed. Of some of the greatest triumphs in debate of Fox, of the younger Pitt and of Sheridan, we have only mangled remnants. One doubtful merit alone seems left; in contradistinction to an orator's published version of his speech, inevitably different from its spoken form and addressed to a reading audience in another mood than that of an excited assembly, they give us, at their best, what was actually said, although in mere fragments, with the reasoning maimed and the fire extinct.

After Burke, Charles James Fox was the senior of the group of great orators in the mid reign of George III. He entered parliament in 1768 while still under age, but it was not till February 1775 that he first showed his powers in a speech in favour of the Americans. Year by year, he grew in ability and debating skill, and Lord Rockingham's death in 1782 left him the undoubted leader of the whigs. But he was now to share his preeminence in oratory with a rival. William Pitt the younger entered the commons in 1781, and his maiden speech at once raised him to the front rank of speakers. Perhaps, English public speaking has never again quite reached the level of those twenty-five years, when Fox and Pitt carried on their magnificent contest. Whichever of the two spoke last, said Wilberforce, seemed to have the best of the argument. Burke, whose eloquence, in his speeches revised for publication, and even in the verbatim report of what he said, stands far higher as literature than theirs, could not compare with them in effectiveness in actual speaking, or in the favour of the House of Commons. It was admitted that their successors, Canning and Grey, belonged to an inferior class of orators. The times were peculiarly favourable. These men spoke on great affairs to a highly critical, cultivated, but not pedantic, audience, which had been accustomed to hear the very best debating and which demanded both efficaciousness of reasoning, clearness of expression and splendour of style. Thus, spurred on by sympathy and success, the two masters of debate established a dual empire over the house. Their powers of persuading those connoisseurs of oratory, whom they addressed, appear, indeed, surprisingly small, when we look at the division-lists · but at least, they cast a triumphal robe over the progress of events.

Like all great speakers, they were improvisers, and, in this line, Fox was admitted to excel. He could come straight from gambling at Brooks's, and enter with mastery into the debate. He had an uncanny skill in traversing and reversing his opponents' arguments, and in seizing on the weak point of a position. Then, he would expose it to the House with a brilliantly witty illustration. Admirable classic as he was, no one understood better the genius of the English language. His thoughts poured out, for the most part, in short vigorous sentences, lucid and rhythmical to a degree. Volubility, perhaps, was his fault, as was to be expected in an extemporary speaker, and there was little that was architectural in his speeches. Without any rambling, they showed but small subordination of parts; one point is made after another, great and small together. Even his speech on the Westminster scrutiny in 1784 has this defect, in spite of his cogent reasoning. As a result, he often reads thin, not from spreading out his matter, but from delaying over unimportant aspects of it. He was convinced that he could refute anything, so he refuted everything. But these blots were scarcely observable at the time. To a marvellous extent, he possessed the ability to reason clearly at the highest pressure of emotion.

> He forgot himself and everything around him. He thought only of his subject. His genius warmed and kindled as he went on. He darted fire into his audience. Torrents of impetuous and irresistible eloquence swept along their feelings and conviction[1].

On the whole, Pitt was more favoured in his delivery than his competitor. Fox's clumsy figure, negligently dressed in blue and buff, seemed unprepossessing; only his shaggy eyebrows added to the expression of his face; his voice would rise to a bark in excitement. Pitt was always dignified and composed:

> In solemn dignity and sullen state,
> This new Octavius rises to debate,

wrote George Ellis, carping, in *The Rolliad*. But his musical voice, in spite of its monotony, enchanted the house, and his manner carried authority with it. He was even more lucid than Fox; the whole course of his argument lay clear even in an unpremeditated speech. And he was far more selective in his reasoning. Only the really decisive considerations were enforced by him, and, in expounding a general policy, he was unequalled. He was architectonic by nature; each speech is a symmetrical building, proceeding from foundation to coping-stone. His diction, the 'blaze of elocution' for which he was renowned, was copious and graceful, but, also, prolix almost beyond endurance, and too often leaves the impression that there is nothing in it, and that Pitt himself either did not intend to say anything or was concealing how little he had to say. The matter, indeed, is generally commonplace, though there is a statesmanlike good

---

[1] Sir James Mackintosh's journal, printed in *Memoirs of the Life of the Rt Hon. Sir James Mackintosh*, ed. by his son, Mackintosh, R. J., 1835, vol. I, pp. 322—5.

sense about it which is unlike the perverse ingenuity of Fox, adding argument to argument to obtain an unwise conclusion. None the less, if Pitt's style be antiquated and, at times, stilted, it can rise, as it does in his celebrated speech on the slave-trade in 1792, to magnificent declamation. His perorations, growing out of his preceding matter as they do, and containing definite reasoning and not mere verbal finery, show him at his best. It was in them that he displayed to the full his skill in the then much prized art of Latin quotation. Every speaker, if he could, quoted Latin verse to point his sayings ; but Pitt excelled all in his felicitous selection. Long-famous passages seemed hardly quoted by him, it seemed rather that the orator's stately period itself rose into poetry.

While Fox shone especially in the witty humour of an illustration, irresistibly quaint and full of a convincing sound sense, Pitt employed a dry contumelious sarcasm, in which severe irony was the distinguishing trait. Thus, he observed of a hopelessly muddled speech that it 'was not, I presume, designed for a complete and systematic view of the subject.' Both orators, however, so far as mere wit was concerned, were outdone by Richard Brinsley Sheridan[1], who almost turned their dual supremacy into a triumvirate of eloquence. But in spite of all his brilliancy, he was manifestly outweighed ; unlike Pitt and Fox, he had entered the period of decline long before he quitted parliament. It is not easy, from the mere reports of his speeches, to give a satisfactory account of his comparative lack of weight and influence. He entered parliament in the same year as Pitt, and his oratorical ability, although, at first, it was somewhat clouded, soon obtained the recognition it deserved ; one speech against Warren Hastings, in February 1787, was declared by the auditors to be the best they had ever heard. But, perhaps, he was too frankly an advocate, and he was too clearly bound, by personal attachment, rather than by interest, to the prince of Wales's chariot-wheels. Although his special pleading by no means surpassed that of his contemporaries, it was more obvious, and his changes of opinion, due to fresh developments of Napoleon's action, were not condoned as were those of others. In 1812, the first debater of the day was left out of parliament through the loss of the prince's favour, and his political career was closed.

Wit—brilliant, sustained and polished to the utmost—distinguished Sheridan from his competitors. Many of his impromptu

[1] Concerning Sheridan as a dramatist, see *post*, chap. xii.

speeches, alone in contemporary literature, have the true Junian
ring, and, were they known by later publication or could they
have been prepared beforehand, doubtless we should have been
told that they were 'tormented with the file.' As it is, we must
own that balanced antithesis and mischievous scoffing were native
to him and his readiest means of expression, even if the *Letters
of Junius* provided him with a favourite model.   Nor did his
merits end with wit.   In the mere physical part of oratory, his
animated gay expression and his trained musical voice exercised
an 'inconceivable attraction,' although it may be that the absence
of 'violence or excess,' which is also recorded, may have led to
an impression that he was not in earnest.   In spite of this, his
gaiety could be very bitter ; and, so far as the words went, his
higher flights could be as impassioned as any.   Yet, his merit was
his defect ; he is not absorbed in his subject like Fox, or delivering
a ruler's oracles like Pitt ; we feel, all along, that here is a celebrated
author, enjoying the use of his powers, impassioned on principles
of taste and arguing with the conscious pleasure of the case-
maker.   He bears print better than the two greater men ; but, in
the real test of an orator—the spoken word—he was, admittedly,
their inferior.

   That weight and respect which Sheridan never gained was
amply enjoyed by his fellow-countryman, Henry Grattan.   Perhaps,
as a statesman from his youth up, whose whole energies were engrossed in politics and government, he had an inevitable advantage
over the brilliant literary amateur.   But the main causes lie deep,
in divergences of genius and temperament.   Grattan had none of
Sheridan's exterior advantages ; his gestures were uncouth, his
enunciation difficult.   He surmounted these impediments, however, almost at once, both on his entry into the Irish parliament,
in 1775, and on that into the parliament of the United Kingdom, in
1805.   In the former case, he led the party which obtained Irish
legislative independence, and inaugurated a period called by his
name ; in the latter, at the time of his death, he had become
venerated as the last survivor of the giants of debate among a
lesser generation.   A certain magnanimity in Grattan corresponded
to the greatness of his public career.   His fiercest invective, however severe in intent and effect, had an old-world courtliness.   Of
persiflage he knew nothing ; his wit, of which he had plenty, was
dignified and almost stern.   'You can scarcely answer a prophet ;
you can only disbelieve him,' he said grimly, in 1800, of the Irish
predictions of Pitt.   He was always, beyond question, in earnest.

The excellence of his speeches does not depend on any of the pettier artistic canons of composition. Rhythmical sentences and periods are both to seek. There is no architectural arrangement of matter; he forges straight ahead, seizing on the crucial points one by one. But he had a magnificent power of states-manlike reasoning and of lucid exposition, and, if he had not Fox's capability of making all argument seem to tend his way, he was quite able to make opposing reasons seem of little worth. He could generalise, too, and state, in a pithy way, maxims of practical philosophy. Pithiness and expressiveness, indeed, were at the root of his oratory. His thoughts came out double-shotted and white-hot; his words are the most forcible and convincing for his meaning, rather than the most apt. It was conviction and force at which he aimed, not beauty. Yet, every now and then, he attains a literary charm, more lasting, because more deeply felt, than the considered grace of Sheridan or Pitt.

CHAPTER III

BENTHAM AND THE EARLY UTILITARIANS

JEREMY BENTHAM is famous as the leader of a school of thought and practice which is known sometimes as utilitarianism, sometimes as philosophical radicalism. Before his day, the philosophical school was not a characteristic feature of English speculation. The greater writers influenced the course of ideas without transmitting a definite body of doctrines to a definite group of followers. Bacon proclaimed a philosophical revolution ; but he sought in vain for assistants and collaborators, and the details of his theory were commonly ignored. Hobbes formulated a compact system, but he had no disciples. Locke struck out a new way which many followed to conclusions often very different from his own. Berkeley never lost courage, but he could not open other eyes to his own vision, and the verdict of the day upon his speculations seems to be not unfairly represented by Hume's statement that his arguments 'admit of no answer and produce no conviction.' For his own sceptical results, Hume himself seemed to desire applause rather than converts. The works of these writers never led to a combination for the defence and elucidation of a creed—to any philosophical school which can be compared with peripateticism, stoicism, or Epicureanism in ancient Greece or with the Cartesian, Kantian, or Hegelian schools in modern thought. The nearest approach to such a phenomenon was of the nature of a revival—the new Platonic movement of the seventeenth century, associated with the names of Cudworth, Henry More and other Cambridge scholars[1]. In this way, the utilitarian group presents an appearance unknown before in English philosophy—a simple set of doctrines held in common, with various fields assigned for their application, and a band of zealous workers, labouring for the same end, and united in reverence for their master.

Jeremy Bentham was born in 1748 and died in 1832, when his fame was at its height and his party was on the eve of a great

---

[1] See *ante*, vol. VIII, chap. XI.

triumph[1]. He was a prodigy from his childhood ; he read history
and French, Latin and Greek, when other boys of his years were
feeding their imaginations with fairy tales ; at the tender age of
thirteen, his religious sensibilities were hurt and theological doubts
raised in his mind when he was required to sign the thirty-nine
articles on matriculating at Queen's college, Oxford ; he submitted, however, completed his course there and afterwards duly
entered upon the study of law in London. His father had marked
his abilities and expected them to raise him to the woolsack ; he
had several causes 'at nurse' for him before he was called to the
bar ; and, when Jeremy neglected the practical for the theoretical
side of his profession, the father said in his grief that the boy
would never be anything more than 'the obscure son of an obscure
attorney.' But he made life easy for his son financially, and
had some compensation for the disappointment of his ambition
in the reputation made by Jeremy's first book, *A Fragment on
Government*, which was published anonymously in 1776, and which
the public voice ascribed to one or another of several great men,
including Burke and Mansfield.

Bentham spent almost his whole life in London or its neighbourhood ; but, for over two years, 1785–88, he made an extended
tour in the east of Europe and paid a long visit to his younger
brother Samuel, who held an important industrial appointment
at Kritchev, in Russia. There, he wrote his *Defence of Usury*
(published 1787). There, also, from his brother's method of in-
specting his work-people, he derived the plan of his 'panopticon'
—a scheme for prison management, which was to dispense with
Botany bay. On this scheme, he laboured for five and twenty
years ; the government played with it and finally rejected it,
giving him a large sum by way of compensation for the still larger
sums which he had expended on its advocacy ; but the failure of
this attempt to influence administration left its mark on his
attitude to the English system of government.

After his return from Russia, Bentham published, in 1789, the
work which, more than any other, gives him a place among philosophers—*An Introduction to the Principles of Morals and
Legislation*. It had been printed nine years earlier, and only the
urgency of his friends induced him to make it public. As an
author, Bentham was singularly careless about publication and
as to the form in which his writings appeared. He worked
assiduously, in accordance with a plan which he formed early in

---

[1] He died on 6 June, the day before the royal assent was given to the Reform bill.

life ; he passed from point to point methodically ; each day he produced a number of pages of manuscript, indicated their place in his scheme and then put them aside and never looked at them again. A doubtful proposition would lead him to turn to a new line of enquiry, which might mean a new book. According to one of the friends of his early years, he was 'always running from a good scheme to a better. In the meantime life passes away and nothing is completed.' This method of working had its effect upon his style. His early writings were clear and terse and pointed, though without attempt at elegance. Afterwards, he seemed to care only to avoid ambiguity, and came to imitate the formalism of a legal document. He was overfond, also, of introducing new words into the language ; and few of his inventions have had the success of the term 'international,' which was used for the first time in the preface to his *Introduction to the Principles of Morals and Legislation.*

It was fortunate for Bentham's reputation that he soon came to be surrounded by a group of devoted friends, who were convinced of the value of his ideas and eager to help in making them known. And he was content to leave in their hands the selection, revision and publication of his more important manuscripts. His first work had brought him to the notice of Lord Shelburne (afterwards first marquis of Lansdowne), at whose house he met a number of the statesmen and political thinkers of the day. There, also, he met Étienne Dumont, who, afterwards, gave literary form to the principles of legislation and administration which Bentham elaborated. Dumont was a citizen of Geneva, who had been minister of one of its churches ; driven from his native town by political troubles, he settled, for some time, in St Petersburg, and, in 1785, came to London as tutor to Lansdowne's son ; in 1788 and, again, in 1789, he visited Paris and was in close relations, literary and political, with Mirabeau. On the earlier of these visits, he was accompanied by Sir Samuel Romilly, with whom he had become intimate and who was already known to Bentham ; Romilly showed him some of Bentham's manuscripts, written in French, and Dumont became an enthusiastic disciple and one of the chief agents in spreading the master's ideas. With Bentham's manuscripts and published work before him, and with opportunities for conversation with the author, he produced a series of works which made the new jurisprudence and political theory known in the world of letters. He translated, condensed and even supplied omissions, giving his style to the whole; but he did not seek to do more than put Bentham's writings into literary form, and, in Bentham's collected *Works*, published after his death, many of the most important treatises are retranslations into English from Dumont's versions. The first of Dumont's treatises appeared in 1802, the last in 1825. It is stated that, by 1830, forty thousand copies of these treatises had been sold in Paris for the South American trade alone.

Other helpers surrounded Bentham during his long life ; but his acquaintance with James Mill, which began in 1808, led, for the first time, to the association of a mastermind with his own in pursuit of common objects. Mill was less of a jurist than Bentham, but more of a philosopher, and better equipped for the defence of their fundamental principles on psychological and general grounds. He was also a man of affairs, familiar with practical business and accustomed to deal with other men, and his influence counted for much in making philosophical radicalism an effective political force. Bentham was a recluse occupied with ideas and projects, infinitely patient in elaborating them on paper, and convinced that they would be carried into effect so soon as he had demonstrated their value. The men who sought him out regarded him as a sage, hung upon his lips and approved his doctrines ; and he expected other men, especially political leaders, to be equally rational. During the first half of his career, he was not a radical in politics ; but the failure of his scheme for a panopticon, which he regarded as an administrative reform of the first importance, and in the advocacy of which he had incurred lavish expenditure, gave him a new—if, also, somewhat perverted—insight into the motives of party politicians, and led to a distrust of the governing classes. His mind was thus fitted to receive a powerful stimulus from James Mill, a stern and unbending democrat, whose creed, in Bentham's caustic phrase, resulted 'less from love to the many than from hatred of the few.'

Up to this time, the utilitarian philosophy had not met with great success as an instrument of political propagandism ; it had failed adequately to influence the old political parties ; an organisation of its own was needed with a programme, an organ in the press and representatives in parliament. The new party came to be known as philosophical radicals. Their organ was *The West-minster Review*, founded by Bentham in 1824 ; their programme laid stress on the necessity for constitutional reform before legislative and administrative improvements could be expected ; and a number of eminent politicians became the spokesmen of the party in parliament. It is not possible to assign to the philosophical radicals their exact share in bringing about the changes which gradually ensued; many other influences were working in the same direction. Their power was not due to their numbers, but to the great ability of many members of the group and to the clear and definite policy which they advocated. Bentham was the head of this party; but, perhaps, it is not too much to say that James Mill was its leading spirit. Mill, also, joined with others in giving literary assistance to Bentham; he edited, with modifications of his own, *A Table of the Springs of Action* (1817); he prepared, from the author's manuscripts, an *Introductory view of the Rationale of Evidence* (printed, in part, in 1812, and published in the *Works*); and his brilliant son, John Stuart Mill, then just out of his 'teens, edited *The Rationale of Evidence* in five volumes[1] (1827). Another prominent assistant was John Bowring, who was the first editor of *The Westminster Review*, wrote from the author's dictation the *Deontology* (a work whose accuracy, as an expression of Bentham's mind, was impugned by the Mills) and became Bentham's biographer and editor of his collected *Works*.

Bentham's *Fragment on Government* is the first attempt to apply the principle of utility in a systematic and methodical manner to the theory of government; it takes the form of 'a comment on the *Commentaries*'—a detailed criticism of the doctrine on the same subject which had been set forth in Blackstone's famous work. Sir William Blackstone[2] was born in 1723; he practised at the bar, lectured on the laws of England at Oxford, and, in 1758, was appointed to the newly-founded Vinerian professorship of law; in 1770, he was made a judge, first of the court of king's bench, afterwards of the court of common pleas; he died in 1780. He edited the Great charter and was the author of a number of *Law Tracts* (collected and republished under this title in 1762); but his fame depends upon his *Commentaries on the Laws of England*, the first volume of which appeared in 1765 and the fourth and last in 1769. It is a work of many conspicuous merits. In it, the vast mass of details which makes up the common and statute law is brought together and presented as an organic structure; the meaning of each provision is emphasised, and the relation of the parts illustrated; so that the whole body of law appears as a living thing animated by purpose and a triumph of reason. The style of the book is clear, dignified and eloquent. Bentham, who had heard Blackstone's lectures at

---

[1] Reprinted in *Works*, vols. VI and VII.   [2] See *ante*, vol. X, p. 499.

Oxford, says that he, 'first of all institutional writers, has taught jurisprudence to speak the language of the scholar and the gentleman.' These merits, however, were accompanied by defects, less obvious to the general reader. The author was more prone to see similarities than differences. His analytical power has been praised; but it was inadequate to the conceptions with which he had to deal. His treatment of natural law, in the second section of the introduction, is a case in point; another instance is the discussion of society and the original contract which Bentham criticises. His emphasis on meaning and purpose adds interest to his exposition, and shows insight into the truth that law is not a haphazard collection of injunctions and prohibitions; but this conception also leads him astray; he does not distinguish clearly enough historical causes from logical grounds; his exposition takes on the character of an encomium; and he is too apt to discover, at every point of the English constitution, 'a direction which constitutes the true line of the liberty and happiness of the community.'

In the preface to his *Fragment*, Bentham offers a criticism of the *Commentaries* in general; but the body of his work is restricted to an examination of a few pages, of the nature of a digression, which set forth a theory of government. In these pages, Blackstone gave a superficial summary of the nature and grounds of authority, in which the leading conceptions of political theory were used with more than customary vagueness. Bentham finds the doctrine worse than false; for it is unmeaning. He wishes 'to do something to instruct, but more to undeceive, the timid and admiring student, ... to help him to emancipate his judgment from the shackles of authority.' He insists upon a precise meaning for each statement and each term; and, while he reduces Blackstone's doctrine to ruins, he succeeds, at the same time, in conveying at least the outline of a definite and intelligible theory of government. There are two striking characteristics in the book which are significant for all Bentham's work. One of these is the constant appeal to fact and the war against fictions; the other is the standard which he employs—the principle of utility. And these two are connected in his mind: 'the footing on which this principle rests every dispute, is that of matter of fact.' Utility is matter of fact, at least, of 'future fact—the probability of certain future contingencies.' Were debate about laws and government reduced to terms of utility, men would either come to an agreement or they would 'see clearly and explicitly the point on which the disagreement turned.' 'All else,' says Bentham, 'is but womanish scolding and childish altercation, which is sure to irritate, and which never can persuade.'

In an interesting footnote, Bentham gives an account of the way in which he arrived at this principle. Many causes, he tells us, had combined to enlist his 'infant affections on the side of despotism.' When he proceeded to study law, he found an 'original contract' appealed to 'for reconciling the accidental necessity of resistance with the general duty of submission.' But his intellect revolted at the fiction.

'To prove fiction, indeed,' said I, 'there is need of fiction; but it is the characteristic of truth to need no proof but truth.'... Thus continued I unsatisfying, and unsatisfied, till I learnt to see that *utility* was the test and measure of all virtue; of loyalty as much as any; and that the obligation to minister to general happiness, was an obligation paramount to and inclusive of every other. Having thus got the instruction I stood in need of, I sat down to make my profit of it. I bid adieu to the original contract: and I left it to those to amuse themselves with this rattle, who could think they needed it.

It was from the third volume of Hume's *Treatise of Human Nature* that the instruction came.

'I well remember,' he says, 'no sooner had I read that part of the work which touches on this subject than I felt as if scales had fallen from my eyes. I then, for the first time, learnt to call the cause of the people the cause of Virtue.... That the foundations of all *virtue* are laid in *utility*, is there demonstrated, after a few exceptions made, with the strongest evidence: but I see not, any more than Helvetius saw, what need there was for the exceptions.'

Hume's metaphysics had little meaning for Bentham, but it is interesting to note that his moral doctrine had this direct influence upon the new theory of jurisprudence and politics. Hume was content with showing that utility, or tendency to pleasure, was a mark of all the virtues; he did not go on to assert that things were good or evil according to the amounts of pleasure or pain that they entailed. This quantitative utilitarianism is adopted by Bentham from the start. In the preface to the *Fragment*, the 'fundamental axiom,' whose consequences are to be developed with method and precision, is stated in the words, 'it is the greatest happiness of the greatest number that is the measure of right and wrong.' Half a century earlier, Hutcheson had formulated this 'axiom' almost in the same words; but Bentham does not seem to have been influenced directly by him. Helvétius, whom he had studied closely, comes very near the same doctrine[1], and Priestley had preceded Bentham in using a similar

---

[1] *La justice consiste ... dans la pratique des actions utiles au plus grand nombre.* De l' Esprit (1758), Discours II, chap. 24.

standard in political reasoning. Priestley is not mentioned in
this place, though the preface begins with a reference to his
scientific discoveries, and Bentham has elsewhere recorded his
youthful enthusiasm for his writings. He even says that he had
found the phrase 'greatest happiness of the greatest number' in
one of Priestley's pamphlets; but, in this, his memory must have
deceived him, for the phrase does not seem to have been used by
Priestley. So far as Bentham was concerned, its origin (as he in
one place suggests) must be traced to Beccaria, the Italian jurist
whose work on the penal law proceeded on the same principles as
Bentham's and had a notable effect upon the latter. Beccaria's
book on *Crimes and Punishments* was translated into English in
1767, and, in this translation, the principle of utility is expressed
in the exact words in which, through Bentham's influence, it soon
became both an ethical formula and a party watchword. Bentham
himself used the word 'utilitarian' as early as 1781, and he asserted
that it was the only name for his creed[1]; but, in later life, he
came to prefer the alternative phrase 'greatest happiness principle.'
'The word *utility*,' he said, in a note written in July 1822[2], 'does
not so clearly point to the ideas of *pleasure* and *pain* as the words
happiness and *felicity* do: nor does it lead us to the consideration
of the *number* of the interests affected.' A few months after the
latter date, the term 'utilitarian' was revived by John Stuart
Mill[3], who seems to have been unaware that it had been previously
employed and afterwards discarded by Bentham; he found the
word in Galt's *Annals of the Parish*, where it is used in describing some of the revolutionary parties of the early nineties of the
preceding century; and, 'with a boy's fondness for a name and a
banner,' he adopted it as a 'sectarian appellation.' After this
time, 'utilitarian' and 'utilitarianism' came into common use to
designate a party and a creed.

The evidence goes to show that the 'greatest happiness principle,' or principle of utility, was arrived at by Bentham, in the
first instance, as a criterion for legislation and administration and
not for individual conduct—as a political, rather than an ethical,
principle. His concern was with politics; the sections of Hume's
Treatise which chiefly influenced him were those on justice;
Beccaria wrote on the penal law; and it was expressly as a
political principle that Priestley made use of 'the happiness of

[1] *Works*, vol. x, pp. 92, 392.
[2] *Principles of Morals and Legislation*, ed. 1879, p. 1 n.
[3] *Autobiography*, pp. 79, 80; *Utilitarianism*, p. 9 n.

the members, that is the majority of the members, of any state,' as his standard. The point is important, seeing that, from the time of Locke, the action of every individual had been commonly interpreted as determined by his own pleasure or pain. It is difficult to reconcile this interpretation (which Bentham accepted) with an ethical theory which makes the greatest happiness of all the end for each. But the same difficulty does not arise when the point of view is shifted from the individual to the state. Indeed, the analogical argument will now be open : since each is concerned with his own greatest happiness, the end for the community may be taken to be the greatest happiness of the greatest number. And, when the 'greatest happiness of the greatest number' has been accepted in this way, it is easy—though it is not logical—to adopt it as not merely a political, but, also, in the strict sense, an ethical, principle.

It is to his *Introduction to the Principles of Morals and Legislation* that we must look for Bentham's fullest and clearest account of the underlying principles, psychological and ethical, of his enterprise. The interests of the individual do not always agree with the interests of the community ; and this divergence sets the problem for penal law. Again, the rule of right is one question, and the causes of action is another question ; and it is important not to confuse the ethical with the psychological problem. This distinction is made, and ignored, in the arresting paragraph that opens the work :

Nature has placed mankind under the governance of two sovereign masters, *pain* and *pleasure*. It is for them alone to point out what we ought to do, as well as to determine what we shall do. On the one hand the standard of right and wrong, on the other the chain of causes and effects, are fastened to their throne. They govern us in all we do, in all we say, in all we think : every effort we can make to throw off our subjection, will serve but to demonstrate and confirm it. In words a man may pretend to abjure their empire : but in reality he will remain subject to it all the while. The *principle of utility* recognises this subjection, and assumes it for the foundation of that system, the object of which is to rear the fabric of felicity by the hands of reason and of law. Systems which attempt to question it, deal in sounds instead of sense, in caprice instead of reason, in darkness instead of light.

These sentences give the gist of Bentham's simple philosophy. Everything rests upon pleasure and pain. They are, in the first place, the causes of all human actions. Man is a pleasure-seeking, pain-avoiding animal. It is true, he has many different impulses, springs of action, or motives ; and, of these, the author essays some account in this book ; and, in *A Table of the Springs of*

Action, he comprehends them all in a diagram with their sources
and their corresponding interests. But the strength of each
impulse or motive lies entirely in the pleasure or pain connected
with it; and there are only quantitative differences among
pleasures themselves, or among pains themselves; and pains can
be compared with pleasures, and marked on the same scale by their
distance below the indifference or zero point where there is neither
pleasure nor pain. To this theory, a later writer[1] has given the
name 'psychological hedonism.' It still counts many psycholo-
gists among its adherents, but Bentham held it in a special form
which hardly admits of defence. It is not the actual pleasure
or pain experienced at the moment of action which, according to
him, determines action, but the estimate formed by the agent of
the probable balance of pleasure that is likely to result to him
from the action. The cause, as well as the standard, of human
action is thus matter of 'future fact' only. Had this phrase been
used by Blackstone, Bentham might have pointed out that, so
long as anything is future, it is not a fact, but only an expectation
of a fact; it is an estimate of probabilities. Not pleasure, therefore, but an idea of pleasure, is the actual motive. Although he
thinks that pleasure is man's only object, Bentham always treats
him as pursuing this object in a deliberate and intelligent way
under the guidance of ideas or opinions; he commits the philosopher's fallacy of substituting a reason for a cause; he overlooks
the fact that man was an active being before he was a rational
being, that he is a creature of impulses, inherited and acquired,
that it is only gradually that these impulses come to be organised
and directed by reason, and that this rationalising process is never
completed.

Bentham's views on this point lend emphasis to the importance
of his hedonic calculus. If men are always guided by estimates of
pleasures and pains, these estimates should be rendered as exact
as possible. For this purpose, Bentham analyses the circumstances
that have to be taken into account in estimating the 'force' or
'value' (notions which, for him, are identical) of pleasures and pains.
A pleasure or pain, he says, taken by itself, will vary in the four
circumstances of intensity, duration, certainty and propinquity[2].

---

[1] Sidgwick, *Methods of Ethics,* Bk I, chap. IV.

[2] Sidgwick points out that, on a rational estimate, propinquity in time (apart from
the greater certainty which it implies) is not an independent ground of value. Bentham
follows Beccaria in introducing it; but Beccaria had a different question in view in his
enquiry, namely, the actual deterrent effect of an immediate, as compared with a remote,
punishment.

If we consider its effects, we must take into account two other circumstances : its fecundity, or the chance of its being followed by other feelings of the same kind ; and its purity, or the chance of its not being followed by feelings of an opposite kind. If more than one person is concerned, then account must also be taken of the number of persons, that is, the extent of the pleasure or pain. If we would estimate the benefit to a community of any particular action, then each person affected by it must be considered separately ; each distinguishable pleasure caused by the action must have its value for him calculated in accordance with the six circumstances first mentioned; and each distinguishable pain must have its value calculated in the same way. When this has been done for every person affected, and the sum of all the pains subtracted from the sum of all the pleasures, then the surplus of pleasure will measure the good tendency of the act ; or, if the pains exceed the pleasures in total amount, then the balance of pain will measure the evil tendency of the act.

This may seem an elaborate calculation, but it gives only a faint idea of the minute detail into which Bentham pursued an estimate of good or evil. The significant feature of his method is that it is quantitative. The same method had been suggested by Hutcheson and others before him ; his contemporary Paley used it to some extent ; but Bentham was the first to follow it out into all its ramifications by an exhaustive enumeration and classification of every conceivable consequence. His aim was to make morals and legislation as precise and certain as the physical sciences. For this purpose, he saw that quantitative propositions were necessary. He did not stop to enquire whether quantity was applicable at all to pleasure and pain ; he assumed that it was; and, perhaps, the assumption was correct. Neither did he seek too curiously for a standard of measurement of these quantities, such as every physical science possesses for its purposes. Even in the exact observations which instruments of precision render possible in the physical sciences, allowance has to be made for the personal equation of the observer. But Bentham almost disregarded the personal equation, even in matters of feeling. He did not adequately allow for the difference of individual susceptibilities, or for the degree in which they change in a single lifetime and in the history of the race ; nor did he avoid the fallacy of arguing as if one man's pleasure were always a safe guide for another. Just as he assumed that men were constantly controlled by intellectual considerations, so here, he also assumes that men are much more alike than they

really are . and the two assumptions account for many of the
weaknesses, and even absurdities, of his projects.

Later utilitarians have avoided some of these difficulties by
laying stress on the importance, in personal and social life, of
the permanent objects which are sources of pleasure, rather than
upon particular pleasant experiences.   Bentham himself, in another
work[1], follows similar lines in enumerating four subordinate ends
in which the happiness of society consists.   These are subsistence,
abundance, equality and security.   Subsistence and security are
the most important of the four : 'without security equality could
not last a day; without subsistence abundance could not exist at all.'
With subsistence and abundance, law has little or no direct concern :

You may order production; you may command cultivation; and you will
have done nothing.   But assure to the cultivator the fruits of his industry,
and perhaps in that alone you will have done enough.

Bentham's treatment of equality is remarkable for certain 'patho-
logical propositions' (as he calls them) which he lays down regarding
the effect of wealth upon happiness.   But the chief care of law is
security; and the principle of security extends to the maintenance
of all those expectations which law itself has created.   Security,
one may say, is a necessity for social life and for any moderate
degree of human happiness ; equality is rather of the nature of a
luxury, which legislation should promote when it does not inter-
fere with security.   As for liberty, it is not one of the principal
objects of law, but a branch of security, and a branch which law
cannot help pruning.   Rights of any kind, especially rights of
property, can be created or maintained only by restricting liberty ;
'in particular all laws creative of liberty, are, as far as they go,
abrogative of liberty.'

These suggestions point to a better way of estimating value
than the enumeration of separate pleasures and pains.   But the
latter is Bentham's prevailing method ; and he brings into clear
light a point which, on any theory such as his, should not be
obscured—the difference between the greatest happiness of an
individual and the greatest happiness of the greatest number.
Even Bentham hesitates, both in his earlier and in his later
writings, to assert that it is each man's duty to promote the happiness of all.   How, indeed, can it be so, in Bentham's view, unless
there is sufficient motive to require such conduct?   He says that
a man is never without motives to act in this direction; he has the
social motive of sympathy and the semi-social motive of love of

---

[1] *Theory of Legislation*, trans. Hildreth, 1876, pp. 96 ff.

reputation. But a man may have, and commonly has, motives which tend in a different direction and may render those insufficient or powerless. The divergence may be read between the lines of the halting sentences in which Bentham speaks of the coincidences between private ethics and legislation. There is no mental fusion between the two classes of motives (the selfish and the social); there is no natural identity between the courses of conduct to which they tend; the identification of self-interest with public interest can only be brought about artificially[1] by means of super-added pleasures and pains, especially the latter. These are the sanctions of the principle of utility, which Bentham reduces to four: the physical, the political, the popular (or moral) and the religious. The physical sanction results from natural law, and is exemplified by the headache that follows intemperance: it sanctions prudence, but not benevolence. The popular sanction results from the illwill of society in any of its non-political expressions; it is often a powerful deterrent, but it is apt to be variable and inconsistent, and it has no exact correspondence with public interest. On the religious sanction, Bentham does not rely. There remains the political sanction, the rewards and punishments employed by society organised as a state. But rewards count for little. The whole weight of the doctrine that general happiness is the rule of right and wrong for individual conduct thus rests upon the penal law; it is the 'duty-and-interest-junction-prescribing principle.' And this principle, also, is found to be imperfect. Even when punishment is neither groundless nor needless, there are cases in which it would be inefficacious and others in which it would be unprofitable—by causing more unhappiness than it would avert. In general, it can compel probity but it cannot compel beneficence. Thus, the doctrine of sanctions fails to establish the thesis of utilitarianism that general happiness is the rule of right. And the failure is not covered by the retort: 'if the thunders of the law prove impotent, the whispers of simple morality can have but little influence.'

In the preface to his *Principles of Morals and Legislation*, Bentham gave a list of the works which he had in preparation or contemplation and in which his great design would be completed. According to this list, works were to follow on the principles of legislation in the following nine matters: civil law; penal law;

---

[1] These terms—fusion of interests, natural identity of interests, artificial identification of interests—describe different solutions of the same problem and have been introduced by Halévy, *Formation du radicalisme philosophique*, vol. I, pp. 15 ff.

procedure; reward; constitutional law; political tactics (that is, rules for the direction of political assemblies so that they may attain the end of their institution); international law; finance; political economy; and these were to be followed by a tenth treatise, giving a complete plan of law in all its branches, in respect of its form, including all that properly belongs to the topic of universal jurisprudence. In the course of his life, he dealt with all these subjects, as well as with many others, in separate works. In the more important and complete of his works, he depended on the literary assistance of Dumont and others. But the ideas and the method were always his own. For the exposure of the anomalies of English law, and for the elaboration of a rational and businesslike system to serve as a model for its reform, he deserves almost the sole credit.

Bentham's power was derived from the combination in his mind of two qualities—the firm grasp of a single principle, and a truly astonishing mastery of details. Every concrete situation was analysed into its elements and these followed out into all their ramifications. The method of division and subdivision was artificial; but it tended to clearness and exhaustiveness, and it could be applied to any subject. Whatever did not yield to this analysis was dismissed as 'vague generality.' Applying this method with infinite patience, he covered the whole field of ethics, jurisprudence and politics. Everything in human nature and in society was reduced to its elements, and then reconstructed out of these elements. And, in each element, only one feature counted, whether in respect of force or of value—its quantum of pleasure or pain. The whole system would have been upset if an independent qualitative distinction between pleasures had been allowed, such as Plato contended for, or John Stuart Mill afterwards attempted to introduce into utilitarianism. 'Quantity of pleasure being equal,' says Bentham, 'pushpin is as good as poetry.' As regards the principle itself, there was no opportunity for originality: Hume had suggested its importance to his mind; Priestley had shown its use in political reasoning; he picked up the formula from Beccaria; and in his exposition of its nature there is, perhaps, nothing that had not been stated already by Helvétius. But the relentless consistency and thoroughness with which he applied it had never been anticipated; and this made him the founder of a new and powerful school.

His method was not that most characteristic of the revolutionary thought of the period. The ideas of the revolution

centred in certain abstract conceptions. Equality and freedom
were held to be natural rights of which men had been robbed by
governments, and the purpose of the revolutionists was to regain
and realise those rights. This mode of thought was represented in
England by Richard Price ; through Rousseau, it came to dominate
the popular consciousness ; in the American Declaration of Independence of 1776, it was made the foundation of a democratic
reconstruction of government. The year 1776 is of note in literary
history, also. It marks the death of Hume, and the publication
of *The Wealth of Nations*, of the first volume of Gibbon's *Decline
and Fall* and of Bentham's *Fragment on Government.* The last-
named work preaches a radical reform, but without appealing to
natural or abstract rights. Although he was an admirer of the
American constitution, Bentham was never deceived by the crude
'metapolitics' (to use Coleridge's word) of the Declaration of
Independence, or by the same doctrine as it was expounded at
greater length, in the 'Declaration of the Rights of Man and the
Citizen,' decreed in the French Constituent Assembly of 1791. His
Anarchical Fallacies, written about this time, is a masterly exposure of the crudities and confusions of the latter document. All
rights, in his view, are the creation of law ; '*natural rights* is simple
nonsense: natural and imprescriptible rights, rhetorical nonsense,—
nonsense upon stilts.' Yet the difference between Bentham's theory
and that of continental and American revolutionists was not immediately obvious. He was in correspondence with some of the
leaders of the revolution, recommended his panopticon scheme for
adoption in France, and offered himself as chief gaoler ; in 1792,
he was made a citizen of France. Nevertheless, his *Anarchical
Fallacies* made his position clear : and it is owing to him that
philosophical radicalism in England, unlike the corresponding
revolutionary doctrines in other countries, was based upon an
empirical utilitarianism and not upon *a priori* ideas about natural
rights. A comparison of his argument in *Anarchical Fallacies*
with his criticism of our 'matchless constitution' in *The Book of
Fallacies* (1824) shows that he was a foe to all kinds of loose
thinking, whether in praise of revolutionary ideals or in the
interests of the established order.

The *Constitutional Code*, which Bentham published towards
the end of his life, exhibits an endeavour to give to the people
concerned the fullest possible control over the acts of government.
The author had become increasingly impressed by the extent to
which 'sinister interests,' especially the personal and class interests

of the rulers, interfered with public interest; and he seeks to check their operation at every turn. His work is intended 'for the use of all nations and all governments professing liberal opinions.' Some years earlier, he had published *Codification Proposals*, offering his services in the matter to any nation that wanted them. Portugal had already applied to him for assistance. He had negotiations of a similar, if less official, kind, with Spain, Mexico, Venezuela, the United States, Russia, Greece and Tripoli. The world seemed to be at his feet, anxious to learn from him the arts of law and government; and he was willing to instruct all comers. But he did not disregard entirely differences of national character and historical conditions. In his essay on *The Influence of Time and Place in Matters of Legislation*, he attributes immutability to the grounds of law rather than to the laws themselves, and rebukes as 'hot-headed innovators' those legislators who 'only pay attention to abstract advantage.'

Bentham's genius was comprehensive and tenacious rather than profound. He covered an extensive field, always following the same clue. He passed from social science to religion, and analysed its influence 'upon the temporal happiness of mankind,' part of his work being edited by a disciple, George Grote, and published under a pseudonym (1822). He wrote, also, a number of papers on education under the title *Chrestomathia* (1816); and he and his friends projected a chrestomathic school in which the youth of the middle and upper classes were to be trained in correct utilitarian principles. Thus, he dealt, in a way, with the deeper things of life, and yet only with the surface-aspect of these things. With forces and values that cannot be measured in terms of pleasure or pain, he had no concern; into history, art and religion he had little insight; but he was unconscious of his limitations, and he attempted to deal with these things by his own scale of values.

Certain of Bentham's occasional papers—those on *Poor Laws and Pauper Management*—appeared in Young's *Annals of Agriculture*. This periodical was started in 1784, and extended to forty-five volumes. Its editor, Arthur Young, was already known as the greatest of English writers on agriculture. At the age of seventeen, he had published a pamphlet on *The War in North America* (1758), and had afterwards written a great variety of works chiefly on English farming, including the records of a series of tours through different districts of England. He was not only an agricultural expert, but, also, a social observer and theorist, as is shown in many of his works, such as *Political Arithmetic* (1774), *Tour in Ireland* (1780) and—most famous of all—*Travels in France* (1792). He had the good fortune to visit France shortly before the revolution, as well as after it had broken out; and his trained power of observation enabled him to see and point out the social conditions which made the continuance of the *ancien régime* impossible. Young's close observation of actual conditions and his apt reflections upon them have made his works important authorities for economists, especially on the question of the relative values of different systems of land tenure. He had also an epigrammatic gift that has made some of his phrases remembered. 'The magic of property turns sand to gold' is one of his sayings which has become famous.

On the ground of his general principles, Thomas Robert Malthus may be counted among the utilitarians; but he was a follower of Tucker and Paley rather than of Bentham. He did not share Bentham's estimate of the intellectual factor in conduct, and the exaggeration of this estimate in other thinkers of the time was the indirect cause of his famous work. Hume had spoken of reason as the slave of the passions; but William Godwin wrote as if men were compact of pure intellect. He, too, was a utilitarian, in the sense that he took happiness as the end of conduct; but he was under the sway of the revolutionary idea; he put down all human ills to government, regarding it as an unnecessary evil, and thought that, with its abolition, man's reason would have free play and the race would advance rapidly towards perfection. It was the doctrine of the perfectibility of man that gave Malthus pause. His criticism of the doctrine was first thrown out in conversation with his father. The elder Malthus, a friend and executor of Rousseau, expressed approval of the idea of human perfectibility set forth, in 1793, in Godwin's *Political Justice* and in Condorcet's *Esquisse d'un tableau historique des progrès de l'esprit humain*. Robert Malthus took a more sombre view of things than his father; he had had a scientific education; and, as a clergyman, he knew something of the life of the people; above all, he was of the new generation, and the dreams of an earlier day did not blind him to existing facts. He saw an obstacle in the way of all Utopias. Even if equality and happiness were once attained, they could not last; population would soon expand beyond the means of subsistence; and the result would be inequality and misery. The argument thus struck out in the course of debate was expanded,

soon after, in *An Essay on the Principle of Population* (1798).
A storm of controversy followed its publication; but its teaching
made notable converts, such as Pitt among statesmen and Paley
among philosophers; and it soon came to be adopted as part of
the orthodox utilitarian tradition.   To his critics, Malthus replied
with the thoroughness of an honest enquirer; he travelled on the
continent, studied social conditions and investigated the actual
circumstances which had kept the numbers of the people and their
food in equilibrium.   The answer came in the second edition of his
Essay (1803), which, in contents, is, practically, a new book.   Even
the title is modified.   The first edition discusses the principle of
population 'as it affects the future improvement of society'; the
second is 'a view of its past and present effects on human happiness.'
The former shattered the picture of a future golden age, to be
reached by the abolition of government or by any communistic
device; the effect it produces on the reader is one of unrelieved
depression; mankind is in the power of an impulse hostile to
welfare; only vice and misery prevent the world from being over-
peopled.   The second edition turns from the future to the past and
the present; it is informed by a fuller study of facts; it finds that
the pressure of the people on the food has diminished with the
advance of civilisation; not vice and misery only, but morality
also, is reckoned among the checks to the increase of population.
Thus, as he says in the preface, he 'tried to soften some of the
harshest conclusions of the first essay.'

The main doctrine of Malthus was not entirely new.   The
question of the populousness of ancient and modern nations had
been discussed by a number of writers, including Hume; there
were anticipations of Malthus in Joseph Townsend's *Dissertation
on the Poor Laws* (1786); and, still earlier, in 1761, Robert Wallace,
in his *Various Prospects of Mankind*, had at first suggested community of goods as a solution of the social problem and then
pointed out that the increase of population, which would result
from communism, was a fatal flaw in his own solution.   But Malthus
made the subject his own, and showed by patient investigation
how population, as a matter of fact, had pressed upon the means of
subsistence, and by what measures it had been kept in check.   He
produced a revolution in scientific opinion and powerfully affected
popular sentiment, so that pure literature took up the theme:

> Slowly comes a hungry people as a lion creeping nigher,
> Glares at one that nods and winks behind a slowly dying fire.

It is hardly too much to say that the prospect weighed on the social mind of the nineteenth century like a nightmare. The mind of the twentieth century has shaken it off like a dream, but it has not answered the main thesis for which Malthus contended. It is true that his exposition is not above criticism. The terms in which he stated his thesis—that population tends to increase in a geometrical ratio and food in an arithmetical ratio—are, at best, inexact. Perhaps, also, he did not allow sufficiently for the effects of new methods and inventions in increasing the supply of food and for the possible reaction of quality upon numbers among men. The darker side of his picture of the human lot may be read in his criticism of the poor law. But he was not blind to considerations of a more favourable kind. He saw that the 'struggle for existence' (the phrase is his) was the great stimulus to labour and a cause of human improvement. Thus, at a later date, Darwin and A. R. Wallace, working independently, found in his book a statement of the principle, of which they were in search, for the explanation of biological development.

The publication of *An Essay on the Principle of Population* determined the career of Malthus, which, thenceforth, was devoted to teaching and writing on economics. His *Inquiry into the Nature and Progress of Rent*, his *Principles of Political Economy* and his correspondence with Ricardo are of importance in the history of economic theory, though they were not fitted to exert any notable influence upon thought and literature in general. In all that he wrote, Malthus kept in close touch with the actual facts of social and industrial life; in this respect, his writings form a contrast in method to the works of Ricardo[1], in whose abstract reasonings the economics of the Benthamite school attained their most characteristic expression.

During the period of Bentham's supremacy, the tradition of a different type of philosophy was carried on by Dugald Stewart. Stewart was born in 1753 and died in 1828; for twenty-five years (1785—1810), he was professor of moral philosophy at Edinburgh. His lectures were the most powerful formative influence upon the principles and tastes of a famous generation of literary Scotsmen, and they attracted, besides, many hearers from England, the continent and America.

'Perhaps few men ever lived,' said Sir James Mackintosh, one of his pupils, 'who poured into the breasts of youth a more fervid and yet reasonable love of liberty, of truth, and of virtue.... Without derogation from his writings, it may be said that his disciples were among his best works.'

[1] He will be treated in a later volume of the present work.

His writings, also, were numerous. The first volume of his *Elements of the Philosophy of the Human Mind* appeared in 1792, the second in 1814, the third in 1827. His *Outlines of Moral Philosophy* was published in 1794, *Philosophical Essays* in 1810, a dissertation entitled *The Progress of Metaphysical, Ethical, and Political Philosophy since the Revival of Letters* (contributed to *The Encyclopaedia Britannica*) in 1815 and 1821, *The Philosophy of the Active and Moral Powers* in 1828; and accounts of the lives and writings of Adam Smith, Robertson and Reid were contributed to the *Transactions* of the Royal Society of Edinburgh.

Himself, in his youth, a pupil of Reid, Stewart remained his follower in philosophy. But he avoided the use of the term 'common sense,' which, as employed by Reid, had produced the impression that questions of philosophy could be decided by an appeal to popular judgment. He speaks, instead, of 'the fundamental laws of human belief, or the primary elements of human reason'; and these he regards not as the data upon which conclusions depend, but, rather,

as the vincula which give coherence to all the particular links of the chain, or (to vary the metaphor) as component elements without which the faculty of reasoning is inconceivable and impossible.

He varied from Reid, also, in many special points, often approximating to the positions of writers of the empirical school; but, according to Mackintosh, he 'employed more skill in contriving, and more care in concealing, his very important reforms of Reid's doctrines, than others exert to maintain their claims to originality.' His works often betray their origin in the lecture-room, and are full of quotations from, and criticisms of, other authors. They are written in a style which is clear and often eloquent, without ever being affected; but the exposition and criticism are devoted to those aspects of philosophical controversy which were prominent in his own day, and they have thus lost interest for a later generation. Nor did he show any such profundity of thought, or even distinction of style, as might have saved his work from comparative neglect. Among his numerous writings, there is no single work of short compass which conveys his essential contribution to the progress of thought.

CHAPTER IV

WILLIAM COWPER

FEW rivers can be traced to a single source. Water from a hundred fields and woods and springs trickles down, to join in a score of streams, which, in their turn, join to make a river. Yet, there is always a point at which it is just to declare any particular stream to be the upper reach of any particular river. So, in the history of English poetry, no single origin can be shown for the poetry of nature and simplicity which, with Wordsworth, became a mighty river, and which is flowing still. To mention but two poets, Gray and Collins poured their tribute of clear water into the stream. But, with Cowper, we come to the upper reaches, and are able to trace thence, with unbroken continuity, the course of the main stream.

Reformers in poetry probably seldom work with a conscious aim, like social and political reformers. A poet writes in a certain manner because that is the only way in which he can write, or wishes to write, and without foreseeing or calculating the effect of his work. This is especially true of Cowper, who owed more, perhaps, than any English poet to what may be called accident, as distinguished from poetic purpose. He did not, like Milton or Tennyson, dedicate himself to poetry. He did not even write poetry primarily for the sake of writing poetry, but to ward off melancholy by keeping his mind occupied. He liked Milton better than Pope, and was careful to show this preference in his versification ; but accident—the bent of his mind and the circumstances of his life—made him the forerunner of a great poetic revival. He drew poetry back to the simple truths of ordinary human nature and the English countryside, because, in the limited outlook on the world which his life allowed him, these were the things that touched him and interested him. Being a man of fine taste, tender feelings and a plain sincerity, he opened the road of truth for the nobler poetic pageants that were to pass along it.

Born in the rectory of Great Berkhampstead, Herts, in November 1731, and becoming poet in earnest nearly fifty years later, he had, meanwhile, fallen under the influence of thought and sentiment which were beginning to break up the old, rigid and, frequently, brutal order. His family, on the father's side, had given distinguished men to the law and the church ; and, in his boyhood and youth, it seemed not wholly unlikely that he would follow in his ancestors' paths and take an active part in life. That he was affectionate and tenderhearted we know from the lines he wrote many years later, *On the receipt of my Mother's Picture out of Norfolk.* How far the bullying which he suffered at his first school may have twisted the development of his nature, it is impossible to say. He was not unhappy at Westminster, where he numbered among his schoolfellows Edward Lloyd, Charles Churchill, George Colman the elder, Warren Hastings and Elijah Impey. True, in after years, he attacked English public schools in *Tirocinium* ; but it is not certain that, in this matter, his boyish feelings tallied with his riper judgment. From Westminster, he went to the office of a solicitor, to be trained for the law. Thurlow was a student in the same office ; and the two young men used to spend much of their time at the house of Cowper's uncle Ashley Cowper, where the chief attraction lay in the daughters, Theodora and Harriet. So far, there is not any trace of the Cowper of later years, though there are already traces of the poet. He fell in love with his cousin Theodora, and wrote verses to her which are far above the average of young men's love-poems. The poems to Delia show, already, the directness, the sincerity and the simplicity which were to be the keynotes of his later work, together with the tenderness which has won him admirers among hundreds to whom most poetry seems unreal. In one of these poems, *On her endeavouring to conceal her Grief at Parting,* occurs the famous verse :

> Oh! then indulge thy grief, nor fear to tell
> The gentle source from whence thy sorrows flow;
> Nor think it weakness when we love to feel,
> Nor think it weakness what we feel to show.

The stanza is completely characteristic of Cowper's mind and manner. The proposed match with Theodora was forbidden by her father, on the ground of consanguinity. To Cowper, the blow, evidently, was severe. In *Absence and Bereavement,* he bewails his fate. The concluding lines of this poem :

> Why all that soothes a heart from anguish free,
> All that delights the happy, palls with me!

suggest strongly the sentiment of a later and finer poem, *The Shrubbery* :

> This glassy stream, that spreading pine,
> Those alders quivering to the breeze,
> Might soothe a soul less hurt than mine,
> And please, if anything could please.
>
> But fixed unalterable care
> Forgoes not what she feels within,
> Shows the same sadness everywhere,
> And slights the season and the scene.

The earlier poem thus seems to foreshadow the melancholy that, afterwards, was to claim the poet. Externally, it is true, there did not appear to be any immediate sign of that melancholy. Cowper bought chambers in the Temple and was called to the bar. Without attempting to practise, he lived the life of a cultivated young man about town, reading Homer and marking the differences between Homer and Pope, writing articles and verses (one or two very popular ballads were among the early works of the author of *John Gilpin*) and helping his brother John with a translation of Voltaire's *Henriade*. Yet, meanwhile, the mischief was growing. He suffered from fits of depression, which, in later life, he believed to have been of religious origin. He found what alleviation he could in the poems of George Herbert ; but, when, in his thirty-second year, he was nominated by his uncle major Cowper to a clerkship in the House of Lords, his depression and his shyness broke into mania, and he tried to kill himself. Thereafter, he was out of the race, but, on that very account, was left the more open to the influences, religious and humane, to which his gentle nature, even in active life, must have been sensible. These were the days of Wesley and Whitefield, of widening hope and freedom in religion ; they were, also, the days of Rousseau and his creed of love and brotherhood. Slaves, animals and 'common wretches' were perceived to have their rights. Cowper was to become the poet of a religious sect, which, though doubtless narrow and unattractive in itself, had its share in breaking up the spiritual ice of the age. He was to sing with power in the cause of slaves, to make his pet hares and his dog famous and to find in rustics some of his best material for poetry. His sympathies were not wide ; but they were on the side of kindness. In politics, he remained 'an old whig' ; but the French revolution was, to him, 'a noble cause,' though made 'ridiculous' by the excesses of a 'madcap' people.

Thus, though living remote from the world, he breathed into the world a spirit of love and freedom. Before that time came, however, he had much to bear. Cured of his mania by a doctor at St Albans, whose religion was of the hopeful kind, he was settled by his brother and friends at Huntingdon; and, here, he maintained his cheerfulness and formed the friendship which proved the most important influence on his life. Morley Unwin was a retired clergyman who taught private pupils. With Unwin, his wife and his son and daughter, Cowper became so intimate that he went to live in their house. Their simple, cheerful, religious life exactly suited his needs. When Unwin was killed by a fall from his horse, Cowper and Mrs Unwin continued to reside together. Theirs is one of the famous friendships of literary history. Henceforth, they never separated; and, in Cowper's letters, in the sonnet, *To Mrs Unwin*, and in the poem, *To Mary*, the woman who devoted her life to Cowper received her reward. Soon after Unwin's death, the family moved from Huntingdon to Olney, in order to be near the curate in charge of that place, John Newton. The house that Newton chose for them was damp and gloomy; Olney was a poor and rather brutal place. Newton, formerly the captain of a slaver, was an evangelist of tremendous power and small tact. More than one of his parishioners (not, perhaps, very delicately organised people) had been thrown off their balance by his 'enthusiasm.' With the best intentions, he did the timid and sensitive Cowper much harm. He forced him to hold forth in public; he robbed him of exercise and gentle pleasures. The result was a severe return of his melancholy. In order to dissipate it, Newton laid upon him the task of writing hymns for a hymn-book which he was compiling.

The collection entitled *Olney Hymns* was published in London in 1779. Cowper's contributions to the volume were initialled 'C.,' and among them occur several hymns still in use, together with three or four which are among the best known of English hymns, to whatever extent people may differ as to their morality. *Oh for a closer walk with God*; *There is a fountain filled with blood*; *Hark, my soul! it is the Lord*; *Jesus! where'er thy people meet*; *God moves in a mysterious way*—these are among the hymns by Cowper in this collection. The salient quality of them all is their sincerity and directness. The poet's actual experiences in the spiritual life are expressed with the simplicity generally characteristic of his work. Their weakness is a lack of profundity, and the absence of that suggestion of the infinite and the awful,

which, as in Crashaw or Newman, sometimes informs religious
poetry less carefully dogmatic than Cowper's. His mind, indeed, was
too precisely made up on matters of doctrine to be fruitful either
of lofty religious passion or of religious mystery ; and, instead of
being great sacred poetry, his hymns are a stay and comfort to
souls experiencing what might be called the practical difficulties
of certain phases of spiritual life. Most of them are hopeful
in tone ; for, though the book was not published till 1779, the
hymns were written by Cowper before 1773. In that year, he had
another outbreak of mania. He imagined himself not only condemned to hell, but bidden by God to make a sacrifice of his own
life. Mrs Unwin nursed him devotedly ; but, more than a year
passed before he began to recover. By 1776, he had resumed, in
part, his correspondence with his friends. In 1779, Newton left
Olney for a London living ; and, the influence of his overbearing
friend being withdrawn, Cowper entered upon what was probably
the happiest period of his life. Carpentering, gardening, horse
exercise, walking and other simple pleasures kept him cheerful ;
and he began again to write poetry. His kinsman Martin Madan
having published a book advocating polygamy, Cowper, in 1781,
printed anonymously a reply to it in the form of a fantastic tale.
Anti-Thelyphthora is not among Cowper's best works ; but it
has a pointed neatness of diction and a descriptive touch which
foretell *The Task*. Mrs Unwin, always anxious to keep him
occupied and to make the best of him, set him to work on a long
poem. She gave him the not very promising subject of the
progress of error ; and, going eagerly to work, he wrote eight
satires : *Table Talk, The Progress of Error, Truth, Expostula-
tion, Hope, Charity, Conversation* and *Retirement*.

Most of Cowper's critics have been unduly severe upon these
moral satires. Doubtless, they are not so good as *The Task*
or many of the shorter poems. Their weakness is obvious.
A satirist, whether he be of the indignant order, like Juvenal, or
the bitter, like Swift, or the genial, like Horace, must begin by
knowing the world that he intends to attack ; and Cowper, who
had been cut off from the world, did not know it. When he
attacks bishops and other clergy who were not of his own
evangelical cast, or newspapers, or town life, it is difficult not to
resent his easy smartness at the expense of things which his
narrowness of outlook prevented him from understanding. Again,
writing, as it seems, with an eye seeking for the approval
of John Newton, Cowper gives too much space to good advice,

and too little to the allurements which should distinguish the
satirist from the preacher.

> The clear harangue, and cold as it is clear,
> Falls soporific on the listless ear

are lines from *The Progress of Error* which have been quoted
against their author ever since the satires first appeared.   And it
may be said in general that, fine as is the famous passage on
Petronius (Lord Chesterfield) in *The Progress of Error*

> Thou polished and high-finished foe to truth,
> Grey-beard corrupter of our listening youth;

Cowper's poetry is not at its best when he is attacking or scolding;
and, writing primarily to distract his mind and to benefit humanity,
only secondarily to produce works of polished art, he is weak in the
construction and arrangement of his poems.   These objections,
however, cannot outweigh the many merits of Cowper's moral
satires.   Their diction is precise and epigrammatic, not so much
because Cowper polished his work minutely, as because his mind
was exact and clear.   Several of his couplets have become familiar
as household words ; and one of them,

> How much a dunce that has been sent to roam
> Excells a dunce that has been kept at home,

achieved the honour of quotation by Bulwer Lytton in his play
Money.   On a higher level is his criticism of Pope:

> But he (his musical finesse was such,
> So nice his ear, so delicate his touch)
> Made poetry a mere mechanic art,
> And every warbler has his tune by heart.

Cowper himself had the tune by heart, no doubt ; but he did not
sing it.   Using the heroic couplet throughout these satires, he
contrives to write quite unlike Pope.   His versification is already
unlike anything to be found in English literature, unless it be the
verse of his former schoolfellow, Churchill, whose work he greatly
admired.   But Cowper's mind was so different from Churchill's
that the resemblance does not go very deep.   In the most successful
portions of these satires—especially in the immortal picture of
the statesman out of office, in *Retirement*—Cowper, both in
matter and in manner, resembles Horace more than he resembles
any other poet.   He shows the same shrewd wisdom, the same
precision and refinement, the same delicate playfulness.   *Retirement*, which is the latest of these satires, is, undoubtedly, the

best; and the perspicacious suggestion has been made[1] that it was written under the influence of Cowper's friend, Lady Austen, to whom we shall return. At any rate, in *Retirement*, as in *The Task*, he is talking of things which he understood and liked for their own sake ; and, since his tender and genial spirit was more responsive to the stimulus of what he liked than of what he disliked, was better, in short, at loving than at hating, in the positive than in the negative, *Retirement* shows him well suited by his subject and happy in its treatment.

The volume was published in 1782 under the title *Poems by William Cowper, of the Inner Temple, Esq.* Besides the satires, it contained thirty-five shorter poems, of which three were in Latin. Those in English include one or two pieces of note : *Boadicea: an Ode*, which has well earned its place in the literature of the schoolroom and its reputation in the world as a fine example of great power and weight attained by perfectly simple means ; the pretty *Invitation into the Country*, addressed to Newton ; some very graceful and delicate translations from the Latin poems of Cowper's Westminster schoolmaster Vincent Bourne; the powerful *Verses supposed to be written by Alexander Selkirk*; and two poems showing Cowper's possession of a gift for writing delicate and suggestive lyric poetry—lyric poetry with the indefinable touch of magic in it—which he did not thoroughly cultivate. One is the poem entitled *The Shrubbery*, to which reference was made above ; the other, the lines 'addressed to a young lady' beginning

> Sweet stream, that winds through yonder glade,
> Apt emblem of a virtuous maid!

a poem which equals the best achievements of Wordsworth or Byron in the same field.

In connection with the satire *Retirement*, the name of Lady Austen was mentioned above. This charming and intelligent widow came into Cowper's life in the year 1781 and touched his spirits and his poetry to fine issues. Unlike Mrs Unwin, she belonged to the world and had a proper appreciation of the external things of life. In suggesting to Cowper a subject for his pen, she gave him not a moral topic but a simple object— the sofa in his room. The idea was very likely thrown off without full prevision of its far-reaching effect ; but, in encouraging Cowper to write about something that he knew, in checking,

[1] By Bailey, J. C., *The Poems of William Cowper*, p. xxxvi.

so far as might be, his tendency to moralise and to preach by fixing his attention on the simple facts of his daily life, she gave him an impulse which was what his own poetry, and English poetry at that moment, most needed. The result of her suggestion was *The Task*, a blank-verse poem in six books, of which *The Sofa* formed the first. Cowper starts playfully, with a touch of the gallantry that was always his. He shows his humour by dealing with the ordained subject in the style of Milton. Milton was his favourite poet; Johnson's life of Milton one of the writings he most disliked. Nevertheless, with his gentle gaiety, he begins his work with a parody of Milton.

> No want of timber then was felt or feared
> In Albion's happy isle. The lumber stood
> Ponderous, and fixed by its own massy weight.
> But elbows still were wanting; these, some say,
> An alderman of Cripplegate contrived,
> And some ascribe the invention to a priest
> Burly and big, and studious of his ease.

Thus, for a hundred lines or so, he plays with his subject. Then, breaking away from it by an ingenious twist, he speaks for himself; and, for the first time, we have a new voice, the voice of William Cowper :

> For I have loved the rural walk through lanes
> Of grassy swarth, close cropped by nibbling sheep
> And skirted thick with intertexture firm
> Of thorny boughs; have loved the rural walk
> O'er hills, through valleys, and by rivers' brink,
> E'er since a truant boy I passed my bounds
> To enjoy a ramble on the banks of Thames;
> And still remember, nor without regret
> Of hours that sorrow since has much endeared,
> How oft, my slice of pocket store consumed,
> Still hungering, penniless and far from home,
> I fed on scarlet hips and stony haws,
> Or blushing crabs, or berries that emboss
> The bramble, black as jet, or sloes austere.

It is, perhaps, difficult to realise nowadays how new such writing as this was when *The Task* was published. Assuredly, these are not 'raptures'

> conjured up
> To serve occasions of poetic pomp.

The truant boy, his pocket store, the berries he ate—there is something in these which his century might have called 'low.' But the berries are exactly described; we feel sure that the boy ate them. The poet who describes them was, himself, that boy;

and, looking back, he sees his boyhood through the intervening sorrow which we know that he suffered. In every line, there is actuality and personality. The diction is still a little Miltonic, for Cowper's blank verse never moved far from his master; but, all the preceding nature poetry might be searched in vain for this note of simple truth—the record of actual experience which the poet perceives to have poetic value and beauty. A little later, he addresses Mrs Unwin in a famous passage, beginning:

> How oft upon yon eminence our pace
> Has slackened to a pause, and we have borne
> The ruffling wind, scarce conscious that it blew,
> While admiration feeding at the eye,
> And still unsated, dwelt upon the scene.

Hitherto, there had been nothing in English poetry quite like the passage that begins with the lines here quoted. The nearest parallel is, probably, Collins's *Ode to Evening*, though that lovely poem wraps its subject in a glow of romance which is absent from Cowper's description. But, when Cowper wrote *The Sofa*, he had never even heard of Collins[1]. He owed as little to Gray's *Elegy*, where the scene is far more 'sentimentalised'; and nothing can deprive him of the title to originality. Here is a very commonplace English landscape, minutely described. The poet does nothing to lend it dignity or significance other than its own. But he has seen for himself its beauty, and its interest; little details, like the straightness of the furrow, the smallness of the distant ploughman, please him. And, because he has himself derived pleasure and consolation from the scene and its details, his poetry communicates that pleasure and that consolation. Familiar scenes, simple things, prove, in his lines, their importance, their beauty and their healing influence on the soul of man. Nature need not any longer be 'dressed up' to win a place in poetry. And, if *The Task* be the forerunner of Wordsworth, its manner of accepting facts as they are, and at their own value, contains, also, the germ of something very unlike Cowper, something that may be found in *The Woods of Westermain*.

The nature poetry in *The Task* is, doubtless, of a humbler order than that of *Tintern Abbey* or *The Excursion*, though, in many passages of simple description, the similarity between Wordsworth and Cowper is striking. Cowper would have been unable to compose the books of *The Prelude: On Imagination and Taste, how impaired and how restored.* He would even

---

[1] *Letters*, ed. Frazer, J. G., 1912, vol. i, p. 282.

have thought them unChristian and reprehensible. Where the great soul of Wordsworth broods over the world of sense, conscious of how it opens and affects the world of the spirit, Cowper hardly even asks how it is that these loved scenes console and enlarge the mind. He is not a philosopher, and he is not a mystic. For him, it is enough that the things he sees are beautiful and dear ; he does not ask for anything more. But the nearness of his object, his familiarity with it and his fine taste in expression result in poetry which, if not, in itself, great, is wonderfully pure and sweet, and prepared the way for profounder work by others. While his simplicity and exactness in description mark him off from all preceding nature poets, even from Thomson, the spirit of his poetry differentiates him equally from Crabbe, who, though even more minute and faithful in detail, always regarded nature as a setting for the emotions of man. There are passages in *The Task* which sound a nobler music than that quoted above. One is the invocation to evening in *The Winter Evening*, beginning :

> Come, Evening, once again, season of peace ;
> Return, sweet Evening, and continue long !

The earlier part of this passage is very like Collins. The whole of it, in spite of certain characteristic words—'ostentatious,' 'modest'— is a little too fanciful and a little too elaborate to be entirely in Cowper's peculiar manner. He is most himself when he is most closely concerned with the scenes and people that, in his restricted life, he had come to know and love. The six books of *The Task* (entitled *The Sofa*, *The Time-piece*, *The Garden*, *The Winter Evening*, *The Winter Morning Walk* and *The Winter Walk at Noon*) contain many passages of sympathetic description that have become classical. Such are the lines on the 'rural sounds' and those on hay-carting in *The Sofa* ; the man cutting hay from the stack, the woodman and his dog in *The Winter Morning Walk* ; the postman and the waggoner in *The Winter Evening* ; the fall of snow, in the same book. Each is the product of the poet's own observation ; each helped to prove, in an age which needed the lesson, that simplicity and truth have their place in poetry, and that commonplace things are fit subjects for the poet. Cowper's simplicity is not the simplicity of *Lyrical Ballads*, any more than it is the glittering artifice of Pope. He is Miltonic throughout ; but he speaks with perfect sincerity, keeping 'his eye on the object.'

There are, no doubt, stretches of didactic verse in *The*

Task. That was almost necessary to Cowper in a poem of this
length.   But it is more important to observe how, in this poem,
one quality, that has endeared Cowper to thousands of readers and
was by no means without its effect on public opinion, finds its chief
expression in his works.   After concluding *The Sofa* with the
famous and beautiful passage beginning :

> God made the country, and man made the town;

he opens *The Time-piece* with a cry for some refuge where the
news of man's oppression, deceit and cruelty might never reach
him.   The love of man for man, the love of man for animals, for the
meanest thing that lives—this is the principal moral message of
The Task.   Doubtless, this kind of 'sentimentalism' was 'in the
air,' at the time.   It belonged, to some extent, to Cowper's section
of the church ; it was spread far and wide by Rousseau.   Yet it
was inborn in Cowper's tender, joyful nature—a nature that was
playfully serene when free from its tyrant melancholy; and Cowper
remains the chief exponent of it in English poetry.

When originally published in 1785, *The Task* was followed in
the same volume by three shorter poems, an epistle to Cowper's
friend, Joseph Hill, *Tirocinium,* to which reference was made
above, and *The Diverting History of John Gilpin.*   In *Tirocinium,*
the attack on the brutality and immorality of public schools may
have been just and is certainly vigorous ; but this is not the kind
of poetical composition in which Cowper excelled.   Of *John Gilpin,*
there is little need to speak at length.   Lady Austen told Cowper
the story.   He lay awake at night laughing over it, and made of
it a ballad in a style of fun peculiarly his own, but not to be
found elsewhere outside his letters.   The more closely one looks
into the poem, the finer seems the characterisation, and the more
delicate and artful the precise simplicity of its manner.   Subsequent editions included twelve more short poems in the volume,
among them *The Rose,* admired by Sainte-Beuve, and the lines
On the Receipt of my Mother's Picture out of Norfolk.   Cowper's
mother had died when he was six years old.   As he tells us in this
poem, nearly half a century afterwards he remembered distinctly
and minutely the event and his feelings, and the poem is one of
the most pathetic and moving in any language.   Thanks to the
poet's use of detail, the woman and her little son live again before
us, and the tenderness of the whole is unsurpassed.   One other of
the shorter poems, *The Dog and the Water-lily,* deserves mention
for the light it throws on Cowper's gentle, animal-loving life ;

and the collection included, also, one or two fables that link him with Prior, Gay and Northcote.

In 1786, Cowper and Mrs Unwin had moved from dreary Olney to a cheerful house and neighbourhood at Weston, not far off, and had enlarged their circle of acquaintances, thanks, partly, to his cousin Harriet (the sister of Theodora), now Lady Hesketh. Cowper's life continued to be happy; and, during these pleasant years, he wrote a number of short poems, which were not published till after his death. Among them were several playful or serious personal addresses, much in the tone of the letters. Others were little narratives or expressions of everyday experience, like *The Colubriad*, an account of a viper which threatened the poet's cat and her kittens, and the epitaph on the poet's hare, 'Old Tiney, surliest of his kind.' The remainder included a few religious poems, several epigrams and translations, one or two tales and some poems on the slave trade, written to order and not showing Cowper at his best. Among these posthumous works four stand prominent: the stanzas *On the Loss of the Royal George*, the sonnet *To Mrs Unwin*, the poem *To Mary* and *The Poplar Field*. The sonnet is one of Cowper's finest achievements; the poem *To Mary* is redeemed by its tenderness from a certain monotony in the form. *The Poplar Field* contains the famous and exquisite second line of the couplet

> The poplars are felled; farewell to the shade
> And the whispering sound of the cool colonnade

which shows Cowper to have had possibilities in lyric poetry never fulfilled by him. Yet, it seems almost unjust to say this in view of *On the Loss of the Royal George*. Written to oblige Lady Austen, who wanted words set to the march in *Scipio*, this poem is one of the noblest dirges ever composed. By the directest, simplest means imaginable, Cowper attains an effect of noble grandeur. The plain statement reaches the sublime.

Cowper was not content to write short poems. In order to stave off its besetting depression, his mind needed regular occupation; and, in 1785, soon after he had finished correcting the proofs of *The Task*, he began, 'merely to divert attention,' turning Homer's *Iliad* into blank verse. The diversion grew into a plan to translate the whole of Homer and publish the work by subscription. Cowper came to his task well equipped. He had known his Homer from boyhood; and how well he knew and appreciated him may be learned from two letters to Lady Hesketh, written in December

1785 and January 1786, which are worth quoting as examples of
judicious and penetrating criticism.

> Except the Bible, there never was in the world a book so remarkable for
> that species of the sublime that owes its very existence to simplicity, as
> the works of Homer. He is always nervous, plain, natural... Homer is,
> on occasions that call for such a style, the easiest and most familiar of all
> writers... Homer's accuracy of description, and his exquisite judgement never,
> never failed him. He never, I believe, in a single instance sacrificed beauty
> to embellishment. He does not deal in hyperbole... accordingly, when he
> describes nature, whether in man or in animal, or whether nature inanimate,
> you may always trust him for the most consummate fidelity. It is his great
> glory that he omits no striking part of his subject, and that he never inserts
> a tittle that does not belong to it. Oh! how unlike some describers that I
> have met with, of modern days, who smother you with words, words, words,
> and then think that they have copied nature; when all the while nature was
> an object either not looked at, or not sufficiently.

Much of this is applicable to Cowper himself; and the writer of
the passage might be held to have been peculiarly well fitted to
translate Homer.   Moreover, Cowper not only knew and loved
Homer (though, indeed, he regretted that this 'most blameless
writer' was 'not an enlightened man'), but he knew Pope's
translation, which he had compared word for word with the original.
To him, Pope's 'faults and failings' were 'like so many buoys
upon a dangerous coast'; and, side by side with his appreciation
of Homer, there runs, in these letters to Lady Hesketh, some
very penetrating examination of the difference between Homer
and the 'two pretty poems under Homer's titles' written by Pope.
So far as criticism goes, therefore, Cowper promised well as a
translator of Homer.   He knew what to aim at, and what to avoid.
The work was finished, well subscribed and published in 1791;
and, today, no one need read it except those who have to write
about it.

The reasons of Cowper's failure are two.   In the first place
though precision and truth of detail are characteristics of both
poets, Cowper's tender, shrinking mind was separated by centuries
and leagues from Homer's.   It was not his to understand the joy
of battle, the fascination of wounds, the fierce, raw passions, still
largely animal, of primitive heroes and heroines, nor to surrender
his convictions to the turbulent folk whom Homer regarded as
gods and goddesses.   In the second place, it is one thing to
realise that Homer is 'nervous, plain, natural,' and another to
achieve those qualities, in learned and sonorous blank verse.
Cowper's Miltonic measures are hardly less unlike Homer than is
Pope's riming jingle.   The movement is completely altered.   It

is ample and stately; it has all the nobility which was one of the qualities demanded by Matthew Arnold in his lectures *On Translating Homer*. It is, also, faithful. Pope had perverted his original in order to find occasion for the brilliant effects of antithesis and epigram in which he excelled. Chapman, an Elizabethan brimful of ideas and curiosity and a spirit of literary adventure, had perverted his original through ebullience of sentiment and fancy. Cowper, priding himself on adhering closely to his original, adhered only in part. He knew exactly what Homer meant to say; he appreciated, in a great measure, Homer's manner of saying it; but his head was full of Milton. He believed Milton's style to resemble Homer's; and, by modelling his blank verse on Milton's, he achieves inversions, pauses and pomposities which are wholly unlike the smooth and simple rapidity of Homer. This is not to say that there are not excellent passages in Cowper's *Homer*, nor that the whole work is not a lofty achievement in scholarship and poetry. But, in avoiding the cleverness of Pope, Cowper fell into the opposite extreme. Homer is grand and lively, Cowper's *Homer* is grand and dull. As translator of the hymns of Mme Guyon, of certain odes and satires of Horace, of Greek songs and the Latin poems of his admired Milton, Cowper was more successful, especially in the case of Horace, with whom, despite the difference between a genial pagan and an evangelical Christian, he had much in common. Perhaps the least disputable title to remembrance which Cowper's *Homer* possesses is that it kept the poet busy and happy, staving off, for a while, his persistent foe, despair.

Despair was to have him in the end. Mrs Unwin sickened and died. The strain of attendance upon her proved too much for Cowper's mental and physical strength; and one of the saddest stories in the world is that of Cowper at and after the death of his heroic friend. Popularity, success, affection, royal favour (in the form of a pension acquired for him partly by the eager, blundering pertinacity of his friend, Hayley[1])—nothing could relieve him. His last original work was a powerful but ghastly poem called *The Castaway*. He died on 25 April 1800.

Cowper, though not among the great poets of England, holds a unique place, partly by virtue of the personality which shines in every line of his poetry, partly by virtue of the sincerity and simplicity which, 'keeping its eye on the object,' saw beauty and

---

[1] Coldicott, H. Rowlands S., 'How Cowper got his pension,' *The Cornhill Magazine*, no. 202, April 1913, p. 493.

consolation in common things, till then neglected, but eagerly seized upon by his successors and transformed into material for their profoundest and noblest art. There is another field in which he holds still a unique position—the field of letter-writing. It seems an error to speak, in connection with Cowper, of the art of letter-writing. If art implies the consideration of their effect upon the public, no letters were ever written with less art. In a letter to William Unwin, Cowper says

It is possible I might have indulged myself in the pleasure of writing to you, without waiting for a letter from you, but for a reason which you will not easily guess. Your mother communicated to me the satisfaction you expressed in my correspondence, that you thought me entertaining and clever, and so forth:—now you must know, I love praise dearly, especially from the judicious, and those who have so much delicacy themselves as not to offend mine in giving it. But then, I found this consequence attending, or likely to attend the eulogium you bestowed;—if my friend thought me witty before, he shall think me ten times more witty hereafter;—where I joked once, I will joke five times, and for one sensible remark I will send him a dozen. Now this foolish vanity would have spoiled me quite, and would have made me as disgusting a letter-writer as Pope, who seems to have thought that unless a sentence was well turned, and every period pointed with some conceit, it was not worth the carriage. Accordingly he is to me, except in very few instances, the most disagreeable maker of epistles that ever I met with. I was willing, therefore, to wait till the impression your commendation had made upon the foolish part of me was worn off, that I might scribble away as usual, and write my uppermost thoughts, and those only.

With the exception of Charles Lamb, all the other great English letter-writers—Gray, Walpole, Pope, Byron—wrote with an eye to the printed collection. Cowper wrote partly for his correspondent, chiefly for himself. His are, in his own phrase, 'talking letters.' He chats about anything that happens to be in his mind. If he is suffering from his mental complaint, he writes a letter unmatched for gloom, a letter that envelopes even a modern reader in a black mist of misery. A few pages later, and he is playful, gay, almost jaunty. His mind was so sweet, and his interest in the little details of life so keen, that the most trivial occurrence—a feat in carpentering, a bed of tulips, the visit of a parliamentary candidate—can interest his reader still. Acute reasoning, sound sense, fine judgment fall into their places with whimsical nonsense, hearty laughter and almost boyish affection. He will break off a criticism on Homer to bid Lady Hesketh 'give me a great corking pin that I may stick your faith upon my sleeve. There—it is done.' The whole of his nature, gay and gloomy, narrow in opinion and wide in sympathy, ever fixed on heavenly things and ever keenly alive to mundane things, is preserved for us in these inimitably vivid letters; and the same taste and scholarship which give point and permanence even to his least elaborated poems have won for these naïve examples of transparent self-revelation an undying value. The more they are read, the better will Cowper be understood and loved.

CHAPTER V

WILLIAM WORDSWORTH

WORDSWORTH'S surprise and resentment would surely have been provoked had he been told that, at half a century's distance and from an European point of view, his work would seem, on the whole, though with several omissions and additions, to be a continuation of the movement initiated by Rousseau. It is, nevertheless, certain that it might be described as an English variety of Rousseauism, revised and corrected, in some parts, by the opposite influence of Edmund Burke. In Wordsworth, we find Rousseau's wellknown fundamental tenets : he has the same semi-mystical faith in the goodness of nature as well as in the excellence of the child; his ideas on education are almost identical ; there are apparent a similar diffidence in respect of the merely intellectual processes of the mind, and an equal trust in the good that may accrue to man from the cultivation of his senses and feelings. The differences between the two, mainly occasional and of a political nature, seem secondary by the side of these profound analogies. For this reason, Wordsworth must be placed by the general historian among the numerous 'sons of Rousseau,' who form the main battalion of romanticism ; though, if we merely regard the ideas he expressed and propagated, his personality may, thereby, lose some of its originality and distinctness. But, resemblance does not necessarily mean repetition and imitation. Moreover, men's ideas are their least individual possessions. The manner in which a man, and, above all, a poet, becomes possessed of his creed, the stamp he puts upon it, are the things that really matter. Now, Wordsworth formed his thoughts and convictions in the light of the circumstances of his own life, whereby they assumed a reality wanting in those of many of his contemporaries. If he thought like others, he always thought by himself. He gives us the impression that, had he lived alone on a bookless earth, he would have reached the same conclusions. His deep influence on a limited, but incomparably loyal, number of readers owes less to his beliefs than to his minute, persevering analysis of every step he made towards them. He appeals to our confidence by his constant recourse to his personal experience. He prides himself on being the least inventive of great poets. He belittles fancy. It is true that he claimed imagination as his supreme gift, but, at the same time, he bestowed on the word imagination a new meaning, almost entirely opposed to the ordinary one. He gave the name to his accurate, faithful and loving observation of nature. In his loftier moods, he used 'imagination' as a synonym of 'intuition,' of seeing into, and even through, reality, but he never admitted a divorce between it and reality. The gift of feigning, of arbitrarily combining the features of a legend or story, which had long been held to be the first poetical prerogative, was almost entirely denied him, and he thanked God for its absence. His hold over many thoughtful and, generally, mature minds is due to his having avowedly, and often, also, practically, made truth his primary object, beauty being only second. Those who had ingenuously turned to his poems for the mere charm of verse were grateful to him inasmuch as they had received, in addition, their first lessons in philosophy. They had gone to him for pleasure and they came back with a train of reflection that followed them through the round of their daily tasks. They were taught by him a new way of looking at men and nature. Wordsworth achieved this result by dint of one-sided pressure, by tenaciousness of aim. Not that his ideas remained the same from beginning to end. Few men, on the contrary, changed more thoroughly. His mind may be represented as continuously shifting along a half circle, so that, finally, he stood at the opposite end of the diameter. The young revolutionist evolved into a greyhaired conservative, the semi-atheist and pantheist into a pattern of conformity. But, all the time, he kept true to his fixed centre, the search for the greatest good. His very contradictions point to one engrossing pursuit. His life was an unbroken series of slow movements which brought him from one extreme to the other, though his eyes were ever bent in the same direction. Because he never ceased to have the same object in view, he was himself imperfectly conscious of the change in his position.

Wordsworth was born in 1770 at Cockermouth, in the north of the lake country, the second child of a fairly prosperous attorney-at-law and of Anne Cookson, daughter of a Penrith mercer. Seen from the outside, without the optimistic prism of *The Prelude*, his childhood does not seem to have been any more privileged, while his youth appears decidedly more vexed and troubled, than those of the common run of men. The child, surely, had pleasant hours with his brothers and sister while playing about the terrace of the family garden which overlooked the Derwent, or when bathing in the river. There were bitter hours, however, when he was taken to his mother's family at Penrith, where harsh grandparents often treated the little ones 'with reproach and insult.' William was particularly unruly and, in consequence, had most to bear from the Cooksons. Hence, we hear of acts of defiance and even of a childish attempt at suicide.

When he was eight years old, his mother died, and, parting from his father, who never recovered his cheerfulness after his bereavement, Wordsworth was sent to Hawkshead grammar school. A very homely one-room house in a very poor village is the place where he was taught. He lodged with one of the old village dames, who, however kind they might be to boys, could only give them coarse and scanty fare. For his companions, he chiefly had farmers' sons, destined for the church, who brought with them the rough manners of their home life. In spite of the delight he found in games, open air life and rambles about hill and lake, it must be admitted that Hawkshead was a very mixed paradise.

Then came his father's death, when the boy was thirteen. The orphan's condition was precarious. Almost all the money left by his father was in the hands of Sir James Lowther, to whom Wordsworth's father had been steward, and Sir James would never hear of paying it back so long as he lived, nor could he be compelled to reimburse. It is true that enough remained to allow William to pursue his studies, and a boy does not take money questions much to heart. But there were wretched holidays at Penrith, in his grandparents' sullen home. Of the frequent distress of the children in that house, we have a vivid picture in the earliest letters of little Dorothy, the poet's only sister, written in the last year spent by William at Hawkshead. Dorothy, whose sweet, affectionate nature cannot be suspected of unjustified complaints, could scarcely bear the loveless constraint she had to undergo. No more could her brothers: 'Many a time have William, John, Christopher and myself shed tears together of the bitterest sorrow.' 'We have no father to protect, no mother to guide us,' and so forth.

From Hawkshead, Wordsworth went to Cambridge in October 1787 and remained there at St John's college till the beginning of 1791. He took little interest either in the intellectual or social life of the university. He never opened a mathematical book and thus lost all chance of obtaining a fellowship. Even his literary studies were pursued irregularly, without any attention being paid to the prescribed course. He did not feel any abhorrence of the students' life, which, at that time, consisted of alternate sloth and wildness. He first shared in it, but soon grew weary of it and lived more or less by himself. In his university years, his only deep enjoyments were the long rambles in which he indulged during vacations. Meanwhile, discussions with his uncles must, at times, have made life rather distasteful to him. He had no money in prospect. All his small patrimony had been spent on his university education ; yet he showed himself vacillating and reluctant when required to make choice of a career. None was to his taste. The army, the church, the law, tutorial work, were all contemplated and discarded in turn. He showed no strong bent except for wandering and writing poetry. He was, indeed, a young man likely to make his elders anxious. In July 1790, just at the time when he ought to have been working hard for his approaching examinations, he took it into his head to start for the Alps with a fellow student, on foot, equipped much like a pedlar—an escapade without precedent. As soon as he had taken his B.A., without distinction, he set fortune at defiance, and settled in London for a season, doing nothing in particular, 'pitching a vagrant tent among the unfenced regions of society.' After this, other wanderings and abortive schemes of regular work followed for more than three years, till he threw aside all idea of a fixed career and settled down to resolute poverty. Such apparent restlessness and indolence could not but be attended by many a pang of remorse. He suffered from his growing estrangement from his relations. He was ill satisfied with himself and uneasy about the future, and these feelings (perhaps darkened by some passages of vexed love) found an outlet in his juvenile poems, all of which are tinged with melancholy.

It seems strange that such a childhood and youth should, afterwards, have furnished him with the optimistic basis of *The Prelude*. Beyond doubt, this poem was meant to be a selection of all the circumstances in his early life that told for joy and hope. Hence, a heightening of bright colours, and a voluntary omission of more sombre hues, in the picture he made of his youth. But the contrast between the dry facts of his early life and his rapture over the same period is, also, owing to a deeper truth. The joy he celebrates in *The Prelude* springs from sources hidden from all eyes, scarcely suspected by the child himself. Whatever shadows might pass over his days, abundant strength and happiness lay beneath the surface. He was not callous to grief, but, somehow, felt all the time that grief was transient, hope permanent, in his breast. His enjoyment of nature gave him those intense delights which are usually unnoticed in the tale of a life. So did his already passionate love of verse. Thus, *The Prelude* is all true, though it does not present us with the whole truth.

Of the young man's passion for nature, his early poems, both published in 1793, furnish direct proof. They are the most minute and copious inventories of the aspects he saw, of the noises he heard, in his native lakes (*An Evening Walk*) or in his wanderings through Switzerland (*Descriptive Sketches*). Such acuteness and copiousness of observation were only possible in the case of a devotee. However contorted and knotty the verse may be, however artificial the diction, the poet's fervour is as manifest here as in the most eloquent of his subsequent effusions. Though he follows in the train of a succession of descriptive poets, he outdoes them all in abundance of precise touches.

But his practice of descriptive poetry was interrupted for several years, at the very time when he was giving the finishing touch to these poems. The influence of the French revolution on this part of his life cannot be overrated. Characteristically, he was rather late in becoming an adept. He uttered no paean on the fall of the Bastille. To move him, it was necessary that his senses should be aroused. Now, the revolution turned her most enticing smile towards him. It so happened that he had first landed at Calais on the eve of the federation of 1790; so, the unparalleled mirth of that time seemed a festivity prepared for his welcome. The glee and hopefulness of the season turned into a charming benevolence, which he tasted with all the relish of a student on a holiday trip. Then came his prolonged stay in France, chiefly at Orleans and at Blois, from November 1791 to December 1792, in times already darkened by civil mistrust and violence. But, chance would have it that he should be eyewitness to heartstirring scenes, such as the enlisting of volunteers and the proclamation of the republic. Above all, he had the good fortune to make friends with one of the true heroes of the day, captain Michel

Beaupuy, whose chivalric nature and generous enthusiasm for the new order warmed the young Englishman. Exquisite is the portrait drawn of Beaupuy in *The Prelude*. The fine traits of his character are all confirmed by what has since become known of his career, with this reservation that, through an irresistible tendency to idealise, Wordsworth may have toned down some of the features. Beaupuy was the revolutionary apostle described by the poet, but there was less of the philosopher and more of the soldier in his composition. It is clear from his letters and diaries that he was an ingenuous and soldier-like reasoner, and, also, that he could utter an oath or two when in a passion. Anyhow, he found Wordsworth a bewildered foreigner and left him a determined revolutionist, one might almost say a French republican. A spirit of revolt and indignation against all social iniquities pervaded Wordsworth for years, together with a sympathy, which never left him, for the poorer and humbler members of the community. When he came back to England, he drew near the Jacobins without becoming one of them; but he was a decided reformer. Alienated from his own country when she went to war with France, he heartily hated king, regent and ministry. His letter to the bishop of Llandaff and his poem *Guilt and Sorrow* (or *Incidents on Salisbury Plain*) are the best testimonies of his feelings. Society appeared to him responsible for the wretchedness, and even the crimes, of individuals—his pity went to vagrants and murderers. His abhorrence of war was shown in insistent and gruesome pictures of war scenes.

When the French revolution passed into the Terror, and especially when the republic changed a defensive into an aggressive war, Wordsworth lost his trust in immediate social reform. He turned more and more to abstract meditation on man and society, chiefly under the guidance of William Godwin—a period of dry intellectualism that went against the grain. He suffered from the suppression of his feelings, from being momentarily deaf to 'the language of the sense.' Besides, his analysis of men's motives soon convinced him that the evils he fought against were not so much the results of social forms as of something inherent in man's nature. A man of commanding intellect may be wantonly cruel and vicious; he may use all the powers of logic for his detestable ends; reason is non-moral; the wicked 'spin motives out of their own bowels.' Hence, a wellnigh absolute, though transient, pessimism, which vented itself in his play *The Borderers*. If the traditional bonds of morality are relaxed, the fixed rules of our actions or the intuitive guidance of the feelings repudiated, then full scope is given to bold, intelligent, bad men ; then are the wellmeaning blinded and betrayed to abominable deeds. Then is the Terror possible. Scarcely any hope of betterment is left. The kindhearted Girondin Marmaduke will be an easy prey to the villainous Montagnard Oswald.

When he wrote this tragedy, Wordsworth had already put an end to his solitary, wandering life and settled at Racedown in Dorsetshire with his sister Dorothy (autumn of 1795). There, they both lived a frugal life, on the meagre income from a legacy of £900 left to the poet by a dying friend. This settlement was the crowning of a longcherished scheme. Brother and sister were passionately attached to each other. Dorothy's letters make their mutual love known to us and let us into depths of Wordsworth's nature, scarcely revealed by his poems. She speaks of 'a vehemence of affection' in him that his readers might not suspect, so careful he usually was, in Hazlitt's words, 'to calm the throbbing pulses of his own heart by keeping his eye ever fixed on the face of nature.' By this discipline, did he, in those years, slowly conquer his besetting thoughts of despondency. Wordsworth and Dorothy were equally fond of natural scenery. Their delight in each other and their daily rambles were the first agents in the young disillusionised republican's recovery. Dorothy made him turn his eyes again to the landscape and take an interest in the peasants near their home. But the poet's mind remained gloomy for a time, as is shown by his pastoral *The Ruined Cottage* (or *The Story of Margaret*), which afterwards found its place in the first book of *The Excursion*. A heartrending narrative, if read without the comforting comments of the pedlar afterwards added to it, a perfect poem, too, such as Wordsworth never surpassed, it points out both the exceeding tenderness often met with in the hearts of the poor and the cruelty of fate aggravated by the existing social order. No doctrine, poetic or philosophical, is perceptible in this poem of simple, chastened beauty. It does not give any token of the message with which Wordsworth was soon to think himself entrusted. His sense of a message only became clear to him after he had, in the summer of 1797, removed from Racedown to Alfoxden, so as to live in daily converse with Coleridge, who was then dwelling at Nether Stowey, in Somersetshire. Till then, the two poets had only exchanged a few visits, after the end of 1795, the first results of which had merely been to encourage Wordsworth to

poetical composition. He had felt raised and exhilarated by
Coleridge's entire, almost extravagant, admiration for his *Salisbury Plain* and *Borderers*. But, when they had become close
neighbours and intimate friends, Coleridge's innate transcen-
dentalism began to affect Wordsworth. It is impossible to define
exactly the share of each in the elaboration of those poetical and
moral tenets which they seemed, for a time, to hold in common,
unconscious of the deep differences between them. Yet, on the
whole, one may say that Wordsworth's share consisted in his
more precise observations of nature and common life. Coleridge,
'with the capacious soul,' influenced his friend by his metaphysical
gifts, 'the power he possessed of throwing out in profusion grand,
central truths from which might be evolved the most comprehensive systems.' An omnivorous reader, with an inclination towards
mystic doctrines, Coleridge talked eloquently to Wordsworth on
Plato and the neo-Platonists, Berkeley's idealism, the pantheistic
system and serene necessitarianism of Spinoza, the intuitional
religion of the theosophists—a new world to one who had not yet
gone beyond the rationalism of the eighteenth century and who
always found his most congenial food in the associationism of
Hartley. Now, Wordsworth, without binding himself to any one
master, was to take hints from all in building up his own doctrine.
But he was not an intellectual dilettante ; all he absorbed from
without had to be reconciled to his personal experience and
turned to a practical aim. He would show men the way to wisdom
and happiness. He would, from his country retreat, give out his
views of nature, man and society. He justified this lofty ambition
to himself because he was conscious, personally, of having issued
out of error into truth, out of despondency into hopefulness. He
thought he knew the reasons why most men in his generation had
fallen into pessimism and misanthropy. He now believed in the
restorative power of nature, in the essential goodness of a man's
heart when unadulterated by the pride of intellect, in the greatness
of the senses which could drink in infinite joys and profound lessons
of wisdom. Thus did he plan his *Recluse*, as early as March 1798,
'the first great philosophical poem in existence,' as Coleridge
anticipated, which was to employ his highest energies for seventeen
years. Though never completed, the monument exists in fragments of imposing magnitude—the first book of *The Recluse*,
properly so called, written in 1800 ; *The Prelude*, written between
1798 and 1805, an autobiography meant as the ante-chapel to
the huge gothic cathedral ; and *The Excursion*, which, though it

includes passages composed as early as 1797, was not finished before 1814. Such intervals of time account better than any other reason for the incompleteness of the edifice, for the poet's ideas changed so much while he was engaged upon his work that no systematic presentation of doctrine, as was first intended, could possibly be achieved. Only the initial impulse remained—the poet's sense of a duty put on him from on high, his earnest wish to benefit his fellow men morally and to make them happier. The reasons for his optimism might and did vary; but the optimistic attitude was preserved to the end, securing the unity of the poet's career.

But, during his stay with Coleridge in Somersetshire, Wordsworth did not only lay the foundations of his *Recluse*. The same intercourse gave birth to less ambitious and more immediate verse, to the famous *Lyrical Ballads* of 1798, a small volume of short poems by Coleridge and himself. It is well known how, after some fruitless attempts at collaboration, the two friends agreed to divide the field of poetry. To the share of Coleridge fell such subjects as were supernatural, or, at any rate, romantic, which he was to inform with a human interest and a semblance of truth. Wordsworth's part was to be the events of everyday life, by preference in its humblest form; the characters and incidents of his poems 'were to be such as will be found in every village and its vicinity where there is a meditative and feeling mind to seek after them, or to notice them when they present themselves.' Thus did Coleridge sing *The Ancient Mariner*, while Wordsworth told the tales *Goody Blake* and *Simon Lee*. Nothing can better show Wordsworth's minute realism, how necessary it was to him to hold a little of his mother earth within his fingers. His homely ballads are so many humble practical illustrations of the philosophy he was at this very time promulgating in lofty blank verse, for instance, in his lyrical hymn of thanks to nature, *Tintern Abbey*. The ballads have 'a something corporeal, a matter-of-factness,' which Coleridge could not help lamenting. They are not only clad in humble garb, but, to a certain extent, are more scientific than poetic in their aim. There survived so much of Wordsworth's former rationalism that he almost gave the precedence to psychology over poetry in these experiments. The preface of the 1800 edition of the *Ballads* really looks like the programme of a man of science. He is inspired by a wish to know more, and make more known, of the human heart. He goes so far as to call poetry 'the history and science of the feelings.'

Perfect unity is not characteristic of this period so much as a gladsome energy exerted in several directions. 'He never wrote with such glee.' His new reading of nature and of man fills him with delight—together with the life he now leads between the most wonderful of friends and the most devoted of inspired sisters. He had such superfluous joy that 'he could afford to suffer with those he saw suffer,' that he was 'bold to look on painful things.' He believed in 'the deep power of joy,' by means of which 'we see into the life of things.' He made joy the chief attribute of poetry, proclaimed poets 'the happiest of men.' He rejoiced in his own boldness, found vent for his surviving republicanism in a sweeping, democratic reform of poetical style—putting down the time-honoured hierarchy of words, abolishing the traditional distinction between high and low, in subjects and diction.

These trustful feelings, this spontaneous optimism, expressive of his unimpaired vitality, sustained him throughout the years from 1798 to 1805, during which period his best and most original poetry was written, whether at Alfoxden, or in Germany, where he stayed with his sister from September 1798 to April 1799, or in the glorious humility of Dove cottage, at Grasmere, in the lake country, where he settled with Dorothy in the last days of the century and where Coleridge was again his frequent visitant, or in his wanderings over Scotland, with both Coleridge and Dorothy, from August to October 1803. A period of 'plain living and high thinking,' made famous by great verse.

One may fix on 1805 as the year in, or about, which this period of Wordsworth's poetical life closes. He had now, if not published, at least written, nearly all that is supreme in his works—his only book of *The Recluse*, all *The Prelude*, the best parts of *The Excursion*, besides many of the best and boldest of his short poems, ballads and sonnets. His great *Ode on Immortality* was all but finished. Had he died then, in his thirty-sixth year, having lived as long as Byron and much longer than Shelley or Keats, he would have left a fame almost as high as he was to attain, though of a different character. His freshness of thought and style being taken together, his works would have stamped him as one of the most daring among the poets of his day. The sedate and sometimes conventional moralising which has been associated with his name comes into existence in his later productions. But it should be added that, for ten years, he was to achieve, in a new direction, some verse that 'one would not willingly let die.'

Outward events and the circumstances of his own life had something to do with the change that took place in him about 1805.
Politically, it was caused by the beginning of the French empire,
the crowning of Napoleon by the pope, 'a sad reverse for all
mankind'; hence, the final overthrow of Wordsworth's sympathies
for the revolution, the decisive proof (so he thought) that his
former ideal was false and treacherous.   This led him to suspect
more and more all that, in his ideas, still savoured of revolt ; it
caused him to rally more closely round the principles of order
and repent his former wishes of social change.   The gray tints
of mistrust slowly overlaid the glowing enthusiasms of yore.   It
is true that Wordsworth's feelings were roused, chiefly by the
Spanish war, to a patriotic fervour that found expression in many
a vigorous sonnet and even turned him into a pamphleteer.   His
eloquent and ponderous *Convention of Cintra* (1809) shows the
fighting spirit that was in him.   But it had the inconvenience of
leading him from verse to prose, from poetry to dialectics, and
thus generated an oratorical habit that was to infect many parts
of his *Excursion.*

Then, in his very home, there happened changes that, whether
fortunate or sad, impressed on his soul new habits and tendencies.
As early as 1802, he had married a Westmorland girl, Mary
Hutchinson, in whom he found one of the greatest blessings of his
life.   The quieting influence of this meek Mary, by degrees, though
not at once, was added to, or even took the place of, the more
impulsive and exciting companionship of Dorothy.   Mrs Wordsworth's nature told for submission and repose.   Besides, the mere
fact of his being married checked gradually, though it did not
suppress altogether, what might be called the guiltless Bohemianism
of his youth.   The duties and cares of the father of a large family
grew upon him.   Five children were born to the pair between 1803
and 1810, two of whom were to die almost simultaneously in 1812.
As early as 1806, the increase of his family had led to a temporary,
then to a definitive, abandonment of the narrow Dove cottage, to
which clung many of his most poetical memories.

Before robbing him of two of his children, death had already
struck Wordsworth a blow that went near his heart, one that ever
after saddened his life—the loss of his brother John, a sailor ship-
wrecked in February 1805.   How deeply he was affected by it is
known, not only by his poems, but from the letters of the Grasmere
household and the journal of Dorothy.   There was another cause
of grievous sorrow in the state of 'the brother of his soul,

Coleridge, now a prey to opium and drink, whose growing distress of body and mind was, for years, a depressing, heartrending sight for his friend, and whose endless idle laments haunted Wordsworth's sleep as well as his waking thoughts. Whether absent or present, Coleridge had become an increasing source of anxiety to Wordsworth. Wordsworth's infinite patience and forbearance, in these circumstances, cannot be too highly praised. But nothing availed. The friends had to part in 1810, Coleridge betaking himself to London. More painful than all the rest, Coleridge, in one of his irresponsible moods, turned in anger against Wordsworth. An estrangement followed which was never wholly healed, and which left a lifelong scar in Wordsworth's heart.

Yet, the change in Wordsworth's poetry had still deeper causes than all these. Though he had little of Coleridge's self-abandonment, he could not help feeling a decay of his strictly poetical powers—of that imagination and joy on which, till then, he had erected the structure of his verse. When Coleridge had written his ode *Dejection* in 1802, Wordsworth could immediately retort with his optimistic *Leech-Gatherer*. But, now, he, also, felt the wane of his 'shaping spirit of imagination.' The earth no longer offered him the splendour it had for him in his youth. A glory had departed from the earth. He had, very early, felt the fading of that glory, but had long checked the onset of the unimaginative years to come by fondly dwelling on the memories of his childhood. In 1805, he had so copiously drawn from the treasure-house for his *Prelude* that the store was becoming exhausted. He understood the meaning of the depression of his vital spirits : he was travelling further away from the springs of energy, drawing nearer to old age and death. This is a sad thought to all men—it was doubly so to him who had rested all his faith on the freshness of the senses and feelings, and on their gladsome guidance.

In want of comfort, he turned to duty. Wordsworth's *Ode to Duty* (1805), produced at the turning-point of his career, is full of import and significance. It throws a light both on the years that went before and on those that were to follow. It also reveals an aspect of the poet's nature not usually apparent. It is common to speak of him as one of the teachers of duty, and to refer to this ode (or to its title) as a proof. Now, he distinctly resigns himself to the control of duty because, at his time of life, a man can do no better. He abjures with regret the faith that, till then, had been his and in which duty had no place, the dear belief that joy and love can guide man to all good—or, rather, he does not renounce it, but still mutters a hope that better days may come when, joy and love reigning supreme, duty can be dispensed with. As for himself, he would still cling to the same creed if he preserved spirit enough to bear the shocks of change and enjoy his 'unchartered freedom.' He retires into the arms of duty as a weary warrior of old might end his days in the quiet shelter of a monastery. He still feels an uncertain convert: 'Thee I now would serve more strictly, *if I may*.' The 'stern lawgiver,' at first sight, inspires him with more fear than love. He only reconciles himself with the 'awful Power' when he has realised that duty wears a smile on her face, that she is beautiful, that, after all, she may be identical with love and joy:

> Flowers laugh before thee on their beds,
> And fragrance in thy footing treads;
> Thou dost preserve the Stars from wrong,
> And the most ancient Heavens through thee are fresh and strong.

a noble stanza, the loftiest of a poem signalised by the almost plaintive appeal that is heard throughout and by the longing, lingering look cast behind.

The *Ode to Duty* seems to have been written just before the death of his brother John. He expressly says that he is still 'untried,' and moved by 'no disturbance of soul.' When the trial came that darkened the world for him, Wordsworth made it his chief task to struggle against grief. He resolutely bade farewell to 'the heart that lives alone, housed in a dream.' He welcomed 'fortitude and patient cheer.' He called his former creed an illusion. His themes now, more exclusively than before, will be the sorrows and tragedies of life. But he must find 'blessed consolations in distress.' He must tell of 'melancholy Fear subdued by Faith.' The consequence is that his exploration of human woes will, henceforth, be guarded and cautious. He now lacks the bold spirit of youth that can haunt the worst infected places without giving a thought to the danger of contagion. He is the depressed visitor of the sick, who must needs beware, and be provided with preservatives. He could no longer offer such harrowing pictures of misery as those to be found in his *Ruined Cottage* or even (in spite of the abrupt conclusion) in his admirable *Michael* (1800). His diminished vitality makes it necessary for him to ward off dejection.

Argument is the process used at wearisome length in *The Excursion*. This noble poem may be described as a long sermon against pessimism, scarcely disguised by a story. Though different speakers are introduced, their speeches are mere ventriloquism. Wordsworth, as the optimistic Pedlar, or Wanderer, assails Wordsworth as the Solitary, or the late enthusiast of the French revolution, now dispirited.   He uses all his eloquence to raise this other self to his own serene mood.   *The Excursion* too often reminds us of the debates between God and Satan at one time set forth in churches for the edification of the people, the rule being that Satan should have the worst of the controversy.   It is the same with Wordsworth's Solitary, who is presented to us in unfavourable colours ; his morals are not of the best.   And, when he vents his misanthropy, he does not seem to be quite so fearless, cogent and impressive an exponent of his own views as he might have been.   We cannot help thinking that, if the author of *Cain* had been entrusted with the part, he would have made it many times more telling. The worthy pedlar's triumph would not have been so easily achieved.

The other manner in which Wordsworth now fought against grief is illustrated by his *White Doe of Rylstone* (1807).   In this poem, he renounced argument and called imagination to his aid.   He found his subject in the romantic past, in an old tale of war and bloodshed, the tragedy of a catholic rebel killed with all his sons in a revolt against queen Elizabeth.   Only one daughter survived, Emily, who, many years after pillage and ruin had passed over the paternal estate, drew comfort from the visitings of a white doe bred by her in her happy days.   The doe is a symbol of the past, the lovely phantom of buried memories.   Her first apparition gives the lady 'one frail shock of pain'; but the pain soon passes into a holy, mild and grateful melancholy,

> Not sunless gloom or unenlightened,
> But by tender fancies brightened.

The awful tragedy has thus been transformed by length of time and strength of habit into something both beautiful and sweet. This is as it should be with the deepest of human woes.

This graceful symbol makes the end of the poem one of the most lovely passages in Wordsworth's poetry.   Yet the poem, as a whole, is languid, and even the moral impression is felt to be less convincing than it might have been.   The reason is that the poet never dares courageously to cope with despair.   He can paint with free energy neither the fate of the rebels, the clang of arms and shocks of death, nor even the pangs and sorrows of Emily. During the battle which is to end in the death of her father and brothers, she, represented as a protestant in a catholic

family, is seen awaiting the issue without even daring to express
a wish for either side. When an old man offers to secure a hiding-
place for her kindred if vanquished, she declines the offer and
declares herself 'with her condition satisfied.' Later, before she
has seen the white doe, she must already have found springs of
comfort, for she is strangely said to be 'sustained by memory of
the past.' Such reticence in the picture of desolation much
enfeebles the effect of the poem. How much more striking it
would have been if it had begun with dark, valiant scenes of tragic
fate ; if Emily's despair had been made so evident that we should
feel for her the want of supernatural comfort, the necessity of the
coming in of the white doe !

Wordsworth, in this period, often defeats his own object by
refusing to describe the power of evil or woe to the full. He stirs
a protest in the reader's mind, incites him to complete the half-
drawn picture of misery. Or else, the strain of his muscles in the
fight against grief, his repeated assaults and his tricks to elude the
grasp of the great adversary, often leave the reader more distressed
than he would be by open pessimistic outpourings. Indeed, the
greatness of Wordsworth, in these years, lies in his stubborn refusal
to confess himself overcome. There is pathos in his optimism, as
in the sight of a strong man that will not weep though timely tears
might do him good. His stoic poem *Laodamia* (1814) is a proof of
this. The Olympian serenity advocated in it makes us feel—and
painfully feel—the distance between the summit where gods dwell
and the lower ground inhabited by men. Well for the gods to
disprove 'the tumult of the soul !' Well for the Elysian fields to
be a place where there are

> No fears to beat away—no strife to heal—
> The past unsighed for, and the future sure !

But poor Laodamia is merely human and lives on this earth of
ours. She cannot 'meekly mourn' for her lost hero. She dies of
a broken heart, and it seems hard that she should be punished for
it as for meditated suicide.

Is this the conclusion of optimism ? How hard, inhuman and,
one might add, despairing ! The poem is great and pathetic,
because Wordsworth, all the time, sympathises with Laodamia,
feels for her tender weakness, is at heart more like her than like
the heroic, dishumanised Protesilaus. But it can scarcely be called
a comforting poem. The same might be said of the other verse
of this period in which Wordsworth insists on proclaiming both

the grandeur and difficulty of hopefulness, when, for instance, he calls hope

> The paramount *duty* that Heaven lays
> For its own honour on man's suffering heart.

We perceive how lofty is the peak—and, also, how hard the climbing.

The rest of Wordsworth's career (1814—50) adds comparatively little to his best verse. No works of magnitude are to be found in it, the most considerable being collected memorials of one or other of the many tours he made either in the British Isles or on the continent, or series of sonnets, like *The River Duddon* (1820) and *Ecclesiastical Sonnets* (1822). Though several of these sonnets or short pieces are as exquisite as any in the former volumes, these gems are now far between, and no new departure is perceptible. The days of original thought and spontaneous creation are over. Perhaps the most lyrical burst of the period is the poem entitled *Composed upon an Evening of extraordinary splendour and beauty*, in 1818, which breathes his former enthusiasm for the aspects of nature ; yet it is to be noticed that an 'extraordinary' magnificence is now needed to revive youthful ecstasies that used to feed on what was common in the beauty of things. The character of his later verse is other than this. Scandalised by the fame of Byron and the success of the new cynical and pessimistic poetry, Wordsworth exaggerates his own sermonising tendencies. There is now a fixed and rigid attitude, a sort of optimistic trick, in the poems which extol the minute joys of life and endeavour to tone down its sorrows. He does his best to convert himself to Anglicanism, which, however, he celebrates with more copiousness than real warmth. His *Ecclesiastical Sonnets* are the Anglican counterpart, on a much narrower basis, of Châteaubriand's *Génie du Christianisme*. In politics, his evolution has become complete to the point of appearing a recantation. He pursues against liberalism the campaign upon which, for liberal reasons, he had entered against Napoleon. He seems to find everything for the best in Europe after the French emperor's overthrow. He approves and upholds the Holy Alliance and opposes, with might and main, every attempt at reform in his own country. He protests against the too advanced instruction which the liberals desire to impart to girls in the lake district, against the spread of mechanics' institutes, against the emancipation of Irish catholics, against the abolition of slavery by parliament, against the abolition of capital punishment, against

parliamentary reform, and so forth.   The one change he supports
is the extension of copyright, which affects his own interests as a
writer.   That he was sincere in all his opinions, and that he had
strong arguments for his absolute conservatism, cannot be doubted.
No apostasy is to be laid to his charge.   The evolution of his ideas,
which made his old age diametrically opposed to his youth, can be
traced, step by step, accounted for by outward circumstances and
earnest meditations.   Yet we cannot help feeling that, all the
same, it is a progress from poetry to prose, from bold imaginings
to timorousness, from hope to mistrust, from life to death.

In the meantime, his worldly prosperity and his public reputation were steadily increasing.   From the gladsome frugality of the
Grasmere days he passed into ease and comfort, thanks to his
appointment, in 1813, as stamp distributor for Westmorland, which
enabled him to remove to Rydal Mount in 1814.   There, he was to
live till his death, courted by members of the nobility and higher
clergy, visited by a growing number of pilgrims, sincere admirers
and mere tourists.   His fame, which was at a low ebb at the
beginning of that period, partly on account of the ridicule thrown
on his poems by reviewers, partly because the public turned in
preference to Scott and Byron, gradually rose after 1820, till it
culminated in a triumphant reception at Oxford in 1839, a state
pension bestowed on him in 1842 and the laureateship in 1843.
Before the close of his life in 1850, Wordsworth could feel assured
that he had become one of the great poetical influences of the age.

It is inevitable that, when retracing Wordsworth's career, one
should insist on the main streams of thought which flowed through
his mind.   The temptation to look upon him as a prophet is great,
and, thus, in any estimate of him, to give chief prominence to the
more or less systematic philosophy woven by him out of experience.
True, few poets blended philosophy and poetry more intimately
together.   Yet, the two remain distinct; they are things of a
different order.   They were in conflict more than once; so, our
estimate of Wordsworth's poetical genius should not be reduced to
an appreciation of his moral code.

He was a great poet when, in 1797, he wrote *The Ruined
Cottage*—he never outdid that pastoral and, indeed, only once
or twice again reached such perfection.   Yet (if we set aside
the words of comfort and resignation wherein, years after, it was
wrapt up), in itself, the tale is most distressing and desolate.
Wordsworth's usual optimism is not to be found in it.   It implies

a protest against the iniquity of society and the harshness of fate. It is one of Wordsworth's masterpieces, but, in a moral sense, can scarcely be called Wordsworthian.

The last of the *Lucy* poems—though written in 1799—is in even more striking contrast to Wordsworth's known teaching. It is one of the most desperate sobs that ever escaped from the heart of a forlorn lover. No glimpse of hope pierces through his vision of the tomb:

> No motion has she now, no force;
> She neither hears nor sees;
> Rolled round in earth's diurnal course
> With rocks, and stones, and trees.

Surely, Wordsworth would have condemned such a fit of blank despair in any other poetry than his own. Yet, he never wrote with more essential strength, and many of his admirers must needs regard this quatrain as, perhaps, the most condensed example of his poetical greatness.

What has been said of his moral doctrine applies, also, to his theory of poetical style. It is now agreed that Wordsworth wrote some of his most beautiful poems in entire opposition to his principles of diction. He had laid it down as a rule that the poet should use the simple language of peasants, merely freed from its errors. Yet, even when he interpreted the feelings of cottagers and made them speak in their own names, he often broke this rule in the most glaring manner. The example pointed out by Myers is so conclusive that it would be idle to look for another one. It is taken from *The Affliction of Margaret*, a pathetic monologue in which a poor widow, who used to keep a shop, laments over the disappearance of her son, and pictures to herself the dangers and sufferings to which he may have been exposed. Not a single phrase in the beautiful stanza ʻPerhaps some dungeon hears thee groanʼ but is raised to the highest pitch of lyrical force and subtlety.

Without recurring to such extreme cases, in which we have the poet at war with the systematic thinker, we must admit that, in many of his finest poems, the characteristics of his thought and doctrine are least evident—whether he gives way to a disturbing melancholy, which he usually condemns, as in *The two April Mornings* or *The Fountain*, or where he imparts to us an impression of nature on which he hangs no moral, as in *The Green Linnet* or *Yew-trees*. The four yew-trees of Borrowdale, ʻjoined in one solemn and capacious groveʼ constitute one of his most impressive pictures. But no philosophy is tagged to the description,

which is self-sufficient. There, you have Wordsworth's power laid
bare, founded on his imaginative vision of natural aspects, yet not
passing from this to a moral lesson. If this dark, powerful piece
of painting had been handed down to us without the author's
name, it is not certain that anyone would have ascribed it to
Wordsworth; or, if so, it would have been on account of the
Westmorland names found in it; for, the bold allegories, the
strange sonorous mythology, would have made many a critic
hesitate.

These instances tend to prove that his poetry is not identical
with his habitual teaching, that it sometimes revolts against it,
that it may here and there go beyond it. Of this conclusion, we
ought not to lose sight, even when we pass on to the examination
of such verses as are both beautiful in themselves and stamped
as Wordsworth's manifest creations, to which no exact parallels
can be found in any other poet.

His chief originality is, of course, to be sought in his poetry
of nature. But it is not the mere fact of his being a poet of
nature that makes him unique. There had been many poets of
nature before, more were to come after, him. It is not even the
minute, precise, loving observation of her aspects that gives him his
preeminence. Certainly, he was one of the most truthful describers
when his task was to describe; though, for accuracy or subtlety of
outward detail, he may have been equalled, nay, surpassed, by other
poets who, at the same time, were botanists or naturalists, writers
as different from each other as were Crabbe and Tennyson. Of
flowers, insects and birds, the latter two knew, perhaps, more
than Wordsworth. His undisputed sovereignty is not there. It
lies in his extraordinary faculty of giving utterance to some of
the most elementary, and, at the same time, obscure, sensations of
man confronted by natural phenomena. Poetical psychology is his
triumph. Apart from the philosophical or moral structure which
he endeavours to raise on data furnished him by his sensations,
these sensations are, in themselves, beautiful and new. By new,
we mean that he was the first to find words for them, for they
must have been as old as mankind.

There was a Boy is one of the most striking instances of this.
The 'gentle shock of mild surprise' felt by the lad who did *not*
catch in due time the answer of the owls to his own hootings, the
sudden revelation to him of the fair landscape while he hung
listening, his thrill of delight at seeing 'the uncertain heaven
received into the bosom of the steady lake'—these were additions

to man's knowledge and enjoyment of his common sensations. The absolute truth of the analysis impresses one simultaneously with its beauty. The emotion is, surely, subtle, but, at the same time universal, and we have it here expressed once and for ever. No psychologist can expect to go further than this, no poet to hit on words more apposite and more harmoniously combined so as to make this little mystery of the soul palpable. When Coleridge read the poem in a letter from his friend, he said that, if he had met with these lines in a desert of Africa, he would have cried out 'Wordsworth' at once. Here, we have, without doubt, one of the essentials of Wordsworth's poetry.

The same character is to be found in *Nutting*, where we are told of 'the intruding sky,' that struck with remorse the boyish nut-gatherer after he had torn the boughs of a virgin bower ; or, again, in *Skating-scene*, where the poet describes the strange appearance of the surrounding hills, which, to the skater who has just stopped short after gliding at full speed, still seem to wheel by 'as if the earth had rolled with visible motion her diurnal round.' Here we have a mere illusion of the senses, but one of the existence of which, as of its weirdness and beauty, no doubt can be entertained.

One English poet only can be compared with Wordsworth here : Shelley, whose senses were endowed with an unusual, almost a superhuman, gift of insight. He, too, was to enrich our knowledge of sensation by his verse. His sensitiveness goes into things even deeper than Wordsworth's. He can see further through the screen, even spy 'the warm light of life.' But few, if any, can follow him to the end, or remember having themselves experienced his wonderful ecstasies. He is alone. On the contrary, Wordsworth has no abnormal and hypertrophied sensitiveness. It was the common healthy sensibility of mankind which he found himself sharing. He merely reveals to us what everyone has felt, or may feel any day.

There may be a poetry of nature less obvious than that founded on a multitudinous notation of her detailed aspects, less subtle than the analysis of exquisite sensations, but, perhaps, of more breadth and grandeur. Hazlitt has said that one could infer that Wordsworth's poetry 'was written in a mountainous country, from its bareness, its simplicity, its loftiness and its depth.' It is not, indeed, by description that the characters of nature are most deeply caught and expressed ; it is by incorporation, so to say, when the image of the outward world, instead of being directly

presented, is reflected in the feelings and shines th
indifferent words; thus deeply had the scenery a
spent his days penetrated into Wordsworth's min
we had to praise him as the poet of mountains
course, choose the noble descriptive pages that
volumes; but, rather than to these, rather than to the famous
mountain scenes in his *Excursion*—which are too conscious—we
should turn to a poem like *Michael*, where scenery, characters
and style form a perfect harmony of lines and tints that could
not have existed without a secret process of assimilation. Lofty
and bare, indeed, is this pastoral; few flowers grow on the
heights where old Michael meant to build his sheepfold. The
land is unadorned. It has no other features than the sheer linea-
ments of its sweeps and pastures or its steep rocks, over which
are spread by turns the naked sky and the winter mists. All this,
together with the bracing air, you feel from the first to the last
line, not less when the poet gives you the speech of his ancient
'statesman' or a glimpse of his stern mind, than when he paints
the landscape itself. Even as the scenery is composed of essentials,
so is the old man's character, and so his language. In such
passages there is not one word of description, and yet the 'pastoral
mountains' are constantly conjured up with their raw atmosphere,
behind the discoursing shepherd. Every syllable he utters is their
emanation.

Another summit is reached by the poet when he freely allows
his creed of the refining agency of the senses to pass into a sort
of waking dream, instead of asserting itself by argument as in
The Prelude, or even, as in *Tintern Abbey*, by lyrical proclamation. Few will deny one of the very first ranks in his verse to
the fourth of the *Lucy* poems, where he tells us how his beloved
had been cared for by nature since her tenderest years, how nature
had vowed to make her 'a Lady of her own,' imparting to her 'the
silence and the calm of mute insensate things,' either bidding the
storm 'mould the maiden's form by silent sympathy,' or causing
'beauty born of murmuring sound to pass into her face.' Here,
Wordsworth joins company with the most aerial of poets. He
drops to the earth, for once, all that matter-of-factness of which
Coleridge complained. He sets common observation at defiance
and simply ignores the objections of common sense, with which he
is elsewhere only too prone to argue. Though most thoroughly
himself when shaping Lucy's natural education, he gives wings,
not feet, to his most cherished belief. We have, in this lyric, 'the

ʌe excess' of poetry. Whatever may be said of these country maids who, though brought up under the clouds and stars, and by the side of dancing rivulets, failed to be informed with grace and beauty, Wordsworth has used his privilege as a poet of embodying a vision made, after all, of mysterious possibilities, perhaps of truths in the making.

But nature never engrossed all his thoughts. Many were given to man, chiefly to the feelings of man. He shows the same mastery in his delineation of the hidden germs of feeling as of those of sensation. He, again, excels when describing the moral emotions in the blending of the subtle and the simple, of the strange and the essential. But the beauty of his verse seems, in this case, to come less from intuitive discovery than from long brooding. Fullness and compactness of meaning now characterise his greatest utterances. All readers catch their pathos at once; few, immediately, if ever, their entire signification. A noticeable instance is the *finale* of the plain prosaic story *Simon Lee*, a short stanza full to overflowing of his prolonged meditations on the present iniquity and harshness of society. Poets and moralists have vied in easy railings at man's ingratitude. Shakespeare, among others, is full of such denunciations. Alas! the greater cause for grief is the existence of gratitude, chiefly of excessive gratitude, which implies that there is a scarcity of fellow-feeling, a dearth of benevolence, a lack of mutual neighbourly assistance in this world. That exaggerated thanks should be offered for the merest trifle, for a deed of easy and imperative kindness, betrays daily uncharitableness and opens vistas of the insensibility of existing society; it shows 'what man has made of man':

> I've heard of hearts unkind, kind deeds
> With coldness still returning;
> Alas! the gratitude of man
> Hath oftener left me mourning.

This is one of his many reflections which are more pregnant and sink deeper into the mind and heart than those of almost any other poet.

From such deep sources do many of his sonnets, chiefly of his political sonnets, draw their rare intensity of moral feeling. It is enough to remind the reader of a few familiar passages: his melancholy on hearing of the extinction of the republic of Venice; his energy of tone when he comforts poor Toussaint Louverture, the liberator of San Domingo, now thrown into a prison; the bitter restrained irony of his 'high-minded Spaniard,' who resents, more than the devastation of his country, Napoleon's so-called benefits, and so forth. In his more strictly English sonnets, the greatness is not due to novelty of thought. It so happens that almost every idea and emotion expressed by Wordsworth in 1802 and the years following had been more than foreshadowed by Coleridge as early as 1798 in his *Ode to France* or *Fears in Solitude.* But the truly Wordsworthian power of the sonnets is owing to the protracted sojourn of these feelings in his breast before he gave utterance to them, to his long reluctance against their admission, to his repeated inward debates. Hence, instead of Coleridge's extemporised effusions, which have been aptly compared, by Angellier, to the sea-scud which is thrown off by a storm, here we have the distilled elixir. Nearly ten years of vexed thoughts went to the making, in 1803, of the final line of the sonnet to England, where, after enumerating and condemning what he calls her many political crimes, he sighs (with a unique mixture of reproof and tenderness, of grief and repressed pride) at the thought that she, nevertheless, is the least unworthy champion of liberty left in the world:

> O grief that Earth's best hopes rest all in thee!

It would be hard to match these ten monosyllables for compactness of historical allusion and complex feeling. Such condensed moral utterances are among the glories of Wordsworth's verse.

Other characteristics ought to be added, regarding his more purely artistic gifts—gifts of verse-writing and style, gifts of composition. But this would land us in endless discussions; for, in these respects, Wordsworth's mastery is surely relative and intermittent. He reaches, at times, so high a degree of excellence that the mere verbal felicity of some of his simplest lines baffles the imitation of the most refined artists:

> Perhaps the plaintive numbers flow
> For old, unhappy, far-off things,
> And battles long ago....

But he frequently mixes the highest poetry with the flatness of unimpassioned, uninspired prose. He also shows himself, in many a period or stanza, devoid of ease, elegance and pliancy. He is more than once awkwardly naïve, clumsily familiar, or, on the contrary, more solemn and pompous than needs be. The talent for construction, niggardly bestowed on the romantic poets of all countries, is particularly weak in him. He could never frame and

fashion a considerable poem with due equilibrium of substance
and form, of thought and story. In this respect, *The Excursion*
is a memorable failure. As to *The Prelude*, it owes its permanent
interest partly to its admirable passages of poetry, partly to its
philosophical or to its autobiographical value, which we feel, as we
read, to be merits not strictly poetic. Only in compositions of
moderate length, like *The Ruined Cottage, Michael, Laodamia*
did he achieve perfect harmony, and in many of his lyrics and
sonnets.

That he often tries to lift us and himself to the poetic mood
rather than takes this mood for granted, cannot be denied. Poetry
often seems to be his object rather than his possession. He made
the training of man to poetry his chief office here below. He
leads us warily from the inlands of prose to the shore, marking out
the way with unprecedented care ; but he is sometimes content
with gazing on the element and leaves it to others boldly to sail
upon it or plunge into it. The main body of his poems is educative
and preparatory. Yet he has left sufficient of absolute verse,
heart-searching and beautiful, enough for a Wordsworthian anthology that will remain among the most enduring treasures of
romanticism.

CHAPTER VI

COLERIDGE

COLERIDGE survives for us as poet: a poet unique in inspiration, unique, also, if sadly fitful, in achievement. But he was also philosopher, critic, theologian, moralist, talker—above all, a talker. And, with the strongest will in the world, it would have been hard for one so variously endowed not to dissipate his genius. Given a will exceptionally infirm, the wonder is that he should have left so much, rather than so little, as a monument of what he was.

The strange complexity of his nature, reflected, as it is, in the whole tenor of his life, is a challenge to all who love to follow the mysterious windings of the soul. His character is an enthralling, as well as a deeply pathetic, study in itself. And it may even be that we shall find it throw some light upon his genius, as a poet.

Samuel Taylor Coleridge was born in October 1772; two years after Wordsworth, one year after Walter Scott. He was crossing the threshold into manhood at the time when the French revolution was rousing the more active minds to revolt against the traditions of the past: a revolt which, in his case as in others, extended to things literary no less than to those social and political. He reached middle life with the reaction which followed the downfall of Napoleon. He died (1834) in the period immediately succeeding the arrest of that reaction: some dozen years later than Keats and Shelley; ten years after Byron; two years after Walter Scott. And, of all the movements connected with those names and events, there was not one, unless we except the creations of Keats and Shelley, which did not, whether by way of action or reaction, leave some trace upon his soul.

From his father he inherited a reverence for verbal niceties which went with him throughout life; a curious strain of pedantry, which crops up in the most unlikely places; above all, a dreamy nature, which always made him a stranger and pilgrim among the bustling figures and harsh incidents of daily life. To his mother, a woman of keen practical instincts, he does not seem to have owed much beyond the priceless boon of affection. And even this was largely lost to him when, on the death of his father, he was despatched, according to the practice even then too common in English households, to school (Christ's hospital) at the age of nine (1781). Henceforth, he was to see his family only at the rarest intervals; and the outlet of home affections was virtually closed.

Even as a child, he had laid hold on all the books—especially, imaginative works—that came within his reach. At school, he became a prodigy of youthful learning and philosophy: 'logician, metaphysician, bard,' the 'inspired charity boy' of Lamb's wistful recollections. For a time, as he tells us—and it was not for the last time—the 'bard' was quite driven out by the 'metaphysician.' And it needed what we should now consider the rather weak stimulus of Bowles's sonnets to rouse him from 'this preposterous pursuit' (1789). The remedy, such as it was, proved undeniably efficacious. For the next five years, sentiment, of the kind represented by Bowles, was the most powerful factor in his growth.

In the excitement of Cambridge life (1791—3)—partly, too, under the spell of love for Mary Evans—his whole being seems to have expanded. But there was nothing to mark him off from the ordinary student of talent until, under the spur of debt or ill-starred love, or both, he suddenly bolted from the university and enlisted in a regiment of light dragoons (December 1793). After four months of this ludicrously unsuitable employment, he was discharged, by the efforts of his friends, and readmitted, with due penalties, to his college. Some two months later (June 1794) began that acquaintance with Southey, then an Oxford undergraduate, which was deeply to colour the next few years of his life.

Up to this time, there is nothing beyond the doubtful evidence of a school exercise to show that the revolution in France had roused any deep interest, or even attention, in his mind. Now, under the tenser will of Southey, he became a fiery revolutionist, of a brand, however, peculiarly his own[1]. In hatred of Pitt and the war, he was, no doubt, at one with the other Jacobins of the time. But the Pantisocracy, which the two friends beat out between them, ran decisively athwart the main stream of revolutionary aspirations. It was intended only for the select few; it was no part of a general

---

[1] 'We never were, at any period of our lives, converts to the system of French politics,' he writes, in an article on Jacobinism (1802). And the lightness with which he dropped the cause of France—as may be seen from his fine, but somewhat rhetorical, *Ode* (1798)—bears witness to the fact.

scheme of social reconstruction. Again, the 'Jacobinism' of Coleridge, though not that of Southey, was always strongly charged with a mystical and religious element, which stands in the sharpest contrast with the purely secular, often atheist, temper more common among the reformers of that day. Lastly—and here, once again, he joins hands with Southey—the whole creed and being of the young convert were drowned in a flood of sentiment which woke in him, for the first time in good earnest, the need of poetic utterance, and which at once sets a barrier between him and most of the leading figures among the rebel band: Godwin, for instance, or Holcroft, or even Thelwall.

It was in pleading the cause of Pantisocracy that he first discovered—to himself, perhaps, as well as to others—his amazing powers of eloquence. His letters of that time are full of boyish delight in the discovery: 'Up I arose, terrible in reasoning' is a typical sentence. And, so long as he could convince, or even vanquish, his opponents, it is clear that he did not much trouble himself to put his convictions into act. Even his breach with Southey, who soon became lukewarm in the cause, would seem to have partly sprung from an uneasy sense that he, too, had said more than he was willing or able to make good, and from the consequent impulse, very natural though not very just, to prove that some one else was yet more guilty than himself. Still more ominous, even in an age of overwrought sentiment, is the sentimentalism of his letters. 'Since I quitted this room,' he writes on his return from the fateful visit to Oxford, 'what and how important events have been evolved! America! Southey! Miss Fricker! Yes, Southey, you are right. Even love is the creature of strong motive. I certainly love her.' It is small wonder that the love which began as 'the creature of strong motive'—that is, Southey's *fiat*—should have ended disastrously for both. A year later (October 1795) the marriage duly took place.

The poetry of these years (1794—6) is a mirror of the man: eloquent, loose-girt, strongly inclined to preach; in all things, the very reverse of the inspired pieces soon to follow. It is, doubtless, the sincere expression of the generous convictions and aspirations which he held in common with others. But it lacks the individuality which is the soul of poetry; and, only in one passage— some three or four lines of *The Eolian Harp*[1]—does it offer even a faint promise of the works by which he lives. It is a glorified

[1] I find that these lines (26—9) were first inserted in the *Errata* to *Sibylline Leaves* (1817). Thus, the one redeeming exception falls to the ground.

version of sermons such as Hazlitt heard in the enchanted walls of the Shropshire chapel. It has nothing in common with *The Ancient Mariner*, or *Christabel*, or even the ode *Dejection*.

It was the genius of Wordsworth—and, with Wordsworth, we must always think of his 'exquisite sister'—that first revealed him to himself. It was in daily intercourse with a stronger spirit than his own—first at Stowey (1797—8), then, more fitfully, in the lake country (1800—3)—that all his enduring poetry was composed. The spell of Wordsworth, however, went far deeper than this. It not only awakened the younger poet to creative energies which had hitherto lain asleep. It was a transforming influence upon his whole cast of thought, upon the whole character of his soul. His whole nature was roused, for the first time, to a full consciousness of its powers; and powers of which he had hitherto given no suspicion were suddenly called to light. A sense of the beauty of outward things, as deep as Wordsworth's, but still more delicate and more subtle; a sense of the boundless mystery of life—the inner yet more than the outer life—and a power of interpreting it in terms of thought: these were the two gifts which came to him with this new birth; and, however idly he may have used them, they remained with him to the end. Well might he say that 'a new earth and a new heaven' were now 'given to him in dower.' For he saw the world with a keener and more radiant vision than had ever been granted to him before; and he saw into it more deeply. In the full sense of the terms, he became, for the first time, both philosopher and poet.

That his use of these magic gifts was not what it might have been, is too clear. But it is only just to remember that this applies more to his work as philosopher than as poet. Poetry 'comes not with observation.' And, if that be true, in a measure, of all poetry, of none is it so true as of that to which the peculiar genius of Coleridge was manifestly ordained. Is it reasonable to suppose that any poet could have gone on living for ever in an air so rarefied as that of *The Ancient Mariner*, or *Kubla Khan*, or *Christabel*? Given circumstances so happy as almost to amount to a miracle, perhaps he might. But the miracle did not happen to Coleridge; and, even if his will had been as strong as it was weak, there is no warrant that it would have happened. To condemn him on this score, however much he himself would have accepted the condemnation, seems, therefore, unwarrantably harsh. But his other gifts lay in a region more under his control. And, had he been a man of ordinary resolution—above all, had he not let himself become the

slave of opium—there was nothing to prevent him from accom-
plishing a giant's work in philosophy and criticism. In criticism
and the theory of criticism, he might have done for his own country
the double work which was done for Germany by Lessing and
Hegel, and something more besides. In philosophy, he might have
recast and even extended the massive fabric of Kant. As it is, in
neither field has he left more than a heap of disjointed, but imposing,
fragments.

The opium habit, the beginnings of which go back as far as 1797,
seems to have grown upon him during his time at Malta (1804—6);
and, by the time he returned to England, the bondage must have
been confirmed. Again and again, he strove to throw off the yoke;
but only to fall back again more helplessly than before. Degraded
in his own eyes, he felt life to be a burden almost too heavy to be
borne; and the letters which, now and again, were wrung from him
by remorse, are, perhaps, among the most terrible ever written. Two
things alone saved him from total shipwreck: the unwearied tenderness of friends, old and new—Poole, Wordsworth, Mrs Clarkson and
the Morgans; and the innate rectitude, winged by a strong religious
impulse, which did not cease to assert itself against reiterated
defeat. At length, after ten years of debasement, he nerved himself
to seek refuge with James Gillman, a physician of Highgate (1816).
And, thanks to the devoted friendship and watchfulness of this man
and his wife—he remained their 'inmate' till his death—he slowly
tore himself loose from the bondage in which he had been held.
That he never wholly gave up the drug, is tolerably clear. But he
so far mastered himself as to take it in rarer and smaller doses;
and, for practical purposes, the hard-fought victory was won. Thus,
the last eighteen years of his life were years of inward peace and
of fruitful service to others. The old weakness, no doubt, still
dogged his steps and prevented the fulfilment of the task—a work
on *Spiritual Philosophy* and half a dozen alternative titles—to
which he was conscious of being called. But, in familiar talk, in
formal lecturing and even in published writings, this was the
richest period of his life; and it left a deep mark upon some of
the strongest and most eager spirits of the younger generation.

The victory was won. But the long years of apparently hopeless
struggle had left scars which nothing could wholly heal. The prime
of his life had been largely wasted. And he had strained the
patience of some of his best friends. Josiah Wedgwood had withdrawn, perhaps with undue harshness, his half of the pension that
he and his brother had granted in days when nothing seemed beyond

the reach of the young poet and thinker. Southey, who had gallantly shouldered the charge of the truant's wife and children, was embittered, if not estranged. Even Wordsworth, by an unguarded utterance made with the best intentions, had caused a breach which could never wholly be made up[1]. This was probably the deepest sorrow of his life; 'all else,' he says, 'is as a flea-bite.' His family life, too—though this was from causes which, in the first instance, at any rate, had little to do with opium—had been entirely broken up. And, though a formal separation was avoided, he never lived with his wife after 1810; and had, in fact, seen as little as he could of her since 1804. The real secret of the estrangement was that, by temperament, the two were ill sorted with each other. But it is impossible not to feel the deepest sympathy with a woman who battled bravely with the hardships of her lot; and hard to check the suspicion that, but for opium, the difficulties might have been smoothed over. In any case, the breach was a worse thing for Coleridge than he was ever willing to acknowledge. It robbed him of the steadying influences of home life, to which he was by nature peculiarly open. And it left a sting in his conscience which he may have ignored, but which, just for that reason, was never healed.

The strangest thing is that, in the very height of the opium fever, he should have been capable of efforts which, though lamentably unequal, still gave evidence of powers which not one of his contemporaries could have rivalled. It was between 1808 and 1815 that he delivered the bulk of the critical lectures which make an era in the history of English literary criticism; that he composed *The Friend*, in its earlier and, doubtless, far inferior version (1809); and, finally, that he wrote all save a few passages of *Biographia literaria* (1815), the only one of his prose works which can be said to survive to the present day. Even in the depth of his debasement, he must have retained an amazing spring, a power of throwing off weights which would have crushed another man, of recovering something, at any rate, of the free flight to which he was born. It was this boundless power of self-retrieval that, at length, enabled him to cast off the yoke of opium. It was this, even more than his genius, which drew men to him as a magnet and never allowed him to forfeit the admiration, and even the respect, of his friends.

---

[1] The details of this misunderstanding are set forth in the MS of Robinson's diary, in the published version of which they are briefly summarised (vol. I, pp. 210—211). See, also, Coleridge's *Letters*, vol. II, pp. 577—8, 586—595.

The work of Coleridge naturally falls under three heads : poetry, criticism and philosophy. It remains to attempt a brief estimate of each.

All that endures of Coleridge's poetry could easily be contained in fifty pages ; and, with few and doubtful exceptions, it was all written during the six years when he was in constant intercourse with Wordsworth (1797—1803). The greatest of all his poems, almost the only one which stands as a rounded and finished whole, *The Ancient Mariner,* is an indirect tribute to the liberating influences which flowed in upon him from the elder poet. And the ode *Dejection,* with the lines written after hearing Wordsworth recite *The Prelude,* is a direct acknowledgment of the same debt. Yet, the powers were there before they were set free by the wand of the enchanter. And it may well be that he had this in mind when he wrote

> O Wordsworth! we receive but what we give,

in the one poem ; and

> Power streamed from thee, and thy soul received
> The light reflected, as a light bestowed,

in the other. So subtle is the action and reaction in such cases that, if this were so, it would be only just. For, after all, the spirit of Wordsworth was here met and answered by one as potent as itself. And what he did for Coleridge was not to mark out the channels along which his genius was to flow, but only to loose the springs of a fountain which, till that moment, had lain half frozen beneath the earth.

A greater contrast than that between the two poets it would, indeed, be hard to imagine: the one drawing his strength from the 'common things of sky and earth,' to which his vision gave a meaning they had never taken before; the other building for himself a gorgeous palace in the clouds, the colours and forms of which may have been reflected from those he had known upon the earth, but which, to us as to him, come charged with a thousand hints of an unearthly, enchanted world, known only to the spirit. As both were well aware, there is a central point where the two visions meet and blend. *Biographia* and the preface to *Lyrical Ballads* speak clearly enough to that. So, to anyone who can read beneath the surface, do the *Ballads* themselves. Still, what is bound to strike us first is not the resemblance, but the difference. And, however much we may recognise the former, the more we live ourselves into the world of the two poets, the less shall we be ready to make light of the latter.

Before 1797, Coleridge had given no promise of what he was to be. 'I cannot write without a body of thought,' he laments in a letter to Southey (11 December 1794). And the 'thought' his poetry embodied had little to distinguish it from what we might expect in the more highly wrought forms of prose. Indignation at the social wrongs of the old order and the wickedness of its rulers, pity for the outcast and oppressed, bitter cries to the Spirit in whom alone is the harmony which can resolve the discord—these form the staple of such poems as *Religious Musings* and *Ode to the Departing Year*; and the style, stiff with Miltonic phrases, rich in echoes of Gray and Collins, is no more original than the matter. Byron was not far wrong when, in his early satire, he mocked at the bard 'to turgid ode and tumid stanza dear.' But the scoff leaves the true Coleridge, the Coleridge of *Kubla Khan* and *The Ancient Mariner*, utterly untouched.

With these poems, the first-fruits of his friendship with Wordsworth, we are in a different world. It is hard to believe they can have come from the same man. The 'body of thought' and the imagery which hung round it like an ill-fitting garment have both vanished. Every idea presents itself unbidden as an image; and every image suggests a world of wonder and enchantment—the world of which he holds the key as no poet has done before or since, and in which, as poet, he was, henceforth, to have his home.

In *Kubla Khan*, an enemy might say that the 'body of thought' does not obtrude itself for the simple reason that there is no thought to obtrude. And it is true that, of all poems, this is the most airy and unsubstantial: a 'vision,' a 'dream,' if there ever was one; as the author himself tells us, an opium dream—the one good service the 'accursed drug' ever did him. This, however, does not rob the poem either of its power or its charm. On the contrary, it is, perhaps, the secret of both. And, even if there were no other argument which forced us to confess it, this one poem would be enough to prove that, while thought alone, however inspiring, is powerless to make poetry, pure imagery and pure music, even without thought (if such a thing be possible), suffice, when working in absolute harmony, to constitute what pedantry alone could deny to be a great poem. And, when a poem is so charged with suggestion, when, at each touch, it transports us into a world of the poet's making, when each shading of the colours, each modulation of the rhythm, presents that world in a new light, when our own mood finds itself forced, step by step, to follow the ever-changing mood of the poet, can we be quite sure that thought is absent?

Reflection is; reasoning is; but that subtler, more impalpable, process, which plays a real part not only in our dreams but even in our waking resolves and inferences—this, assuredly, is not. Unconscious though this may be in the process, it is conscious enough in the result. It brings about a frame of mind as distinct, as unmistakable, as any of those universally recognised to be 'thought.'

In the case of *The Ancient Mariner*, no such question could be raised. There, we have an ordered story which moves on unchecked, doubtless through a world of wonder, from mysterious preface to inevitable close. Each incident stands out clear-cut and vivid; each corresponding change in the soul of the mariner is registered, no less distinctly, as upon the plate of an enchanted dial. That is one side of the matter; and a side which sets the poem in the sharpest contrast with the phantasmagoria of *Kubla Khan*. On the other hand, each incident in that long succession—the sailing of the ship, the gradual disappearance of the landmarks, the southward voyage and the rest—is presented not with the shorthand brevity which suits the needs of daily life, but in the successive images, distinct and single, which struck the eye of the mariner at the moment; and this with a persistency which is clearly intentional, and which it would be hard to parallel from any other poem. It is here that the method of *Kubla Khan* repeats itself.

In one respect, indeed, *The Ancient Mariner* carries that method a step further. In *Kubla Khan*, there is a general sense of colour diffused throughout the poem. But, when we come to ask how that impression is conveyed, it is impossible to lay our finger upon anything more definite than the

> forests ancient as the hills,
> Enclosing sunny spots of greenery.

In *The Ancient Mariner*, on the other hand, we are not at loss for a moment. The ice 'as green as emerald,' the 'copper sky' of the tropics, the moonbeams 'like April hoar-frost spread upon the sultry main,' the moonlight that 'steeped in silentness the steady weathercock'—these are but a remnant of the lavish store of colour which brightens the whole poem. And the touches which mark the more unearthly moments of the mariner's sufferings are still to add:

> The water, like a witch's oils,
> Burnt green and blue and white;

> The charmed water burnt alway,
> A still and awful red;

not to speak of the ghastly colours which 'patched the bones' of Death, in a verse which the subtle instinct of Coleridge led him subsequently to strike out. Of all the elements that blend to make an image, colour is the most potent. And, if there be any poem which drives this truth home, it is *The Ancient Mariner*.

As to the significance of this imagery—above all, in the supernatural episodes of the poem—Coleridge himself has done something to mislead later critics. Even to friendly readers, such as Lamb and, perhaps, Wordsworth, 'all the miraculous parts' seem to have been things suspect. And Southey, with however ill a grace, was probably giving voice to the common verdict when he pronounced the poem to be 'an attempt at the Dutch sublime.' It is small wonder, therefore, that Coleridge, who was never too confident in his own genius, should have taken fright. And, in *Biographia*, he is a shade too anxious to explain that his stress lay not on the incidents themselves, but on their working upon the soul of the mariner. That there is some truth in this, is certain. But it is not the whole truth, nor anything like it. The incidents themselves—and, not least, the marvels—have a compelling power upon the imagination; the story, as a mere story, is among the most thrilling ever told. And, when we remember that this story shapes itself in a succession of images unsurpassed for poetic power and aptness, how is it possible to deny that all this counts, and counts unspeakably, in the total imaginative effect? It is, no doubt, still more surprising that, when all is said, these things should be no more than an element in a larger whole; that, side by side with these outward incidents and images, we should have to reckon, and reckon at least as largely, with their reflection in the soul of the man who saw and suffered from them; that, from beginning to end, we should see them through his eyes and feel them through his spirit. But this is the miracle of Coleridge. And it is a poor tribute to his genius if we insist upon isolating one element and asserting that it is all he had to give. It is only by taking both elements together and giving full allowance to both that we do justice to the unique quality of this 'miraculous' poem.

The first part of *Christabel* was written almost immediately after *The Ancient Mariner*, and shortly before the little band of Stowey was broken up, never again to meet under such 'indulgent skies.' The theme is of the same nature as in the preceding poem. It is handled with more artifice; but, just for that reason, perhaps with less of inspiration; certainly, with less of buoyant and exultant freedom. The 'spring of love' that had gushed from the poet's heart, as, for the first time, he saw and felt how 'excellently fair' were the 'outward shows of sky and earth' and how deep the

meaning that lay hidden within, could never again gush 'unaware.'
And, when he speaks once more of the vision that had come in the
first instant of his awakening, it is only to lament that it had been
withdrawn almost as soon as it was given and had left nothing but
yearning and self-reproach behind. In any case, the personal note,
which is very strong in *The Ancient Mariner* and which some
have thought has found its way too loudly into its closing verses,
is deliberately banished from *Christabel*; or finds an echo only in
the poignant passage about broken friendship, which he himself
considered 'the best and sweetest lines he ever wrote,' and in the
epilogue to the second part, which is partly an obvious suggestion
from the 'breeze-borne' elfish nature of his son, Hartley, partly a
lament over the difficulty—the impossibility, as it proved—of the task
which he had set himself: the solution of which, unlike the hopes and
longings of the child, was always to seek and never, alas, to find.

The same elaboration is manifest, also, in the metre. Never
before had the four-foot couplet been used with such variety and
subtlety of effect. As the author himself points out, that effect is
largely produced by a frequent use of the anapæstic movement,
which had already found its way into the ballad measure of *The
Ancient Mariner*; as in the lines—

> For the sky and the sea, and the sea and the sky
> Lay like a load on my weary eye,
> And the dead were at my feet.

But it is here invoked still more persistently; as, indeed, in
general, there is a subtlety, not to say a *finesse*, about the
rhythmical movement of this poem, which would have been quite
out of place in the rushing narrative and more homely metre of
the other. It is one more proof of the wide gulf by which, in
spirit and in total effect, the two poems are divided. Of the
subtlety which went to the creation of the metre in *Christabel*
there could be no clearer illustration than the failure both of
Scott and Byron—the one in the opening lines of *The Lay of the
Last Minstrel*, the other in a cancelled introduction of *The Siege
of Corinth*—to catch anything like the cadence of the rhythm
which, avowedly, served for their model.

It has been said that 'the thing attempted in *Christabel* is
the most difficult in the whole field of romance: witchery by
daylight.' And nothing could come nearer the mark. The
miraculous element, which lies on the face of *The Ancient Mariner*,
is here driven beneath the surface. The incidents themselves are
hardly outside the natural order. It is only by a running fire

of hints and suggestions—which the unimaginative reader has been known to overlook—that we are made aware of the supernatural forces which lie in wait on every side. The lifting of the lady across the threshold, the moan of the mastiff bitch, the darting of the flame as the enchantress passes—to the heedful, all these things are full of meaning ; but, to the unwary, they say nothing ; they say nothing to Christabel. Yet, the whole significance of the poem is bound up with these subtle suggestions ; though it is equally true that, if they were more than suggestions, its whole significance would be altered or destroyed. It would no longer be 'witchery by daylight,' but by moonlight; which is a very different thing.

To take a world not markedly different from that given to us in nature, and fill it with the presence, unseen but felt, of the supernatural ; to tell a tale of human joys and sorrows, and make it seem 'a story from the world of spirits'—this, indeed, was the aim of Coleridge. But no one was more keenly aware than he what were the obstacles to its achievement. 'I have, as I always had,' he said about a year before his death, 'the whole plan entire from beginning to end in my mind'—it may be suspected that this is one of many similar delusions—'but I fear I could not [now] carry on with equal success the execution of the idea, an extremely subtle and delicate one.' So subtle and delicate, in truth, that it is doubtful whether even a man of stronger will and more mastery of self could ever have ended the poem in the same tone in which it was begun. Even of the fragment, as it now stands, it can hardly be said that the second part carries out the design so perfectly as the first. The localisation of the scene in a familiar country may, as has sometimes been said, have something to do with this comparative failure. But it is due much more to other causes : to an almost inevitable inability on the poet's part to maintain himself indefinitely in the doubly distilled imaginings which were the essence of his undertaking. Even in the earlier part, it would seem that the right note had not always come to him at the first effort. For, if we are to believe a contemporary reviewer—it may have been Hazlitt—in *The Examiner* (2 June 1816), the original version of

> A sight to dream of, not to tell!

was

> Hideous, deformed, and pale of hue;

and there are other instances of the same kind. The reviewer scornfully remarks that the rejected reading was 'the keystone to the whole poem,' and that it was rejected by the author for that very reason. In his heart, he must have known better. It is of the essence of the poem not to feed the mind with facts—still less, with gruesome facts—but to spur the imagination by a sense of mystery. It is manifest that the original reading renounces the latter purpose for the former. And, if this be the case, it is clear that Coleridge would have ruined his poem by retaining it.

The sketch of the projected continuation, which Gillman gives on the authority of the poet, reads poorly enough. But it is impossible to say what it, or any other raw material, might have become under the transforming breath of inspiration. Still, temperament and opium between them had so clouded the sense of fact in Coleridge that it would be rash to pronounce whether this was really the plan which he had in his mind from the beginning, or nothing more than the improvisation of the moment.

How did Coleridge stand towards outward nature? and what was his place in the poetic movement of his time? It is impossible to leave his work, as poet, without a few words on each of these crucial, but widely different, matters.

This was the golden age of 'the poetry of nature'; and Coleridge may claim his place in it with the best. It is a place entirely to himself; and it depends upon two qualities. The first is a faculty of minute and subtle observation, which he may have learned, in the first instance, from Wordsworth, but which he fostered to a degree of delicacy to which neither Wordsworth himself, nor, perhaps, any other 'worshipper of nature,' Keats excepted, ever quite attained. The 'creaking of the rook's wing' and the branchless ash,

> Unsunned and damp, whose few poor yellow leaves
> Ne'er tremble in the gale, yet tremble still,
> Fanned by the waterfall,

in *This lime-tree bower, my prison*, and that 'peculiar tint of yellow-green' which marks the sunset sky in the ode *Dejection*, together with whole poems such as *The Nightingale*, bear witness to this extraordinary power. And, if more were wanted, it is supplied in abundance, though rather as raw material than as poetic creation, by the notes written when he was once more in constant communion with Wordsworth (1803), and published in the book which, of all others, throws most light upon the secret springs of his genius, *Anima Poetæ* (pp. 34—52). Nor does this command of minute detail in any sense bar the way to an equal mastery of broad, general effects. What picture was ever painted with broader brush than that of the ice-fields or the tropical ocean in *The Ancient Mariner*? What general effect was ever caught more precisely than that of the moonlight 'steeping in silentness the steady weathercock' of the same poem, or of April as the month 'of dark brown gardens and of peeping flowers' in the ode *Dejection*? It may be doubted whether full justice has even yet been done to this side of the poet's genius.

Yet, even this quality, great though it be, would have availed little, if it had not gone hand in hand with one of a very different order. With such a store of observed images at his command, there must have been a constant temptation to lavish it at every turn. Nothing is more surprising than the reserve, the sleepless sense of poetic fitness, with which it is employed by Coleridge. Even this, indeed, does not give us the whole truth. It is not only that such images recur seldom; but that, when they do, they are lifted into a rarer atmosphere, a more remote region, than that of mere outward vision. In all his greater poems—*The Ancient Mariner*, perhaps, alone excepted—we are made to feel, and we should hardly have entered into their spirit unless we did feel, that the outer world is presented to us not directly, but through a veil of mystery, which softens all that is harsh in outline or colour; by a kind of second sight, which rather recalls objects, once familiar, to the memory, than offers their actual image to the eye. 'Sir George Beaumont,' he notes in *Anima Poetæ*, 'found great advantage in learning to draw from nature through gauze spectacles.' And, with a success which we may be very sure Sir George never approached, he seems to have applied a like process to the forms of nature, as reflected in his poetry. Not that his eye was ever shut even to the crudest effects of the 'inanimate cold world.' The very chemists' jars of 'blue and green vitriol,' as reflected in the stagnant reaches of a London canal, win an entry in his note-book[1]. But when they appear in his poetry, it is—or, did dates allow, it would be—as the 'witch's oils' that 'burnt green and blue and white' around the waterlogged vessel in the 'charmed water' of the tropical sea. Nothing, in short, that he found in the outer world attained its rightful value for him until, 'by sublimation strange,' it had passed into the 'realm of shadows' which Schiller conceived to be the true region both of poetry and of action[2].

---

[1] *Anima Poetæ*, p. 28.

[2] See *Das Ideal und das Leben*, of which the original title was *Das Reich der Schatten*.

Of his place in the poetic movement of his time there is no need to speak at length. It was the hour of romance. And, of all that is purest and most ethereal in the romantic spirit, his poetry is the most finished, the supreme, embodiment. No doubt, some of the strands which went to make up the intricate web of the romantic tissue appear but faintly, if at all, in the poetry of Coleridge. Medievalism, which plays a large part in the work of Scott and others, is to Coleridge commonly no more than a vague atmosphere, such as would give the needful sense of remoteness and supply the fit setting for the marvellous which it is his purpose to hint at or openly display. Once only does he go palpably beyond this : in the shadowy picture of

> The chamber carved so curiously,
> Carved with figures strange and sweet,
> For a lady's chamber meet.

But, even this touch of medievalism is studiously vague ; nor are the allusions to trial by combat which follow in the second part of *Christabel* any more precise. Contrast these with the description of Madeline's chamber in *The Eve of Saint Agnes* or of the feudal castle and the moss-troopers in *The Lay of the Last Minstrel*; and we have the measure of the gulf which parts Coleridge from other romantic poets in this matter.

Of the historic instinct, strong both in Scott and Byron, Coleridge, in truth, was defiantly destitute.

'Of all the men I ever knew, Wordsworth himself not excepted,' he writes, 'I have the faintest pleasure in things contingent and transitory.... Nay, it goes to a disease with me. As I was gazing at a wall in Carnarvon Castle, I wished the guide fifty miles off that was telling me, In this chamber the Black Prince was born—or whoever it was,'

he adds, as well he might. It is true that, when the first cantos of *Childe Harold* appeared, he had the courage to assert : 'It is exactly on the plan that I myself had not only conceived six years ago, but have the whole scheme drawn out in one of my old memorandum books[1].' But this was a pure delusion, of the same kind as that which led him to declare he had conceived a poem, with Michael Scott for hero, much superior to Goethe's *Faust*[2]; with this difference, that, whereas *Faust* lay within his field of vision, *Childe Harold*, or any other poem that should make appeal to 'the sense of a former world,' after the manner of Byron, assuredly did not.

---

[1] *Letters*, vol. II, p. 583.
[2] See *Table-Talk*, vol. II, pp. 108—113.

It was in the subtler, more spiritual, regions of romance that Coleridge found his home. As to his treatment of the marvellous, ever 'the main region of his song,' little need be added to what has been said already. In one form or another, the theme never ceased to haunt his mind during the brief flowering time of his genius; and *The Ancient Mariner*, *Christabel* and *The three Graves* stand for three quite distinct modes of approaching it. In *The Ancient Mariner*, the poet openly proclaims his marvels, and exults in them. In *Christabel*, they are thrown into the background, and conveyed to our mind rather by subtle suggestion than direct assertion. Finally, in *The three Graves*, neither incidents nor persons have, in themselves, anything of the marvellous; it appears solely in the withering blight brought by a mother's curse upon three innocent lives. It is here that Coleridge most nearly approaches the field and method of Wordsworth; whose *Peter Bell*—in another way, perhaps, *The Thorn*—offers a curious analogy with this powerful but, as usual, unfinished poem. In the homelier region, he was, manifestly, less at ease than among the marvels and subtleties of the two other poems ; and it is rather there that the secret of his unique genius must be sought.

Two things, in particular, may be noted. The indirectness by which the elusive touches of *Christabel* are made to work their cumulative effect may be contrasted with the directness of the method employed by Keats in his treatment of a like theme, the transformation of a serpent into the guise of a woman, in *Lamia*. But it is more important to bear in mind that, if Coleridge is haunted by the marvellous, it is less for its own sake than as a symbol of the abiding mystery which he, like Wordsworth, found everywhere in life, within man and around him ; a sign of the spiritual presence which, in his faith, bound 'man and bird and beast' in one mystical body and fellowship ; a token of the love which is the life of all creation, and which is revealed to us in 'the blue sky bent over all.' It is this faith which gives a deeper meaning to these fairy creations than they bear upon the surface, and which raises the closing verses of *The Ancient Mariner* from the mere irrelevant appendage they have seemed to some critics, to an expression of the thought that lies at the core of the whole poem. And, if this be true, his wellknown retort to Mrs Barbauld—'Madam, the fault of the poem is that it has too much moral'—would take a wider significance than has commonly been supposed. Only, the self-depreciation of the poet must not be taken more seriously than it deserves.

In treating of Coleridge as literary critic, there is no alternative but to speak either very briefly or at considerable length. The latter is here impossible. All that can be done, therefore, is to indicate the main avenues which his criticism opened out.

The only written monument of his critical work is that contained in *Biographia Literaria* (1815—17), and in a short series of articles contributed to Farley's *Bristol Journal* a year or two earlier (1814)[1]. All else has to be gleaned from the very imperfect reports of his lectures, recorded by Collier, Crabb Robinson and others. These lectures, of which there were, in all, some dozen courses, were delivered, partly in London partly at Bristol, between the years 1808 and 1819. Their avowed subjects, apart from a course on the history of philosophy (1818—19), were, mainly, the drama in general, or Shakespeare and Milton. But Coleridge was never the man to be bound down by a syllabus ; and his audience had, on occasion, to bear, as best they could, a defence of school-flogging, an attack on 'the Lancastrian system of education' and other such irrelevancies, when they had come to hear a discourse on *Romeo and Juliet.* Yet, in spite of these glaring faults, the lectures were not seldom worthy both of their subject and of their author. And, with the written pieces, they form a body of work such as makes an epoch in the history of English—it would hardly be too much to say, of European—criticism.

Coleridge concerns himself not only with the practice of criticism, but, also—perhaps, by preference—with its theory. On both sides, he offers the sharpest contrast with the critics of the century, and, not least, of the generation, preceding. The Wartons and Hurd, no doubt, stand apart from the men of their day. In sentiment, they rebel against the canons of the Augustans ; and, so far, they are at one with Coleridge. But they were content to defend their instinctive judgments on purely literary grounds, and made no attempt to justify them on more general principles. Indeed, they seem never to have suspected that their revolt against the established taste in poetry carried with it a revolt against the established system in philosophy. Coleridge, on the other hand, was philosopher just as much as poet. He lived in the full tide of a philosophical, no less than a poetic, revival. He was himself among the leading figures in both. He had, therefore, on both sides, a far richer store of material to draw from than had been open

---

[1] They are reprinted in the appendix to Cottle's *Early Recollections.* To the works mentioned above should be added a pregnant section of *A Preliminary Treatise on Method,* prefixed to *Encyclopædia Metropolitana.* It was written in 1817 and published in 1818.

to the earlier rebels. And it was the first instinct of his nature to weave, or force, every side of his experience into a consistent whole.

At the first step, he rules out the assumption, which, from Horace onwards, had wrought such havoc in criticism, that the object of poetry is to instruct; or, as a less extreme form of the heresy had asserted, to make men morally better. That this may be an effect of poetry—of much that is noblest in poetry—he is not in the least concerned to deny. That, however, is no more than an incidental result. And the true end, or function, of poetry is to give immediate pleasure: pleasure, he explains in a somewhat disconcerting addition, 'through the medium of beauty[1].'

This may not carry us very far. But, at least, it serves to warn us off from the wrong road, and to set our feet at the beginning of the right one. More than this: by further additions and modifications, Coleridge so expands his original doctrine as to bring us considerably further on the path. In the first place, the assertion that the pleasure which imaginative art aims at giving is wrought 'through the medium of beauty,' however much it may check the logical flow of the argument, at least serves to enforce the truth, already laid down by Aristotle, that imaginative pleasure differs in kind from all other forms of pleasure: nay, that one form of imaginative pleasure differs in kind from all other forms of imaginative pleasure: that given by poetry, for instance, from that given by sculpture or painting; that given by the drama from that given by lyric or by epic. In the second place, his own analysis of that which constitutes 'beauty' is so illuminating, his own exposition of the conditions necessary to poetic pleasure is so subtle, as to bring us a great deal further on the road than, at the first moment, we may have been aware. The former throws a flood of light upon the points in which the various arts differ from each other, as well as upon those they have in common. The latter—enforced, as it is, by a criticism of Shakespeare's early poetic work, and reinforced by an equally delicate criticism of the charm attaching to the consummate presentment of 'common form' in poetry, particularly by the Italian poets of the later renascence—is one of the most satisfying things ever written in this kind. In applying the principles which he had already laid down in theory, the author succeeds both in defining them more closely and in extending them more widely; in the very statement of his theory, he contrives to offer a model of the method which critics should aim at following in practice.

[1] Farley's *B. J.* art. 1.

Of the rest of his work in practical criticism, no account can be offered. It must suffice to mention his criticism of Wordsworth in *Biographia*, and that of Shakespeare, as dramatist, in various courses of his lectures. The former, in itself, is a fine and discriminating piece of work. But it is more than doubtful whether Coleridge was the man to have undertaken it. He was aware that the slightly astringent touch, which he felt justice demanded, would give offence to his brother poet. And, considering the relation between the two men—a relation once of the warmest friendship, now of strained forbearance—it would have been more gracious to keep silence. Indeed, so far as the criticism deals with Wordsworth's theory of 'poetic diction,' it cannot but strike the reader as carping; not to mention the appearance of treachery involved in attacking a theory for which he himself was commonly held, and, probably, with some justice, to be, in part, responsible. As critic of Shakespeare's dramatic genius, his part is less ambiguous, though even this is complicated by questions of unacknowledged debts to Schlegel. He was the first English writer to insist that every work of art—in this instance, every play—is, by its very nature, an organic whole ; and that, if this is harder to discern in the complicated structure of Shakespearean and much other modern drama, it is because, at least in the nobler examples, such plays are not less, but more, vitally articulated ; not less, but more, spontaneous and organic. Structure, scenic effect, poetry, character—all are shown to spring from the same common root in the spirit of the poet ; each to enhance the imaginative effect which, instinctively, he had in view. And he enforces this, not as a mere abstract doctrine—though it lies at the core of his theory of beauty—but by an exposition of individual masterpieces which, for subtlety and suggestiveness, had certainly, if we except Goethe's masterly criticism of *Hamlet*, never been approached. It remains true that, having done so much, he might justly have been expected to do even more ; and that nothing but his own nervelessness, at once the cause and effect of the opium habit, could have prevented him from doing it.

If, in literary criticism, there has sometimes been a disposition to exaggerate the value of the work actually accomplished by Coleridge, in philosophy, the tendency has almost always been to give him less than his due ; certainly, as to what he achieved in the way of writing ; too often, even as to his intrinsic capacity. Yet, his importance in the history of English philosophy is not to be denied. It is neither more nor less than to have stood

against the current which, for the last century, had swept everything before it; to have assailed the mechanical philosophy
which, from the time of Locke, had firmly entrenched itself in
this country and in France; and, however much he may have
been overborne by the prejudices of the moment, at least to
have paved the way for their ultimate exposure and defeat. Even
at the moment, in the high tide of Bentham's influence, his
labours were by no means in vain. As writer—still more, in his
talk and in his personal influence—he served for a rallying point
to all who felt, if they could not explain to themselves, the
inadequacy of the prevailing system: the one man who was
capable of laying bare its fallacies, the one man who was able
to give a reasoned account of the larger faith after which they
were blindly groping. The evidence of this is to be found in
the lives of such men as Arnold and Maurice; or, more com-
pactly, in the generous essay of Mill and the brilliant, but not
too generous, chapter devoted to the subject in Carlyle's *Life
of Sterling*.

In philosophy, as he himself would have been the first to
acknowledge, he was building on the foundations laid by Kant
and, to a less degree, by Fichte and Schelling. At what time
he became acquainted with the writings of Kant, is a disputed
point. He himself seems to place it in 1800[1]; and, though he was
constitutionally inaccurate about all matters of fact, it is hard to
see why this date, the period immediately following his return
from Germany, should not be accepted. The question is hardly
one of supreme importance. For, despite some unlucky borrowings
from Schelling (alas! unacknowledged), he was in no sense a mere
adapter, still less a mere copyist, from the Germans[2]. He worked,
as all philosophers must work, on hints furnished by his predecessors; and that is all.

His aim was to show the necessity of replacing the mechanical
interpretation of life and nature, which he found in possession
of the field, by one consistently spiritual, indeed religious. And
he carries out this purpose over the whole field of experience:
in metaphysics and philosophy; in ethics and politics; not to
mention his application of the same principle to imaginative
creation, as briefly indicated in the preceding section. In

---

[1] *Biographia*, chap. IX.

[2] The passage in *Biographia*, chap. XII (pp. 124—7), which forms the introduction
to Coleridge's metaphysical system, is an unblushing translation (with a misquotation
from Horace faithfully reproduced) of Schelling's *System des transzendentalen Idealismus*,
§§ 1, 2. The rest of the chapter is largely an adaptation from the same work.

metaphysics, his work is probably less satisfactory than in any other branch of his vast subject. And that, partly because he is here more ready than elsewhere to follow the hazardous guidance of Schelling ; partly because the temptation to press speculative truth into the service of a particular religious creed was more than he was able wholly to resist. Hence, with all his subtlety, he does not succeed in driving home the essentially creative action of the mind in the process of knowledge—and that, after all, is the main point at issue—at all as clearly as Kant had done before him. And, by his use of the distinction between the 'reason' and the 'understanding'—a distinction originally due to Kant—for the purpose of bolstering up opinions originally derived from a wholly different source, he opens the door to all kinds of fallacies and perversions. With Kant, the distinction between the reason and the understanding has a purely restrictive purpose. Its effect is to deny to the former anything more than a 'regulative' or suggestive function in the ordering of knowledge; and to claim from the latter, which, from its nature, must always go hand in hand with a sensible intuition, the sole title to the discovery of truth. In other words, it is a distinction which leads straight to what have since come to be known as agnostic conclusions. To Coleridge, it serves a purpose exactly the reverse. So far from separating the spheres of the two faculties, he sweeps away all barriers between them. He allows to the one an apparently unlimited power of re-affirming what the other had found it necessary to deny; and thus exposes himself to Carlyle's sarcasm that he had discovered 'the sublime secret of believing by the reason what the understanding had been obliged to fling out as incredible.' It would be grossly unfair to say that this exhausts the teaching of Coleridge in the region of metaphysics. His criticism of the mechanical system—and, in particular, of the theory of association, as elaborated by Hume and Hartley— would, in itself, suffice to overthrow any such assertion[1]. But it can hardly be denied that this is the side of his doctrine on which he himself laid the heaviest stress ; nor, again, that it is the side upon which he is most open to attack.

In the kindred field of psychology, his results are both sounder in themselves and more absolutely his own. His records of the working of the mind, especially under abnormal or morbid conditions, are extraordinarily minute and subtle. It would hardly be too much to say that he is the founder of what has since

---

[1] *Biographia*, chaps. v—viii.

become a distinct, and most fruitful, branch of philosophy : the study of experimental psychology. And this, which is fully known only to those who are familiar with *Anima Poetæ*, is, perhaps, his most original contribution to philosophy.

In ethics, he is more upon the beaten track. But it was a track almost unknown to Englishmen of his day. And it is his lasting service, at the moment when the utilitarian scheme of things swept all before it, to have proclaimed the utter insufficiency of any doctrine which did not start from the postulate of duty. Here, once more, he bases his teaching upon that of Kant. But he enters a just protest, as Schiller had done before him, against the hard saying that the highest goodness is that which tramples upon the natural instincts of the heart. And, throughout his exposition, as given in *Aids to Reflection*, he shows (as, from his personal experience, he well might) a sense of human frailty—a sense, that is, of one of the two main elements of the problem—which the noble stoicism of Kant had been too apt to treat as matter for nothing but shame and contempt.

Few, probably, now think of Coleridge in connection with political philosophy. Yet, there is no subject to which, throughout life, he gave more time and thought; from the days of *Conciones ad populum* and *The Watchman* (1795—6) to those of *The Friend* (1809—10 ; 1818), or of *The Constitution of Church and State* (1830). Coleridge habitually spoke of himself as the heir of Burke. And that constitutes at once the strength and the weakness of his position as political philosopher. More systematic, but with far less of imaginative and historic insight than his master, he inherited, in fact, both the loves and the hates of *Reflections* and *Letters on a Regicide Peace*.

On the negative side, he is the fiery foe of the rights of man, of Jacobinism, of the sovereignty of the people. And he makes no effort to disentangle the truth which—under a crude form, no doubt—found expression in watchwords which, in his early manhood, had shaken Europe to her depths and had in no sense lost their power when he died. To the end, he was unable to see that no state, which does not draw its will from the whole body of its members, can be regarded as fully organised or developed ; and that this was the ideal which the French revolution, perhaps before the time was ripe, certainly through many crimes and blunders, was striving to make good. Against this ideal, he had nothing to propose but that of a government, based upon the will of the propertied classes only, and imposing itself upon the rest

of the community from above.   The result is that, at the present
day, his theory seems ludicrously out of date : far more so than
that of the Jacobins, or of *Le Contrat social*, which he does his
best to cover with ridicule and contempt.   So childish, indeed, was
his fear of Jacobinism, so keen his scent for the faintest breath of
its approach that, when Erskine brought in a bill, the first of its
kind, for the prevention of cruelty to animals (1809), he denounced
it, in his largest capitals, as 'the strongest instance of legislative
Jacobinism[1].'   It was bad enough that rights should be demanded
for men ; to concede them to animals was iniquitous and absurd.
In spite of these follies, it is right to acknowledge that his criticism
of Jacobinism and of *Le Contrat social*, however little we may
agree with it, reveals powers beyond the reach of any man living
in England at the time ; probably, if we except Hegel, beyond the
reach of any man in Europe[2].

Yet, as with all thinkers worthy of the name, it is in expounding
the positive side of his doctrine that his powers are seen at their
brightest and most convincing.   The core of his creed, as of Burke's,
lay in the conviction that the civic life of man is the offspring not
of deliberate calculation, 'the cautious balancing of comparative
advantages,' but of instincts, often working unknown to himself,
which are rooted in the deepest fibres of his nature.   He is assured
that the state, so far from being a cunning piece of mechanism,
put together at the will of individuals and to be taken to pieces at
their pleasure, is something larger and more enduring than the
individuals who compose it.   He knows that, in a very real sense,
it has a life of its own : a life which, at countless points, controls,
no less than it is controlled by, theirs.   He believes that the moral,
as well as the material, existence of men is largely determined by
the civic order into which they are born.   And he infers that, if
this order be roughly shaken, the moral, as well as the material,
well-being of those who belong to it is grievously emperilled.
These are the vital principles which lie behind all that he wrote
on political matters, and which find their best expression, characteristically barbed by a bitter attack on Hume, in an eloquent
passage of one of his *Lay Sermons*[3].

[1] *Letters*, vol. II, p. 635.
[2] *The Friend*, ed. 1837, vol. I, pp. 240—266; vol. II, pp. 28—30.   *Essays on his own Times*, pp. 543—550.
[3] *The Statesman's Manual*, 1816.

CHAPTER VII

GEORGE CRABBE

GEORGE CRABBE was born at Aldeburgh, on the coast of Suffolk, on 24 December 1754. His father, a collector of salt-duties at the harbour, was a man of both high tastes and low. Rather disreputable in his later years, he had, as a young man, kept school, and used to read Milton, Young and other poets aloud to his family. Destined for the profession of medicine, George was apprenticed to a medical practitioner in Wickhambrook, near Bury St Edmunds, from whose surgery, three years later, he passed into that of a doctor at Woodbridge. Here he remained from 1771 to 1775, and became acquainted with Sarah Elmy, who, though ten years were to pass before they were married, exercised from the first a softening and brightening influence on the rather grim nature of the unformed youth. Just about the time of their meeting, Crabbe made his first known appearance in print as a poet. In 'the poets' corner' of a ladies' magazine in 1772 appeared several pieces of verse, some signed 'G. Ebbare' and one 'G. Ebbaac,' which are held to be by Crabbe[1]. One of these, consisting of two very pretty stanzas, called *The Wish*, celebrates the poet's 'Mira,' which was the poetical name given by Crabbe to Sarah Elmy.

In 1775, just before the close of his apprenticeship at Woodbridge, Crabbe put his powers to a severe test, by publishing with an Ipswich bookseller a poem, in three parts, entitled *Inebriety*. From the description of the cottage library in part I of *The Parish Register*[2] and other references in Crabbe's works, we know that, in boyhood, his favourite reading had been romantic; but, by the time he wrote *Inebriety*, he must have made a close study of the poetic dictator of the day, Pope. Much of *Inebriety* is composed of frank imitation, or parody, of *An Essay on Man* and *The Dunciad*; while, here and there, Crabbe proves his knowledge of Gray. Echoes of these poets, being mingled with language drawn

---

[1] *George Crabbe*, ed. Ward, A. W., Cambridge English Classics, vol. I, pp. v—viii.
[2] ll. 95—126. See, also, *The Borough*, letter xx, *Ellen Orford*, ll. 11—119.

by the doctor's apprentice from his art, and presented in rimed heroic verse, at once laboured and slipshod, leave *Inebriety* one of the rawest poems ever written. Yet, if there is plenty of affectation about the youthful satirist, it is not sentimental affectation. Crabbe shows signs already of that revolt against idealisation which was to inspire his mature work. To him, inebriety is an evil, and he describes with vigour and point its evil effects in all classes of life.

His apprenticeship over, Crabbe returned home to Aldeburgh, without any prospects and with very little knowledge of the science of healing. Owing to his mother's illness and his father's intemperance and violent nature, his home was unhappy. During these years, the iron must have entered into his soul. He tried to practise his profession at Aldeburgh, and was appointed parish doctor. Meanwhile, however, he was studying nature, and especially botany, with results which, if of no service to him as doctor, were to be of great value to his poetry. He continued to read much and to think much, and he found his mind turning definitely to faith and piety. Sarah Elmy was his consolation and hope (many years later, in one of the *Tales* called *The Lover's Journey*, he wrote a famous description of a visit to her); and he went on writing poetry, a little of which has survived. To the years 1775—9 belong several religious poems, an impressive little piece on Mira[1], which tells how she drew the author from the relief of 'false pleasures' to 'loftier notions,' and a blank verse work entitled *Midnight*, which, if very gloomy, ends on a note of sane and sturdy courage.

At length, he could not endure life at Aldeburgh any longer. Towards the end of 1779, he made up his mind to stake his all on literary work in London and, in April 1780, with assistance from Dudley North, a relative of the prime minister, he set sail from Slaughden quay. In London, he took a lodging close to the Royal Exchange, near some friends of Miss Elmy who lived in Cornhill, and set to work revising a couple of plays and some prose essays which he had brought with him, studying botany and entomology in the country round London, and keeping a journal addressed to Mira. The year was to him one of privation and disappointment. Among the poems that, without success, he attempted to publish were an epistle, in his favourite couplets, to prince William (afterwards William IV), a satirical *Epistle from the Devil* (apparently a revised version of an earlier poem, *The Foes of Mankind*) and

---

[1] Ward, *u.s.* vol. I, p. 38.

an *Epistle to Mira,* in both of which he uses anapaests. No publisher would accept these poems, in spite of a biting introduction by their author, under the pseudonym 'Martinus Scriblerus.' Lords North, Shelburne and Thurlow, one after another, turned a deaf ear to the author, though his compliment in verse to Shelburne deserved some reward. And when, probably in August 1780[1], he found a printer willing to print two hundred and fifty copies of another poem, it did not bring him in anything but one or two slighting reviews. Crabbe, who, in several works of this period, describes his own feelings and condition, hereupon addressed to 'the Authors of the *Monthly Review*' a letter in verse, in which he practically asks them to advise him whether he should persevere in poetry or not, bestowing on himself, by the way, some satirical advice on the methods that lead to success. There is nothing remarkable about the poem except the amazing simplicity of the idea.

The kindness of the wigmaker with whom he lodged, occasional help from Sarah Elmy's family and the pawning of his possessions just sufficed to save Crabbe from destitution; but his condition was very bad indeed when, in something like despair, he wrote, probably in February or March 1781, a letter to Edmund Burke. This letter, which is still extant[2], he left, with some specimens of his poetry in manuscript, at Burke's house in Charles street, St James's. Burke granted an interview, found Crabbe to have 'the mind and feelings of a gentleman,' gave him money for his immediate needs and became his patron. Among the poems then submitted by Crabbe to Burke was *The Library*; and this was the poem which Burke recommended for publication. First, however, it must be revised; the thoughts were often better than the verses. The revision was carried out under Burke's eye. *The Library* was published by Dodsley, 24 July 1781. It did not bear any author's name, and there is not anything in the poem itself to declare it Crabbe's. It smacks throughout of Pope and of the poetical commonplace of the day. The author imagines himself in a library and utters his glib reflections upon the provinces of theology, history and so forth, and upon the relief from care afforded by reading. Any other of the poets of the day might have written it, and it did not advance Crabbe's reputation.

With the next publication, the case was different. The packet left with Burke had contained portions of a poem which attempted to contrast village life, as the writer knew it, with the Arcadian

[1] Huchon, R., *Un Poète Réaliste Anglais,* p. 139, n. 1.
[2] It is reproduced in facsimile by Huchon, *u.s.*

life described by authors of pastorals. When completed, the poem
was published as *The Village*. Before, however, its appearance
turned the fortunes of Crabbe as poet, his fortunes as a man had
already been turned through the influence of Burke. Burke invited him to stay at Beaconsfield, introduced him to his powerful
friends, Fox, Reynolds, Thurlow (who presented him with £100 and
forgave him an old insult), and then, finding the bent of his mind to
be towards holy orders, recommended him to the bishop of Norwich,
who ordained him, December 1781, when he was all but twenty-
seven years old, to the curacy of Aldeburgh. At Aldeburgh,
Crabbe, as usual, was not happy. His father was proud of him ;
but the neighbours regarded him as an upstart. Change from one
awkward situation to another came with the offer of the post of
private chaplain to the duke of Rutland at Belvoir, whither Crabbe
went in 1782. In spite of 'the mind and feelings of a gentleman,'
which Burke had found in him, there seems to have been a kind
of bluntness, perhaps merely that of a strong and sincere mind
(Thurlow once said that he was 'as like Parson Adams as twelve
to a dozen'), which unfitted him for a ducal chaplaincy; and,
though the portrait of 'my lord,' in *The Patron*, is not drawn
from the duke of Rutland, who treated Crabbe with kindness and
consideration, some of John's difficulties there set out were,
doubtless, borrowed from the poet's own experience. However,
he was now free from anxiety, constantly meeting people of learning and taste and blessed with plenty of leisure for his poetic
work.

Crabbe went to Belvoir in or about August 1782. In May
1783, the publication of *The Village* revealed his peculiar qualities
as a poet. The poem had been completed and revised under
Burke's guidance, and submitted by Reynolds to Johnson, who
declared it 'original, vigorous, and elegant,' and made an alteration
which cannot be wholly approved[1]. The originality of the poem
won it immediate success[2]. Such a work may, almost, be said to
have been needed. The taste for pastorals, running down from
the Elizabethan imitations of Theocritus and Mantuan to Ambrose

---

[1] *The Village*, I, ll. 15—20. Crabbe's original lines may be seen in *Works* (1834),
114, n. 4.

[2] The daring novelty of Crabbe's poetic treatment of the poor may be gauged by a
curious parallelism between *The Borough*, letter XVIII, *The Poor and their Dwellings*,
ll. 354 *sqq.*, and the lines recited by 'the poet' in letter XXX of Goldsmith's *The Citizen
of the World*. Goldsmith's lines were written as burlesque; Crabbe's, written in all
seriousness. The present writer is indebted to Canon A. C. Deane of Great Malvern
for pointing out this loan.

Philips, Allan Ramsay and Thomson, had worn itself out. Gay's
Shepherd's Week, with its parody of Philips, had helped to kill it;
and Crabbe, certainly, owed something to the form and tone of
Gay's poem. Yet, the impulse had continued in another form.
Goldsmith, in *The Deserted Village*, and Gray, in *An Elegy
Written in a Country Churchyard*, though completely free from
pastoral affectation, had, at any rate in Crabbe's opinion, idealised
the life and character of the villager. Crabbe, who, perhaps
from early youth, had contrasted his knowledge of life round
Aldeburgh with the 'smooth alternate verse' read aloud to him
by his father, where

> fond Corydons complain,
> And shepherds' boys their amorous pains reveal,
> The only pains, alas! they never feel[1],

conceived the idea of telling the truth about country folk as he
saw it. For this task, he was peculiarly well equipped. He knew
the life of the country poor by personal experience; and his studies
in botany and other branches of natural science—possibly, even the
mental shortsight which, all his life, kept his vision very close to
its object—enabled him to substitute for the graceful vagueness
of pastoral poets a background drawn with minute exactness. In
seven consecutive lines of *The Village*, thistles, poppies, bugloss,
mallow and charlock are mentioned by name, each in a manner
which proves it to have been closely observed; and it is said that
Aldeburgh, Great Parham and the country around Belvoir are all
recognisable in the several descriptions of scenery. As with his
background, so with his persons. The desire to tell the truth as
he saw it was the intellectual passion which governed Crabbe in
all his mature poetry. The side of truth which he saw was,
however, nearly always the gloomy side. 'Nature's sternest
painter, yet her best' Byron said of him, in a wellknown line,
of which the first part probably remains true, while the second
seems to overlook the fact that even village life has a bright side.
This may be found in *The Cotter's Saturday Night*. An unhappy
youth spent in a rough home may have tinged Crabbe's mind;
but his sturdy dislike of sentimentalism was an enduring characteristic. So he becomes linked with the 'realists' of later times.
Man is not to be served by iridescent visions of what he is not,
but by pity awakened by the knowledge of what he is.

In spite of this revolt against sentimentalism, *The Village*, like

[1] *The Village*, I, ll. 12—14.

Crabbe's later poems, shows substantial fairness. Its picture is not all gloom. If we contrast his clergyman with the parson of *The Deserted Village*, the poem is entirely free from the note, to be described, perhaps, as petulant, which occurs more than once in Cowper's satires, which had been published, with not much immediate success, a few months before *The Village*.

The workmanship of *The Village* reaches a point which Crabbe never passed. The poem had the advantage, as we have seen, of revision by Burke and Johnson, and the heroic couplets, which were always Crabbe's favourite metre, lack the fluency of *The Library*, and the rugged carelessness of his later poetry. They are sufficiently polished, without losing any of his peculiar sharpness ; and his love of epigram and of antithesis, that amounts almost to punning, is kept in check. The 'originality and vigour,' if not the ' elegance,' of the poem, were immediately recognised. Burke put extracts from it into *The Annual Register* for 1783, where Scott read the description of the workhouse so earnestly that he could repeat it more than ten years later. As Horace Walpole wrote to Mason, Crabbe 'writes lines that one can remember.'

To *The Annual Register* for 1783, Crabbe contributed an obituary notice of his patron's brother, Lord Robert Manners, whose death in a seafight, while in command of *The Resolution*, he had sung in some fine lines feebly tacked on to the end of *The Village*; but he did not publish any more poetry for nearly two years. And, then, he did not give the public anything worthy of him. It is difficult to believe that *The Newspaper*, a satire published March 1785, was not an early work, written, perhaps, just after Burke had given his approval to *The Library*, which it closely resembles. In fact, after *The Village*, Crabbe did not publish any important poetry for more than twenty-two years. During most of these years he was writing verse and destroying it; during some of them, no doubt, he was living it, rather then writing it, for, on 15 December 1783, he was married to Sarah Elmy. During the years that followed, Crabbe wrote three prose romances and, on his wife's advice, destroyed them; withdrew, before publication, on the advice of a friend, a projected volume of poems; and worked hard at various branches of science and at reading in several languages.

At length, in October 1807, at the age of nearly fifty-three, he published another volume, which contained, besides reprints of *The Library*, *The Village* and *The Newspaper*, some new poems. Of these, the longest and most important, *The Parish Register*,

develops the theme of *The Village* and first brings Crabbe into
prominence as a teller of stories. A country clergyman (such is
the scheme of the poem) is looking through his registers, and
utters the reflections and memories stirred in him, in turn, by the
entries of births, marriages and deaths. Crabbe's desire to be
just is evident from his inclusion of certain happy scenes (suggested, probably, rather by his own parishes than by his recollections of Aldeburgh) and of fortunate people; but the bent of
his mind is equally evident in his manner of turning away from the
description of the charming cottage, with its pictures, its books and
its garden,

> To this infected row we term our street.

The Parish Register contains some of the best and the best-
known passages in Crabbe's poems, notably the story of Phoebe
Dawson, which touched the heart of Fox during his lingering death
in the autumn before its publication. Meeting Crabbe at Dudley
North's house, Fox urged him to publish more poetry, and
offered to read and revise his manuscript. *The Parish Register*,
then, had the benefit of Fox's advice, as *The Village* had enjoyed
that of Burke and Johnson; and Crabbe, as he tells us in his
preface to the volume, had followed it scrupulously—doubtless to
the advantage of the couplets. In subject and treatment, the
poem was sufficiently novel to create some stir. It has been pointed
out[1] that the impulse given to English fiction by the Roger de
Coverly papers in *The Spectator* was exhausted. With the
exception of Miss Edgeworth, there was not any novelist then
telling stories that approached the truth about humble and
ordinary folk; and, in *The Parish Register*, Crabbe revived an
impulse that passed on, in course of time, to George Eliot and,
after her, to living writers[2].

As in all his poetry, the moral purpose is made very clear.
Most of the unhappiness related is ascribed to the ungoverned
passions or the weaknesses of the characters, to the lack of that
prudence, moderation and selfcontrol which he consistently advocated, in matters temporal and spiritual. He desires to warn
all who might find themselves in like circumstances, and, at the
same time, to rouse pity in the minds of his readers for sinning
and suffering humanity. The first requisite for a poet with these
aims is a sympathetic understanding; and Crabbe, later, was to

---

[1] *E.g.* by Ainger, *Crabbe* (English Men of Letters), p. 103.
[2] For Crabbe's attitude towards romantic tales in general, see, especially, *The
Borough*, letter xx, *Ellen Orford*, ll. 11—119.

show, even more clearly than he shows in *The Parish Register*, his mastery of what novelists know as psychology.

Of the other poems in the 1807 volume, *The Hall of Justice* is a strong and horrible narrative, in stanzas, of the life of a gipsy woman; while *The Birth of Flattery* is a pompous allegory showing how flattery is the fortunate child of poverty and cunning. More remarkable is *Sir Eustace Grey*, a poem very different from Crabbe's usual pedestrian and minutely 'natural' work. In or about 1790, Crabbe had been recommended by his doctor to take opium for severe indigestion; and opium-taking became a habit. It was suggested by Edward FitzGerald that opium influenced Crabbe's dreams, and, through them, *Sir Eustace Grey* and *The World of Dreams*, a poem of somewhat the same nature, which was first printed after his death. The scene of *Sir Eustace Grey* is a madhouse, where a patient, once rich and happy, relates to his physician and a visitor his downfall and the visions of his madness. Parallels have been found between some of these imaginings and those recorded by De Quincey in *The Confessions of an Opium-Eater*. The poem, which is written in eight-line stanzas with linked rimes, is wild and forcible in a very high degree; but Crabbe, with fine art, allows it to sink gradually to rest with Sir Eustace's account of his conversion by what the poet admitted to be a 'methodistic call,' his singing of a hymn and the reflections of the physician.

Crabbe's next publication was *The Borough*, a poem in twenty-four parts or 'letters,' published in April 1810. Like *The Village* and *The Parish Register*, it describes life and character as the poet had seen them in Aldeburgh. Yet, not in Aldeburgh only; for this borough might, to some extent, stand for any country town of moderate size. In a series of letters to a correspondent, the author gives an account of the town, the church, the religious bodies, the politics, professions, amusements, the workhouse, the poor, the prisons, the schools and many other features of the town's life. As the work is much longer than its predecessors, so it shows an increase in Crabbe's scope and power. There was no one now to revise his writings; and *The Borough* remains a very uneven work, both in matter and in versification; yet, Crabbe, who had spent eight years upon the poem, was not then so indifferent to craftsmanship as he became later. Parts of *The Borough* are very dull; excess of detail makes other parts tedious; and there is much clumsiness and flatness of expression. Nevertheless, *The Borough* contains some of Crabbe's finest work, and shows an advance in his power of divining motive and depicting character. The portraits of the clergy and the ministers, and of the inhabitants of the almshouses, show rare penetration and vigour in description; and, if Crabbe found himself unable to construct in verse, or in prose, a novel in which the characters should act and react upon each other, he remains a master of the individual portrait. For poignancy and poetic beauty, nothing in all his work, perhaps, equals the description of the condemned felon's dream of his youth at home[1].

Little more than two years elapsed before Crabbe published another volume of poetry, in some ways his best. *Tales*, issued in September 1812, shows an advance on *The Borough* in the art of revealing character by narrative. Many of the twenty-one stories are constructed on the same plan—initial happiness converted gradually into misery by intellectual pride or ill-regulated passion; but the variety of the treatment and of the characters prevents monotony. And, if any one were tempted to accuse Crabbe of a lack of humour, *Tales* should avert such a charge. In this set of stories, more than in any other, he exhibits a humour, bitter, no doubt, but profound, searching and woven into the very stuff of the tale. *The Gentleman Farmer*, with its exposition of the daring free-thinker enslaved in three different kinds of bondage—to a woman, a quack doctor and an ostler turned preacher; *The Patron*, with its picture of the noble family's reception of their poet-*protégé's* death; the masterly comedy of the wooing of a worldling and a puritan in *The Frank Courtship*—these and several others show Crabbe in complete control of his material, and exercising upon it more of the poet's (or, rather, perhaps, of the novelist's) intellectual and emotional labour than he usually bestowed upon the fruits of his observation. Two of the tales have extraneous interests. Tennyson knew and admired Crabbe's poems, and may have made use in *Enoch Arden* of his recollections of *The Parting Hour*; and Charles Lamb founded on *The Confidant* a comedy called *The Wife's Trial*[2], which, in turn, gave Maria Edgeworth an idea for *Helen*.

After *Tales*, Crabbe did not publish anything more for seven years. He was now a poet of wide reputation, and was welcomed by Rogers, Campbell and others on the visits to London which his wife's death in 1813 set him free to pay. In the spring of 1814, he was appointed to the cure of Trowbridge in Wiltshire, where he was within reach of William Lisle Bowles, of Lord Bath and of the

---

[1] *The Borough*, letter xxiii, *Prisons*, ll. 289—329.
[2] Printed in *Blackwood's Magazine*, December 1828.

interesting people who lived in Bath or came there to take the waters. He appears to have worked meanwhile, with the regularity of an Anthony Trollope, at his poetry; and the results of this manner of work may be detected in his next volume, *Tales of the Hall*, published in July 1819. He had always been a careless or a wilful workman. Left to himself, and more careless than ever, now that his fame was established and his age advanced, he indulged more freely than before in unnecessary detail, in sentences distorted for the sake of a rime, in flatness approaching doggerel, in verbosity and antithesis. Some of his critics, among them Jeffrey, had complained of the lack of connection between the stories in his earlier volumes. The objection seems trivial; and, in *Tales of the Hall*, Crabbe's device of making brothers who are scarcely acquainted with one another exchange stories seems futile, when all these stories clearly bear the impress of a single mind. As usual, Crabbe took most of his material from people and events he had observed, or from true stories related to him; and one very interesting passage in *Tales of the Hall*[1] appears to be a portrait of himself. The time had gone by when Crabbe could justly be accused, as he had been by Jeffrey, of 'disgusting representations.' *Smugglers and Poachers* in *Tales of the Hall* is a terrible story; but, in most of these poems, as in *Tales*, Crabbe is dealing with people of a higher social grade than his early models. Though most of the stories are sad, there is less scope for brutality, and more for minute and sympathetic study of the finer shades of thought and temper. *The Widow* is a fine piece of high comedy; the twice-widowed lady's letter to her third suitor[2] is shrewdly ironical; while a passage in *Delay has Danger*[3], describing a peevish wife, is, perhaps, the best example that could be chosen of the sharp and vivid effect to which Crabbe could attain by his epigrammatic, antithetic manner.

Tales of the Hall was the last volume of poems by Crabbe published in his lifetime. At Trowbridge, he lived in comfort, winning, by degrees, the esteem of his parishioners (a tribute which, in other cures, he had not wholly gained), working hard at poetry and paying visits to his friends. At the house of the Hoares in Hampstead, he met Wordsworth, Southey, Rogers, Joanna Baillie and others; and he paid a memorable visit to Scott in Edinburgh. He died at Trowbridge, in February 1832. At his death, many volumes of poetry in manuscript were found in his

---

[1] Book xiv; *The Natural Death of Love*, ll. 3—42.   [2] Book xvii, ll. 407—445.
[3] Book xiii, ll. 733—744.

house, and selections from these were printed in the collected edition of his works, edited by his son, George Crabbe, which was published in 1834. They include one delightful tale, *Silford Hall; or, The Happy Day*, which describes the visit of a poor boy to a great house over which he is shown by the housekeeper; and one shrewd piece of comedy, *The Equal Marriage*, in which a male and a female coquette marry to their joint discomfort. *The Farewell and Return* is a series of short poems describing the fortunes of a man's acquaintances before and after his long absence from his native town. They contain some admirable work, such as the poem called *The Ancient Mansion*, which tells how the local great house had been bought and spoiled by a newcomer. But, in reading these posthumous tales, it is just to remember that they had not been finally passed for the press by the author, whose reputation they do little to enhance. The lyric was not his best means of expression, and he used it rarely; but the quatrain, *His Mother's Wedding-Ring*, shows a beautifully turned thought, and the short poem on his dead wife, *Parham Revisited*, is simple and passionate. The unpublished poems by Crabbe, collected from manuscripts in the possession of the university of Cambridge and printed in the Cambridge English Classics edition of his works, include other examples of his work in lyric poetry.

Between the publication of Crabbe's first work and of his last, a revolution had come over English poetry. He began to write in a barren time, when the power of Pope was waning, and nothing new had yet arisen to take its place. Almost contemporaneously with *The Village*, his first characteristic poem, appeared the first volume of Cowper. During Crabbe's long silence, the influence of Cowper was to spread; and, by the time of Crabbe's death, Coleridge, Wordsworth, Scott, Campbell, Byron, Shelley and Keats had done their work for English poetry. It says much for one who, though an innovator in subject, belonged to the previous age in execution, that he held his own throughout life and for some time afterward. He told the plain truth about peasants; yet he called them 'swains,' as if *Lyrical Ballads* had never been published. Poetry took on a hundred new or revived forms; yet he clung, with very few re-missions, to his couplets. In spite of all, his work was read and admired by the very men who were trying to set poetry free from the shackles in which he continued to labour. Almost alone among the voices of the new school, Hazlitt's was raised against him; and Hazlitt's wellknown attack[1] can best be explained by

[1] *The Spirit of the Age.* Waller and Glover's *Hazlitt*, vol. IV, pp. 348 ff.

a moment of spleen.   The admiration of Wordsworth for Crabbe's
work was warm.   *Lyrical Ballads* had not done anything to affect
Crabbe's style, and the two poets, both starting from the same point,
a recognition of sympathetic interest in common life, had followed
widely different paths; but, like Tennyson, at a later date, Wordsworth valued highly the independence and truth of Crabbe's sturdy,
old-fashioned poetry, and saw in it, what Hazlitt failed to see, the
beauty born of poetic passion.

Though Crabbe has paid the penalty of neglect, exacted from
all poets who are careless of form, he was undoubtedly wise to
keep almost exclusively to his couplets.   No metre could be better
suited to his close sketches of character or to the level development
of his tales.   When at its worst, his work is very bad, and an easy prey
to clever parodists like the authors of *Rejected Addresses*, who, in
a few trenchant lines, brought all its faults into the light.   When at
its best, it is more than good narrative verse.   In certain passages,
particularly in passages of description, it rises to an intense and
passionate beauty, all the minute details which Crabbe liked to
record being caught up into the dramatic mood of the moment,
in a manner which, it is sometimes supposed, was unknown before
Maud.   A notable example of this dramatic propriety may be
found in *The Patron*, the fifth of the *Tales* (ll. 426—433), where
the presumptuous *protégé's* too happy summer in his patron's
country house is at an end, and his doom is approaching.   Save
for the word 'melancholy,' the passage consists of description
which might be termed bald.   Crabbe does not make any attempt,
as a 'pastoral' poet would have done, to explain to his readers
the mood inspired by the scene; but the intensity of his observation and his choice of the most effective among the details bring
the scene itself vividly to the mind's eye.   A parallel passage, which
contains also a touch of poetic magic, is that in *Delay has Danger*,
the thirteenth book of *Tales of the Hall* (ll. 703—724), where
the halfhearted betrothed, already wishing himself free, looks out
of his window.   Such economy, and the resulting intensity, are rather
the exception than the rule with Crabbe.   Too often, as in the early
part of *Amusements*, the ninth letter of *The Borough*, he spoils
the effect of beautiful passages of sympathetic description, like that
of the boat leaving the ship, by dwelling too long on the 'species
of the medusa (sea-nettle),' or the 'marine vermes,' or other such
things, that interested the man of science rather than the poet.   In
spite of this excess, he gave the poetry of nature new worlds to
conquer (rather than conquered them himself) by showing that

the world of plain fact and common detail may be material for poetry; just as, in dealing with the characters of men and women, he enlarged the scope of both poetry and fiction. He was not, like Wordsworth, a lofty and passionate dreamer; so far is he from possessing the engaging tenderness of Cowper, that often, even at his finest moments, he repels by his ruthless insistence upon the truth as he sees it. On the other hand, his keen, if rugged, sympathy widely separates his 'realism' from the dreary chronicle of a Zola; and his not infrequent doggerel comes from his saying too much, not from saying anything beside the mark. He has left some vivid and beautiful passages of descriptive poetry, some admirably told tales and a long gallery of profound and lively portraits; and, by the intensity of his vision, the force of his mind and his sturdy sincerity, he ploughed for future workers wide tracts which, before him, poetry had allowed to lie fallow.

CHAPTER VIII

SOUTHEY

LESSER POETS OF THE LATER EIGHTEENTH CENTURY

THERE are few English writers who have been the subject of more controversy in different kinds than Robert Southey. Estimates of his positive worth as a poet have varied from the certainly rather excessive notions of it entertained by himself and by Landor, to the mere impertinence of Emerson's 'Who is Southey?' Very few persons have endeavoured to give full value to that singular combination of proficiency and performance in the two harmonies wherein he has, perhaps, only one rival in English literature. The absence—an absence which, perhaps, is the chief instance of a scandal that too often affects English, as compared with foreign, literature—of even an attempt at a complete edition of at least his bookwork, has complicated the difficulty of dealing with him. Even though the old *odia*—political, theological and other—have, to some extent (by no means wholly), settled down, he is—it may be admitted partly by his own fault—apt to rouse them in single cases and passages after a disturbing fashion. And there is one pervading condition of a dangerous kind attending his work, from which he was almost the first, if by no means the last, to suffer.

This condition was the difficulty—which his prudence and self-denial reduced to some extent, but which weighed on him all his life and finally killed or helped to kill him—of adjusting the *vita* to the *vivendi causae*. If Southey had had a private fortune or a lightly burdened office or benefice of any kind ; if he had had the gift of bachelorhood and the further gift of a college fellowship; if he had been able to draw profit from professional work which left time for writing ; if several other 'ifs and ands' had transformed themselves in the practical fashion of the saying—not merely would he, probably, have died in perfect mental health, but he would have left us work (if he had left any at all, which is an important proviso) including more definite masterpieces than he actually achieved. But fate would not have it so. He had no fortune ; and, more than once, he rather stood in the way of his own luck. He was a born 'family man'; and, what is more, a most hospitable, charitable and generous person[1]. He not only refused, after some efforts, all professional work, but was, probably, in a measure, incapable of any. He would not have been able to live his own life anywhere except in the depths of the country ; but he could only live that life there by spending what would have been now enormous, and must, even then, have been considerable, sums upon a vast library. To supply these necessities, there was only one way—hackwork for the press. He began this at a very unfavourable time, when, as he has somewhere said, a whole day's work would bring him in some ten shillings, and, though he lived into a more golden age, he never, as had even Coleridge at one time, had that regular work for daily and weekly periodicals which alone really makes an income. Even so, there might have been difficulties ; for he did not like being 'edited'; he would not, as he says himself, 'regard pen-and-inkmanship as a trade'; and the consequence was that, while he was perpetually interrupting his more ambitious work to 'boil the pot,' these interruptions merely performed that office and seriously interfered with the other.

Thus, being not a mere gutter journalist but a man of letters of the higher, if not highest, rank, he was ill content with this hackwork. He wanted to do, and he did, great work in prose and verse ; and, with such work, after a, perhaps, treacherously pros-perous beginning, he had scarcely any luck—perhaps because, as Scott thought, he mismanaged his affairs with his publishers. As for the pensions which were constantly thrown in his face by his political decriers, the facts are simply these. He had—and, for some time, could hardly have lived without it—an allowance of £160 a year from his rich schoolfellow Charles Wynn; he gave this up when he received a government pension rather less than more than it in value (it was nominally £200, but was largely reduced by fees and taxes) ; the laureateship added less than £100 (the whole of which, and a little more, he at once devoted to life in-surance), and, very late in his life, Sir Robert Peel gave him £300 more. In 1816, he had declined offers from Lord Liverpool which,

---

[1] Literary coincidences are sometimes amusing. It so happens that, as Grosvenor Bedford, the father, was a frequent agent of Horace Walpole's charities, so was Grosvenor Bedford, the son, of Southey's, and we have numerous letters, from principal to agent, on the subject, in both cases. Horace was by no means stingy in this way; but it is rather curious to compare his scale of benefaction and Southey's, remembering that the one was a richly endowed sinecurist and bachelor, the other a man with a rather large family, who lived almost wholly by ill-paid exertions of his own.

though apparently somewhat vague, would certainly have tempted most men, at a time when he was actually pressed for money. A little later, he refused the editorship of *The Times* with, it is said, £2000 a year attached. It may be taken as certain that, if his gains, including these pensions, during a lifetime of almost unbroken work, resulting, occasionally, in firstrate literature, were summed up and divided yearly, the average income would be found to be not half of that of some places since created for persons of no merit who perform services of no value.

Southey's life was what is called uneventful; but its circumstances were too intimately connected with the character of his work to permit complete neglect of them. He was born (1774) in Bristol, of a Somerset family, old, entitled to bear arms, in one of its branches possessed of some fortune, but not of any historical distinction, and, so far as his own immediate connections were concerned, obscure and unfortunate. His father, who was a linendraper, failed in business, and died early ; but Southey received unusual, if, on one side, fitful, assistance from his mother's relations. His uncle, a clergyman named Thomas Hill, was almost a father to him ; and his half-aunt, Miss Tyler, made him free of her house till his own eccentricities, and her wrath at his marriage, drove him out. From his very earliest childhood, he seems to have been a devourer of books, especially in English literature, and more especially in poetry. His uncle sent him to Westminster, where he made valuable friends. But the 'strong contagion' of the French revolution caught him there ; and he was expelled for his concern in a school magazine the principles of which are sufficiently indicated by its title, *The Flagellant.* He was thus cut off from proceeding, as usual, to Christ church, but he went to Balliol (1792), where he stayed for a year and a half 'working,' in the strict sense, not at all, but reading immensely, advancing in Jacobinism, making the acquaintance of Coleridge and, with him and others, starting the famous scheme of 'pantisocracy' or 'aspheterism,' a miniature socialist republic to be carried out anywhere or nowhere. The vicissitudes of this association are not for us ; but they ended, so far as Southey was concerned, in his relinquishing the scheme and marrying (1795) Edith Fricker, but starting from the church door, and alone, for Portugal, to comply with the demands of his uncle, who was chaplain at Lisbon.

How he there laid the foundation of that knowledge of the peninsular literatures which formed one of the special studies of his life and supplied the subjects of more than one of his chief works; how he returned, lived with his wife at Bristol or London and elsewhere, dutifully tried the law, but found it as hopelessly uncongenial as he had previously, in his hotter Jacobin time, found the church and medicine; how he paid a second visit (1800) to Lisbon, this time with his wife, and how, after trying various abodes and giving himself up to the press and various employments, including a private secretaryship to the chancellor of the Irish exchequer Corry, he settled, where Coleridge had already established himself (and, at first, with him), at Greta hall, Keswick, thus becoming 'a Lake poet,' would take long to tell. But, rolling stone as he had been for some thirty years, he here found his resting-place (though that was hardly the term for a home of Southey) for life. He never left it again, save for short holiday absences; he became, after being, in a way, Coleridge's guest or, at least, his house partner, the host and, for a time, the supporter of Coleridge's family; he collected the great library already mentioned; he begat sons and daughters, and was passionately fond of them, suffering intensely from the deaths of some of them, especially those of his eldest son, Herbert, and his youngest daughter, Isabel. At last, in 1834, his wife's mind gave way, and she soon died. The shock completed what, if it had not altogether caused, inordinate brainwork[1] had, beyond all doubt, helped, a mental breakdown in his own case. He found a second wife, or, rather, a nurse, in the poetess Caroline Bowles; but she could only attend upon his decline, and he died of softening of the brain in 1843.

It is impossible wholly to pass over that question of political tergiversation which plays a large part in Southey's actual history, owing, partly, to the time at which he lived, and, partly, to the rather unscrupulous ability of some of his enemies; but, partly, also, it must be confessed, to that rather unlucky touch of selfrighteousness which was almost the only fault in his otherwise blameless character. The present writer has never seen the question of the character and duration of Southey's political and religious unorthodoxy examined at length; and there is not room for such an examination here; but there are ample and final materials for it in his *Letters*. It was, undoubtedly, brought on by that 'prince of the air,' a momentary epidemic of popular opinion, and by the common, though not universal, opposition of clever boys to the powers that be; it was hardened by the unwise

---

[1] The manner, as well as the amount, contributed. As he says himself (*Letters*, vol. III, p. 64), 'I am given to works of supererogation, and could do nothing to my own satisfaction if I did not take twice as much labour as any other person would bestow upon it.'

severity of William Vincent at Westminster; it was shaken so early as the execution of Marie-Antoinette and the downfall of the Girondists; and, by 1796, the patient had got to writing: 'as for pigs, they are too like the multitude.' All was safe after that; though a few minor relapses follow for a short time. It may be allowed, even by the most sympathetic judgment, that Southey had not a political head; in fact, he admitted it himself when choosing his subjects for *The Quarterly*. His account of the matter in his famous reply to William Smith as to the resuscitation of *Wat Tyler*—one of the finest things of the kind, for matter and style, ever written—to the effect that he had 'always had an ardent desire for the melioration of mankind,' but that 'as he grew older his ideas as to the best means of that melioration changed,' is adequate, accurate and final. But the position which it indicates is, obviously, an incomplete one. As Coleridge had too much logic, Southey had too little ; and he was always laying himself open to reproaches of actual inconsistency, which is important, as well as of retrospective inconsistency, which is futile. He never had been a thorough Jacobin, and he never became a thorough tory. To the end of his life, he had odd semisocialist ideas ; he never could see Pitt's greatness, not because he detected that statesman's real faults, but because the old 'nervous impression' of dislike remained ; and he never forgave the *Anti-Jacobin* attacks on himself. Not at any period of his life, for fear or favour, was it possible for Southey to acquiesce in what he did not think right; but what he thought right generally depended, not on any coherent theory, not on any sound historical observation, but on a congeries of personal likings, dislikings, experiences and impressions generally. This is really the conclusion of the whole matter respecting his politics, and no more need be said about it.

As is probably the case with all great readers and most copious writers, Southey began both processes, in more than the school sense of reading and writing, very early. He seems to have had almost congenital affinity to poetry and romance, and this, or mere accident, sent him, when almost a child, from Tasso (in translation, of course) to Ariosto, and from Ariosto to Spenser, in a way which the most critical pedagogue could not have improved. As a child, also, he filled quires, if not reams, with verse ; and, though he had too much sense to preserve, or, at least, to print, any of these *plusquam juvenilia*, it is probable that we should not have found in them anything like the striking difference from his future work which is discernible in those of Milton, of Coleridge, of Shelley and of Tennyson. His early letters, too, contain specimens of the halfdoggerel anapaests, which Anstey[1] had made popular a generation earlier, and which continued, for at least another, to be written with a familiar and current pen by persons of good, as well as of indifferent, wits. But (speaking under correction) the earliest thing that he regularly published and acknowledged—the *Ode to Horror*, dated 1791, when the author was seventeen—is a somewhat better than Della Cruscan (*v. inf.*) effort to follow Collins very far off. Some other pieces (of the same kind, mostly, but including a terribly flat monodrama on, of all subjects, Sappho) date from the next year or two; and, then, we come to the notorious *Wat Tyler*, 'written in three days at Oxford' during the year 1794, and surreptitiously and invidiously published from a stolen copy twenty-three years later Southey failed in recourse to the law owing, perhaps, to one of the most extraordinary 'quillets' of a legal mind[2] ever recorded. Therefore he himself included it in his works and very sensibly made not the slightest correction, merely explaining the date and circumstances of its composition. *Wat Tyler* remains most cheerful reading. It is a short drama in verse of three acts only, and of, perhaps, some eight or nine hundred lines. If its actual authorship and circumstances were not known, a good critic might take it for a deliberate and very happy parody of the cruder and more innocent utterances of sentimental republicanism. Wat and his fellows clothe these utterances in the wellknown theatrical lingo of the time; and arrange them in unexceptionable, if slightly uninspired, blank verse. For an intelligent and educated audience, the thing might still make a most laughable 'curtain-raiser' or afterpiece, more particularly as its fustian fallacies are of a kind constantly revived. But, as a serious composition, it is not, and could not be, of the very slightest value. It remained, however, as has been said, unknown for all but a quarter of a century; but, at the same time, and, indeed, earlier, the author had been busy on an epic, *Joan of Arc*, which appeared in 1795, was received with something like enthusiasm and, by actually passing through five editions, showed the nascent taste which was to grow to the advantage of Scott and Byron. Southey altered it a good deal, and, little as he was disposed to undervalue his own work, always acknowledged its

---

[1] Cf. p. 173, *post*.

[2] Lord Eldon held that, as it was a mischievous work and contrary to the public welfare, there could not be any property in it—and, consequently, no means of stopping the mischief and the public danger.

'great and numerous faults.' It is doubtful, however, whether he ever saw, or would have acknowledged if it had been pointed out to him, the most fatal fault of all—a fault shared by most— fortunately not by all—of his longer poems that followed. That fault is the adoption of blank verse for a long narrative poem, a proceeding which nobody, save Milton and Tennyson, has ever carried out successfully, while Tennyson himself, and others who have come near success, have usually broken up the single narrative into a cluster of shorter pieces.

For, to achieve such success, the verse must have qualities of its own, like those of Milton or Tennyson, which are almost independent of the subject, and which reinforce its interest to such an extent that the reader never thinks of saying 'A good story ; but it would have been better in prose.' Some readers, certainly, do say this, not merely in reference to *Joan*, but to *Madoc* and *Roderick*. Southey's blank verse is, indeed, never bad ; but it also never, or in the rarest possible instances, has this intrinsic character; and it is a remarkable instance of the almost invariable soundness of his general critical principles, however the *de te fabula* may have sometimes escaped him, that he expressly recognised[1] 'the great difficulties of the measure, and its disadvantages in always exposing the weak parts' of a long poem.

During the time when he was loyally endeavouring to repay his uncle's -kindness by adopting some profession, he partly suspended his 'long-poem' writing. But, in the last years of the century, he produced many smaller pieces, generally good, sometimes all but consummate and really important to history. There is still rubbish : many of those poems on the slave trade which have gone some way towards avenging the poor African by the boredom if not anguish which they have inflicted on the white brethren of his oppressors; *Botany Bay Eclogues* (but, indeed, these were earlier and contemporary with *Wat Tyler*), the much ridiculed, and, no doubt, wrongly constructed, sapphics and dactylics, which reflect the same temper. But, especially during his sojourn at Westbury, near Bristol, he also wrote lyrics and ballads of very much greater value. Here, in 1798, was composed that admirable *Holly-Tree* which softened even Hazlitt, and which, with *My days among the Dead are passed*, twenty years later, shows Southey at his very best both as a poet and as a man.

But the most important productions of this time, if not the best, were the *Ballads*. Most of the best of these were written

[1] *Letters*, vol. II, p. 354.

between 1796 and 1798 ; and, although none of them possesses
anything like the poetical power of *The Ancient Mariner*, it is
nearly certain that Southey preceded Coleridge in his appreciation
and practice of the ballad principle of anapaestic equivalence in
mainly iambic measures, though he may have followed others,
from Anstey down to Lewis, in adopting the pure anapaest. From
another point of view, he deserves the credit of blending the spirit
of the then popular terror-novel with touches of humour, so as to
produce the effect for which there is, perhaps, no single word except the French *macabre*. This, which was afterwards pushed still
further by Hood, Praed and Barham, has provided English with a
sort of hybrid style, capable of easy degeneration in various ways,
but, at its best, almost peculiar and quite delectable. Southey
himself was sometimes content with the mere singsong of the
eighteenth century ballad, and sometimes overstepped the
treacherous line which keeps ghastly humour from bad taste.
But, in divers instances, such as *The Cross Roads, Bishop Hatto*
and the famous *Old Woman of Berkeley*, he has hit the white ;
while, in less mixed modes, *The Well of St Keyne, The Inchcape
Rock*, the almost famous *Battle of Blenheim* and, perhaps, *Queen
Orraca* should be added to his tale of complete successes. From
the point of view of form, they had a most powerful influence in
loosening the bonds of eighteenth century metre ; and, from that
of combined form and matter, they exercised the same influence
more widely. It ought never to be forgotten, though it too often
is, that Southey was particularly influential in the days when better
poets of his own age were still forming themselves and when other
better poets, younger as well as better, had not produced anything.

Yet, all this was itself the work of a very young man; in the
earlier cases, of a mere boy ; and, when Southey returned to the
long poem with *Thalaba* (1801, but very long in hand), he was only
six- or seven-and-twenty. But this was not only by far the most
ambitious, it was, also, though less important and much less well inspired than the *Ballads*, the most audaciously experimental of the
work he had yet tried. Rimeless metres outside the regular blank
verse were, of course, not absolutely novel in English. Campion
had tried them and gone near to beauty two centuries earlier ;
Collins had tried them in the last generation and gone nearer ;
just before Southey himself and Frank Sayers (*v. inf.*) had used
them on a larger scale. But nobody had adventured a really
long poem in them. Southey did, and with the same remarkable
appreciation of metrical theory as well as practice which he had

shown in the ballad case. The great danger of unrimed verse in English is that (from that natural tendency of the language which showed itself as early as Chaucer's prose) it will fall into more or less complete and continuous iambic decasyllables, unless it is arranged, either into somewhat un-English line-moulds as it had been by Campion, or into very definitely marked and identical stanzas, as it had been by Collins—with the result, in both cases, of a monotony which would be intolerable in a long poem. Sayers had notoriously fallen into the trap, as have, since, Matthew Arnold and W. E. Henley. Southey, with his eyes open to it, determined that he would avoid it, and he did. *Thalaba*, though not quickly admired, was much liked by good wits of his own generation, and not without reason. The story is by no means uninteresting and, if not exactly the characters, the situations are good. There are far finer passages in it than in *Joan of Arc*; indeed, some of the incidents, and more of the descriptions, are really poetical. But the unfamiliarity and aloofness of the whole thing are not carried off by the *diable au corps* of *Vathek* or the sheer story interest of *The Arabian Nights* themselves; and the unrimed versification perpetually harasses and hampers the reader as something, perhaps, admirable, but, somehow, not enjoyable—in other words, as a disappointment and a mistake.

Besides *Joan of Arc* and the *Minor Poems* written before and during the Westbury sojourn, Southey, in 1794, had collaborated with Coleridge in the worthless *Fall of Robespierre*, and with his other brother-in-law, Lovell, in a small collection of lesser verse. He had also issued the first of his many volumes of prose as *Letters from Spain and Portugal* (1797). This, without *Wat Tyler*, then unpublished, but with *Thalaba*, made more than half-a-dozen volumes in hardly more than as many years. But a longer gap occurred—one, indeed, of four years—till, though he did not quite know it, he had settled down at Keswick, and started on the career which was only to close with his death, and to leave plentiful matter for posthumous publication. In 1805, however, he re-appeared with two volumes of verse—*Metrical Tales* and *Madoc*. The former contained not a little of the nondescript, but acceptable, work above described; the latter, which had been many years on the stocks, was introduced with a flourish ('Come, for ye know me! I am he who sung'), warranted by classical precedents rather than in accordance with the modesty expected from English poets. Although, like *Thalaba*, it sold very slowly and disappointed the hopes which the reception of the far inferior *Joan of Arc* had raised in its author, it was very much admired by no common judges; and there are, I believe, one or two among the now infrequent readers of Southey who rank it highly. To others, the peculiar curse referred to above seems to rest on it. The adventures of the son of Owen Gwyneth in his own land and in Mexico are neither uninteresting nor ill-told. But some rebellious minds cannot away with the vehicle of telling—

> This is the day when in a foreign grave
> King Owen's relics shall be laid to rest—

and are wholly unable to perceive anything in it to be desired above 'This is the day when King Owen's relics shall be laid to rest in a foreign grave.'

There can, however, be no doubt that *Madoc* greatly raised Southey's position as a poet; for Scott was only beginning, the world would not have anything of Wordsworth, Coleridge was silent and the greatest of the younger poets had not begun. In the next seven or eight years before his appointment to the laureateship in 1813, he produced his very best works, in verse and prose respectively, *The Curse of Kehama* and *The Life of Nelson*; he joined (1809) *The Quarterly Review*, which was almost his main source of income for the rest of his life (though, for a very few years, he drew considerable sums from Ballantyne's *Annual Register*); he began the mightiest of all his works, *The History of Brazil* (1810–19), originally planned as merely a part of a still huger *History of Portugal*, and (besides revising the old translations of *Amadis* and *Palmerin* and executing the charming one of *The Chronicle of the Cid*) he wrote two popular miscellanies, as they may be termed, *The Letters of Espriella* (1807) and *Omniana* (1812).

As a historian and reviewer, Southey may be considered here generally; some remarks on the two lighter books may follow; but *Kehama* and the *Nelson* cannot be left without separate notice.

If almost the widest possible reading, a keen curiosity and interest in the things both of life[1] and literature, common sense tempered by humour, unwearying application, a disposition, if with some foibles and prejudices, on the whole singularly equable and amiable and an altogether admirable style, could make a good historian and a good reviewer, Southey ought to have been one of the very best of both classes. It would, perhaps, be too much to say that he actually

---

[1] His observed knowledge of human nature was extraordinary. The wonderful and should-be famous letter about Hartley Coleridge as a child is the master document of this; but there are hundreds of others.

was. In history, he was apt to attack too large subjects, and to exhibit, in dealing with them, a certain absence of that indefinable grasp of his subject which the historian requires in order to grasp his reader. Episodes, as in the later *Expedition of Orsua* (1821), or short statements, as in *Nelson* itself, he could manage admirably; and, for this reason, his reviews are much better than his histories, though it is not easy to judge the former exhaustively, since they have never been collected and are believed to be, in some cases, impossible of identification. But the magisterial style which the early *Reviews* affected (though he himself sometimes protested against it) was rather a snare to Southey, and it cannot be said that his best work is there.

The two productions of a lighter character mentioned above deserve a place on that shelf or in that case of books for occasional reading with which the wise man should always provide himself. Southey's earlier *Letters from Spain and Portugal* were written before he had thoroughly mastered his own inimitable style : but those, two years later, 'from England,' assigned to an imaginary young Spaniard Don Manuel Alvarez Espriella, are much better. They belong to a wellknown class, and, no doubt, cannot compete with the work of such masters in that class as Montesquieu or Goldsmith. But they contain, perhaps, a more accurate picture of English ways in the very beginning of the nineteenth century than exists anywhere else, as well as some curiosities, such as the accounts of Brothers and Joanna Southcott. *Omniana* has interest of a different kind or kinds. It is not (as it has been sometimes pronounced to be) a mere commonplace-book : it is a commonplace-book made original. The enormous store of reading which supplied the posthumous *Commonplace Books* of the author, and which was more substantively utilised in *The Doctor*, does, indeed, supply the texts; but, for the most part, if not always, these are retold or, at least, commented on in that author's own words. An additional piquancy undoubtedly lies in the fact that Coleridge undertook to be, and, to a small extent, was, a contributor; though, as usual, he defaulted save to that small extent. To anyone who reads the book for a first time, or even for a second or a third, at an interval long enough to allow him to forget the exact whereabouts or subjects of Coleridge's contributions, it is no small amusement to stumble on the Estesian 'proofs.' No prose can be pleasanter to read or more suitable to its wide range of subjects than Southey's ; but, when you come to such a sentence as ' A bull consists in a mental juxta-position of incongruous ideas with the sensation but without the sense of connection' you know that another than Southey has been there.

It might not be a bad question from the point of view of the arrest of hasty criticism: 'What rank would you have accorded to Southey as a poet, if he had left no long poems but the best parts of *Thalaba* and *The Curse of Kehama*, and no short ones but the half-dozen ballads and lyrics noticed above?' It is difficult to see how even the positive verdict could have been anything but a very high estimate indeed; while nine critics out of ten would probably have added that 'If Southey had been permitted or had cared to pursue poetry further, there is no knowing, etc.' In almost all respects but one, *Kehama* is invulnerable. The verse stanzas of the *Thalaba* kind, but longer, more varied and rimed, are extremely effective. The story, in itself, is interesting and well managed; the conclusion is positively dramatic; the characters have at least epic, if not dramatic, sufficiency. As for pure poetry of execution, anybody who denies this to the curse itself, to Landor's favourite picture of the 'gem-lighted city' and to a dozen other passages, is either blind by nature or has made himself so by prejudice. But the one excepted point remains—the injudicious choice of subject and the attempt to make it more acceptable by a mass of quasi-learned notes. It is said by Englishmen who have taught orientals that, to them, if you can elicit their genuine feeling, western romance, especially of the supernatural kind, appears simply absurd—the most passionate passages evoking shouts of laughter. It is certain that, except in the rarest cases and under the most skilful treatment, Hindu romance, especially of the supernatural kind, has, to western readers, an element not so much of absurdity as of extravagance and boredom which it is possible for very few to get over. That, and that only, is the weak point of *The Curse of Kehama*.

It is not easy to say anything new about *The Life of Nelson*; in fact, it would be impossible to do so without availing oneself of mere rhetoric or mere paradox epigram, both of which are absolutely foreign to the book itself. The *Life* established itself, if not immediately, very soon, as, perhaps, the best short biography of a plain and straightforward kind in the English language; it has held that position almost unchallenged till a very recent period; and it may be said, without offence, that the charges since brought against it have certainly not weakened, if they have not even positively strengthened, its position. For, all that anyone has been able to make good against Southey is that he was not in possession of all the documents on the subject; that he was not a professional seaman or strategist; and that, on some disputed points of fact or opinion, it is possible to hold views different from his. What has not been shown and, it may be said without fear, cannot be shown, is that the most abundant technical knowledge of naval, or the most recondite study of military, affairs could have bettered such a book as this; that the points of disputed opinion cannot possibly be accepted as Southey accepts them; or that material advantage could have been obtained for such a book as this from the documents that could not be consulted. The specification of it might be put, after Aristotelian fashion, thus: 'A short, clear, well written narrative displaying Nelson's acts and showing forth his character, with all necessary accuracy of fact, with sympathy not too partial or indiscriminate, in such a manner as to make the thing for ever a record of heroism and patriotism in the past, and a stimulus to them in the future.' The great majority of competent judges, some of them by no means inclining to Southey's way of thought in political or other senses, has unhesitatingly declared the material part of this specification to be amply achieved. As for the formal or literary part, there never has been even one such judgment which has failed to pronounce *The Life of Nelson* such a model of the more modern 'middle style,' with capacities of rising to something grander, as hardly exists elsewhere. The scale saved the writer from his own fatal fancy for quartos, and from the opportunities of prolixity and divagation which quartos bring with them; his own patriotism, in which he was the equal of Chatham or of Nelson himself, gave the necessary inspiration; his unwearied industry made him master of details even to the extent of avoiding any serious technical blunders; and those quaint flashes of the old Jacobinism which have been noticed occur just often enough to prevent the book from having the air of a mere partisan pamphlet. These things, with Southey's own sauce of style, were enough to give us a somewhat larger and more important *Agricola*; and we have it here.

From the time of the publication of *Nelson*, which was also that of Southey's laureation, he had thirty years of life allowed him, and at least five-and-twenty of life in full possession of his faculties. During the whole of this last-named period, he worked in the portentous fashion more than once described in his letters, practically taking up the whole of his time from waking to sleeping, except that allotted to meals (but often encroached upon) and to a little exercise. This work was by no means, as it has been absurdly described, 'compiling and translating from the Spanish,' but its results cannot be very fully commented on here. His *Quarterly* reviewing was, fortunately (for it provided his main income), continuous: and, after a time, was very well paid, the regular 'ten guineas a sheet' passing into comfortable lump sums of fifties and hundreds. But he never fully reconciled himself to it; and there were unpleasant misunderstandings about the editorship in the interregnum between Gifford's and Lockhart's. The taskwork of the laureateship (of which, in accepting it, he had thought himself relieved, but which continued for, at any rate, some years) he hated still more, but discharged with almost too great conscientiousness, the chief results being the unluckily named *Lay of the Laureate* on princess Charlotte's wedding, and the unluckily composed *Vision of Judgment* on George III's death. As to the latter, it is enough to caution the unwary against concluding from the undoubted cleverness of Byron's parody-attack, that Southey's original is worthless. The English hexameters may be a mistake, but they are about the best of their special pattern of that probably hopeless form; and the substance, though displaying, occasionally, the want of tact which now and then beset the author, is, sometimes, very far from contemptible. But the occasions when Pegasus has shown his true form in official harness are, as is too well known, of the rarest; and Southey's work does not furnish one of the exceptions.

To complete the notice of his poetry: in 1814, he had published another long poem which, as was usual with him, had been on the stocks for a great while, had been much altered and more than once renamed. It appeared, finally, as *Roderick the last of the Goths* and is probably the best of his blank verse epics, but does not quite escape the curse above mentioned. *The Poet's Pilgrimage to Waterloo* is not in blank verse; but here, also, especially after reading his pleasant letters on the journey and the home-coming, the old question may be asked. He was, even at this time, beginning two other pieces of some length—*A tale of Paraguay*, which appeared ten years later, in 1825, and which is of good quality, and *Oliver Newman*, which was only posthumously published, and adds little to his fame. Had he, in fact, produced much great poetry in the hardly existing intervals of his task-work in prose, he would have been unlike any poet of whom time leaves record. But a few of his smaller pieces, especially that admirable one noticed above and written (1818) in his library, are poetry still. The last independent volume of verse which he issued was *All for Love* (1829); but he collected the whole of his poems published earlier,

in ten volumes (1837—8), almost at the close of his working
life.

The prose itself gave frequent nourishing and invigorating crops,
if nothing of the rarest fruit. *The Life of John Wesley* (1821)
is not much inferior to that of *Nelson*: the differences are chiefly
that it has a less interesting subject and is longer. *The History
of the Peninsular War* (1823—32)—second of the big histories on
which he spent and, indeed, wasted much time—failed of success,
as was common with him, partly by his own fault, but much more
by his ill-luck. It was his fault that he set himself against
the duke of Wellington's wishes with that supererogatory conscientiousness which was one of his main failings, and thus lost an
almost indispensable support; it was his misfortune that, owing
to the pressure of bread-winning work, it was not finished till
after the appearance of Napier's much more brilliant and professional, though, perhaps, not altogether trustworthy, book. But
it is much to be regretted that, in place of this, we have not a
Life of George Fox and one of Warren Hastings, on which,
according to his wont, he wasted much time in preparation,
and which would almost certainly have been very good.

The same mixture of fault and fate from the first beset some
more original productions of the same period—*The Book of
the Church* (1822), *Vindiciae Ecclesiae Anglicanae* (1826), *Colloquies* (1828), rather unfairly described in Macaulay's essay, and
Essays Moral and Political (1834), part of which was Rickman's
work. All were quite admirably written, as, indeed, Macaulay
himself confesses, *Colloquies* especially containing passages of
almost consummate execution; and the caution above given as to
Byron may be repeated in reference to their matter. But Southey's
defects as a political writer have been frankly acknowledged
already, and he suffered from the same defects, or others like
them, in matters ecclesiastical. He had entirely got over his early
unorthodoxy, here, also, on important points; but, even in his ortho-
doxy, there was a good deal of private misjudgment; and he carried
the disapproval of Roman catholicism, and of all forms of protestant
dissent, which, when held and expressed moderately, is logically
incumbent on an Anglican, to fantastic and extravagant lengths.
Fortunately, these things were succeeded in his last decade, while
it was yet time—not merely by an edition of Cowper, which, though
prevented by insuperable obstacles from being quite complete,
is, in the circumstances, a most remarkable example of combined
industry and judgment, but, also, by two original works: one, *The
Lives of the Admirals*, which has been almost universally admitted

to contain delightful matter, admirably told, and another, almost an *opus maximum*, which has not been so fortunate.

Few books, indeed, have been the subjects of more different judgments than Southey's last, unfinished and, indeed, unfinishable work *The Doctor*, in seven volumes (1837—47), part being posthumous. It has been pronounced by some to be actually delightful and by others to be intolerably dull. An impartial, experienced and acute thirdsman, even without knowing the book, would, in such a case, perceive easily enough that there must be something in it which appeals strongly to one taste or set of tastes and does not appeal to, or actually revolts, another. Yet, inasmuch as the tastes and appreciations to which *The Doctor* appeals are positive, and those to which it does not appeal are negative, it seems that the admirers have the most to say for themselves. The book has been called 'a novel,' which it certainly is not; 'a commonplace-book' pure and simple, which it, as certainly, is not; and 'a miscellany,' which it, as certainly, is. But the last description is, perhaps, as inadequate as the two former are incorrect. To speak with critical accuracy, materials of the most apparently heterogeneous sort, derived from the author's vast reading, are in it digested into a series, as it were, of articles, the succession of which is not without a certain contiguity of subject between each pair or batch, while the whole is loosely strung on a thread, now thicker now thinner, of personal narrative. This last history, of Dr Daniel Dove of Doncaster and his horse Nobs, seems, originally, to have been a sprout of Coleridge's brain; but, if it ever had, as such, any beginning, middle or end, they are certainly not recorded or retained in any regular fashion here. The extraction, early and later homes, marriage, horse-ownership and other circumstances of the titular hero serve as starting-points for enormous, though often very ingeniously connected, divagations which display the author's varied interests, his quaint humour and his unparalleled reading. To a person who wants a recognisable specimen of a recognised department of literature; to one, who, if not averse from humour, altogether abhors that nonsense-humour which Southey loved, and which his enemy Hazlitt valiantly championed as specially English; to any-one who does not take any interest in literary *quodlibeta*, *The Doctor* must be a dull book, and may be a disgusting one. To readers differently disposed and equipped, it cannot but be delightful. Attempts have sometimes been made at compromise, by excepting from condemnation, not merely the famous *Story of the Three Bears*, but the beautiful descriptions of the Yorkshire dales, the history of the cats of Greta hall and other things. But the fact is that, to anybody really qualified to appreciate it, there is hardly a page of *The Doctor* which is not delightful.

To understand, not merely this his last book, but Southey himself, it is expedient and almost necessary that the immense mass of his letters (even as it is, but partially published) should be perused; and any reader who is not daunted by mere bulk may be assured of agreeable, as well as profitable, reading. Neither his son's collection, in six volumes, nor his son-in-law's, in four, (somewhat more fully and freely given) is very judiciously edited, and there is, in the latter especially, considerable duplication; but those to his second wife were more fortunate, and, from the three collections, with very little trouble, the man, and a very different man from some conceptions of him, becomes clear[1]. Coleridge's ingeniously epigrammatic and rather illnaturedly humble remark 'I think too much to be a poet: he [Southey] too little to be a great poet' has a certain truth, though one might retort that thinking too much neither prevented *The Ancient Mariner* and *Kubla Khan* or *Christabel* from being great poetry nor, indeed, makes any particular appearance in them[2]. Except in the moral line, Southey was not a philosopher: but neither was he the commonplace Philistine that he is often thought to have been. Like some other men, he obtained the desires of his heart—family life and a life of letters—only to find that the gods seldom fail to condition their gifts, if not exactly with curses, with taxes and fees like those over which he groaned in reference to his earthly pensions. There are evidences in his letters not merely of deep sentiment but even of a tendency to imaginative speculation; but neither was 'in the day's work,' and so he choked the former down with stoicism, the second with common sense. In such an unbroken debauch of labour as that to which he subjected himself, it is marvellous that he should have done such things as he did. And most marvellous of all is his style, which—not, as has been said, quite attained at first—was very soon reached, and which, in all but fifty years of incessant and exorbitant practice, never became slipshod or threadbare or wanting in vitality.

Therefore, whatever may be his shortcomings, or, to put it more exactly, his want of supremacy, it must be a strangely limited history of English literature in which a high position is not

---

[1] It is unfortunate that only scraps, though very amusing and acute scraps, from the letters of his principal correspondent, Grosvenor Bedford, have been published. Those of another remarkable friend, Rickman, have been very recently drawn upon for publication.

[2] It is fair to Coleridge to say that his acknowledgment of Southey's superiority as a prose-writer was unqualified.

allowed to Southey. For, in the first place, as must be once more repeated, he has actual supremacy in one particular department and period of English prose style. It is difficult to imagine any future time, at which his best and most characteristic, though least mannered, achievements in this way can ever become obsolete— precisely because of their lack of mannerism. And this must be credited to him as a pure gift of individual genius, though he stands in the race and lineage of a perhaps still greater writer of his own class, as to whom more presently. For this extraordinary combination of clearness and ease will not come by observation, or even by reading the fourteen thousand books which constituted Southey's library. Such a polyhistor, for variety, for excellence of matter and for excellence of form, it may be doubted whether any other language possesses.

If not quite such high praise can be given to his verse, it is not in regard to form that he fails. On the contrary, there are strong reasons for assigning to him the first clear perception of the secret of that prosodic language which almost everybody was to practise in Southey's own time and ever since. Whether, in actual date, his early ballads preceded *The Ancient Mariner* and the first part of *Christabel* in the use of substitution, it may be difficult to decide absolutely; though, even here, the precedence seems to be his. But, what is absolutely certain is that his formulation of the principle in a letter to Wynn is twenty years earlier in time than Coleridge's in the preface to the published *Christabel* and very much more accurate in statement. There are many other references to *res metrica* in his work, and it is a curious addition to the losses which the subject suffered by the non-completion of Jonson's and Dryden's promised treatises, that Guest's *English Rhythms*, which was actually sent to him for review, reached him too late for the treatment which he, also, designed. And, in general criticism, though his estimate of individual work was sometimes (not often) coloured by prejudice, he was very often extraordinarily original and sound. For a special instance, his singling out of Blake's 'Mad Song' may serve; for a general, the fact that, as early as 1801, he called attention[1] to the fact that

there exists no tale of romance that does not betray gross and unpardonable ignorance of the habits of feeling and thought prevalent at the time and in the scene,

thereby hitting the very blot which spoils nearly all the novel-writing of the time, and which was first avoided by Scott, much later. To those who have been able to acquire something of what has

[1] *Letters*, vol. I, p. 173.

been called 'a horizontal view' of literature—a thing even better,
perhaps, than the more famous 'Pisgah sight,' inasmuch as the
slightly deceptive perspective of distance is removed, and the
things pass in procession or panorama before the eye—there are,
with, of course, some striking differences, more striking resem-
blances in the literary character and the literary fates of Southey
and Dryden. The comparison may, at first sight, be exclaimed
against, and some of its most obvious features—such as the charges
of tergiversation brought against both—are not worth dwelling on.
But there are others which will come out and remain out, all the
more clearly the longer they are studied. The polyhistoric or
professional man-of-letters character of both, though equally
obvious, is not equally trivial. Both had a singularly interchange-
able command of the two harmonies of verse and prose; and, in
the case of no third writer is it so difficult to attach any 'ticket'
to the peculiar qualities which have placed the prose style of each
among the most perfect in the plain kind that is known to English.
Their verse, when compared with that of the greater poets of their
own time—Milton in the one case, half a dozen from Coleridge to
Keats in the other—has been accused, and can hardly be cleared,
of a certain want of poetical quintessence. Dryden, indeed, was as
much Southey's superior intellectually as, perhaps, he was morally
his inferior: and, neither as poet nor as prose writer, has the later
of the pair any single productions to put forward as rivals to *An
Essay of Dramatick Poesie, All for Love,* the great satires, the
best parts of the *Prefaces,* and the best *Fables.* He will, therefore,
perhaps, never recover, as Dryden, to a great extent, has recovered, from the neglect which lay upon him from about 1830
to about 1880. In regard to Southey, this attitude was begun,
not by Byron or Hazlitt or his other contemporary detractors
—who really held him very high as a writer, though they might
dislike him in other ways—but by the more extreme romantics
of a younger generation, and by persons like Emerson. That it
will be wholly removed, or removed to the same extent as the
neglect of Dryden has been, would, perhaps, be too much to expect.
But there is still much that should and can be done in the way
of altering or lessening it; and a sign or two of willingness to
help in the work, has, perhaps, recently[1] been noticeable.

---

[1] It is, however, a rather unfortunate revenge of the whirligig of time that, while
Southey's detractors, in his own day, usually made him out to be a very bad man of
genius, some of his rehabilitators seem to see in him a very good man of no genius
at all.

LESSER POETS OF THE LATER EIGHTEENTH CENTURY

It has been thought proper to group, round or under Southey, like gunboats under the wings of a 'mother' frigate, certain lesser poets of the mid- and later eighteenth century, notice of whom may continue that given to others of their kidney in previous volumes. It would, indeed, be possible, without very extravagant fancifulness, or wiredrawing, to make out more than an accidental or arbitrary connection between him and at least some of them. For, beyond all doubt, he was much indebted to Anstey for patterns of light anapaestic verse, and more so to Sayers for an example of rimelessness. Long before he knew Coleridge, he, also, felt that curious influence of Bowles's *Sonnets* which supplies one main historical vindication and reason for existence to minor poetry. Hayley was his friend and Merry his acquaintance. His connection with Hanbury Williams is, indeed, a sort of 'back-handed' one; for he tells us that he had refused, twenty years before its actual appearance, to edit the existing collection of Williams's *Poems*, disapproving of their contents; and this disapproval would certainly have extended, perhaps in a stronger form, to Hall Stevenson. But these are points which need no labouring. Moreover, which is strictly to the purpose, he was himself all his life distinguished by a catholic and kindly taste which he showed not only to minorities of his own time from Kirke White downwards, but in collecting three agreeable volumes[1], of seventeenth and eighteenth century writers to follow Ellis's *Specimens*. These volumes may still, in no unpleasant fashion, revive half-forgotten memories of Amhurst and Boyse and Croxall, of Fawkes and Woty and William Thompson, while they may suggest once more, if, perhaps, in vain, the removal of more absolute forgetfulness if not original ignorance, in the cases of Constantia Grierson and Mary Leapor, of Moses Mendez and Samuel Bellamy.

For such as these last, however, only a chronicle planned on the scale of *L'Histoire Littéraire de la France* and destined to be finished, if ever, in a millennium, could well find room. We may notice here Anstey, Hanbury Williams and Hall Stevenson among writers distinctly earlier than Southey; Darwin, Hayley, the Della Cruscans, Bowles, Sayers and one or two more among his actual contemporaries, older and younger.

[1] To himself, they gave a good deal of trouble—as usual, because he had thought to spare himself some by devolving part of the work on Grosvenor Bedford. He never did it again.

The three lighter members of the group, Anstey, Stevenson and
Hanbury Williams, were by far the eldest: if Williams had not died
prematurely, he would have been a man of over sixty at Southey's
birth, and, though Anstey lived to the year of *Madoc*, he was fifty
when Southey was born.   All three, in a manner, were survivals of
the school of sarcastic and social verse which had been founded by
Prior and Swift, and taken up by Gay.   Nor did Anstey, though
his verse is somewhat 'freer' than taste has permitted for nearly
a century, exceed limits quite ordinary in his own day.   He is
remarkable as being, in poetry, a 'single-speech' writer, that is to
say as having, like Hamilton himself, by no means confined himself
to a single utterance, but as having never achieved any other that
was of even the slightest value.   An Etonian and a Cambridge man
of some scholarship; a squire, a sportsman and a member of
parliament, Anstey, in 1766, produced the famous *New Bath
Guide*, a series of verse letters, mainly in anapaests of the Prior
type, which at once became popular, and which still stands
preeminent, not merely among the abundant literature which
Bath has produced or instigated, for good humour, vivid painting
of manners, facile and welladapted versification, and fun which
need not be too broad for any but a very narrow mind.   Anstey
lived, chiefly in the city of which he had made himself the laureate,
for forty years, and wrote much, but, as has been said, produced
nothing of worth after this history of 'The Bl[u]nd[e]rh[ea]d
Family' and their adventures.

A charitable epigrammatist has divided 'loose' writers of any
merit at all into those who sometimes follow the amusing across
the border of the indecent and those who, in the quest of the
indecent, sometimes hit upon the amusing.   If Anstey deserves
the indulgence of the former class, Hanbury Williams and Hall
Stevenson must, it is feared, be condemned to, and by, the latter.
It is true that, in Williams's case, some doubt has been thrown on
the authorship of the grossest pieces attributed to him, and that
most other things recorded of him—except a suspected showing of
the white feather—are rather favourable.   He appears, both in
Horace Walpole's letters and in Chesterfield's, as a man extremely
goodnatured and unwearied in serving his friends.   It is certain,
however, that the suicide which terminated his life was preceded,
and probably caused, by a succession of attacks of mental disease;
and, in some of the coarsest work assigned to him in the singularly
uncritical hodgepodge of his *Works*, a little critical kindness may

trace that purely morbid fondness for foulness which mental disease often, if not always, brings with it. On the whole, however, Williams's asperity and his indecency have both been exaggerated. He took part ardently on the side of Sir Robert in the 'great Walpolian battle' and was never weary of lampooning Pulteney. But his most famous 'skits'—those on Isabella, duchess of Manchester, and her way of spending her morning and her subsequent marriage to the Irishman Hussey—are neither very virulent nor very 'improper.' The fault of Williams's political and social verse is a want of concentration and finish. In these points, the notes which his editor (Lord Holland?) gathered from Horace Walpole in prose are frequently far superior to the verse they illustrate. But the verse itself is full of flashes and phrases, some of which have slipped into general use, and many of which are far superior to their context. Compared with the brilliant political verse, first on the whig, then on the tory, side, of the last twenty years of the century, Sir Charles is pointless and dull; but, in himself, to anyone with a fair knowledge of the politics and persons of the time, he is far from unamusing. Sometimes, also, he could (if the *Ballad in Imitation of Martial*, 'Dear Betty come give me sweet kisses,' written on Lord and Lady Ilchester, be his) be quite goodnatured, quite clean and almost as graceful as Prior or Martial himself.

The notorious John Hall Stevenson, Sterne's Eugenius, master of 'Crazy Castle' and author of *Crazy Tales*, had, beyond all doubt, greater intellectual ability than Williams; and, though eccentric in some ways, was neither open to the charge, nor entitled to plead the excuse, of insanity. He wrote a good deal of verse—much of it extremely slovenly in form, though, every now and then—as in the lines on Zachary Moore, the description of the Cleveland deserts at the back of his house and of the house itself and some others—showing a definite poetical power, which was far above Sir Charles. But the bulk of his work consists either of political squibs largely devoted to abuse of Bute (*Fables for Grown Gentlemen, Makarony Tales*, etc.) or of the 'Crazy' compositions above referred to. The former, for a man of such wellauthenticated wit as Stevenson, are singularly verbose, desultory and dull. If anyone has derived his ideas of what political satire ought to be, say, from Dryden in an earlier, and Canning in a later, age, he will be woefully disappointed with *A Pastoral Cordial* and *A Pastoral Puke*, which, between them, fill eighty or ninety

mortal pages, and contain hardly a line that could cheer a friend
or gall an enemy. A very few purely miscellaneous pieces like the
lines to 'the Pumproom Naiad,' Polly Lawrence of Bath, show,
once more, that, if Stevenson had chosen to be goodnatured and
clean, he might have been a very pleasant poet. As for *Crazy
Tales*, some of them are actual French *fabliaux* of the coarser
kind translated or adapted, and the rest are imitations of the
same style. It would be unfair to bring up La Fontaine against
them; but anyone who knows, say, the nearly contemporary
gauloiseries of Chamfort—himself neither the most amiable, nor
the cleanest minded, nor the most poetical of men—will find
English at a painful disadvantage in the prosaic brutality of too
much of Stevenson's work. He, sometimes, succeeds even here in
being amusing; but, much more often, he only succeeds in proving
that, if the use of proper words will not by itself produce wisdom,
the use of improper ones will still less by itself produce wit.

Who now reads Erasmus Darwin? Yet he pleased both Horace
Walpole and William Cowper, his verses were called by the latter
'strong, learned and sweet,' and by the former 'sublime,' 'charming,' 'enchanting,' 'gorgeous,' 'beautiful' and 'most poetic.' It
is idle to assign Darwin's poetic extinction to Canning's parody,
admirable as that is, for, if there is one critical axiom universally endorsed by good critics of all ages, schools and principles,
it is that parody cannot kill—that it cannot even harm—anything that has not the seeds of death and decay in itself. The
fact is that Darwin, with a fatal, and, as if metaphysically aided,
certainty, evolved from the eighteenth century couplet poetry all
its worst features, and set them in so glaring a light that only
those still under the actual spell could fail to perceive their
deformity. Unsuitableness of subject; rhetorical extravagance
and, at the same time, convention of phrase; otiose and padding epithet; monotonously cadenced verse; every fault of the
mere imitators of Pope in poetry, Darwin mustered in *The
Botanic Garden*, and especially in its constituent *The Loves of
the Plants*. It is true, but it is also vain, to say that the subject,
in itself, is interesting and positively valuable; that the rhetoric,
the phraseology, the effort, are all very craftsmanlike examples of
crafts bad in themselves. The very merits of the effort are faults
as and where they are; and it has none of the faults which, in
true poetry, are not seldom merits. Although one would not lose
The Loves of the Triangles for anything, it is superfluous as a

mere parody. *The Loves of the Plants* is a parody in itself and of itself, as well as of the whole school of verse which it crowned and crushed. Time is not likely to destroy, and may rather increase, the credit due to Darwin's scientific pioneership: its whirligig is never likely to restore the faintest genuine taste for his pseudo-poetry.

For Darwin's *opus*, however, one cannot, though it may, at first sight, seem inconsistent to say so, feel actual contempt. It is simply a huge, and, from one point of view, a ludicrous, but still a respectable, and, from another point of view, almost lamentable, mistake. The works of Hayley, the other great idol of the decadence of eighteenth century poetry, are contemptible. *The Loves of the Plants* is not exactly silly. *The Triumph of Temper* is. That puerility and anility which were presently to find, for the time, final expression in the Della Cruscan school, displayed themselves in Hayley with less extravagance, with less sentimentality and with less hopelessly bad taste than the revolutionary school were to impart, but still unmistakably. Hayley himself, as his conduct to Cowper and to Blake shows, was a man of kindly feelings; indeed, everybody seems to have liked him. He was something of a scholar, or, at the worst, a fairly wellread man. His interests were various and respectable. But, as a poet, he is impossible. Southey, in deprecating one of Coleridge's innumerable projects— a general criticism of contemporaries (which would certainly, if we may judge from the wellknown review of Maturin's *Bertram* in *Biographia*, have been a field of garments rolled in blood)— specified Hayley as a certain, but halfinnocent, victim, urging that 'there is nothing bad about the man except his poetry.' Unfortunately, on the present occasion, nothing about the man concerns us except his poetry; and the badness, or, at least, the nullity, of that it is impossible to exaggerate. A fair line may be found here and there; a fair stanza or passage hardly ever; a good, or even a fair poem, never.

For the nadir of the art, however—which, as if to justify divers sayings, was reached just before the close of the eighteenth century, and just before those ascents to the zenith which illustrated its actual end, and the early nineteenth—one must go beyond Darwin, beyond even Hayley, to Robert Merry and those about him—to the school commonly called the Della Cruscans, from the famous Florentine academy to which Merry actually belonged, and the title of which he took as signature. Darwin, as has been said, is a pattern of mistaken elaborateness, and Hayley one of well-intentioned nullity. But Darwin was not imbecile; and Hayley was not, or not very, pretentious. The school just referred to was preceded in its characteristics by some earlier work, such as that of Helen Maria Williams and Sir James Bland Burges (later Sir James Lamb). But, in itself, it united pretentiousness and imbecility after a fashion not easy to parallel elsewhere; and was, inadequately, rather than excessively, chastised in the satires of Gifford and Mathias. It does not appear that all its members were, personally, absolute fools. Merry himself is credited by Southey and others with a sort of irregular touch of genius: and 'Anna Matilda'—Mrs Cowley, the author of *The Belle's Stratagem* —certainly had wits. But they, and still more their followers, 'Laura,' 'Arley,' 'Benedict,' 'Cesario,' 'The Bard,' etc. (some of whom can be identified, while others, fortunately for themselves, cannot) drank themselves drunk at the heady tap of German *Sturm-und-Drang* romanticism, blending it with French sentimentality and Italian trifling, so as to produce almost inconceivable balderdash. Even the widest reading of English verse could hardly enable anyone to collect from the accumulated poetry of the last three centuries an anthology of folly and bad taste surpassing the two volumes of *The British Album*, the crop of a very few years and the labour of some half-a-dozen or half-a-score pens.

Of the last constituents of the group under present review, it is, fortunately, possible to treat Bowles and Sayers, both of them possessing, as has been said, some special connection with Southey, in a different fashion. Neither, so far as poetic inspiration goes, was even a secondclass poet; but both exercised very great influence over poets greater than themselves, and, therefore, have made good their place in literary history. William Lisle Bowles, slightly the elder, and very much the more longlived, of the two, has left (as in that life of many years he might easily do without neglecting his duties as a country clergyman) a very considerable amount of verse, which it is not necessary for anyone save the conscientious historian or the unwearied explorer of English poetry to read, but which can be read without any extraordinary difficulty or disgust. Bowles, indeed, never deserves the severer epithets of condemnation which have been applied in the last page or two. His theories of poetry (of which more presently) were sound and his practice was never offensively foolish, or in bad taste, or even dull. He lacks distinction and intensity. But he lives, in varying degrees of vitality, by two things only that he did, one at the very outset of his career, the other at a later stage of it. His first claim, and by far his highest, is to be found in *Fourteen Sonnets* (afterwards reinforced in number), which originally appeared in 1789, and which passed through nearly half-a-score of editions in hardly more than as many years. Grudging critics have observed that they were lucky in coming before the great outburst of 1798— 1824, and in being contrasted with such rubbish as that which we have been reviewing. It would be uncritical as well as un-generous not to add that, actually, they did much to start the movement that eclipsed them; and that, whatever their faults may be, these are merely negative—are, in fact, almost positive virtues—when compared with the defects of Darwin and Hayley and the Della Cruscans. Although Bowles was not the first to revive the sonnet, he was the first, except, perhaps, Bampfylde, to perceive its double fitness for introspection and for outlook; to combine description with sentiment in the new poetical way. It is no wonder that schoolboys like Coleridge and Southey, gluttons alike of general reading and of poetry, should have fastened on the book at once; no wonder that Coleridge, unable to afford more printed examples, should have copied his own again and again in manuscript for his friends. And it is one of the feathers in the cap of that historic estimate which has been some-times decried that nothing else could enable the reader to see the real beauty of Bowles's humble attempts, undazzled and un-blinded by the splendour of his followers' success. *Tynemouth* and *Bamborough Castle, Hope* and *The Influence of Time on Grief* are not very strong meat, not very 'mantling wine'; but they are the first course, or the *hors d'œuvre*, of the abounding banquet which followed.

Bowles's second appearance of importance was rather critical than poetical, or, perhaps, let us say, had more to do with the theory, than with the practice, of poetry. Editing Pope, he, not unnaturally, revived the old question of the value of Pope's poetry: and a mildly furious controversy followed, in which classically-minded poets of the calibre of Byron and Campbell took part, which produced numerous pamphlets, rather fluttered Bowles's Wiltshire dovecote, but developed in him the fighting power of birds much more formidable than doves. As usual, it was rather a case of the gold and silver shield; but Bowles's general con-tention that, in poetry, the source of subject and decoration alike should be rather nature than art, and Byron's incidental insistence (very inconsistently maintained) that execution is the great secret, were somewhat valuable by-products of a generally unprofitable dispute.

Frank Sayers, a member of the almost famous Norwich literary group of which William Taylor was a sort of coryphaeus, contributed less to the actual body of English verse than Bowles. His life was much shorter; he was, at any rate for a time, a practising physician, and had a considerable number of other avocations and interests besides poetry. But he touches the subject, in theory and practice both, at one point, in a fashion which was to prove decidedly important, if not in actual production, yet influentially and historically. Whether Sayers was originally attracted to unrimed verse, not blank in the ordinary restricted sense, by the Germans, or by his own fancy, or by the reading which, after his own practice, he showed to a rather remarkable extent in a dissertation-defence on the subject—does not seem to be quite clear. The dissertation itself, which was published in 1793, shows the persistent extension of knowledge of English poetry, which was doing much to prepare the great romantic outburst that followed. Collins's *Evening*, and the now deservedly forgotten choruses of Glover's *Medea*, would have been known to anyone at the time, and, perhaps, Watts's *Sapphics* (Cowper's were not published). Most men must have known, though, perhaps, few would have brought into the argument, Milton's 'Pyrrha' version. But Sidney's practice in *Arcadia, The Mourning Muse of Thestylis*, which was still thought Spenser's, and Peele's *Complaint of Oenone* would have been present to the minds of very few.

But whether he had known all these before he wrote, as Southey almost certainly did, or whether it was learning got up to support practice, Sayers's own earlier *Dramatic Sketches* had supplied the most ambitious and abundant experiments in unrimed verse since Sidney himself, or, at least, since Campion. He does not entirely abjure rime; but, in *Moina, Starno* and his version of the Euripidean *Cyclops*, he tried the unrimed Pindaric; and (in a rather naïve, or more than rather unwisely ambitious, manner) he actually supplemented Collins's ode with one *To Night*, on the same model. Elsewhere, it is perfectly plain, not merely from his rimelessness but from his titles and his diction, that the influence of Ossian had a great deal to do with the matter. He adopts, however, in all cases, regular verse-stanzas instead of rhythmed prose. Sayers's poetical powers—wildly exalted by some in that day of smallest poetical things and of darkness before dawn—are very feeble: but he intends greatly, and does not sin in either of the three directions of evil which, as we have seen, Darwin and Hayley and the Della Cruscans respectively represent. But the most interesting thing about him is the way in which, like nearly everybody who has made similar attempts except Southey (*v. sup.*), he succumbs, despite almost demonstrable efforts to prevent it, to the danger of chopped decasyllables, which unite themselves in the reading and so upset the intended rhythm. Such things as the parallel openings of *Thalaba* and of *Queen Mab* he was incapable of reaching; but, if he had reached them, their inherent poetry might have carried off the almost inevitable defect of the scheme. As it is, that effect is patent and glaring.

Sir William Jones, who, in a life which did not reach the half century, accumulated a singular amount of learning and of well-deserved distinction, was more of an orientalist and of a jurist than of a poet. But he managed to write two pieces—the *Ode in imitation of Alcaeus*, 'What constitutes a state?' and the beautiful epigram *From the Persian*, 'On parent knees a naked new-born child,' which have fixed themselves in literary history, and, what is better, in memories really literary. If there is in these at least as much of the scholar as of the poet, it can only be wished that we had more examples of the combination of such scholarship with such poetry.

CHAPTER IX

BLAKE

WILLIAM BLAKE, born 28 November 1757, was the son of a London hosier, who is said to have had leanings towards Sweden-borgianism. This may explain Blake's acquaintance with writings that exercised a marked influence upon his later doctrines and symbolism, though he always held that the Swedish mystic failed 'by endeavouring to explain to the reason what it could not understand.' The boy never went to school, on account, it is said, of a difficult temper. He 'picked up his education as well as he could.' According to one authority[1], Shakespeare's *Venus and Adonis, Lucrece* and *Sonnets,* with Jonson's *Underwoods* and *Miscellanies* were the favourite studies of his early days. To these must be added Shakespeare's plays, Milton, Chatterton and the Bible, 'a work ever at his hand, and which he often assiduously consulted in several languages'; for he acquired, at different times, some knowledge of Latin, Greek, French, Italian and Hebrew. Ossian and Gesnerian prose were less fortunate influences.

At the age of fourteen, he was apprenticed to James Basire, the engraver, who sent him to make drawings of monuments in West-minster abbey and other ancient churches in and about London. Thus, he came under the direct influence of Gothic art, which increased its hold upon his imagination, till it finally appeared to him the supreme expression of all truth, while classicism was the embodiment of all error. After leaving Basire, he studied for a time in the antique school of the Royal Academy, and then began work as an engraver on his own account. Shortly after his marriage in 1782, Flaxman introduced him to Mrs Mathew, a famous blue-stocking. The outcome of this was the printing of *Poetical Sketches* (1783) at the expense of these two friends. In the *Advertisement,*

---

[1] Benjamin Heath Malkin, author of *A Father's Memoir of his Child* (1806), the dedicatory epistle to which contains a valuable note on Blake.

by another hand than Blake's, the contents of this slight volume are
said to have been written between the ages of twelve and twenty ;
while Malkin, apparently quoting Blake, asserts that the song
'How sweet I roam'd from field to field' was composed before his
fourteenth year.   But his earliest writings seem to have been in
the distinctly rhythmical prose of the fragment known as *The
Passions*, which, like similar pieces included in *Poetical Sketches*,
is a juvenile essay in the inflated style and overstrained pathos
that gave popularity to Gesner's *Death of Abel*.

But Blake's early verse stands in quite another class.   Much
of it, indeed, is more directly imitative than his later work ; yet
this is due less to slavish copying than to an unconscious
recognition of the community between his own romantic spirit and
that of our older poetry.   Spenserian stanza, early Shakespearean
and Miltonic blank verse, ballad form, octosyllabics and lyric
metres, all are tried, with least success in the blank verse, but
often with consummate mastery in the lighter measures.   One who
met Blake in these years says that he occasionally sang his poems
to melodies of his own composing, and that 'these were sometimes
most singularly beautiful.'   It is, therefore, not improbable that
these lyrics were composed to music, like the songs of Burns or of
the Elizabethans.

His genuine delight in the older verse preserved him from the
complacency with which his age regarded its own versification.
Like Keats, but with more justice, he laments, in his lines *To the
Muses*, the feeble, artificial and meagre achievement of the time.
His notes are neither languid nor forced, but remarkably varied
and spontaneous.   Even in his less perfect work, there is not any
abatement of fresh enthusiasm, but, rather, an overtasking of
powers not yet fully equipped for high flights.   So, in the midst of
Fair Elenor, a tale of terror and wonder, and sorry stuff in the
main, occur passages like the stanza beginning

> My lord was like a flower upon the brows
> Of lusty May! Ah life as frail as flower!

while there is something more than promise in the youth who could
capture the sense of twilight and evening star so completely as
Blake in the lines

> Let thy west wind sleep on
> The lake: speak silence with thy glimmering eyes
> And wash the dusk with silver.

The six songs, which include almost all Blake's love-poetry,
illustrate the versatility of his early genius.   'How sweet I roam'd'

anticipates, in a remarkable way, the spirit and imagery of *La Belle Dame*, though, perhaps, it has less of romantic strangeness and the glamour of faerie than of sheer joy, the Elizabethan wantonness of love, so wonderfully reembodied in *My silks and fine array*. The remaining four pieces are in a homelier vein, and more closely personal in tone. Like his poems on the seasons, they reveal, in spite of a slight conventionality in expression, a sincere delight in nature, quickening rural sights and sounds into sympathy with his own mood. Yet, he was so far of his age that he shrank from the idea of solitude in nature; knowing only the closely cultivated districts of Middlesex and Surrey, he held that 'where man is not, Nature is barren.' But, apart from their freer, if still limited, appreciation of natural beauty, these songs are noteworthy by reason of their revelation of a new spirit in love. Burns was to sing on this theme out of pure exuberance of physical vitality; in Blake, love awes passion to adoration in the simple soul.

The wide range of poetic power in Blake is proved by the distance between the gentleness of these pieces and the tense emotion of *Mad Song*. Saintsbury has dealt at length with its prosodic excellence: particularly, in the first stanza, the sudden change in metre carries a vivid suggestion of frenzy breaking down, at its height, into dull despair. Stricken passion seems bared to the nerves; each beat of the verse is like a sharp cry, rising to the haunted terror of the closing lines.

The incomplete chronicle-play *King Edward the Third* is chiefly of interest as indicating Blake's juvenile sympathies and the limitations of his genius. He had little of the dramatic instinct, as his 'prophetic' writings prove, while his vehement denial of the validity of temporal existence cut him off from the ordinary themes of tragedy and comedy. And, even in this early work, he is chiefly occupied, not with any development of the plot, but with the consideration of abstract moral questions. His characters are all projections of his own personality, and the action halts while they discourse on points of private and civic virtue. Yet, the spirit behind the work is generous, and occasional passages come nearer to Shakespeare than most of the more pretentious efforts of the time. So, too, *A War Song to Englishmen*, though over-rhetorical in parts, is a stirring thing in an age that produced little patriotic verse.

The incomplete manuscript known as *An Island in the Moon* has been described as 'a somewhat incoherent and pointless precursor of the *Headlong Hall* type of novel.' Intended to satirise

the members of Mrs Mathew's learned coterie, its offence against
decency would be inexpiable were it not almost certain that no
eye but Blake's ever saw it in his lifetime. As literature, the work
has little value, except that it contains drafts of three of the *Songs
of Innocence*, as well as the quaint little *Song of Phebe and
Jellicoe*. The satirical verse is generally coarse and noisy, and but
rarely effectual, though the piece *When old corruption first begun*
is powerful in an unpleasant way. The prose has the faults of the
verse, being too highpitched and too uncontrolled to give penetra-
tive power to the caricature of a learned circle such as Blake had
known at Mrs Mathew's. It contains, however, an interesting,
though, unfortunately, incomplete, account of the process adopted
later for producing the engraved books. There are also indications of antipathies which were afterwards developed in the
'prophetic' books, notably a contempt for experimental science
and 'rational philosophy.'

A comparison of *Songs of Innocence* (1789) with *Poetical
Sketches* shows that the promise of Blake's earlier poetry has,
indeed, been fulfilled, but in a somewhat unexpected way.
Naturally, the maturer work is free from the juvenile habit of
imitation ; it is, however, of interest to note in passing the
suggestion that the hint of the composition of these *Songs*
may have come from a passage in Dr Watts's preface to his
Divine and Moral Songs for Children[1]. Moreover, the baneful
Ossianic influence is suspended for a space. But the vital
difference is that here, for the first time, Blake gives clear
indication of the mystical habit of thought, which, though at
first an integral part of his peculiar lyrical greatness, ultimately
turned to his undoing. In *Poetical Sketches*, his vision of life is
direct and naïve : he delights in the physical attributes of nature,
its breadth and its wonders of light and motion, of form and
melody. But, in *Songs of Innocence*, his interest is primarily
ethical. The essence of all being, as set forth in the piece called
The Divine Image, is the spirit of 'Mercy, Pity, Peace and Love';
and, as, later, he uses the terms 'poetic genius' and 'imagination'
to express his conception of this fundamental principle, so, here,
the 'Divine Image' is his vision of that spirit which is at once

[1] John Sampson makes the conjecture in the general preface to his edition of
Blake's *Poetical Works* : 'In the preface to that popular work Watts modestly refers
to his songs as "a slight specimen, such as I could wish some happy and condescending
genius would undertake for the use of children, and perform much better"; and it is
likely enough that Blake may have rightly felt himself to be this destined genius.'

universal and particular, God and Man. Under the inspiration of this belief, the world of experience fades away : there is nothing of death, pain or cruelty, except in the opening couplet of *The Chimney Sweeper*, and, even then, the idea of suffering is almost lost in the clear sense of a sustaining presence of love in the rest of the poem. Every other instance shows sorrow and difficulty to be but occasions for the immediate manifestation of sympathy. God, as the tender Father, the angels, the shepherd, the mother, the nurse, or even the humbler forms of insect and flower, as in *The Blossom*, or *A Dream*,—all are expressions of the same universal ethic of love. But, perhaps, the most remarkable illustration of this belief, particularly when contrasted with Blake's later criticism of public charity, is *Holy Thursday*. Clearly, in the world of these *Songs* there is not any suspicion of motives, no envy or jealousy. To use a later phrase by Blake, it is a 'lower Paradise,' very near to the perfect time wherein the lion shall lie down with the lamb : as in the poem *Night*, the angels of love are always by, to restrain violence or to bring solace to its victims.

The theological reference in this simple ethic is slight. God and Jesus are but visions of the love that animates all forms of being. Hence, at this period, Blake's position is distinct from that of mystical poets like Henry Vaughan, in whom a more dogmatic faith tends to overshadow the appeal of the natural universe. So, too, Blake's poetry has more of the instinct of human joy. Mercy, pity, peace and love, the elements of the Divine Image, are 'virtues of delight,' and nothing is clearer in these *Songs* than his quick intuition and unerring expression of the light and gladness in common things. In this, he returns to poems in *Poetical Sketches* like *I love the jocund dance*, rather than to the more formal pieces of nature-poetry. His delight in the sun, the hills, the streams, the flowers and buds, in the innocence of the child and of the lamb, comes not from sustained contemplation but as an immediate impulse. There is not as yet any sign of his later attitude towards the physical world as a 'shadow of the world of eternity.' His pleasure in the consciousness of this unifying spirit in the universe was still too fresh to give pause for theorising ; and, perhaps for this reason, such pieces as *Laughing Song, Spring, The Echoing Green, The Blossom* and *Night*, sung in pure joy of heart, convey more perfectly than all his later attempts at exposition the nature of his visionary faith. In Blake's later writings, there is a wide gulf between the symbol and the reality it conveys ; so, the reader must first grapple with a stubborn mass

C.E.L. VOL. XI   13 of symbolism. But, in *Songs of Innocence*, this faculty of 'spiritual sensation' transfigures rather than transforms. Thus, in *The Lamb*, pleasure in the natural image persists, but is carried further and exalted by the implication of a higher significance. It is the manifest spontaneity of this mystical insight that carries Blake safely over dangerous places. A little faltering in the vision or straining after effect would have sunk him, by reason of the simplicity of theme, diction and metre, now the sources of peculiar pleasure, into unthinkable depths of feebleness. Contrast with the strength of these seemingly fragile lines the more consciously didactic pieces like *The Chimney Sweeper* and *The Little Black Boy*. These, indeed, have the pleasant qualities of an unpretentious and sincere spirit; but their burden of instruction brings them too near to the wellmeant but somewhat pedagogic verse that writers like Nathaniel Cotton and Isaac Watts thought most suitable for the young. Blake regarded children more humanly, as the charming 'Introduction' to these *Songs* bears witness, or the poem *Infant Joy*, a perfect expression of the appeal of infancy. And, in *The Cradle Song*, almost certainly suggested by Watts's lines beginning 'Hush! my dear, lie still and slumber,' Blake's deeper humanity lifts him far above the commonplace moralisings of his model.

The Book of Thel was engraved in the same year (1789), though its final section is almost certainly later in date. The regularity of its unrimed fourteeners, the idyllic gentleness of its imagery and the not unpleasant blending of simplicity and formalism in the diction, proclaim the mood of *Songs of Innocence*. It treats of the same all-pervading spirit of mutual love and selfsacrifice. In response to the 'gentle lamentations' of the virgin Thel, to whom life seems vain, and death utter annihilation, the lily of the valley, the cloud, the worm and the clod, rise up to testify to the interdependence of all forms of being under the law of the Divine Image, and to show that death is not final extinction, but the supreme manifestation of this impulse to 'willing sacrifice of self.' Blake's original conclusion to this argument is lost, for the last section has not any perceptible connection in its context. In it, the whole conception of life is changed. This world is a dark prison, and the physical senses are narrow windows darkening the infinite soul of man by excluding 'the wisdom and joy of eternity,' the condition of which is freedom. The source of this degradation is the tyranny of abstract moral law, the 'mind-forged manacles' upon natural and, therefore, innocent desires; its symbols are the silver rod of authority and the golden bowl of a restrictive ethic that would mete out the immeasurable spirit of love. Here, Blake is clearly enough in the grip of the formal antinomianism that produced the later 'prophecies.'

The undated manuscript *Tiriel* apparently belongs to this period. It is written in the measure of *Thel*, but is less regular, and the Ossianic influence is strong in its overwrought imagery and violent phrase. Blake's purpose in writing this history of the tyrant Tiriel and his rebellious children is not clear; perhaps, he was already drawing towards the revolutionary position of the later books. The final section, which appears to be a later addition, repeats with greater vehemence the substance of the last part of *Thel*.

But this early spirit of revolt is most notably expressed in *The Marriage of Heaven and Hell* (1790), the only considerable prose work engraved by Blake. It is a wellsustained piece of iconoclastic writing, full of *verve* and abounding in quite successful paradox. Critically regarded, Blake's position as the devil's disciple, maintaining the 'great half-truth Liberty' against 'the great half-truth Law,' is not unassailable; yet the abiding impression is one of exuberant satirical power, of youthful freshness and buoyancy and of unflagging energy. Blake shows himself the master of firmly-knit, straight-hitting phrase, entirely without artifice, and he displays a wonderful fertility of apt illustration, in aphorism, in ironic apologue and in skilful reinterpretations of familiar episodes, chiefly biblical. The vivid scene wherein Blake and the angel contemplate their 'eternal lots' is in the spirit of Swift's early work, though its imagery has greater breadth and shows an artist's sense of colour.

Of the tangled strands of opinion in this work, the two chief would seem to be Blake's theory of reality and his denial of authority. Here, as before, he lays stress on the identity of the universal and the particular spirit, the oneness of God and man; though now, and in the contemporary *No Natural Religion* plates, he calls this prime essence the 'Poetic Genius,' or the soul, of which latter, body is but a partial and modified percept, due to narrowed physical senses. From this, it follows, first, that there cannot be any valid law external to man, and, secondly, that the phenomenon of absolute matter is an illusion, due to empirical reasoning. For, since all forms of being are coextensive with the 'Universal Poetic Genius,' it must be that all knowledge is intuitive. So, it comes to pass that Blake runs tilt against all civil, moral and religious codes and all exercise of reason, while, on the positive side, he affirms the sufficiency and sanctity of natural impulse and desire, of 'firm persuasions' and 'the voice of honest indignation.' Energy is exalted; to attempt to limit or divert it is to threaten man's spiritual integrity. The strong man resists such tyranny, the weak succumb; yet, unable wholly to repress natural instincts, they veil their inevitable gratification under legal sanction, by their hypocrisy generating all forms of moral, spiritual and physical corruption. By cunning, the weak come to power in this world, and, setting up their slave-moralities as the measure of truth, call themselves the righteous, the elect, the angels and heirs of heaven, while those whose clearer vision refuses obedience are cast out as of the devil's party[1]: they are the rebels in Hell. Angels repress joy as sin; devils hold it to be the justification of all action.

The original purpose of *The Marriage* was to expose Swedenborg's inconsistency, in that, while pretending to expose the fallacy of the normal religious acceptance of moral distinctions, he was himself infected with the same error. But, this particular intention is soon absorbed in the general onslaught upon the legalist positions, though the earlier purpose is recalled from time to time, particularly in the remarkably virile satire of *Memorable Fancies*, written in mockery of the Swedish mystic's *Memorable Relations*.

It is strange that, having thus proved his power as a writer of clean-limbed muscular prose, he should have returned almost immediately to the fourteener, and developed therein what is too often the windy rhetoric of the 'prophetic' books. He seems to have aimed at creating a body of *quasi*-epic poetry, dealing with the origin, progress and ultimate purpose of mortality. To this end, he invented his mythology, wherein the passions and aspirations of man, and the influences that made for or against vision, appear in human form, but magnified to daemonic proportions. It is clear that he was largely influenced by Milton, whom he regarded as the great heresiarch, and whose theological opinions he felt himself called upon to confute. This is explicit in *The Marriage* and in the book called *Milton*, as well as in recorded passages of Blake's conversation, while much of his imagery, and occasionally, his rhythm and diction, are reminiscent of the older poet. But there are also evidences of Biblical, Ossianic and Swedenborgian

---

[1] The present account of the doctrines of Blake's 'prophetic' books must, necessarily, from considerations of space, be brief and, in a measure, dogmatic. It may, however, be stated that the interpretation here given is based upon a long and detailed study of these works, undertaken by the present writer in conjunction with Duncan J. Sloss.

influences in works written between the years 1793 and 1800, the period of his residence in Lambeth.

A brief examination of the Lambeth books will show how the freight of ideas gradually broke down the frail semblance of form with which they started. The first, the recently rediscovered *French Revolution* (1791), is in almost regular fourteeners, and its style, though distorted and over-emphatic, is comparatively intelligible. Only the first of seven books appears to have been printed; it opens the series of what may be called visionary histories, and embodies Blake's interpretation of events in Paris and Versailles between 5 May and 16 July 1789, though it does not describe the actual attack upon the Bastille (14 July). Its literary interest is slight: what is, perhaps, the most striking passage describes the various towers and the prisoners in the famous fortress, when premonitions of its impending fate are in the air. Otherwise, the work is only of value for its indications of ideas developed later. For Blake, the stand made by the *tiers état* marks the first step towards universal emancipation from the thraldom of authority. Yet, his portrayal of Louis XVI has none of his later violence towards kings, for the French monarch is seen as one overborne by circumstances and the influence of his nobles. But, Blake's lifelong feud against priestcraft utters itself in an attack upon clericalism in the person of the archbishop of Paris.

The French Revolution was printed by Johnson, and it may have been about this time that Blake became one of the circle—of which Paine, Godwin, Holcroft and Mary Wollstonecraft were also members—that used to meet at the publisher's table. It is, therefore, natural to conclude that this society, to a considerable extent, was responsible for the extreme revolutionary spirit of the Lambeth books, and it is likely that those which deal with the rebellions in France and America may have owed something, in the way of suggestion or information, to Paine. *The French Revolution* was followed by *A Song of Liberty*[1] and *America* (1793). The former, being, substantially, a *précis* of the latter, is only remarkable because of its form, being cast into short numbered paragraphs like the verses in the Bible. But *America*, one of the most beautifully engraved of these books, marks a considerable advance in the use of symbolism. Here, the conflict between England and her colonies is interpreted as presaging the imminent annihilation

---

[1] This work, from the fact that it is sometimes bound up with *The Marriage of Heaven and Hell*, has generally been ascribed to the year 1790. But its symbolism would seem to put it later than *The French Revolution* (1791).

of authority and the reestablishment of the Blakean ideal of a condition of complete licence. On the side of law stands Urizen, the aged source of all restrictive codes ; his ministers are the king, councillors and priests of England. On the opposite side stands Orc, the fiery daemon of living passion and desire, the archrebel, 'Antichrist, hater of Dignities, Lover of wild rebellion and transgressor of God's Law,' and, therefore, the liberator of man from the power of law : he inspires the colonial leaders, Washington and the rest. But Blake handles history much more freely here than in *The French Revolution*, for the fact that he wrote after the successful issue of the revolt made it possible for him to claim it as a vindication of his own anarchic theory. Ever after, in his symbolism, the western quarter, either America or the sunken continent of Atlantis, stands for the visionary ideal of perfect liberty, from which fallen man, in Europe and Asia, is cut off by the floods of moral fallacies, the 'Atlantic deep.' This concept appears in *Visions of the Daughters of Albion* (1793), which, in its vigorous enthusiasm and comparative buoyancy, most nearly resembles *America*. Like that work, too, it is easily intelligible, but deals with the physical and moral, rather than with the political, tyranny of legal codes. The myth tells how the virgin Oothoon, 'the soft soul of America,' the spirit of delight, plucks the flower of instant and complete gratification of desire ; further, she is ravished by a violent daemon, Bromion. On both these accounts, she is condemned and mourned over by the spirit of prudential morality, and the major part of the book is a vehement vindication of physical appetite. The whole argument, of course, is very unreal ; yet the force of Blake's conviction gives his statement of the case a certain vitality, and keeps it unfalteringly above the low places of thought.

Up to this point, Blake's writings preserve the spontaneity and confident strength that mark *The Marriage* : his faith in the immediate efficacy of passion to free itself by revolt gives energy and freshness to the measure and language. But, from this time, his outlook becomes increasingly overcast. He comes to see that the will to freedom is not all-powerful, but must endure, for a time, the limitations of temporal experience. Salvation is still to come through passionate revolt, and, in an indefinite way, this is associated with the French revolution ; but, Blake now emphasises the strength of the moral heresy, and the impetuous enthusiasm of *America* and *Visions* is, to a considerable degree, checked. The simplest indications of this change occur in *Songs of Experience*

(1794) and those poems in the Rossetti MS belonging to the same period. The contrast between these and *Songs of Innocence* is not merely formal, but is the direct expression of the change already referred to. In the early collection, there are no shadows : to Blake's unaccustomed eyes, the first glimpse of the world of vision was pure light. But, in the intervening years, experience had brought a fuller sense of the power of evil, and of the difficulty and loneliness of his lot who would set himself against the current of this world. So he writes of himself

> The Angel that presided o'er my birth
> Said, ' Little creature, formed of Joy and Mirth
> Go, love without the help of anything on Earth.'

The title-page for the combined *Songs of Innocence and of Experience* describes them as 'Shewing the Contrary States of the Human Soul' while, in the motto, he writes, in a spirit of disenchantment,

> The Good are attracted by Men's perceptions
> And think not for themselves;
> Till Experience teaches them to catch
> And to cage the Fairies and Elves,

the catching of the fairies and elves, apparently, signifying the deliberate searching after the hidden mystical meaning of things, in place of a docile acceptance of other men's faith.

Signs of the change lie on every hand. If the introduction in *Songs of Experience* be compared with its earlier counterpart, the piper is seen to have become the more portentous bard, the laughing child upon a cloud gives place to ' the lapsèd Soul weeping in the evening dew.' And there is, also, apparent, at times, the vague consciousness of 'some blind hand' crushing the life of man, as man crushes the fly. This, however, is not quite constant, though something of the same mystery lies behind the question in *The Tiger*,

> Did he who made the Lamb make thee?

More commonly, Blake lays stress upon the fallacy of law, and this, chiefly, in its relation to love. Thus, in *The Clod and the Pebble*, his own ethic of the love that 'seeketh not itself to please,' is set against the concept of love governed by moral duty, and, therefore, cold and interested. Similarly, in *Holy Thursday*, there is white passion beneath the simplicity and restraint of his picture of the little victims of a niggard charity ; perhaps, nothing gives so complete an impression of the change in Blake as the comparison of the earlier and later poems under this title. Moreover, he always opposed any interference with the natural development of the individual genius. 'There is no use in education,' he told Crabb Robinson, 'I hold it wrong. It is the great Sin.' This text he develops in *The Schoolboy* and in the two versions, manuscript and engraved, of *Infant Sorrow*. Something of the kind appears in *A Little Boy Lost*, though there is also a return to the baiting of the Philistine with paradox, as in *The Marriage*. For, here, as before, churches and priests represent the extreme forms of obscurantism and repression, and the exaltation of the letter of a rigid law above the spirit of love that transcends mere obligation. But, by far the greater bulk of the engraved and manuscript verse of this period repeats the theme of *Visions*, the infallibility of the human instinct towards gratification of appetite, and the iniquity of all that interferes with it. Hence, modesty, continence and asceticism become glosing terms, hiding the deformity and corruption that arise from the covert satisfaction of desire; they are the fair-seeming fruit of the poison-tree, the tree of moral virtue.

Such is a summary of the main ideas embodied in these *Songs*. There are, indeed, moments when this passion of disputation tells heavily against the verse, prosodically perfect though it is; only the unfaltering sincerity and directness of Blake's spirit bears him safely through. Indeed, he never surpassed the best work of this period. Notably in *The Tiger*, his imagination shakes off the encumbrances of doctrine, and beats out new rhythm and new imagery for a more exalted vision of life. The poem proceeds entirely by suggestion; its succession of broken exclamations, scarcely coherent in their rising intensity, gives a vivid impression of a vast creative spirit labouring at elemental furnace and anvil to mould a mortal form adequate to the passion and fierce beauty of the wrath of God, the 'wild furies' of the human spirit: it is as though the whole mighty process had been revealed to him in vivid gleams out of great darkness. Of a lower flight, but still unequalled before Keats, are poems in the 'romantic' mood of human sorrow, in harmony with the more desolate aspects of nature. Such are the *Introduction* and *Earth's Answer*, the lovely first stanza of *The Sunflower* or the manuscript quatrain, almost perfect in its music, beginning 'I laid me down upon a bank.' Yet, Blake could ruin the effect of such lines by adding an atrocious verse in crude three-foot anapaests on the iniquity of moral law. He gives his own version of this obsession in another manuscript poem:

Thou hast a lap full of seed
And this is a fine country.
Why dost thou not cast thy seed,
And live in it merrily?

Shall I cast it on the sand
And turn it into fruitful land?
For on no other ground
Can I sow my seed,
Without tearing up
Some stinking weed.

Yet, some seed of song fell into the sandy wastes of Blake's ethical disputations, and sprang up and blossomed in spite of the tearing up of noxious moral heresies in their neighbourhood. Such are the delicate minor melody of *The Wild Flower's Song*, the lines *I told my love, To My Myrtle*—a notable instance, by the way, of Blake's rigorous use of the file in his lyrics—and *Cradle Song*. He still has his old delight in natural beauty, though his perverse antipathies often stood in the way of its expression ; and his utterance is almost always singularly clear, concise and un-forced.

But, in the remaining Lambeth writings, Blake is no longer controlled by the exigencies of lyrical form, and the first freshness of his revolutionary enthusiasm is past; hence, his energy turns to exposition or affirmation, not so much of his own faith as of the errors of the opposite party. To this end, he invented the mystical mythology which is chiefly contained in *The Book of Urizen* (1794), with its complements *The Book of Ahania* and *The Book of Los* (1795). These trace the fallacies of the moral law to their pre-mundane source. *Europe* (1794) and *The Song of Los* (1795) though they have the same mythological basis, come rather nearer in tone to *America*. The *Urizen* series, too, is written in a shorter and very irregular measure, generally containing three or four stresses. The other two works combine the fourteener and the shorter line.

Blake's antagonism to Milton's theodicy led him to reinterpret the story of the fall, affirming that it was not Satan, but the God of this world, the author of the moral codes, or, in Blake's mytho-logy, Urizen, who fell. Hence, *The Book of Urizen* contains obvious inversions of Miltonic episodes. But, here, as elsewhere in Blake, the root-idea is that existence is made up of two great bodies of contraries ; on the one side, the eternals. the expression of the ideal ethic, on the other, Urizen. This latter daemon plots to impose his will upon the eternals, but fails, and is cast out into chaos, wherein is ultimately developed the world of time and space. This process of evolution is not directed to any discernible end, except that it gives extension and duration to the unreal forms begotten of Urizen's perverted moral and intellectual sense, which become apparent as the phenomena of a physical universe, wherein man forgets 'the wisdom and joy of eternity' and shrinks, spiritually and bodily, to mortal stature. But, since Urizen is the negation of all creative activity, Blake is constrained to introduce a forma-tive agent in Los, the eternal prophet—though, as yet, there seems little to justify this title. Labouring at his furnaces and anvils, he gives permanence to the successive modifications of the Urizenic substance of which this new world is made, binding them in the chains of time. From him, also, derive two important develop-ments, the 'separation' of the first female, the manifestation of Los's pity for the sterile universe, and the birth of Orc. But, apparently because *The Book of Urizen* is incomplete, nothing comes of these episodes, and the work concludes with the enslave-ment of all mortality beneath Urizen's net of religion. In this myth, Blake's main purpose is to demonstrate, by reference to their origins, the falsity of the ethical spirit and the unreality of the material universe. In *The Book of Ahania,* he further identifies Urizen, as the author of the Mosaic code, with Jehovah. He also emphasises, in new symbols, the antagonism of morality, first to 'masculine' or positive energy, and, secondly, to physical desire, imaged in the female Ahania. In the remaining member of this trilogy, *The Book of Los,* the strangeness of the symbolism makes interpretation too much a matter of conjecture to warrant any conclusion as to its place in the development of Blake's ideas.

In *Europe* and *The Song of Los,* Blake turns from universal history to consider the present portents of immediate emancipation through the French revolution. This change is reflected in the greater prominence given to Los and Enitharmon, who, as regents of this world, act as the ministers of Urizen to transmit to men his systems of religion and philosophy, from that of 'Brama' to the Newtonian 'Philosophy of the Five Senses.' But the most im-portant point is that Blake here utters his plainest criticism of Christianity. According to his own statement in *Africa,* the first section of *The Song of Los,* the asceticism of Jesus's gospel would have depopulated the earth, had not Mohammedanism, with its 'loose Bible,' that is, apparently, its laxer moral code, been set to counteract it. And, in *Europe,* the Christian era is the period of the 'Female dream,' the false ideal that makes passivity a virtue and the gratification of innate desire a sin. Thus, Enitharmon is the typical female, at once the source and the symbol of repressive morality.

The next work, the manuscript originally called *Vala*, belongs to two distinct periods of Blake's development. The earlier portion, dated 1797, extends and elaborates the symbolism of *The Book of Urizen*, with certain modifications, of which the most important is that man is conceived, ideally, as a harmony of four spiritual powers, Urizen, Luvah, Urthona—apparent in time as Los—and Tharmas. It may be that these, later known as the Zoas, have a psychological significance, as the symbols of reason, emotion, energy and instinct or desire ; but the indications are too vague and contradictory to admit of assured interpretation. Further difficulties arise with the four females joined with the male qua-ternion. But, this elaborate symbolism, like most of Blake's attempts in this kind, soon falls through, and may safely be ignored. As before, the real basis is a dualism of liberty and law. The first 'Nights' of *Vala* repeat, under a bewildering variety of imagery, the now familiar criticism of the ethical spirit as a dis-ruptive force, destructive of the ideal unity in man, and the cause of the difficulty and darkness of mortality, through the illusions of materialism and morality. The remaining sections develop the antithesis of authority and anarchy in Urizen and Orc, and, though the former triumphs at first, its manifold tyrannies are ultimately consumed beneath the cleansing fires of Orc's rebel spirit of passion, so that, after the final 'harvest and vintage of the Nations,' man reascends to his primal unity in a state of perfect liberty.

The arid symbolism and uncouth style of the later Lambeth books mark a zeal that has overridden inspiration, till the creative spirit flags beneath the continual stimulus of whip and spur, and, almost founders in barren wastes of mere storm and splutter ; and though, by sheer strength, Blake occasionally compels his stubborn matter into striking forms, the general effect is repellent in the extreme. Then came his visit to Felpham, at the invitation of William Hayley, and the three years (1800—1803) passed there influenced him most deeply, as his letters and later 'prophecies' clearly show. Perhaps the shock of transition from the cramped London life to the comparative freedom of his new surroundings awakened him to consciousness of the extent of his divergence from the sounder and more human faith of his early manhood. But, whatever the cause, his old attitude changed, coming nearer

to that of *Songs of Innocence*, as he himself writes to captain
Butts:

And now let me finish with assuring you that, though I have been very
unhappy, I am so no longer. I am again emerged into the light of day;
I still and shall to eternity embrace Christianity, and adore Him who is the
express image of God[1].

In this spirit he took up *Vala* and, renaming it *The Four Zoas*,
attempted to bring it into harmony with his new vision by grafting
additions, and rewriting the whole or considerable parts of various
'Nights.' But the basis of *Vala*, like that of the other Lambeth
books, is purely necessitarian: the eternals stand apart from mundane life, having neither sympathy with it, nor foreknowledge of
its end. Mortal existence is totally evil, and is not in any way
connected with man's regeneration, which is conceived as coming
through mere rebellion, and consisting in a return to anarchy. It
was to this crude stock that Blake sought to join an unusually
vivid faith in a divine providence, apparent, to visionary sight,
either as God or Jesus, in whom the eternals were united in a
divine family watching over the life of man, to lead it to ultimate
salvation through the mediation of such spiritual agencies as the
daughters of Beulah, or Los and Enitharmon. These latter, as
time and space, embody Blake's new valuation of mortal life. The
former criticism of the phenomenon of absolute physical reality, as
being a delusion due to reason and sense-perception, is still maintained; but Blake now finds an ulterior significance in mundane
forms, as the symbols of spiritual ideas revealed to the inspired
man by divine mercy. This higher revelation is mediate through
Los and Enitharmon, who give it expression fitted to the enfeebled
powers of man. They are also associated with a corresponding
change in the estimate of the mortal body. As Blake states the
matter, spirits at the fall become 'spectres,' 'insane, brutish, de-
formed,' 'ravening devouring lust'; but Los and Enitharmon create
for them 'forms' or 'counterparts,' 'inspir'd, divinely human,' and
apparently indicating an endowment of visionary inspiration.
Thus equipped, man passes through this world, subject to the
temptations of metaphysical and moral error in the forms of
Satan, or the feminine powers, Rahab, Tirzah, or Vala.

But, in his mortal pilgrimage, he is, also, sustained by spiritual
influxes transmitted by 'angels of providence,' such as the
daughters of Beulah, through natural objects, trees, flowers, birds
and insects. The supreme revelation, however, comes through the

[1] Letter to captain Butts, 22 November 1802.

incarnation and crucifixion of Jesus, wherein the whole mystical
faith is manifested to corporeal understanding, becoming subject
to the conditions of mortality in order ultimately to reveal their
falsity and annihilate them.   But, though all this has a metaphysical reference, Blake lays most stress upon its ethical
significance.   In the Lambeth books, he attacks conventional
morality on the ground of its inhibition of physical desire ; but
now, though this criticism is not entirely retracted, the emphasis
shifts to the false concept of love as a religious obligation towards
an extrinsic deity, whose law is essentially penal, 'rewarding with
hate the loving soul' by insistence upon repentance and vicarious
sacrifice.   Such is the religion of Satan, symbolised by the false
females, Rahab and Tirzah, or by Babylon, the harlot of *Revelation.*
This is clearly a development of the concept of Enitharmon noticed
in *Europe.*   Against this, Blake sets the gospel of brotherhood
and unconditional forgiveness, revealed to man in the incarnation
of Jesus.   Here, there is a reversion to the ethic of *Songs of
Innocence.*

It was, apparently, the impossibility of fusing the old and
new elements in *The Four Zoas* that led to its abandonment.
Judged as literature, it suffers by reason of its formlessness and
incoherence ; yet, though it is often little better than mere clamour
and outrageous imagery, there are scattered passages of much
cogency and imaginative power.   But it is chiefly of interest as a
document in the history of Blake's development.   In 1804, he
began to engrave *Milton* and *Jerusalem.*   The former work de-
cribes the nature of his new inspiration, and also, as it would seem,
the manner of its transmission.   It tells how Milton redescended
from his place in eternity—for, as Blake told Crabb Robinson, the
author of *Paradise Lost,* in his old age, turned back to the God
he had abandoned in childhood—in order to annihilate the error
to which he had given currency in his great epic.   To achieve this
end, he entered into Blake at Felpham.   Thus inspired, Blake
becomes the prophet of the new ethic and proclaims the necessity
to subdue the unregenerate self, the spectre which is in every man.
And, in a variety of mythical episodes, he assails the fallacy of
retributive morality, the natural religion of Satan, god of this
world, and preaches the gospel of Jesus, the law of continual selfsacrifice and mutual forgiveness.   But the main points of his later
creed are comprehended in his theory of imagination, the most complete and intelligible statement of which is contained in the prose
note in the Rossetti MS on the design for *A Vision of the Last*

Judgment. The following quotation shows how Blake returned to and elaborated his earlier doctrines of the Divine Image and the Poetic Genius.

> The world of imagination is the world of eternity. It is the divine bosom into which we shall all go after the death of the vegetated [*i.e.* mortal] body. This world of imagination is infinite and eternal, whereas the world of generation is finite and temporal. There exist in that eternal world the eternal realities of everything which we see reflected in this vegetable glass of nature. All things are comprehended in the divine body of the Saviour, the true vine of eternity, the Human Imagination, who appeared to me coming to judgment ... and throwing off the temporal that the eternal might be established.

For Blake saw all things under the human form: 'all are men in eternity.' And, to Crabb Robinson, he said 'we are all co-existent with God; members of the Divine body, and partakers of the Divine nature'; or, again, concerning the divinity of Christ, 'He is the only God ... And so am I and so are you.' From this follows the insistence on vision, the immediate perception of the 'infinite and eternal' in everything; literally, 'To see a World in a grain of Sand.' In such a theory of knowledge, reason and sense-perception cannot have place; they, with the phenomenon of a corporeal universe, are part of the error of natural religion, the fallacies of moral valuation and of penal codes completing it. Even Wordsworth's attitude to nature is condemned as atheism. Thus 'all life consists of these two, throwing off error ... and receiving truth.' In the former case, the conflict is against the unregenerate influences within and without; man must 'cleanse the face of his spirit' by selfexamination, casting off the accretions of merely mundane experience, till the identity of the individual with the universal is established in what Blake calls the Last Judgment. The positive aspect of visionary activity in mortality is a constant seeking after the revealed truths of imagination, which are comprehended in Jesus.

> 'I know of no other Christianity' he writes 'than the liberty both of body and mind to exercise the Divine Arts of Imagination ... The Apostles knew of no other Gospel. What were all their spiritual gifts? What is the Divine Spirit? Is the Holy Ghost any other than an Intellectual Fountain? .. What are the Treasures of Heaven which we are to lay up for ourselves? Are they any other than Mental [*i.e.* Imaginative] Studies and Performances? What are the Gifts of the Gospel? are they not all Mental Gifts?'

What Blake states thus impressively in his prose, is stated under a bewildering variety of apparently unconnected symbolic episodes, in *Jerusalem.* Man, or Albion, is the battle-ground wherein the forces of imagination contend against the forces of natural religion:

Jesus against Satan : Los against his spectre : Vala or Babylon against Jerusalem, till error is consumed and Albion reascends into the bosom of the Saviour.   Yet, in spite of formlessness and incoherence in statement, the underlying body of doctrine is remarkably consistent. In the later Lambeth books, Blake seems to have written under a jaded inspiration. Here, however, the very intensity of his conviction and the fecundity of his imagination, militated against lucidity and order. Moreover, he deliberately adopted the symbolic medium as translating his visions with less of the distracting associations of ordinary experience than must have beset normal speech. And, if his visions were unintelligible, the fault lay in the reader, who had neglected to cultivate his imaginative faculty; in Blake's sweeping condemnation, they were ' fools ' and ' weak men,' not worth his care.   Aesthetically, *Jerusalem* suffers much from this perversity, though the poet in Blake at times masters the stubborn mass of his symbolism, turning it for a brief space to forms of beauty or power.   And there always remains the high nobility of the gospel which he proclaimed, and according to which he lived.

The theme and dramatic form of *The Ghost of Abel* (1822) were suggested by Byron's *Cain*, wherein, as Blake believed, the scriptural account of the punishment of Cain is misinterpreted in conformity with the heresy of the churches, which declare Jehovah to have been the author of the curse. Blake, however, attributes it to Satan, ' God of this World,' the ' Elohim of the Heathen': for the gospel of Jehovah is ' Peace, Brotherhood and Love.'   Then, in the *Laocoon* aphorisms, he turns, for the last time, to his doctrine of imagination, and gives it final form by identifying Christianity and art. Jesus and his apostles were artists, and who would be Christians must practise some form of art, for, as Crabb Robinson reports him, inspiration is art, and the visionary faculty, equally with every other, is innate in all, though most neglect to cultivate it.

Such, in brief, seems to have been the course of Blake's development. It still remains to notice the more formal verse and the prose of this latest period. The first, which, during Blake's lifetime, remained in the Rossetti and Pickering MSS, is, though slight in bulk, of remarkable quality. It includes such lovely lyrics as *Morning*, *The Land of Dreams*, or the penultimate stanza of *The Grey Monk*. But the most singular are the abstruse symbolic poems *The Smile*, *The Golden Net* and *The Crystal Cabinet*, which seem to embody the visionary's consciousness of the unholy beauty and seductiveness of the natural world. Unfamiliar as is their language, they make a real, though illusive, appeal, which may ultimately lie in the romantic cast and spontaneity of the imagery, as well as in their perfection of lyrical form. The other symbolic poems, such as *The Mental Traveller* and *My Spectre around me*, lacking this directness and unity of expression, fall short of a like effectiveness. But all these poems stand aloof from purely human feeling. Except *The Birds*, a most un-Blakean idyllic duologue, they rarely touch the common lyric chords. They are primarily spiritual documents. *Mary, William Bond* and *Auguries of Innocence* illustrate this. The lastmentioned poem, though it has passages of real force and beauty, depends, for its adequate understanding, upon the doctrine underlying it, the identity of all forms of being in the divine humanity : 'all are Men in Eternity.' The recognition of this principle gives cogency and deep truth to what must otherwise appear exaggerated emphasis of statement. But, the reserve of poetic power in Blake is most clearly revealed in *The Everlasting Gospel*. Metrically, it is based upon the same octosyllabic scheme as *Christabel*, though it is handled so as to produce quite different effects. In spirit, it comes nearest to *The Marriage*, developing, with wonderful fertility of illustration, the theme of Jesus as the archrebel. Yet, its value as a statement of Blake's position is subordinate to its poetic excellences, its virile diction and its sturdy, yet supple, metre, following, with consummate ease, the rapid transitions from spirited declamation to satire or paradox.

Blake's prose has the directness and simplicity that distinguish his poetry. Except for the *Descriptive Catalogue*, for the engraved pieces, such as the introductions to the 'books' of *Jerusalem*, and for the letters, it lies scattered in the Rossetti MS and in marginalia to Reynolds's *Discourses* and other works. Yet, in spite of its casual character, it is a quite efficient instrument, whether for lofty declaration of faith, as in the addresses *To the Deists* or *To the Christians* or for critical appreciation, as in the famous note on *The Canterbury Tales* admired by Lamb. It also served as a vigorous, if sometimes acrimonious, medium for expressing Blake's objections to those whose opinions or artistic practice ran counter to his own. But, it is almost always perfectly sound, though without conscious seeking after style. His letters have the same virtues, but their chief interest would seem to lie in the insight which they give into his character and the light they throw upon the symbolism of the prophetic books.

Blake's peculiar method of reproducing his writings, and the comparative seclusion in which he lived, prevented his works from exercising any influence on their age, though Wordsworth, Coleridge, Southey and Lamb knew and admired portions of them, Yet, few responded so directly and in so many ways to the quickening impulse of the romantic revival. It is true that his early years coincided with an awakened interest in our older literature, which was already exercising a limited influence on contemporary work; and, moreover, as has been seen, his juvenile reading was in this field. But the root of the matter seems to have lain deeper. The whole temper of his genius was essentially opposed to the classical tradition, with its close regard to intellectual appeal and its distrust of enthusiasm. In the *Laocoon* sentences and in the engraved notes *On Homer's Poetry* and *On Virgil*, he identifies it with the devastating errors of materialism and morality, and, in the *Public Address*, he is vehement in denouncing Dryden's presumption in 'improving' Milton, and Pope's 'niggling' formalism: as he puts it, the practitioners of this school 'knew enough of artifice, but little of art.' Such a judgment, though not wholly just to classicism at its best, was the fighting creed of the romantics, and Blake maintained it more uncompromisingly than most. His mystical faith freed him from the barren materialism of his age, and opened to him in vision the world lying beyond the range of the physical senses. Hence, the greater warmth of his ethical creed; and his preoccupation with the supernatural, which he never consciously shaped to literary ends, is yet the source of the peculiar imaginative quality of his work. It also looks forward to the use of the supernatural in such works as *The Ancient Mariner* and *Christabel.* Though he probably intended it otherwise, the effective and complete revelation of the new spirit within him is made, not in his definitely dogmatic writing, but in his verse, which he seems to have rated below his other work; he scarcely ever speaks of it as he does of his art or his mystical writings. Yet, his lyric poetry, at its best, displays the characteristics of the new spirit some years before it appeared elsewhere. His first volume of poems contained songs such as had not been sung for more than a century; the nearest parallel in time is Burns. While Wordsworth was still a schoolboy, Blake had found, and was using with consummate art, a diction almost perfect in its simplicity, aptness and beauty. His earlier attitude to nature, as has already been noticed, has none of the complacency that distinguishes his age: to him, it was the revelation of a universal spirit of love and delight, the Divine

Image, less austere than Wordsworth's 'overseeing power.' It has also been seen that he had the romantic sympathy with quaint or terrible imaginings, such as appeared later in Keats and Shelley. His passion for freedom was, also, akin to that which moved Wordsworth, Coleridge and Southey in their earlier years, though, in its later form, it came nearer to Shelley's revolt against convention. There is, indeed, an unusual degree of fellowship between these two : the imagery and symbolism, as well as the underlying spirit, of *The Revolt of Islam, Alastor* and *Prometheus Unbound* find their nearest parallel in Blake's prophetic books. Both had visions of a world regenerated by a gospel of universal brotherhood, transcending law ; though, perhaps, the firmer spirit of Blake brought his faith in imagination nearer to life than Shelley's philosophic dream of intellectual beauty. For the final note of Blake's career is not one of tragedy : his own works and the record of others show that he had subdued the world to his own spirit ; he died singing.

CHAPTER X

BURNS

LESSER SCOTTISH VERSE

In the annals of English literature, Burns is a kind of anomaly. He defies classification. He stands apart in isolated individuality. If he is something of a prodigy, his accidental singularity helps to convey this impression. The preceding English poetry of the eighteenth century did not give any prognostication of the possibility of anyone resembling him. His most characteristic verse is outside its scope, and is quite dissimilar from it in tone, temper and tendency. He was influenced by this English verse only in a superficial and extraneous manner. However much he may have tried, he found it impossible to become a poet after the prevailing English fashion of his time. Not from the brilliant generations of English bards can he claim poetic descent. So far as concerned general literary repute, his chief poetic ancestors were, if not lowly, obscure and forgotten. Whatever their intrinsic merits, they were almost unknown until curiosity about them was awakened by his arrival.

The old school of Scottish verse did not, however, deserve its fate. As may be gathered from previous chapters, it was by no means an undistinguished one. It included one poet, Dunbar, of an outstanding genius closely akin to that of Burns, and, if not possessed of so full an inspiration or so wide and deep a sympathy, vying with him in imaginative vividness, in satiric mirth, in wild and rollicking humour and in mastery of expression, while more than his equal as a polished metrist. Other names famous in their generation were Henryson, Douglas, Kennedy, Scott, Montgomerie and David Lyndsay. In addition to these were unknown authors of various pieces of high merit, and, besides them, what Burns himself terms the 'glorious old Bards,' of 'the Ancient Fragments' and of various old songs of tradition: bards, whose 'very names are,' as he says, 'buried amongst the wreck of things that were.' This school of Scottish poetry perished, or all but perished, in its prime. Its line of succession was cut short by the reformation, which had been followed by an almost complete literary blank of a century and a half. During this interval, the spoken dialect of Scotland had been undergoing processes of change, and the language of the old verse, by the time of Burns, had become partly a dead language. The forms and methods of its metre had also become largely antiquated, and were not akin to modern English usage. Moreover, the bulk of the old poetry that had escaped destruction was still wrapped in oblivion. It lay *perdu* in manuscripts, though more than a glimpse of what was best of it was obtainable from the selections that had appeared in Ramsay's *Evergreen* and other publications. But, while it could thus be known to Burns in only a fragmentary fashion, he was largely indebted to it directly or indirectly. Like many Scots of past generations, he was familiar with much of the verse of 'Davie Lyndsay'; as perused by him in the modernised version of Blind Harry's poem by Hamilton of Gilbertfield, 'the story of Wallace,' he tells us, had 'poured a Scottish prejudice' into his veins; he had dipped, if little more, into Gawin Douglas; in addition to *The Evergreen*, he knew Watson's *Choice Collection* (1706—11); and, before the publication of the Kilmarnock volume, he may have read Lord Hailes's *Ancient Scottish Poems* (1771) and Herd's *Ancient and Modern Scottish Songs* (1769 and 1776). At the same time, he did not know the old 'makaris' as they are now known; of the individualities of some of the principal of them he had no very definite idea; and even the poetic greatness of Dunbar had not dawned upon him. Again, though he had an acquaintance with the older poets, similar to that possessed by Ramsay, Fergusson and others, from the very fact that they had preceded him, he did not come so immediately under the influence of the older writers. Later writers had already formed a kind of new poetic school, and it was more immediately on them that he sought to model himself: their achievements, rather than those of the older writers, were what he sought to emulate or surpass. His special aim, as stated in the preface to the Kilmarnock volume, was to 'sing the sentiments and manners he felt and saw in himself and his rustic compeers around him, in his and their native language.' As a lyric poet, his commission was rather more comprehensive; and, here, he could benefit but little by the example either of Ramsay—great as had been his vogue as a song writer—or even Fergusson. Other contemporaries had done as good lyric work as they; but, here, the best, and, also, the chief, exemplars of Burns were 'the glorious old Bards,' of 'the Ancient Fragments.' The greatness of his lyric career was, however, only faintly foreshadowed in the Kilmarnock volume (1786) or in the Edinburgh edition of the following year. The former contained only three songs, the best of which, *Corn Rigs*, was suggested by one of Ramsay's; and, in the latter, only seven additional songs were included, the best being *Green grow the Rashes o'*, related to an old improper song, and *The Gloomy Night*, which is less a song than a personal lament. The others are not in the same rank with these, and one, *No Churchman am I*, in the strain of the bottle songs of the collections, is hardly better than its models.

It is vain to enquire whether, without the example of Ramsay, Fergusson and their contemporaries, Burns would have succeeded so well as he has in his special aim; but he could hardly have succeeded so soon, nor could he have done so in quite the same fashion. In his preface to the Kilmarnock volume, he says that he had 'these two justly admired Scotch poets' often in his 'eye in the following pieces though rather with a view to kindle at their flame than for servile imitation.' A critical study of Burns and these two predecessors will fully corroborate both statements. Another statement is in quite a different category. While scouting servile imitation, he yet disowns pretensions 'to the genius of a Ramsay or the glorious dawnings of the poor unfortunate Fergusson.' On the part of one so greatly gifted, this was a strange declaration enough, whether it expressed his real convictions—as he took care to protest it did—or not. But Burns was always excessively generous in his appreciation of other poets, and his own case was, also, a very exceptional one. Both his social experiences and his knowledge of literature were, at this period of his life, rather circumscribed; and though, as he says, looking 'upon himself as possest of some poetic abilities,' he might hesitate to suppose that he had much scope for the display of genius in singing 'the sentiments and manners' of himself and 'his rustic compeers.' But, however that may be, his glowing tribute to these two predecessors must be taken as evidence of the immense stimulus he had received from them, and the important part they had had in aiding and shaping his poetic ambitions.

The pieces included in the Kilmarnock volume were written when Burns had, though a considerable, still a comparatively limited, acquaintance with English poetry or prose. Exceptionally intelligent and well-informed as was his peasant father, he could not provide his sons with very many books, and these were mainly of a grave and strictly instructive character. One of Burns's school books, Masson's *Collection of Prose and Verse*, contained, however, Gray's *Elegy*, and excerpts from Shakespeare, Addison, Dryden, Thomson and Shenstone. Before 1786, he had, also, in addition to Ramsay, Fergusson and other Scottish versifiers, made acquaintance with several plays of Shakespeare, a portion of Milton, Ossian and the works of Pope, Thomson, Shenstone and Goldsmith. Among prose works, his 'bosom favourites' were *Tristram Shandy* and *The Man of Feeling*; and the influence of both occasionally manifests itself in his verse. *The Lark*, a collection of Scottish and English songs, 'was,' he says, his '*vade mecum*,' and he was also a voluminous reader of 'those Excellent New Songs that are hawked about the country in baskets, or exposed in stalls in the streets.'

The influence of his study of *The Lark* and of the 'New Songs' was shown in various tentative efforts which he did not publish in the Kilmarnock volume—and some of which he did not publish at all—as *Handsome Nell, O Tibbie I hae seen the Day, The Ruined Farmer, The Lass of Cessnock Banks, Here's to the Health* and *My Father was a Farmer*. The roistering songs in *The Jolly Beggars* are also modelled on the songs of the *Collections*, or of Ramsay's *Tea-Table Miscellany*, including even the bard's song, though there is an older model for it; and neither in language nor in poetic form are they so purely Scottish as the graphic vernacular recitativos. Such experiments, again, as *A Tragic Fragment* and *Remorse*—neither of which he published—are inspired by the eighteenth century English poets. In the Kilmarnock volume, these poets, supplemented by the metrical Davidic *Psalms*, are responsible for such pieces as *The Lament, Despondency, Man was made to Mourn, A Prayer in the Prospect of Death* and *To Ruin*, all purely English. Then, *The Cotter's Saturday Night*, in the Spenserian stanza—which Burns got from Beattie, not from Spenser, but which is of purely English descent and had not been used by any Scottish vernacular poet—is a kind of hybrid. Though partly suggested by Fergusson's *Farmer's Ingle*, and professedly descriptive of a lowly Scottish interior and of 'the sentiments and manners' of the Scottish peasants in their more hallowed relations, it is not, like Fergusson's poem, written 'in their native language,' but, substantially, in modern English, with, here and there, a sparse sprinkling of Scottish, or Scoto-English, terms. Much of its tone, many of its sentiments and portions of its phraseology are reminiscent of those of the English poets whom he knew—Milton, Gray, Pope, Thomson and Goldsmith. It is a kind of medley of ideas and phrases partly borrowed from them, mingled with reflections of his own and descriptions partly in their manner but derived from his own experience, and may almost be termed a splendidly specious adaptation rather than a quite original composition. On the whole, the artistic genius and the afflatus of the poet prevail, but in a somewhat shackled, mannered and restrained form, as becomes manifest enough when we compare it with the spontaneous brilliancy of the best of his more vernacular verses in old traditional staves.

In other important pieces in the Scots staves, such as *The Vision* and *The Epistle to Davie*, where the sentiment is mainly of a grave and lofty character, and especially when he abandons his 'native language' for pure English, we have occasional echoes from English poets, though he is sometimes charged with having borrowed from poets he had never read, and with having appropriated from certain English poets sentiments and reflections which were really current coin to be found anywhere. In occasional stanzas of other poems, we also meet with traces of his English reading, but, in the case of the thoroughly vernacular poems, they are so rare and so slight as to be negligible. These poems are Scottish to the core; and it is here that we have the best, the truest and fullest, revelation of his mind and heart. The sentiments, thoughts and moods they express are of a very varied, not always consistent, and sometimes not quite reputable, character; but they are entirely his own, and, such as they are, they are set forth with peculiar freedom and honesty and with rare felicity and vigour, while, in the presentation of manners, scenes and occurrences, he manifests a vivid picturesqueness not surpassed, and seldom excelled, by other writers of verse.

At a later period of his life, Burns—it may be partly at the suggestion of Dr Moore, that he 'should abandon the Scottish stanza and dialect and adopt the measure and dialect of modern English poets'—began to consider the possibility of escaping from his vernacular bonds, and made somewhat elaborate experiments in English after the manner of eighteenth century poets. But, though the mentors of Burns might be excused for giving him this advice, it could not be carried out. It was too late for him to transform himself into a purely English poet; and, in the end, this was perceived by him. In Scots verse, as he wrote to George Thomson, he always found himself at home, but it was quite otherwise when he sought to model himself on English predecessors or contemporaries. He had a quite different poetic mission from theirs; his training, his mode of life, his social circumstances especially fitted one of his temperament and genius to excel as a rustic Scottish bard, and, in this capacity, he compassed achievements, which, apart from their intrinsic merit, possess a special value due to their uniqueness. When, on the other hand, he essays purely English verse, English in method and form as well as language, his strong individuality fails to disclose itself; his artistic sensibilities cease to serve him; his genius remains unkindled; he is merely imitative and badly imitative. *From Esopus to Maria* and the *Epistles to Graham of Fintry* are very indifferent Pope. *Lines on the Fall of Fyers* and *Written with a Pencil at Taymouth* are only inferior Thomson. Such pieces as *Birthday Ode for* 31*st December* 1787, *Ode Sacred to the Memory of Mrs Oswald, Ode to the Departed Regency Bill, Inscribed to the Hon. C. J. Fox* and *Ode to General Washington's Birthday* are all, more or less, strained and bombastic. The ability they display is not so remarkable as its misapplication, and they are, mainly, striking illustrations of the ineffectiveness of a too monotonous and unmeasured indulgence in highflown imagery and bitter vituperation. With certain qualifications and with outstanding exceptions, these remarks apply to his epigrams and epitaphs, but less to those in the vernacular, some of which, even when not quite goodnatured, are exceedingly amusing, as, for example: *In Lamington Kirk, On Captain Grose, On Tam the Chapman, On Holy Willie, On a Wag in Mauchline, On John Dove, Innkeeper* and *On Grizzel Grimme.* *The Bard's Epitaph* is unique as a pathetic anticipation of the sad results of the poet's own temperamental infirmities; and, though in a quite opposite vein, the elegies *On the Death of Robert Ruisseaux* and *On Willie Nicol's Mare* are evidently written *con amore*; but those *On the Death of Sir James Hunter Blair* and *On the Death of Lord President Dundas,* and even that *On the Late Miss Burnet of Monboddo* are, as he candidly confesses of one of them, 'quite mediocre.' They are too elaborately artificial to stir the feelings with mourning and regret; indeed, their inveterately ornate expression of grief seems almost as purely formal and official as that represented in the trappings of funeral mutes. There is more true pathos in the admirable, though mostly humorous, vernacular *Ode to The Departed Year,* 1788; but his elegiac masterpieces are all in the traditional stave in *rime couée.*

The main benefit, as a poet, gained by Burns from what was,

evidently, a close and repeated perusal of certain English poets, was an indirect one. It stimulated his thought, it quickened his sensibilities, it widened his mental outlook, it refined his tastes, it increased his facility in the apt use even of his own 'native language.' In this last respect, he seems to have been specially indebted to Pope. His style is admirable, pellucidly clear and brilliantly concise, and, in his best pieces, the same 'finishing polish' manifests itself. He greatly underrated his own accomplishments, even in 1786, when he modestly declared that he was 'unacquainted with the necessary requisites for commencing Poet by rule'; and Carlyle displays a strange obliviousness or misapplication of facts in affirming that he had merely 'the rhymes of a Fergusson or a Ramsay as his standard of beauty.' To accept this view, while rather slighting at least Fergusson, would ignore the relations of both to the older classics, would fail to take into account what Burns knew of the classics and of the Scottish lyrists of past generations and would disregard the minute study of certain English poets with which he started, and which, later, was not only augmented by a fairly comprehensive course of English reading, but supplemented by a perusal of the chief French poets. He had undergone some intellectual discipline, even if it were a little unsystematic and haphazard. Strikingly exceptional as was his poetic career, it was not inexplicably miraculous. It is quite the reverse of truth to state that he had 'no furtherance but such knowledge as dwells in a poor man's hut'; and, so far as he was concerned, to talk of 'the fogs and darkness of that obscure region,' only tends 'to darken counsel by words without knowledge.' His alleviations and his physical and mental calibre being such as to prevent him succumbing too early to the evils of his lot, he even found himself in a position which specially fitted him to become the great poet of rustic life and the representative Scottish poet that he was.

The character of his environment in itself gave Burns, as a vernacular Scottish poet, a certain advantage over both Ramsay and Fergusson. Though, in the eighteenth century, the vernacular was in fuller, and more general, use in conversation, even by the educated classes in Scotland, than it is now, both these poets made literary use of it with a certain air of condescension, and as the specially appropriate medium of lowly themes. Burns employed it more variously, and often with a more serious and higher intent, than they. He was also in closer and more perpetual contact with humble life than was either of them; the vernacular, as he says, was his 'native language,' the usual medium of the thought and expression of himself and his 'compeers'; and, in his verse, he seems to revel in the appropriation of its direct and graphic phraseology. While, also, as a poet of rustic life, more favourably placed than any of his later Scottish predecessors, he had a special superiority over those poets, Scottish or English, who, as he says, 'with all the advantages of learned art, and perhaps amid the elegances and idlenesses of upper life, looked down on a rural theme.' In the case of a rural theme, he is entirely in his element. Here, he exhibits neither affectation, nor condescension, nor ignorant idealisation, nor cursory and superficial observation; everywhere, there is complete comprehension and living reality. He was himself largely his own rural theme, and he is unstintedly generous in his selfrevelations. Apart, also, from his lyrical successes, he attains to the highest triumphs of his art in depicting the manners and circumstances of himself and his fellow peasants; in exhibiting their idiosyncrasies, good and bad, and those of other personalities, generally, but not always, quite obscure and, sometimes, disreputable, with whom he held intercourse, or who, otherwise, came within the range of his observation; in handling passing incidents and events mainly of local interest; and in dealing with rustic beliefs, superstitions, customs, scenes and occasions. He did not need to set himself to search for themes. He was encompassed by them; they almost forced themselves on his attention; and he wrote as the spirit moved him. His topics and his training being such as they were, his rare endowments are manifested in the manner of his treatment. It betokens an exceptionally penetrating insight, a peculiarly deep sympathy, yet great capacity for scorn, an abounding and comprehensive humour, a strong vitalising vision and a specially delicate artistic sense; and, thus, his opportunities being so close and abundant, he has revealed to us the antique rural life within the limits of his experience and observation with copious minuteness, and with superb vividness and fidelity. But, of course, he has, therefore—though some would fain think otherwise—his peculiar limitations. His treatment of his themes was so admirable as to secure for them almost a worldwide interest; but, ordinarily, his themes do not afford scope for the higher possibilities of poetry. He could not display his exceptional powers to such advantage as he might have done, had he been allowed a wider stage and higher opportunities; nor, in fact, were they trained and developed as they might have been, had he been sufficiently favoured of fortune.

For his vernacular verse, Burns had recourse mainly to the
staves already popularised by Ramsay, Fergusson and other poets
of the revival. As with them, the most common medium of his
verse was the favourite six-line stave in *rime couée,* used by
Sempill in *Habbie Simson.* Following their and Sempill's
example, he usually adopted it for his vernacular elegies, of
which we may here mention those on *Poor Mailie, Tam Samson*
and *Captain Matthew Henderson.* The first, an early production,
is more in the vein of *Habbie* than the other two, and its opening
stanza is almost a parody of that of Sempill's poem. In it and
Tam Samson, he also adopts throughout the Sempill refrain
ending in 'dead'; but, in the more serious elegy *Captain Matthew
Henderson* he has recourse to it in but one verse, and that
accidentally. The *Samson* elegy, like those of Ramsay, is in a
humorous, rather than in a pathetic, vein—a fact accounted for by
the sequel—but the humour is strikingly superior to that of Ramsay
in delicacy, in humaneness, in copious splendour, while the poem
is, also, specially noteworthy for the compactness and polish of its
phrasing. A marked feature of *Tam Samson,* but, more especially,
of the *Henderson* elegy, is the exquisite felicity of the allusions to
nature. This last, the best of the three, is pitched in a different
key from the others; pathos prevails over humour, and the closing
stanzas reach a strain of lofty and moving eloquence.

Following the example of Ramsay and Hamilton of Gilbertfield,
Burns also employed the six-line stave for most of his vernacular
epistles. In their tone and allusions, they are also partly modelled
upon those of his two predecessors, and, occasionally, they parody
lines and even verses, which he had by heart; but they never do this
without greatly bettering the originals. Most of them are almost
extempore effusions, but, on that very account, they possess a
charming naturalness of their own. Special mention may be
made of those to *John Lapraik, James Smith* and *Willie Simpson.*
Here, we have the poet, as it were, in undress, captivating us by
the frankness of his sentiments and selfrevelations, by homely
allusions to current cares and occupations, by plain and pithy
comments on men and things and by light colloquial outbreaks
of wit and humour, varied, occasionally, by enchanting, though,
apparently, quite unstudied, descriptions of the aspects of nature.

One or two of his epistles, as those *To John Rankine,* and
Reply to a Trimming Epistle received from a Taylor, are in a
coarser vein; but, even so, they are equally representative of
himself and of the peasant Scotland of his time. They are

occupied with a theme concerning which the jocosity of the peasant
was inveterate. They are not to be judged by our modern
notions of decorum; and Burns, it may be added, is never so
merely squalid as is Ramsay. In the epistolary form and in the
same stave is *A Poet's Welcome to his Love-Begotten Daughter*,
in which generous human feeling is blended with sarcastic defiance
of the conventions. The attitude of the peasant towards such
casualties had been previously set forth in various chapbooks of
the period, both in prose and verse.

In the same stave as the epistles are *Scotch Drink* and *The
Author's Earnest Cry and Prayer*, which mirror the strong
social sentiments of the Scottish rustic, and the close association
in farming communities—an association still surviving—of strong
drink with good fellowship.

This stave is, further, employed by Burns with superb effect in
the satiric narrative of *Death and Doctor Hornbook*, containing
the eerie midnight interview of the 'canty' bard with the awful
'Something,' whose name, it said, was death, and its grimly jocose
discourse on the medical skill of 'the bauld apothecary,' a village
schoolmaster, who sought to eke out his small salary by the sale of
drugs; but, on the whole, the masterpieces in the stave are *The
Address to the Deil, Holy Willie's Prayer* and *The Auld Farmer's
New Year Salutation to his Mare Maggie*. They differ greatly in
their tone and the character of their theme, but each, after its own
fashion, is inimitable. The first two have an ecclesiastical or theological *motif*. Of these, *The Address to the Deil* is a boldly
humorous sketch of the doings of the evil personality, who figured
prominently in the 'Auld Licht' pulpit oratory of the poet's time
and of the preceding centuries, and became transformed into the
'Auld Hornie,' 'Nickie Ben' and 'Clootie' of peasant conversation
and superstition. It is preceded by a motto of two lines from
Milton's *Paradise Lost*, 'O Prince,' etc., which piquantly contrast
in tone and tenor with the opening verse of the poem itself, the first
two lines—a kind of parody of a couplet in Pope's *Dunciad*—being

> O thou! whatever title suit thee,
> Auld Hornie, Satan, Nick or Clootie.

The tone of comic humour is maintained throughout, and, in
the last stanza, as in the second, comicality and pathos are
delicately blended in suggesting scepticism of the diabolic personality's existence:

> I am wae to think upo' yon den
> Ev'n for your sake.

Apart from its weird comedy, the poem is remarkable for the graphic and condensed vividness of its descriptions, as, to quote only a few lines and phrases:

> Whyles on the strong-winged tempest flyin,
>> Tirlin' the kirks
> Or where auld ruined castles grey
>> Nod to the moon
> Aft yont the dyke she heard you bummin
>> Wi' eerie drone
> Awa ye squattered, like a drake,
>> On whistling wings

Holy Willie's Prayer, again, is wholly satirical in tone, a mere metrical chain of brilliantly relentless mockery. This mockery is made to serve both a general and a special purpose. While, by a skilful series of burlesque parodies, it exposes, with deadly effect, the hypocritical selfrighteousness of an ignorantly opinionated ruling elder in Mauchline, who had a prominent part in an unsuccessful prosecution of the poet's friend and landlord, Gavin Hamilton, it, also, lampoons the narrow puritanic Calvinism of the 'Auld Licht' party in the kirk, towards whom Burns, being what he was, was bound to cherish an almost un- measured antipathy. The antipathy, only indirectly and in glimpses revealed in *The Address to the Deil*, is, in *The Twa Herds*, in portions of *The Holy Fair*, in *The Ordination* and in *The Kirk's Alarm*, manifested in the form of uproarious derision. Though, in his later years, something of a social democrat, and, even from early manhood, cherishing a certain jealousy of those above him in station, and easily offended by airs of con- descension towards him, his antipathy to the 'Auld Licht' clergy, the favourites of the people, made him a strong opponent of the anti-patronage movement, which he contemptuously scouted as an attempt to 'get the brutes themselves the power to choose their herds.' The proposal is, incidentally, ridiculed with great gusto in *The Twa Herds*—in the six-line stave—but more at length and more directly in *The Ordination*, while the jingling *Kirk's Alarm* deals very unceremoniously with the characters and qualifications of the principal clerical prosecutors in a heresy case; but these three pieces, though admirably fitted to arouse the derision of the multitude, are a little too boisterous and violent. For us, at least, they would have been more effective had they been less lacking in restraint; and their method cannot compare with the mock seriousness, the polished innuendo, the withering irony, the placid scorn of *Holy Willie's Prayer*.

But, vastly and variously entertaining as are his ecclesiastical diatribes, these controversial topics have now lost much of their savour even for Scotsmen; and it is a relief to turn from such bitter and mocking satires, and the old ecclesiastical disputes they embalm, to the scene of rustic concord, content and happiness conjured up in *The Auld Farmer's Salutation.* Here, the poet's rustic heart-strings are touched, and his tenderer and more genial feelings have full, uninterrupted play. He is at peace with the world and himself, and his appeal is primarily to our benevolent sympathies. In language more thoroughly and curiously vernacular than that of most of his verse and with an air of artless and frank simplicity, just as if the words had come from the lips of the hearty old farmer, it supplies a realistic biographic sketch of the lifelong partnership between him and his favourite mare Maggie— their mingled toils and pleasures and their joint achievements from the time when, in the bringing home of his 'bonnie Bride,' the mare outran all the other steeds of the company, until he and she had 'come to crazy years together'; and all is so delicately true to nature as to entitle the poem to rank as a kind of unique masterpiece.

The Auld Farmer's Salutation is partly, but only imperfectly, paralleled in *Poor Mailie, The Death and Dying Words of Poor Mailie* and in portions of *The Twa Dogs*; but, in these, it is more the animals themselves than their owner and his relations with them that are portrayed; his connection with them is only indirectly hinted. Again, *To a Mouse,* delicately fine as are its descriptive stanzas, and strikingly as it appeals to the sense of the hard case of a large part of the animal creation in their relations to one another and to man, hardly expresses the sentiments of the average ploughman or farmer and, it may be, not altogether those of Burns. Here, and in *To a Mountain Daisy,* he partly assumes the 'sensibility' pose; and English influence is also specially visible in the character of the reflection in the concluding stanzas. In striking contrast with both is the broad rustic humour of *To a Louse.* While all three— in the same six-line stave—are but sparsely sprinkled with the pure vernacular, it is in the last employed here and there with graphic drollery. But, in this stave more particularly, Burns could write occasional stanzas in pure English to splendid purpose, as witness the nobly serious poem *The Vision,* though, in the opening stanzas depicting the poet's rustic situation and sur-roundings, he, with admirable discretion, has recourse mainly to the vernacular.

Next to the six-line stave in *rime couée,* the favourite stave of Ramsay, Fergusson and other poets of the revival was what may be termed the *Christis Kirk* stave, which, though probably the invention of the author of that poem and of *Peblis to the Play,* is, also, the metre of what—from a reference of Sir David Lyndsay— must be regarded as a very old poem, *Sym and his Brudir,* and is used by Alexander Scott in his *Justing and Debait.* It is formed by the addition of a bobwheel to the old ballad octave in rollicking metre as represented in, for example, *The Hunting of the Cheviots,* and Henryson's *Robene and Makyne.* Burns, like Ramsay and Fergusson, contracted the bobwheel into a refrain of one line ; but, unlike Ramsay, he did not vary the ending of the refrain. He uses the stave for five pieces: *The Holy Fair, Halloween, The Ordination, A Dream* and *The Mauchline Wedding* and for a recitativo in *The Jolly Beggars.* In *Halloween* and in *The Jolly Beggars* recitativo, the final word of the refrain is 'night'; in the others, it is 'day.' In *A Dream, The Ordination* and the recitativo, he, like Ramsay, adheres to the ancient two-rime form of the octave ; but, in *The Holy Fair, Halloween* and *The Mauchline Wedding,* he follows Fergusson in breaking up the octave and making use of four and, occasionally, three, rimes. *A Dream* is really a series of advices, mostly couched in semi-satirical or jocular terms, but, notwithstanding some clever epigrams, it must, on the whole, be reckoned of that order of merit to which most of his political, or semipolitical pieces belong. *The Ordination* has been already referred to. Like it, the other three—as in the case of *Christis Kirk* and other old poems, as well as those of the revival—are humorously descriptive narratives. *The Mauchline Wedding* is unfinished; *The Holy Fair* and *Halloween,* as presentations of scenes and episodes in humble life, rank, almost, with *The Jolly Beggars* and *Tam o' Shanter,* though they lack the full inspiration and irresistible *verve* of both.

The Holy Fair, in its general form, is modelled on Fergusson's *Leith Races* and his *Hallow Fair.* Like them, it is the narrative of a day's diversion and, like them, it concludes with a hint that the result of the day's pleasuring may, in some cases, be not altogether edifying or pleasant. In intent, it differs somewhat from them. Unlike them, it has a definite satirical purpose, and there runs throughout a prevailing strain of ridicule, though not so much of his fellow peasants—whose idiosyncrasies and doings are portrayed with a certain humorous toleration—as of the occasion itself, and of the oratorical flights, especially of the 'Auld Licht' clergy, whom Burns makes the subjects of his unsparing wit. The first six stanzas are a kind of parody of the first five of Fergusson's *Leith Races*, but, however excellent, in their way, are Fergusson's verses, the parody by Burns, in picturesque vivacity and in glowing realism, quite surpasses the original. It has further been pointed out that certain stanzas resemble rather closely, in their tenor, portions of a pamphlet published in 1759, *A Letter from a Blacksmith to the Ministers and Elders of the Church of Scotland.* Burns probably knew the pamphlet. It may have partly helped to suggest the writing of the poem; and, having a very retentive memory, he may have got a phrase or two from it; but, throughout the whole poem, it is evident enough that he is describing the details of an actual 'sacramental occasion' in Mauchline, from his own direct knowledge; and, whatever small hints he may have got from the pamphlet, his matchless sketch of the humours of the oldworld scene of mingled piety, superstition and rude rustic joviality owes its rare merit to his own penetrating observation and vivifying genius.

But, *Halloween* is the finer poem of the two—mainly, because mere satire is absent and mirthful humour prevails. It conjures up a quite different rustic scene, one where ecclesiasticism, either to good or bad purpose, does not intrude; and all is pure fun and merriment. He had a suggestion for the poem in Mayne's *Halloween*, and faint reflections of it, as well as of lines in Montgomerie, Ramsay, Fergusson, Thomson and Pope, are discernible in some of the stanzas, just as similar faint reminiscences of their predecessors or contemporaries are discernible in the work of most poets of eminence; but they do not affect in the slightest the main texture of the poem, which, throughout, is, characteristically, his own. In the fine opening stanza, he adds to the descriptive effect by introducing internal rimes:

Upon that night when fairies light,

and he has also partial recourse to this device in some other stanzas. Near the close of the poem, he suspends, for a moment, his mirthful narrative of the Halloween adventures and misadventures to surprise and enchant us by his consummate picture of the meanderings of a woodland stream:

Whyles owre a linn the burnie plays.

But this is a mere casual interlude. It is with the exploits and ludicrous mishaps of the 'merry, friendly country folks' that the poem is chiefly concerned.

Another important stave of Burns is that used by Montgomerie in *The Cherrie and The Slae*. In this stave, Thomas Howell also wrote *A Dreame*, published in his *Devises* 1581[1]; but *The Cherrie and The Slae* was, probably, written before Howell's poem; and, in any case, there is proof of the use of the stave in Scotland before Howell's volume appeared, and of its earliest use by a Scottish poet having been by Montgomerie: *Ane Ballat of ye Captane of the Castell* (1571), is described as 'maid to the tone of *The Bankis of Helicon*,' of which Montgomerie was the author. The peculiarity of the stave is the final wheel of four—properly six—lines, borrowed from a stave of the old Latin hymns, and affixed to a ten-line stave, common from an early period in English verse.

Though revived by Ramsay for *The Vision* and other poems, there are not any examples of it in Fergusson. With Burns, however, *The Cherrie and The Slae*, which he had doubtless seen in Watson's *Choice Collection*, was a special favourite, and he refers to *The Epistle to Davie* as in the metre of that poem. Besides *The Epistle to Davie*, he had recourse to it for *To the Guidwife of Wauchope House*, and for the purely English *Despondency*, *To Ruin*, *Inscribed on a Work of Hannah More's* and *The Farewell*. All these, more or less, are gravely reflective or didactic in tone, as, indeed, is also *The Cherrie and The Slae*; but, in the two opening, and the final, recitativos of the boisterous *Jolly Beggars*, he made use of it for humorous descriptive purposes with a picturesque felicity not surpassed in verse.

For the other descriptive recitativos of this unique cantata, he employed the ballad octave of two rimes, of which there is also an example in his *Man was made to Mourn*; the French octave or ballad royal (which, though not found in Ramsay or Fergusson, was used by Alexander Pennecuick for his semi-vernacular *Truth's Travels*, but which Burns—who, later, used it for the *Lament* and the *Address to Edinburgh*—probably got from *The Evergreen*), very properly recommended by James VI for 'heich and grave subjects,' but, on that very account, all the more effective where gravity is burlesqued; the octo-syllabic couplet, used, also, in *The Twa Dogs* and *Tam o' Shanter*; the six-line stave in *rime couée*; the common ballad stave of four rimes, of which there are various

---

[1] See *ante*, vol. III, p. 188.

examples in Ramsay, and to which Burns had recourse for *An Address to the Unco Guid* and *Epistle to a Young Friend*; and the *Christis Kirk* stave. The cantata thus samples all his principal Scots staves, though omitting the *Sir Thopas* stave of *The Epistle to Lord Daer* and *Fintry My Stay*, the modified *Killychrankie* form of the ballad stave, as exemplified in *Guildford Good* and the heroic couplet of the partly English and partly Scots *Brigs of Ayr*. Compact and short as are the recitativos of *The Jolly Beggars*, Burns never employed their staves to more brilliant purpose. The songs, again, with which they are interspersed, are, as already stated, modelled after those to be found in the *Choice Song-Books* or in Herd's *Collection*; and very similar songs, though ruder in their form and coarser in their expression, may actually have been sung by different members of the ragged fraternity, in the course of the carousal of which Burns was a witness.

Burns was unacquainted with the bulk of old English plays, treatises and songs, dealing with the fortunes of beggars, vagabonds and outlaws; but he had probably read Gay's *Beggars' Opera*; he knew, of course, the clever Scottish ballads *The Gaberlunzie Man* and *The Jolly Beggar*; and he evidently got faint hints from *The Happy Beggars*—an excerpt from Charles Coffey's ballad opera, *The Beggars' Wedding*—and *The Merry Beggars* of Ramsay's *Tea-Table Miscellany* and the song-books. The poem is, also, modelled on the burlesque odes and cantatas of the period; but the wonder is that, such being the case, the curious metrical medley should be such a captivating masterpiece. True, it has a certain advantage, even in its complete singularity, as an assortment of old Scottish staves, interlaced with songs characteristically Scots or Anglo-Scots in their style and manner. All this aids the vivid picturesqueness of the presentation; but only the fact that the subject appealed, in a very special way, to peculiarities of the poet's temperament and genius can account for the striking character of his artistic triumph.

Carlyle was the first to claim for *The Jolly Beggars* a superiority over *Tam o' Shanter*. Few, perhaps, will admit so complete a superiority as he asserts, but the value of the criticism, so far as regards the praise of *The Jolly Beggars*, originally, in many quarters, only faintly tolerated, is now generally admitted. Here, we have a more varied and more intimate and vital presentation of certain types of human nature than in *Tam o' Shanter*; and the detailed record of the vagabonds' high festival affords wider scope for picturesque effects than the comparatively conventional and respectable carousal in the village alehouse.   On the other hand, it seems a strange belittlement or misjudgment of *Tam o' Shanter* to describe it as less a poem than 'a piece of sparkling rhetoric,' and a still more questionable statement that it 'might have been written all but quite as well by a man who, in place of genius, had only possessed talent.'   Most other critics are still convinced that here, as in *The Jolly Beggars*, we have a superbly characteristic example of the rare genius of Burns, as developed by his special environment and his peculiarly mingled poetic training.   Scott says: 'I verily believe *Tam o' Shanter* to be inimitable, both in the serious and ludicrous parts, as well as in the happy combination of both.'   As to the relative merits of the two poems, *Tam o' Shanter* is the more studied and mature production: when he wrote it, Burns was a more fully experienced, a better-read and a more highly trained, artist, than when, in a fit of fine inspiration, he dashed off *The Jolly Beggars*; and he himself says of it that it 'shewed a finishing polish,' which he 'despaired of ever excelling.'   The felicity and terse compactness and vividness of its phrasing—notwithstanding an occasional looseness, as was customary with him, in riming—are unsurpassable; and, as for the alehouse fellowship of Tam and Souter Johnie, and the skelping ride of the primed farmer through the eerie region in the wild night, genius could hardly better these; while the thunder and lightning storm, and the witches' hornpipes and reels at haunted Alloway, with Auld Nick himself as musician, are certainly more strictly poetical and more thrilling than the presentation of squalid revelry in the low Mauchline lodging-house.   But the poems are really so dissimilar in theme and method that a comparison of their respective merits is somewhat difficult and, more or less, futile.   In both, Burns affords us a more splendid glimpse than elsewhere of his poetic possibilities, had fortune favoured their full development.

But the dilemma of Burns was that the very circumstances which favoured him in making him become the unique peasant poet that he was, tended, also, to preclude the adequate fulfilment of his poetic aspirations; and there were, also, certain peculiarities in his case which made the adverse circumstances in the end all-powerful.   Thus, apart from songs, *Tam o' Shanter* and *Captain Matthew Henderson* are the only poems of any special importance produced by him after 1787; though various election pieces, if not particularly excellent specimens of wit, cleverly reproduce the manner and style of the old ballads.   Except as a song-writer, the really fruitful period of his genius is confined to the year or two, when, together with other members of the family, he occupied Mossgiel, in the stable-loft bothy of which—where, for lack of room in the farmhouse, he took up his quarters with the farm-servant—he, in the evening, elaborated the verses he had been conning over during his daily avocations. Hard and toilsome as was his daily round of labour, and dreary and disappointing as were his immediate prospects as a farmer, the horizon of his future had not yet been definitely circumscribed and hope was still strong within him. While his misfortunes as a farmer overset, as he says, his wisdom, made him careless of worldly success and caused him to seek consolation in social diversions not always of a quite harmless character, they augmented, rather than diminished, his poetic ambitions; and when, after the enthusiastic reception in Ayrshire of the Kilmarnock volume, he left the plough to seek his fortune in Edinburgh, it was probably with high hopes of a possible future essentially different from his bleak and toilsome past.

To pass immediately from his lowly toil and from the rustic scenes and company of Mossgiel and Mauchline to the fashionable society of the capital and the learned and cultured converse of its lawyers, professors and doctors might well seem a rather adventurous experiment; but, what might have proved, even to most persons of ability in his position, a very trying ordeal, was, to him, a highly interesting and entertaining experience; and, as regards his main errand, he was successful quite beyond his highest expectations. Through the introduction of Dalrymple of Orangefield, the earl of Glencairn and the famous advocate Henry Erskine, brother of the eccentric earl of Buchan, took him, as he says, 'under their wing'; and, at the instance of Glencairn, William Creech, the chief Edinburgh publisher of the time, whose levees were frequented by all the distinguished dignitaries and *literati* of the city, condescended to undertake the publication of the proposed volume of his verse.

Meantime, the social popularity of the 'illiterate ploughman of Ayrshire,' so 'Jupiter' Carlyle terms him, was quite extraordinary. In the houses of the gentry he was warmly welcomed as a kind of rustic wonder; and he charmed everyone by his perfect, yet modest, selfpossession, and the easy felicity of his conversation. His 'address to females'—as recorded by Scott from the testimony of the duchess of Gordon—while extremely deferential, had always 'a turn to the humorous or the pathetic which engaged their attention particularly'; and the duchess affirms that she never 'saw a man in company with his superiors in station and information more perfectly free from either the reality or the affectation of embarrassment.' The fact was that, whatever his deficiencies in certain kinds of information, and his ignorance of the current interests of the higher Edinburgh circles, he had a remarkable ease in estimating the character and mental calibre of those with whom he held intercourse. He, therefore, soon recognised that, at least in natural gifts, he was the inferior of none with whom he mingled; and, even in the more learned companies, he did not hesitate to express his own opinions, sometimes with greater emphasis than was customary in polite society, but, says Hugh Walker, 'though somewhat authoritative, it was in a way that gave little offence.' Dugald Stewart further tells us that Burns charmed him 'still more by his private conversation than he had ever done in company.' But, in the society of the middle-class burghers, in taverns where memories still lingered of Ramsay and Fergusson, and, more especially, in the company of the jovial and outspoken wits of the Crochallan club, he was more entirely at his ease, and, doubtless, shone more brilliantly than in the somewhat grave and constrained circles frequented by Dugald Stewart.

What, however, we have more especially to note, is his supreme popularity everywhere, and the effect of his social success on the subscriptions to his forthcoming volume. No fewer than three thousand copies were printed—a remarkable number for a book of rustic verse, and twice as many as were contemplated when the book was sent to press—for one thousand five hundred subscribers, Creech himself subscribing for five hundred copies, and purchasing for one hundred pounds the copyright of any subsequent editions. Burns, in the end, gained five hundred pounds by his Edinburgh venture, as compared with twenty pounds for the six hundred copies of the Kilmarnock volume. He was now completely relieved from the stress of poverty which had been his sore affliction from childhood. Petted and *fêted* by Edinburgh grandees, he might almost have fancied that he had passed into another world than that of his sordid past. With his greatly widened fame as a poet, and with many influential friends to further his interests, he might surely count on a future comparatively free from the old worldly anxieties by which he had, hitherto, been greatly hampered, and latterly almost overwhelmed, so that he had been meditating escape from them, by becoming, as he states, 'a poor negro-driver,' in Jamaica. Soon, however, he discovered that his patrons, greatly as they were charmed by his rustic personality, and much as they admired his rustic muse, had but lowly notions of the sphere of activity that was suitable for him. All that, apart from subscriptions to his volume, he ever obtained through his patrons—and he obtained even this with difficulty—was a nomination for the excise. Only one of his new friends, Mrs Dunlop, manifested any deep concern about his future well-being. She advised him to become a candidate for the then discussed chair of agriculture in Edinburgh university; and, likewise, mentioned to him the possibility of his becoming a salt officer, the duties of which would be both pleasanter and less engrossing than those of the excise. But, neither of these, or other, suggestions made by her bore fruit. Dugald Stewart affirms that, from the conversation of Burns, he 'should have pronounced him to be fitted to excel in whatever walk of ambition he had chosen to exert his abilities'; and his aptitudes, doubtless, were great and various; but, then, his circumstances were exceptional and he had the defects of his qualities. Had he been less entangled with his obscure and somewhat tumultuous past, and had he practically known more than he did of 'prudent, cautious self control,' he might well have been able to have secured for himself a fair amount of worldly success as an Edinburgh citizen. But, even his flirtations with Mrs Maclehose, to say nothing of other amatory adventures in the capital, would have rendered his settlement there a rather unwise experiment; and, besides, having, at last, as a man of some means, and, even, of great repute, found favour in the eyes of the parents of his rustic sweetheart, Jean Armour, and having come to the conclusion that 'humanity, generosity, honest pride of character and justice to' his 'happiness in after life' necessitated his acknowledging her as his wife, he resolved to banish from his thoughts whatever brighter day dreams he might have cherished and to venture what, after a loan to his brother, remained of his small capital, in the lease of the farm of Ellisland, Dumfriesshire.

While this was, perhaps, the best resolve that, in the circumstances, he could have taken, it was rather with chastened and placid resignation than with perfect content that he decided to return to the old occupation associated from his childhood with years of hopeless drudgery. In a letter to his special friend, William Dunbar, he refers to his Edinburgh sojourn as 'my late hare-brained ramble into life'; and, from various expressions in his other letters, it is clear that, great as was both the social and material success of his Edinburgh venture, he had cherished certain anticipations about it which were only in part fulfilled. He had set out to the capital, apparently with some hope that he might escape from his past and begin a new life. In this, he was disappointed, and Edinburgh was, ever afterwards, very sour grapes to him. In one letter, he remarks that, in his 'scene of domestic comfort the bustle of Edinburgh will soon be a business of sickening disgust'; but we seem to have a better insight into the real state of his feelings, when, in reference to the friendships he had formed there, he writes to Dunbar: 'from my uncouthness when out of my native sphere and my obscurity in that sphere, I am obliged to give most of them up in despair of a mutual return.' Partly, it may be, from his own faults, but, mainly, owing to his previous circumstances, he felt himself a kind of alien in the sphere of life which best accorded with his aspirations; and, though the 'obscurity' of his position is always referred to by him in a manly and independent fashion, his rooted discontent manifested itself more and more as time went on.

> The heart of man and the fancy of the poet [he wrote to Mrs Dunlop] are the two grand considerations for which I live; if miry ridges and dirty dunghills are to express the best part of the functions of my soul immortal, I had better have been a rook or a magpie at once.

The support of his wife and family was always his first care, but the only thing that made his social 'obscurity' tolerable to him was the hope that, as a farmer, he might enjoy sufficient leisure and sufficient freedom from care to enable him, as he put it, 'to pay court to the tuneful sisters.' To Lady Elizabeth Cunningham he wrote: 'I had the most ardent enthusiasm for the muses when nobody knew me but myself, and that ardour is by no means cooled now that My Lord Glencairn's goodness has introduced me to all the world.' To bishop Geddes, brother of the poet, he intimated his determination 'to try if the ripening and corrections of years' could enable him 'to produce something worth preserving,' and he proposed to communicate to him when he saw him in Edinburgh, 'some large poetic plans that are floating,' so he writes, 'in my head, or partly put in execution.' Of these plans, he makes more definite mention in a letter to Lady Elizabeth Cunningham. He was, he said, not 'in haste for the press,' and he continues:

> I am aware that though I were to give performances to the world superior to my former works, still if they were of the same kind with those, the

comparative reception they would meet with would mortify me. For this reason I am determined if possible to secure my great friend Novelty on my side by the kind of my performances;

and he further went on to say that he had 'thoughts on the drama':

not the stately busk of the Tragic Muse, but considering the favourite things of the day, the two or three act Pieces of O'Keefe, Mrs Inchbald etc.—does not your Ladyship think that an Edin. Theatre would be more amused with the affectation, folly and whim of true Scottish growth, than manners which by far the greatest part of the audience can only know at second hand?

Later, with a view to some such purpose, he set himself to collect the works of English and French dramatic authors.

Doubtless, in cherishing such intentions, as in his occasional experiments in purely English verse, Burns was partly influenced by the comparatively low esteem in which Scots vernacular verse was then held by the more cultured of his countrymen. Some have also expressed the opinion that, in contemplating becoming a dramatist of any kind, he was mistaking his true vocation as much as he did in aspiring to become an accomplished English poet. Necessarily, he was lacking in stagecraft; but, then, he had a marvellous genius for comedy, and anything he wrote was certain to be at least delightfully amusing reading. Even at the worst, he might have considerably eclipsed Ramsay's *Gentle Shepherd*; indeed, when we consider that *The Jolly Beggars* was the random product of his early and untutored years, it is difficult to say what he might not have accomplished as a writer of, at least, a certain type of comedy-opera libretto.

Then, in the *Tam o' Shanter* of his more mature and more fully disciplined genius, he did actually achieve a splendid success in a species of verse quite different from any of his earlier pieces; and, given the leisure that assists inclination, he might well have delighted the world with a series of similar tales. But the melancholy fact is, that, apart from songs, it remains almost the one solitary sign that he had it in him to fulfil the promise of his Mossgiel productions by the execution of more mature and finished work. Notwithstanding his repeatedly expressed resolve 'to produce something worth preserving,' he never did seriously set himself to carry out his meditated plans; no trace was found among his papers of even abortive attempts to do so. The last nine years of his life—the period when his powers might be supposed to be at their best—were, apart from songs, almost a poetic blank. He may have been partly led astray by a passing ambition to excel in English verse; but the chief explanation seems to be that, as he well might, he partly succumbed, doubtless, at first, reluctantly, but, in the end, apathetically, to his circumstances. The mere return to his old farming tasks, implying, as it did, the definite dissipation of his more sanguine day-dreams, was, however brave a face he might put on it, a very disheartening experience ; and, when, to the old gin-horse round of toil and care was conjoined the old impossibility of making farming pay, his highest poetic intentions were bound to remain unfulfilled. By obtaining an excise commission for his own rural district with a salary of fifty pounds, he was able to save himself from bankruptcy ; but this supplement to his income did little more ; and, all things considered, he concluded that his only chance of bettering himself in life was through the excise. Having, therefore, at a break in the lease, relinquished his farm, he removed to Dumfries at a salary of seventy pounds, which, in September 1792, when he was appointed port officer, was raised to ninety pounds ; but this was the extent of his promotion, for his outspoken approbation of the French revolutionaries, both in conversation and in occasional verse, brought him into bad odour with his official superiors and even endangered the retention of his office. This greatly embittered and disheartened him ; towards his closing years, he partly lost hope ; and his higher poetic ambitions remained in suspense until fate conclusively decided against them by the long painful illness which, 21 July 1796, terminated in his death.

Happily, however, he all along found some encouragement and opportunity for the exercise of his gifts as a song writer. While in Edinburgh, he made the acquaintance of James Johnson, an engraver and music-seller, who was then preparing the first volume of his *Scots Musical Museum.* To the first volume, he contributed two songs ; and, from the autumn of 1787 almost until his death, he was largely both literary and musical editor of the work. He wrote the prefaces probably of volume II and certainly of volumes III and IV ; volume V did not appear until shortly after his death, but it includes some of his best songs and adaptations, among them *A Red, Red Rose, Auld Lang Syne* and *It was a' for our Richtfu' King* ; while volume VI, though not published until 1803—doubtless largely due to the lack of his supervising help—was in course of preparation before his death, and contains some twenty of his contributions. All that he did for the publication was, with him, a mere labour of love. He received no remuneration for it, nor would he have accepted any. In his efforts on its behalf, he was influenced partly by the desire to help 'a good, worthy, honest fellow' in a patriotic undertaking, the lucrative character of which was very doubtful, and which, without his guidance and help, seemed almost certain to collapse. But to assist in it was, besides, a pure delight : he confided to the poet Skinner that he had 'been absolutely crazed about the project,' and was 'collecting stanzas and every information respecting their origin, authors, etc.' Most of this did not involve any protracted mental effort. He could amend songs with easy facility, and he could even partly compose others during his labours on the farm, or in the course of his excise excursions, which, also, supplied him with opportunities for obtaining old songs and airs from tradition.

While Burns was still busy assisting Johnson, George Thomson —a government clerk in Edinburgh and an amateur musician— invited him, in September 1792, to contribute songs to his *Scottish Airs with Poetry*, to which Pleyel had promised accompaniments; and, without remitting his diligence in assisting Johnson, he could not resist immediately informing Thomson how delighted he was with his proposal, which, he said, 'will positively add to my enjoyment in complying with it.' But, though Thomson, also, mentioned that he would pay him any reasonable price he might demand for his contributions, Burns replied : 'As to remuneration, you may think my songs either *above* or *below* price, for they shall absolutely be the one or the other.' In his difficult worldly circumstances, it was a noble, though almost Quixotic, resolve ; but, apart from the fact that he was not receiving any remuneration from Johnson, he was determined to be influenced by no other considerations than love of his art, and to be perfectly free and independent in the exercise of it. He did not object to change lines and words when he thought that, while satisfying his own judgment, he might better meet the wishes of Thomson ; he did not resent even Thomson's most absurd suggestions; but he was adamant when convinced that any alterations would be for the worse, though he told Thomson repeatedly, and evidently with perfect candour, that he would not be in any degree offended by his rejection of any songs that did not please him.

The prosecution of his art, even in this circumscribed fashion, became, to Burns, the sheet-anchor of his life, and his main solace during the troubles and frustrations of his later years. On the whole, the best of his work was that which he did for Johnson. He began it when hope was still high within him, and here he was,

besides, his own editor. Moreover, although, in his first letter to
Thomson, he had written: '*Apropos*, if you are for *English*
verses there is an end of the matter,' he was ultimately induced,
entirely against his better judgment, to oblige Thomson by not
unfrequently breaking his resolution. 'Whether in the simplicity,'
so he had written, 'of the Ballad or the pathos of the Song, I can
only hope to please myself in being allowed at least a sprinkling
of my native tongue'; and the justness of his preference is
abundantly proved by his performances.

If lyric verse did not afford Burns adequate scope for the
exercise of his best poetic powers, it quite accorded with a certain
strain of his complex personality. He found an entirely congenial medium for the expression of poetic emotion and
sympathetic humour, and the exercise of his rare artistic
sensibilities, in writing new songs to old airs, in giving a new,
and an artistically improved, expression to some of the freer
songs of tradition, in inimitable amendments of other old songs—
sometimes merely by the substitution, here and there, of a new
word, or phrase, or line, or the partial reconstruction of a stanza;
often by a combined process of omission, condensation and
addition, so that a merely halting and vulgar, if, in some respects,
clever, doggerel ditty, becomes transformed into a noble and
finished masterpiece; or, again, by utilising merely the burden
or chorus of an old song, or a mere fragment of verse preserved
in floating tradition, so as, while preserving the spirit and
essence of the sentiment, to inspire it with higher emotional
efficacy and provide it with the artistic setting necessary for its
full lyrical expression. Unlike many song writers, he, also, even
when the words were entirely his own, wrote his songs for
particular airs, and most of them for old traditional airs, some
of which he himself collected. His inspiration was thus, in part,
derived from the old national music.

> Until [so he wrote to Thomson] I am a complete master of a tune in my
> own singing (such as it is) I never can compose for it. My way is: I consider
> the poetic sentiment corresponding to my idea of the musical expression;
> then choose my theme.

Again, even of the advantage of having only the old title, when
the song has been lost, and 'composing the rest of the verses
to suit that line,' he says:

> This has always a finer effect than composing English words, or words
> with an idea foreign to the spirit of the old title. When old titles of songs
> convey any idea at all, they will generally be found to be quite in the spirit of
> the air.

But, apart from the burden, or the fragments, or the title, or the air, much of his direct lyrical inspiration was derived from, or modified by, the past. Here, it was not Ramsay or Fergusson, or any other bards of the revival that he strove to emulate, but 'the glorious old bards' of an earlier period. The special character of his success, even when the theme was entirely his own, was largely due to his comprehensive knowledge of old minstrelsy; he was pervaded by its spirit, and, besides fashioning his verses for its music, moulded them in the manner of its expression. It was, also, mainly because of the large and various inheritance of old verse, which he was free to manipulate and reshape, that he was able to supply the world with so rich an assortment of popular songs, and, more especially, to appeal in them, so fully and irresistibly as he does, to Scottish sentiment and emotion. The best of his lyrics—both those entirely or mainly his own and those which he partly refashioned or almost re-created—differ entirely in their manner and spirit from those of the principal English poets. Much of their special virtue derives from their antique ingenuousness and simplicity, and the marvellous art of Burns is manifested in the manner in which, while preserving the antique charm, he has enriched each song with his own individual vitality. Only an exceptional poetic artist could have so finely utilised Burns's opportunities, but his opportunities were, themselves, exceptional. His peasant origin and environment specially aided him in preserving the primitive simplicity of the old songs; and his achievements as lyrist indicate, also, extraordinary gifts of sympathy, humour, sentiment and emotion, combined with a great mastery of expression and a singularly delicate artistic sense; but they could never have been so great, varied and unique as they are, except for his partial partnership with older bards.

To give a few illustrations. The lyric by which he is best known throughout the world is *Auld Lang Syne*: its universal and immortal popularity depends on the fine fervour and simplicity of its appeal to old memories of social fellowship; but it is not wholly Burns's own: he got its burden and the essence of its sentiment, however defectively it was expressed, from an old anonymous song, itself derived from an ancient and lost original. Again, of *MacPherson's Farewell* and specially of the chorus, Carlyle remarks: 'Who, except Burns, could have given words to such a soul?' This is true enough, but Carlyle did not know that the chorus of Burns is merely a masterly modification of that of a broadside, contemporary with MacPherson's execution, from which, moreover, the whole outlaw sentiment of the song—matchless though its expression of the sentiment is—is borrowed. A much less striking but, so far as the theme would permit, equally complete, example of the deftness of Burns in utilising the burden and sentiment of an old song is *Up in the Morning Early*. 'The chorus of this,' he himself tells us, 'is old; the two stanzas are mine'; but, had he not got the chorus, he would not have written the stanzas, nor could he have written anything at all resembling them. Those three lyrics differ widely in their sentiment and manner, but this, mainly, because in each case, Burns borrowed the sentiment and the manner of different old songs.

Of another, and quite dissimilar, method of utilisation we have an example in the piquantly humorous sketch of rustic courtship in *Duncan Davison*. The song was suggested by, and borrowed something from, an old song of the same name in *The Merry Muses*; but its last stanza is, as regards the first half, a mere assortment of lines borrowed from old ballads and songs, while the second half was snatched almost verbally from the Herd MS. As illustrating his art of re-creation, in which a matchless process of revision is combined with condensation, omissions and slight additions, it may suffice to mention *How Lang and Drearie is the Night, Charlie he's my Darling, A Red, Red Rose* and *It was a' for our Richtfu' King*. The two last rank with the very finest specimens of lyric verse; and many would rank them above any of Burns's songs of which the *motif* was entirely his own. True, most Scots probably agree with Carlyle that *Scots Wha hae* is the best war ode 'ever written by any pen'; but, here, there is a possibility of patriotic bias. There are some, again, who think that Burns reached the height of his achievement in *Is there for Honest Poverty*, which, though a kind of parody of an older song, or older songs, is, like *Scots Wha hae*, Burns to the core, and, though not faultless as regards the temper of its philosophy, offers, on the whole, a splendidly glowing forecast of the final triumph of human worth over all artificial restrictions; but the piece is apt to be overestimated or underestimated according to the predilections of the reader.

Of the more purely lyrical pieces which he claims as his own, though they are suggested by older songs, characteristic examples are *John Anderson My Jo, O Merry Hae I been, What Can a Young Lassie, Wha is that at My Bower Door, O Leeze me on my Spinnin Wheel* and *Comin Thro' the Rye.* On the other hand, while the majority of his lyrics were not expressive of sentiments due to his actual experience, and, though some of this sort—especially the artificial kind produced for Thomson by putting himself 'in the regimen of adoring a fine woman'—are but mediocre, they also include such varied and excellent specimens of his art as *The Rantin Dog the Daddie O't, Of a' the Airts, The Banks o' Doon, Ye Banks and Braes and Streams Around, Yestreen I had a pint o' Wine, Willie Brew'd a Peck o' Maut, The Blue-eyed Lassie, Mary Morison* and *O Wert thou in the Cauld blast.*

As regards his purely English songs, it may suffice to quote two of his own remarks to Thomson : 'You must not, my dear Sir, expect your English songs to have superlative merit, 'tis enough if they are passable' ; and : 'These English songs gravel me to death. I have not the command of the language that I have of my native tongue. In fact I think my ideas are more barren in English than in Scottish.' Some, even of his Scottish songs or adaptations, are not of 'superlative merit' ; the character of the theme or sentiment does not always permit of this ; but there are few that do not, in their tone or expression, exhibit traces of his felicitous art ; and, taken altogether, his achievement as a lyrist—partly on account of its peculiar relations to the older bards—is, for comprehensiveness and variety, unmatched by any other poet. For the same reason, it is, in its character, in some respects, unique ; and, while the general level of its excellence is very high, it often, notwithstanding a pervading rustic homeliness, exercises the complete captivating charm which is the highest triumph of lyric verse.

Thus, while, in other respects, the poetical aims of Burns were largely frustrated, he was, as a lyrist, even, in some respects, peculiarly favoured by fate. Here, he fulfilled, and even more than fulfilled, the promise of his earlier years ; and if, as seemed to Carlyle, all the writings he has left us are 'no more than a poor mutilated fraction of what was in him,' his very peasant circumstances—which, in some ways, greatly hampered and narrowed his endeavours—were, also, the means of enabling him to bequeath a poetic legacy more essentially Scottish than, probably, it could otherwise have been, and, at the same time, of such vital worth as to secure him a high place among the **greater poets of Britain.**

LESSER SCOTTISH VERSE

The Scottish literary revival inaugurated by Ramsay was associated with a widespread interest among educated and fashionable ladies in the old national airs and songs, and it is not therefore surprising that several of the most talented of them essayed song writing. Lady Grizel Baillie, Lady Wardlaw, Mrs Cockburn and Jane Elliot have been already mentioned[1]. These and other ladies, besides songs that have been published, wrote various others which were circulated only privately among their friends; and the fashion continued into the nineteenth century. Here, however, our chronicle of poetesses begins with Joanna Baillie, who was more of a professional authoress than most of the others. In 1790, she published a volume of *Fugitive Pieces*; and, while she devoted her main efforts, occasionally with marked literary success, to playwriting, it is probably mainly by her songs that she will be remembered. In 1823 appeared *Metrical Legends*, and her poems were published in one volume in 1841. Burns considered her *Saw Ye Johnie Comin*, which appeared anonymously in volume I of Johnson's *Museum*, unparalleled for 'genuine humour in the verses and lively originality in the air.' Among her happier contributions to Thomson's *Scottish Airs* are a version of *Woo'd and Married and a'*, beginning 'My Bride he is winsome and bonnie,' and *Poverty parts Good Company*, both in the old Scottish manner; and the same sprightly humour manifests itself in some of her ballad tales, as *It was on a morn* and *Tam o' the Lin*, a parody of the *Tomy Lin* ballad in Ritson's *Northern Chorister*, which is related to a very old rime.

The very popular sentimental song *Auld Robin Gray*, which first appeared in a very imperfect form in Herbert Croft's novel *Love and Madness* (1780), and, afterwards, in volume III of Johnson's *Museum*, was written by Lady Anne Lindsay of Balcarres (afterwards Lady Anne Barnard) as words to the air of an old song *The Bridegroom Greets* [weeps] *When the Sun gae's doon,* sung by a much older lady at Balcarres, who 'did not,' says Lady Anne, 'object to its having improper words.' A version revised by Lady Anne, with a continuation, was, in 1829, edited for the Bannatyne club by Sir Walter Scott, who was also entrusted with other poems and songs by Lady Anne and other members of the Lindsay family for publication; but the permission to publish was, afterwards,

---

[1] See *ante*, vol. IX.

withdrawn. The only other piece known to be by Lady Anne is a short poem in *The Scots Magazine* for May 1805, *Why Tarries My Love*. Susanna Blamire, the 'muse of Cumberland,' though of English descent and birth, spent much time in Scotland, owing to her elder sister's marriage to colonel Graham, of Gartmore, and became specially interested in old Scottish songs and airs. To Johnson's *Museum*, she contributed two songs, somewhat in the Scottish style: *What ails this heart of Mine*, and the better known *And Ye shall walk in Silk Attire*; and her *Nabob* is a kind of parody of *Auld Lang Syne*. Mrs Grant of Carron (afterwards Mrs Murray of Bath) is the authoress of the sprightly *Roy's Wife of Aldivalloch*, admirably suited to the air *The Ruffians Rant*, to which it is set. It appeared in volume III of Johnson's *Museum* (1792); and, some time after its publication there, Burns, in his long critical letter to Thomson, of September 1793, thus refers to it:

I have the original, set as well as written by the Lady who composed it [it was probably sent to the editor of Johnson's *Museum* after the publication of the song there], and it is superior to anything the public has yet seen;

but this version of the song has disappeared. Mrs Grant of Laggan, authoress of *Letters from the Mountains*, 1806, published, in 1803, a volume of *Poems*, and, in 1814, *Eighteen hundred and Thirteen a Poem*; but only her song, *O Where tell me Where*, has escaped oblivion. Elizabeth Hamilton, authoress of the Scottish tale *The Cottagers of Glenburnie* and other works, is known as the writer of only one song, the simple and homely, but very happily expressed, *My Ain Fireside*. Mrs John Hunter, wife of the famous anatomical professor, published a volume of *Poems* in 1802. Her song, *Adieu Ye Streams that Swiftly Glide*, appeared in *The Lark*, in 1765, as a proposed setting to the old air *The Flowers of the Forest*, and it is the third set to that tune in volume I of Johnson's *Museum*; but, of course, it is quite overshadowed by the first two versions, by Mrs Cockburn and Jane Elliot respectively; and she is now mainly remembered by her *My Mother bids me bind my hair*, which was set to music by Haydn. Burns sent to Johnson's *Museum* two songs by Mrs Maclehose ('Clarinda'), *Talk not of Love* and *To a Blackbird*. They are quite as good as most of the sentimental English lyrics of the period; but it was mere flattery on his part to assert of the former that the latter half of its first stanza 'would have been worthy of Sappho.'

Caroline Oliphant, Lady Nairne, who began to write as the career of Burns was prematurely drawing to a close, outvies all other songstresses of Scotland in the average excellence and

variety of her songs. Early though she began to write, most of
her best-known songs were first published—under the signature
B. B.—in *The Scottish Minstrel*[1]. Though she was largely inspired
by the example of Burns, and, like him, wrote many new versions
of old songs, she has been likened to him rather inaptly; for the
feminine strain is even more marked in most of her songs than it
is in several of the songs of the women already mentioned. Such
a strain in a woman writer is, of course, rather an excellence than
a defect, just as the strong manliness of Burns lends a special
compelling charm to his verse. At the same time, Lady Nairne's
love songs, such as *The Lass of Gowrie* and *Hunting Tower*,
somewhat lack afflatus, and are rather hackneyed and conventional
in their sentiment. On the other hand, pathetic feeling is finely
expressed in such songs as *The Auld Hoose, Here's to Them that
are Gane, The Rowan Tree* and *The Land of the Leal*, though the
last has not been improved by the traditional substitution of 'Jean'
for 'John' as the person addressed—a change perpetuated, partly,
because of the quite mistaken supposition that the song was meant
to express the dying words of Burns—for the sentiment of the
song is essentially that of a woman. *Caller Herrin*, a kind of
blend of humour and pathos, is, as set to the air by Niel Gow,
a very realistic representation of the cries of picturesque New-
haven fishwives in Edinburgh streets, mingled with the peal of
bells in St Andrew's church, George street. *John Tod* and *The
Laird of Cockpen*—the latter suggested by an older song—are
wittily humorous portraits of antique eccentrics; and *The Hundred Pipers* is quite irresistible in its combination of Jacobite
defiance and comical mirth. Though written when Jacobitism
had become little more than a pious opinion or a romantic memory,
Lady Nairne's Jacobite songs are inspired by a fervent Jacobite
ardour, derived from old family predilections. Among the best
known are *Wha'll be King but Charlie, Will Ye no come back
again?, He's O'er the Hills that I lo'e weel* and *Charlie is
My Darling*, a more Jacobite, but very inferior, reading of the
Burns adaptation in Johnson's *Museum*.

Among the more voluminous contributors to Johnson's *Museum*
was Burns's friend, the blind poet, Dr Blacklock; but the character
of his lyrics is sufficiently indicated in the words of Burns, so far as
they apply to his friend. 'He,' he says, in his tactfully and modestly
polite fashion, 'as well as I, often gave Johnson verses, trifling
enough perhaps, but they served as a vehicle for the music.'

[1] Edited by Smith, R. A., in six volumes (1821—4).

Blacklock's contributions, all in pure English, are, in fact, quite commonplace and characterless. There is, however, some poetic feeling in the contributions, mainly in English, of Richard Gall, an Edinburgh printer, whose *Poems and Songs* were published posthumously at Edinburgh, in 1819; but, neither his *Farewell to Ayrshire*, sent by him to Johnson's *Museum* with the name of Burns attached to it, nor his *Now Bank and Brae*, wrongly ascribed to Burns by Cromek, is of greater merit than the more indifferent lyrics of Burns. John Hamilton, a music-seller in Edinburgh—mainly remembered for the additions to *Of a' the Airts*, which he ventured to make as he was accustomed to do to other songs which he sold with the music in sheets—contributed several songs to Johnson's *Museum*; but none of them call for mention here. Burns sent to the *Museum* two songs by the John Lapraik of his poetic *Epistles* : *When I upon thy Bosom Lean*, the 'song that pleased me best' of the *Epistle*, and *Jenny was Frail and Unkind*. Because of a somewhat different version of the former song having appeared in *Ruddiman's Magazine* in 1773, Lapraik's authorship of it has been questioned ; but he included it in his published *Poems* (1788). John Lowe, an episcopal clergyman of Kirkcudbrightshire, is represented in volume I of Johnson's *Museum* by the tragic song, in pure English, *Mary's Dream*, of which a forged vernacular version, doubtless by Allan Cunningham, appeared in Cromek's *Remains* as the original. *Pompey's Ghost*, also, is attributed to Lowe by Burns ; but it appeared in *The Blackbird* in 1764, when Lowe was only fourteen years old.

Hector MacNeil, though the senior of Burns by thirteen years, did not publish his ballad legend *The Harp* until 1789. His poetic tales, *Scotland's Scaith or the History of Will and Jean* (1795), and the sequel, *The Waes of War or the Upshot of the History of Will and Jean* (1796), were meant to expose the evils of the convivial habits of the period. The stories, rather trite in their general tenor, are tersely rimed ; and their homely commonplace and moral wisdom secured them a wide circulation among the people ; but neither these nor other tales by him in prose and verse, also of didactic intent, are any longer read ; and his memory is kept green mainly by various excellent contributions to Johnson's *Museum*. The ballad *Donald and Flora*, in that publication, though well expressed, is rather mannered and artificial; but, in the vernacular *Mary of Castle Cary*, *My Boy Tammy* (founded on an old song of which at least one broadside copy still exists), *Come Under my Plaidie* and *Dinna think Bonnie Lassie*, homeliness of sentiment is blended to very good purpose with quiet or lively humour.

A considerable contributor to the *Museum* was James Tytler—known as 'Balloon Tytler,' from his construction of a balloon in which he made the first ascent in Scotland—latterly an Edinburgh hackwriter (until, owing to his revolutionary principles, he emigrated to America, where he became somewhat more prosperous), but of good education and of accomplishments ranging from science to theology. He was editor, and largely compiler, of the second and third editions of *The Encyclopaedia Britannica*, at, according to Burns, the remarkable salary of half a guinea a week, though, it is said, with an advance in the case of the third edition. Burns describes him as 'an unknown drunken mortal,' who 'drudges about Edinburgh as a common printer, with leaky shoes, a skylighted hat and knee-breeches as unlike George by the Grace of God as Solomon the Son of David.' Of the songs which he contributed to the *Museum*, the best known are two in the vernacular : *The Bonnie Brucket Lassie*, which preserves two lines of an old free song of that name, and *I hae laid a Herring in Saut*, an adaptation from a song in the Herd MS related to a very old wooing song, containing the line 'I canna come every day to Woo.'

John Mayne, born in Dumfries the same year as Burns, contributed to *The Dumfries Journal*, in the office of which he was a printer, twelve stanzas of *The Siller Gun*, published, in 1779, in an expanded form in two cantos. Written in the six-line stave in *rime couée*, it gives a spirited vernacular account of the annual shooting-match at Dumfries for the silver gun presented by James VI. From his *Halloween*, published in *Ruddiman's Magazine*, in 1780, Burns got some hints for his poem of that name. In 1787, Mayne became editor of *The London Star*, where, in 1789, appeared his version of *Logan Water*—founded on an older song —which, in popular esteem, has justly superseded the semi-political version by Burns, composed, he tells Thomson, 'in my elbow chair, in three quarters of an hour's lucubrations.'

Sir Alexander Boswell, of Auchinleck, the eldest son of Johnson's biographer, inherited his father's love of literature. As an Ayrshire man, he was specially interested in the career of Burns, in honour of whom he initiated the movement for the erection of a monument on the banks of Doon. Boswell's pastoral dialogue *Ah! Mary, sweetest maid, Farewell*, first published as a sheet song, appeared in the sixth volume of Johnson's *Museum*; and he contributed songs to George Thomson's *Welsh Airs*, his

Irish Airs and his *Scottish Airs* and to Campbell's *Albyn's Anthology*. In 1803, he published, anonymously, *Songs Chiefly in the Scottish Dialect*; in 1812, he wrote *Sir Albyn*, a burlesque of Sir Walter Scott's poetic methods; and, at his private printing press at Auchinleck, he published various short poems written by himself, as well as reprints of some old works. His squib, *The New Whig Song* in *The Glasgow Sentinel*, led to a challenge from James Stuart, of Dunearn, and, in the duel which followed, 26 March 1822, Boswell was fatally wounded. His *Taste Life's Glad Moments* and *Paddy O'Rafferty* are still well known; but his most characteristic pieces are his humorous vernacular sketches and songs, such as *Skeldon Haughs or the Sow flitted*, *Jenny's Bawbee* and *Jenny Dang the Weaver*, and the singularly realistic domestic quarrel and reconciliation detailed in *The East Neuk of Fife*.

In striking contrast with the songs of Boswell are the love lyrics of the Paisley weaver and chief of many Paisley poets, Robert Tannahill, who published a volume of *Poems and Songs* in 1817. The rather monotonous amorousness of Tannahill's songs is relieved by the felicity of his references to nature : he conveys the impression that he is quite as much enamoured by nature's charms, as by those of the imaginary sweethearts he elects to bear him company in his saunterings. The truth is that, having been at an early period of life disappointed in a very serious love affair, he was, henceforth, a lover merely in a poetical or a reminiscent sense. He first won general fame by his *Jessie the Flower of Dunblane* (an imaginary personage), which was set to music by his fellow townsman, R. A. Smith, afterwards of Edinburgh ; and, among other songs still popular are *The Lass of Arrinteenie* (not in Paisley, but on the banks of loch Long!), *Gloomy Winter's noo Awa'*, *The Bonnie Wood of Craigielea*, *Loudon's bonnie Woods and Braes* and *The Braes o' Balquither*. He is, also, the author of a clever humorous song *Rob Roryson's Bonnet*. Another Paisley poet, who began life as a weaver, and then blossomed into a travelling packman, was Alexander Wilson, who, in 1790, got a volume of his poems printed, which he sold on his itineraries. Later, he resided in Edinburgh and became a poetic contributor to *The Bee*; but, on account of republican sentiments inspired by the French revolution, he emigrated to America, where he won lasting fame as an ornithologist by his work on American birds. Wilson's lengthy and rather homespun and squalid ballad *Watty and Meg*, published anonymously, in 1792, was hawked through Dumfries by one Andrew Hislop, as a new ballad by Robert Burns; upon which Burns is stated to have said to him: 'That's a lee Andrew, but I would make your plack a bawbee if it were mine': a dark saying, which could hardly be meant, as is often supposed, as a compliment to the merits of the ballad. Of higher social station and literary pretension than either Tannahill or Wilson was William Motherwell, who, though a native of Glasgow, where he was born in 1797, was brought up in Paisley, under the care of his uncle, and, after some years spent in the sheriff-clerk's office there, became editor of *The Paisley Advertiser* and, later, of *The Glasgow Courier*. In 1817, he also began *The Harp of Renfrewshire*, to which he contributed various songs as well as an essay on the poets of Renfrewshire. In 1827, he published his *Minstrelsy Ancient and Modern*, which included various ballad versions collected and, probably, somewhat 'improved' by himself. His *Poems Narrative and Lyrical* appeared in 1832 ; and, together with James Hogg, he brought out, in 1834—5, an edition of the *Works* of Burns. He was a facile versifier, with small poetic inspiration; he wrote some ballads in an affectedly antique style, but is best known by his vernacular songs, which, however, have little individuality ; *Jeanie Morrison* is a little too cloying in its sentimentality.

Next to Burns, by far the most considerable poet of humble birth was James Hogg, the Ettrick shepherd; and, though, in richness of natural endowments, he is not to be compared to Burns, his poetic career was, in some respects, more astonishing. His record, in his autobiography, of how he became the poet that he was, is a plain and simple statement of unexaggerated fact; but it reads almost like a sheerly impossible romance. In all, he was not more than six months at school, and, when he left, at the age of seven, he had only 'advanced so far as to get into the class that read the Bible'; and, in writing, he was able only to scrawl the letters, 'nearly an inch in length.' In his early years, his poetic tendencies did not receive any instruction or fostering influence except that derived from his peasant mother's imperfect recital of ballads and fairy tales. From his eighth year, his hours from daybreak to sunset were spent in the fields as a herdboy and, later, as a shepherd. Until his eighteenth year, the only verses that he had seen in print were the metrical *Psalms* of David, and, when he obtained access to *The Life and Adventures of Sir William Wallace* and *The Gentle Shepherd*, he could make very slow progress in reading them: 'The little reading that I had learned,' he says,

'I had nearly lost, and the Scottish dialect quite confounded me.' While a shepherd with Laidlaw, of Blackhouse, he was, however, supplied by him with a number of books, which, he says, he 'began to read with considerable attention'; and, 'no sooner,' he relates, 'did I begin to read so as to understand them, than, rather prematurely' (he was, however, twenty-six years of age) 'I began to write.' His first compositions 'were songs and ballads made up for the lassies to sing in chorus.' 'I had no more difficulty,' he naïvely tells us, 'in composing them than I have at present, and I was equally well pleased with them.' His main difficulty was in writing them out after he had composed and corrected them in his mind; he had 'no method of learning to write save by following the Italian alphabet'; and, with laborious toil, he could not do more than 'four or six lines at a sitting.' So isolated was he in his southern solitudes, that, he says, 'the first time I heard of Burns was in 1797, the year after he died,' when a half-daft man came to him on the hill and surprised and entranced him by repeating to him *Tam o' Shanter*. This 'formed,' so he writes, 'a new epoch of my life. Every day I pondered on the genius and fate of Burns. I wept and always thought with myself what is to hinder me from succeeding Burns?'

The ambition of Hogg—recorded by him with characteristically ingenuous vanity—may well seem rather extravagant. His career as a poet, remarkable though it was, cannot be said to entitle him to rank as a second Burns. Save that, like Burns, he was a Scottish peasant, he has very little in common with him. He lacks his predecessor's marked intellectuality as well as his strongly passionate temperament. Emotion, imagination, a good musical ear, a faculty for riming, a strong sympathy with nature, created by years of solitary converse with her, were his principal gifts. He had an excellent eye for scenery, and his descriptions are remarkably fine and truthful; but he is somewhat superficial; the vigour and penetration of Burns are beyond him. As he possessed, however, a peculiarly lightsome and joyful disposition, his hardships, disappointments and misfortunes did not, as in the case of Burns, give him any very deep concern.

One may think [he writes], on reading over this memoir, that I have worn out a life of misery and wretchedness; but the case has been quite the reverse. I never knew either man or woman who has been so universally happy as I have been; which has been partly owing to a good constitution, and partly from the conviction that a heavenly gift, conferring the powers of immortal song, was inherent in my soul.

The wide difference in the individualities of Burns and Hogg is

shown in their relations with Edinburgh. Lacking the personal
prestance of Burns, Hogg could not attain there to the great personal
success commanded by Burns; his rustic simplicity, combined with
his vanity and certain eccentricities of manner, partly created by his
early circumstances, even made him a kind of butt in the higher
literary circles of which he was proud to be reckoned a member ;
and, to many, he is now best known by the unfair caricature of him
as the irrepressible 'Shepherd,' in *Noctes Ambrosianae*. But,
unlike Burns, he made a definite attempt, and, considering his ante-
cedents, with quite marvellous success, to establish himself as a
littérateur in Edinburgh. Having lost, in farming, the money gained
by the publication of *The Mountain Bard*, he, as late as 1810—when
he was forty years of age—set out to the capital on his adventurous
quest. 'I tost,' he writes, 'my plaid about my shoulders, and
marched away to Edinburgh, determined, since no better could be,
to push my fortunes as a literary man.' He even set up, as he puts
it, for 'a connoisseur in manners, taste and genius,' by founding
a weekly critical journal *The Spy*; and, fresh from wielding his
shepherd's crook in the wilds of Ettrick, essayed to supply literary
guidance and direction to the enlightened denizens of the metropolis. This paper—a literary curiosity of which, unhappily, no
copy is now known to survive—written three-fourths by himself,
was carried on for more than a year; and, largely for his own
mental discipline, he set on foot a debating society, the Forum,
where his speeches must have been sufficiently amusing. But,
by his publication of *The Queen's Wake*, he more than surprised
even his warmest admirers. ''Od,' said one of his vernacular
acquaintances, 'wha wad hae thought there was as muckle in that
sheep's head o' yours?' It firmly established his reputation as
a poet; but, owing to the failure of his publishers, his fortunes
were yet to seek, when the duke of Buccleuch bestowed on him
the farm of Altrive in Yarrow, at a nominal rent. Here, until his
death in 1835—with occasional visits to Edinburgh and the lakes
—he continued to spend a life in which farming and sports were,
not in a pecuniary sense very successfully, but, otherwise, happily
enough, combined with literary labours, his conviction of his
supreme success in which made him blissfully content with his,
from a worldly point of view, comparatively humble lot: 'Yes,' so
he wrote in his old age :

> Yes—I hae fought and won the day;
>   Come weel, come woe, I care na by;
> I am a King! My regal sway
>   Stretches o'er Scotia's mountains high

> And o'er the fairy vales that lie
> Beneath the glimpses of the moon,
> Or round the ledges of the Sky
> In twilight's everlasting noon.

The poetry of Hogg is more akin to that of Scott than that of Burns. Properly, he does not belong to the Scottish poetic school of the revival. His poetic powers were first nourished by, and received their special bent from, old border tales and ballads. He was nearly thirty years of age before he had even heard of Burns; and if, latterly, he was well read in Scottish vernacular verse, he, while employing a kind of Scots in certain of his pieces, did not make any use of the old traditional Scottish staves. Long before he had studied the vernacular bards, he had become acquainted with the works of various English poets. Thus, unlike Burns, he never had, in a literary sense, any strong vernacular bias; and, since a great period of poetic revival had now begun, both in Scotland and England, he, necessarily, received from it much stimulus and guidance; in fact, it was with these later poets he loved to be classed, and he reckoned himself by no means the least of the brilliant galaxy. While, therefore, his verse, like himself, displays, now and again, a certain naïve rusticity, and is occasionally marred by superficial solecisms, it is not only distinguished by the native charm derived from his early nurture on adventurous ballad tales and fairy lore, and from his mode of life as a solitary shepherd in a beautiful pastoral region, but, also, bears tokens of cultured refinement. Unlike Burns, he wrote English verse with perfect facility. His excessive fluency, his *extempore* voluminousness, his inability to condense—due, partly, to his insufficient mental discipline in early life—is, in truth, the occasion of his chief literary sins as a writer both of prose and verse; his larger poems as well as his ballads are, generally, too long drawn out. Yet, he has his passages of high inspiration. The concluding portion of *The Witch of Fife* in *The Queen's Wake* is a quaintly unique specimen of fantastic eeriness, touched with humour, *e.g.* the flight of the bewitched old man from Carlisle:

> His armis war spred and his heid was hiche.
>   And his feite stack out behynde;
> And the laibis of the auld manis cote
>   War wauffing in the wynde.
> And aye he nicherit, and aye he flew,
>   For he thochte the ploy sa raire;
> It was like the voice of the gainder blue,
>   Quhan he flees throw the ayr.

Bonny Kilmeny—which most critics unite to praise—in the same
poem, is in a quite different vein. Though it has certain superficial
faults, he here succeeds with delicate imaginative art in invoking
to admirable purpose the old mystic fairy spells, faintly preserved
in what remains of the old ballad stories of tradition. Many, also, of
the ballad imitations in the same poem, though lacking in concise-
ness, have much spirit; the eleventh bard's song, *The Fate of
Macgregor* ('Macgregor, Macgregor remember our Foemen'), is,
also, a splendidly vivid and impressive recital, and the poem
abounds in finely descriptive passages, somewhat after the manner
of Scott, with others more airily mystical. In *Mador of the Moor*,
he employs the Spenserian stanza with perfect success: he tells
us, in characteristic fashion, that he 'had the vanity to believe,'
that he was 'going to give the world a new specimen of this stanza
in its proper harmony'; and, if the story is badly constructed, the
narrative flows on with perfect ease and smoothness. He is, also,
pretty near the truth when he remarks, with his usual self-satisfac-
tion, 'There is no doubt whatever that my highest and most
fortunate efforts in rhyme are contained in some of the descriptions of nature in that poem'; and the remark applies more
particularly to the delineation of the hunting episodes, the
mountain and river scenery and the weather effects in canto I.
In the rather fantastic *Pilgrims of the Sun*, he attempts more
daring imaginative flights, but not always quite happily; and, in
the long historic poem *Queen Hynde*, he still more mistook his
powers, notwithstanding his firm opinion that it 'was the best
epic poem that ever had been produced in Scotland.'

The reputation of Hogg now rests, mainly, on *The Queen's Wake*,
and several of his shorter pieces. In 1810, he published *The Forest
Minstrel*, two-thirds of which were written by himself, and the rest
by his acquaintances, including the pathetic *Lucy's Flittin* by
William Laidlaw, Scott's steward. Of the songs in this volume,
Hogg himself frankly says: 'In general they are not good,
but the worst of them are all mine, for I inserted every ranting
rhyme that I had made in my youth, to please the circles about the
firesides in the evening.' Such was the shepherd's own opinion of
what were, in present day slang, uncommon good 'folk songs';
and, on the whole, his opinion of them is correct. They are, most
of them, merely 'ranting rhymes,' much better versified and
written and cleverer than the average example of their genus, but,
on the whole, best fitted for the appreciation of those for whom
they were primarily intended. On the other hand, there is

admirable spirit and fire in such later war odes and Jacobite songs
as *M' Kinnon, Rise Rise Lowland and Highland Man, Lock the
Door Lauriston, Cam Ye by Athol* and *The Gathering of the
Clans*; his grotesque sketch of the wicked village of 'Balmqu-
happle,' in Fife, is quite worthy of Burns; and, while his love songs,
for the most part, are a little cold and commonplace, *O Weel Befa'*
(in *The Haunted Glen* : not the longer version of the song) and
When the Kye comes Hame are charmingly fine pastorals; though
the most perfect of his lyrics and of his shorter pieces is *The
Skylark*, itself sufficient to justify his proud conviction that he
possessed in his soul the gift of immortal song.

John Leyden, like Hogg, the son of a shepherd, was associated
with him in supplying Scott with ballad versions for *The Minstrelsy
of the Scottish Border*; and he also contributed to it two imitation
ballads, *Lord Soulis* and *The Cout of Keeldar*, an *Ode to Scottish
Music*, and *The Mermaid*; and he wrote a few lyrics for *The
Scots Magazine*, which he edited for some months in 1802. Before
proceeding, in 1803, as a surgeon to India—where he afterwards
held the chair of Hindustani in Bengal and distinguished himself
by his linguistic and ethnological researches—he wrote, as a sort
of farewell, a long reminiscent poem *Scenes of Infancy*, somewhat
after the manner of Thomson, which, though tastefully written, can
hardly be termed poetical. *The Mermaid* is his only poem which
displays true poetic glamour.

Allan Cunningham, a native of Dumfriesshire—who, though of
middle-class descent, became a stonemason, but, later, was secretary to the sculptor Chantrey, and combined with his secretarial
duties miscellaneous literary work for the magazines and publishers—supplied Robert Hartley Cromek with most of the pieces
and information contained in his *Remains of Nithsdale and
Galloway Song* (1810); its poetic contents being mainly fabricated
by him, though, in some cases, he merely modified traditional
versions of old songs. In 1820, he published a drama, *Sir Marmaduke*, which, though praised by Scott as poetry, did not find
acceptance on the stage; and, in 1833, *The Maid of Elvar*, a
rustic epic in twelve parts. His *Songs of Scotland Ancient and
Modern* (four volumes, 1825), include some of his own compositions.
In his imitations of the older minstrelsy, Cunningham showed
varied dexterity, his attempts including traditional ballads, love
lyrics, Jacobite songs and plaintively pious covenanting effusions,
though their fictitious character becomes evident enough on a
careful perusal. *The Young Maxwell*, for example, is too much

a mere echo of ballads in general; *Hame Hame, Hame* is too prettily sentimental for an original Jacobite song ; *She's Gane to dwell in Heaven* is far too elaborately refined in expression to express the sentiments of the average pious peasant ; and the heroine of *Bonie Lady Anne,* evidently, never had any existence in Nithsdale or elsewhere. Several, however, both of his acknowledged and unacknowledged pieces, enjoy a wide popularity—among them the humorous *John Grumlie,* a condensed revision of *The Wyfe of Auchtirmychty* ; the funnily vituperative, if not very witty, *Wee, Wee German Lairdie;* *My Nannie O,* a kind of modified version of the song by Burns and quite as good as the original, and the classic sea-song *A Wet Sheet and a Flowing Sea.*

Thomas Mounsey Cunningham, an elder brother of Allan, is now best known by his *Hills o' Gallowa,* which, when it appeared anonymously, was attributed to Burns, but only echoes some of his mannerisms. In 1797, Cunningham's *Hairst Kirn* (harvest home) appeared in Brash and Reid's *Poetry Ancient and Select,* and he contributed to Hogg's *Forest Minstrel, The Scots Magazine* and *The Edinburgh Magazine.*

William Tennant, a native of Anstruther, who, in 1834, became professor of oriental languages in St Andrews university, published, in 1812, while a schoolmaster at Denino, in Fife, his *Anster Fair,* a kind of mock heroic description, in English verse, of that now discontinued rural gathering, not lacking in cleverly humorous or even in poetic touches. His *The Dingin doon O The Cathedral*—descriptive of the destruction of St Andrews cathedral by the reformation mob—and his *Tangier's Giant* are good specimens of graphic vernacular ; but his *Thane of Fife,* and his two dramas *Cardinal Bethune* and *John Baliol,* all in English, are now quite forgotten.

Of the songs and other pieces of the still less important versifiers of the later period which have escaped oblivion, it may suffice to mention the rapturous and rather finely imaginative *Cameronian's Dream* of James Hyslop; Robert Gilfillan's plaintive emigrant song *O Why Left I my Hame* ; the weird *Brownie of Blednock* by William Nicholson, known as 'the Galloway poet'; William Glen's *Wae's me for Prince Charlie* ; and the grotesque masterpiece *Kate Dalrymple,* at one time claimed for professor Tennant, but now known to be by William Watt, a Lothian poet, who also wrote the picturesque *Tinkler's Waddin.*

By the side of the purely secular verse of the revival there also

244 Lesser Scottish Verse [CH. X

flourished intermittently a kind of school of sacred verse of which the earliest and most elaborate specimen is Blair's *Grave*, noted elsewhere[1]. A chronic controversy still prevails in Scotland as to the authorship of several of the metrical paraphrases of Scripture adopted by the general assembly of the church of Scotland in 1781. Two students of humble birth, Michael Bruce and John Logan, studied together at Edinburgh university Bruce died in 1767, at the age of twenty-one; and, in 1770, Logan published, from papers supplied by the family, *Poems on Several Occasions by Michael Bruce*, with the information that 'with a view to make up a miscellany some poems wrote by different authors are inserted.' In 1781, Logan, now minister of South Leith parish, published a volume of poems containing an improved version of *The Cuckoo*, which had appeared in Bruce's volume, and a number of the paraphrases adopted by the church of Scotland. *The Cuckoo* and the paraphrases have been claimed for Bruce; but Logan's *Braes of Yarrow* and other poems in the volume show as great poetic aptitude as any pieces by Bruce. In 1783, Logan's tragedy *Runnamede* was accepted for Covent garden theatre, but was condemned by the censor on account of its political allusions. Among Bruce's poems is one on loch Leven, after the manner of Thomson, and an *Elegy on Spring*, a pious farewell to nature in view of his approaching death from consumption. James Grahame, a native of Glasgow, who, finally, became curate at Sedgefield, Durham, published various volumes of verse, including the dramatic poem *Mary Queen of Scots* (1801), and *The Birds of Scotland* (1806), but is best known by his meditative poem *The Sabbath* (1804), in blank verse, in which commonplace musing and pattern sentiments are conjoined with elegant and tasteful, if rather tedious, description.

Our record closes with Robert Pollok's *Course of Time*, published in 1827, a long elaborate dissertation in blank verse, modelled upon Milton, on human destiny, which professor Wilson considered, though not a poem, 'to overflow with poetry,' and which, at one time, enjoyed much popularity in more serious circles, but which has now ceased to be read.

---

[1] See *ante*, vol. IX, p. 167.

CHAPTER XI

THE PROSODY OF THE EIGHTEENTH CENTURY

In dealing with the subject of the present chapter, the procedure of our last chapter on that subject[1] has to be directly
reversed. We had, there, to give account of complicated and
largely changing practice, with hardly any contemporary theory to
accompany it—with almost no theory in a developed and extant
form. In the present case, a very short survey of the practice will
suffice. But we shall have to take into consideration a body of
prosodic study, no member of which is of very great interest in
itself, but which practically founded that study in English literature.

Yet, if the space allotted to metrical practice at the time is
small, it is not because that practice is negligible. On the
contrary, the sentence in our earlier chapter that 'it established in
the English ear a sense of rhythm that is truly rhythmical' deserves repetition and emphasis. So strongly was this establishment
based, buttressed and built upon, that it practically survived all
the apparent innovations in practice of the nineteenth century
itself, and has only been attacked in very recent years and, as yet,
with no real success. But it was, almost, of the nature of this
process that the prosodic exercises of the eighteenth century should
be comparatively few and positively simple. With the exception of
the rhythmical prose-verse or verse-prose of Ossian, which, with its
partial derivative, that of Blake, may be left to separate treatment
later, and of the recovery of substitution by Chatterton, which
may also be postponed, almost the entire practical prosody
of the period confines itself to two main, and a very few subordinate, forms, all of which are governed by one general prosodic
principle. This principle directs the restriction of every line—
with the fewest and most jealously guarded licenses—to a fixed
number of syllables, the accentual or quantitative order of which
varies as little as possible. Over the decasyllabic couplet, the
sovereign of the prosodic seas at this time, over its attendant
frigate the octosyllabic, over the not very numerous lyrical

[1] *Ante*, vol. viii, chap. ix.

fly-boats that complete the squadron, this flag of syllabic and accentual regularity floats—only one or two privateer or picaroon small craft daring to disregard it.

The heroic couplet of Dryden, already sufficiently discussed, underwent, in the earliest years after Dryden's death, changes which, considering the natural tendencies of humanity, may be called inevitable. By his own almost inimitable combination of skill and strength, and by the mechanical devices of triplet and Alexandrine, Dryden himself had kept off the monotony which the regular stopped couplet invites. But the invitation was sure to be accepted by others; indeed, they might plead that they were only realising the ideal of the form. As Waller and others before Dryden, wittingly or unwittingly, had hit upon the other devices of sententious balance and a split in the individual lines, and of pendulum repetition in the couplets: so, after Dryden, first Garth and then Pope, no doubt with their eyes open, rediscovered these; and the extraordinary craftsmanship of Pope carried the form to its highest possible perfection. If —and it is difficult to see how the assertion can be denied—the doctrine expressed in various ways but best formulated by De Quincey that 'nothing can go wrong by conforming to its own ideal' be true, the couplet of Pope, in and by itself, is invulnerable and imperishable.

But it very soon appeared that a third adjective of the same class, which indicates almost a necessary quality of the highest poetic forms, could not be applied to it. It was not inimitable. The admitted difficulty, if not impossibility, of deciding, on internal evidence, as to the authorship of the books of *The Odyssey* trans- lated by Pope himself, as compared with those done by Fenton and Broome, showed the danger; and the work of the rest of the century emphasised it. Men like Savage, Churchill and Cowper went back to Dryden, or tried a blend of Dryden and Pope; men like Johnson and Goldsmith new-minted the Popian couplet, in the one case by massive strength, in the other by easy grace of thought and phrase and form. But the dangers of monotony and of convention remained; and, towards the end of the period, they were fatally illustrated in the dull insignificance of Hoole and the glittering frigidity of Darwin.

From one point of view, it is not fanciful or illogical to regard all other serious, and most other light, measures of this time as escapes from, or covert rebellions against, this supremacy of a single form of heroic; but, as has been pointed out above, one

metre stands in somewhat different case. The octosyllabic couplet
had been little practised by Dryden, though, when he tried it, he
showed his usual mastery ; and it evidently did not much appeal
to Pope. But Butler had established it with such authority that,
till well into the nineteenth century, it was called specifically
'Hudibrastic' ; and two of the greatest verse writers of the early
eighteenth, Swift and Prior, had used it very largely and very
successfully, so that it could not be regarded as in any way insignificant, oldfashioned, or contraband. It was, in fact, as much
the recognised metre of the century for light or brief narrative
and miscellaneous purposes not strictly lyrical, as the heroic was
for graver and larger work. But, as Dyer showed early and others
later, it served—owing to the earlier practice of Milton more
especially—as a not ineffectual door for smuggling in variations
of line-length and foot-arrangement which were contraband, but
of very great value and efficacy.

Another of these centres of free trade in verse was the
Spenserian stanza. The dislike of stanzas of all kinds which, as
we saw, grew during the seventeenth century, was, as shown below,
seriously formulated at the beginning of the eighteenth, and may
be said to have been more or less orthodox throughout its course.
But the exceptional charm of Spenser broke through this ; and
no small body of imitations—bad enough, as a rule, but saved by
the excellence of at least part of *The Castle of Indolence*, and,
perhaps, *The Schoolmistress*, as well as by the influence, if not the
intrinsic merit, of *The Minstrel*—found its way into print.

The most formidable rival, however, of the heroic was blank
verse. The practice of this inevitably arose from, and, in most
instances, continued to be the imitation of, Milton, which, sparse
and scanty for the first generation after his death, grew more
abundant as the eighteenth century itself went on and, in
The Seasons, almost ceased to be mere imitation. Fine, however,
as Thomson's blank verse is, and sometimes almost original, it
suffered not a little, while all the blank verse of the century
before Cowper's latest suffered more, from undue generalisation in almost all cases, and in most from positive caricature,
of Milton's mannerisms. The worst of these (so far as prosody
is concerned) was the exaggeration of his occasional, and always
specially effective, use of the full stop in the interior of a verse
by chopping up line after line in this fashion to an extent
ridiculous to the eye and mind, and destructive of all harmony
to the ear. The practitioners of blank verse, also, too often agreed

with its enemy Johnson that, if it was not 'tumid and gorgeous,' it was mere prose; and, though they frequently failed to make it gorgeous, they almost invariably succeeded in making it tumid. Even in *Yardley Oak*, Cowper's masterpiece of the form, these defects exist: and the eighteenth century strain in Wordsworth himself never completely freed itself from them.

It is, however, in lyric measures that the limitations of this period of more or less rigid drill show themselves most. In what has been called 'the greater ode,' the terrible irregular 'Pindarics' of the later seventeenth century continued; but they gradually died out, and the establishment of stricter forms (in which respect Congreve is not to be forgotten), speedily and luckily inspired with fuller poetic spirit by Gray and Collins, did much to appease the insulted ghost of the great Boeotian. In smaller and lighter work, the adoption of the anapaest by Prior was almost as fortunate as his patronage of the octosyllable, and we have not a few graceful trifles—'free' in no evil sense—not merely by Prior himself but by Gay and by Byrom, by Chesterfield, Pulteney, Shenstone and others.

Still, as a rule, the lyric poet of the eighteenth century was confined, or confined himself, to very few metres. Stiff and sing-song 'common' or ballad measure; rather better, but too uniform, 'long' measure or octosyllabic quatrains alternately rimed; and (somewhat curiously) the old romance-six or *rime couée* (8 8 6 8 8 6 *a a b c c b*) with occasional decasyllabic quatrains, of which the great *Elegy* is the chief, will probably account for three-quarters, if not even more, of the lyrical verse of the period; and almost the whole of it displays that submission to a cast-iron law of syllabic number and accentual distribution to which reference has been made. The reason of this we shall understand better when we have surveyed the preceptist or theoretical literature of prosody which, almost for the first time since the Elizabethan period, makes its reappearance.

For if, during this period, practical prosody enjoyed or suffered from a kind of stationary state, it was very much the reverse with prosodic theory. It is, in fact, from the second year of the eighteenth century that attempts to deal with English prosody as a subject practically date. Gascoigne's examination was too slight, Puttenham's too ineffectually systematised, the studies of the other Elizabethans, directed too much to one particular, and for the most part non-essential, point (classical versing) and all too little historical; while the, possibly, more pertinent treatises of Jonson and Dryden are not extant, and the very distribution or trend of them is only to be guessed.

In 1702, there appeared, written or compiled by an obscure person by name Edward Bysshe, an *Art of Poetry*, which (after a custom set on the continent for some considerable time past and already followed here by Joshua Poole) consisted principally of a riming dictionary and an anthology of passages containing similes and so forth. The book became popular and was often reprinted (at first with considerable additions) during the century. The bulk of it has long been mere waste-paper; indeed, a riming dictionary may be said to be, in itself, almost the greatest achieved, if not the greatest possible, insult to the human understanding. But its brief introduction, 'Rules for Making English Verses,' is one of the two or three most important *points de repère* of the whole subject; though, even at the present day, and even by serious students of prosody, that importance is sometimes denied and oftener belittled. It has even been said that Bysshe merely represents 'the traditional view'; to which it can only be replied that exhaustive examination of every previous treatment of the subject has failed to discover any expressed tradition of the kind or any sign that such tradition had 'materialised itself' to anybody outside an extremely variable practice.

What Bysshe does is to formulate, with extraordinary fidelity, a system of versification to which the practice of the foregoing century had certainly been more and more tending, but which had never been expressed in theory before. His own principle is strictly syllabic. There are no feet in English—merely a certain number of syllables. Moreover, he would preferentially admit only verses of ten (with an extra one for double rimes), eight and seven; though he does not absolutely exclude others. These syllables, in a heroic, must be arranged so that there is a pause at the fourth, fifth or sixth, and a strong accent on the second, fourth and sixth. So absolutely devoted is he to syllables and accents that he only approaches verses of triple (dactylic or anapaestic) time (while he uses none of these terms), by the singularly round-about way of describing them as 'verses of nine or seven syllables with the accent on the last,' and dismisses them as 'low,' 'burlesque' and 'disagreeable,' unless they occur in 'compositions for music.' He is, of course, a severe advocate of elision: the 'e' of the article must always be cut off before a vowel; 'violet' is, or may be, 'vi'let.' But he disapproves of the seventeenth century practice of eliding such vowels as the 'y' of 'by.' As for stanzas of intermixed rime (*i.e.* Spenserian, rime royal, etc.), 'they are now wholly laid aside' in longer poems.

Now, this gives us a miserably restricted prosody; but, in the first place, it is the prosody of the eighteenth century, and, in the second place, it had never been thus formulated before.

But, although hardly any poets except Chatterton and Blake (for Gray and Collins themselves do not show any formal rebellion) were rebels to this until Southey and Coleridge broke it down at the end of the century, the preceptive prosodists—who, in most cases, were not poets at all—by no means showed equal docility, although their recalcitrance was seldom of the right kind. Pope, indeed, in almost his only prosodic passage, the early *Letter to H. Cromwell* (1710[1]), follows Bysshe literally in some points, virtually, in almost all. On the other hand, Pope's enemy Gildon (who, like Dennis, has of late years been 'taken up' in some quarters) revolted against Bysshe's syllables and accents, and, though in a vague manner, introduced a system of employing musical terms and notes to prosody—a specious proceeding which has had many votaries since. He, also, with John Brightland and one or two more, started another hare—the question of accent *v.* quantity—which has been coursed ever since, and which, also, will probably never be run down. This latter point attracted much attention, especially as it connected itself with a contemporary discussion, to which Foster, Gally and others contributed, on accents in the classics. Henry Pemberton was so ferocious a champion of accentuation that he would have rewritten Milton, altering, for instance

> And towards the gate rolling her bestial train

into

> And rolling towards the gate her bestial train.

Edward Mainwaring followed the musical line, and began a practice, frequently revived to the present day, of turning the heroic topsy-turvy and beginning with an anacrusis or single syllable foot

> And | mounts ex|ulting | on tri|umphant | wings.

The catalogue of eighteenth century prosodists, thenceforward, is a long one, and it cannot be said that a thorough student of the subject is justified in neglecting even one of the following: Harris (*Hermes* Harris), Say, Lord Kames, Lord Monboddo, Webb, Abraham Tucker, Herries, Thomas Sheridan, Steele, Tyrwhitt, Young, Nares and Fogg. But, with some notice of Steele and

---

[1] Nov. 25. This was the subject of one of Pope's extraordinary falsifications. He changed it into one to Walsh dated four years still earlier.

XI]   *Joshua Steele*

Young, we may pass here to half-a-dozen others (four of whom
are of general interest and one of real importance)—Shenstone,
Gray, Johnson, John Mason, Mitford and Cowper.

Joshua Steele undoubtedly exercised great influence on many
prosodic students, some of whom acknowledged it and some did
not, while he has been recently hailed as 'a master' by authorities
who deserve respect. Yet, these same authorities, strangely enough,
acknowledge that Steele's actual scansion is 'utterly wild.' It is
not incumbent on a survey like the present to attempt the reconciliation, or at any length to expose the incompatibility, of two
such statements. It is, perhaps, sufficient to say, on the first head,
that Steele's 'mastery' seems to be shown in the fact that, for the
first time, he proclaimed verse to be essentially matter of musical
rhythm, and applied musical methods frankly and freely to the
notation of metre; that he discarded syllabic feet; and that he
gave the metrical franchise to pauses as well as to spoken syllables.
As to the second head, it should be still more sufficient to state that
he allowed from six to eight 'cadences' in a heroic line; that he
scans a famous verse

> O | happiness | our | being's | end and | aim

and starts *Paradise Lost* as

> Of | Man's | first diso|bedience | and the | fruit.

By what logic it can be contended that a system which leads
to such 'monstrosities' (the word is that of an admirer of Steele)
as this is 'masterly,' some readers, at any rate, will find it
difficult to imagine. Either Steele's scansions are justified by his
principles or they are not. If they are, these principles are self-
condemned; if they are not, the perpetrator of the scansions must
have been a man of so loose a way of thinking that he cannot be
taken into serious consideration. In either case, he cannot have
had an ear; and a prosodist without an ear may surely be asked
to 'stand down.' There is much of a similar kind to be said of
Young. On the other hand, Tyrwhitt, in his justly famous edition of
Chaucer, showed himself a real prosodist and, early as it was, came
to very sound conclusions by the simple process of taking the
verse first and getting it satisfactorily scanned. Of the rest, most
are chiefly remarkable for curiosities of a theory which always
neglects large parts of English poetry, and sometimes sets at
naught even the practice that it recognises. Perhaps the best is
Johnson's despised 'Sherry,' whose prosody is, certainly, in many
points heretical, if Johnson's own is orthodox.

Wrong as they generally went, fruitless as were, too often, their attempts, flitting shadows in an arid desert as some may think them, history cannot entirely omit these enquirers; but she certainly turns to a few others with some satisfaction. Shenstone, Gray, Johnson and Cowper were poets[1] who turned their attention definitely to prosody. Mason (John, not William) and Mitford were prosodists who, in the first case, at least, appreciated the beauty of poetry, and, in the second, made large excursions into the more than contemporary history of it. Shenstone's actual poetical value may not be very high; but the merest glance at the variety of his poetical forms should prove something of a tell-tale about him, and his prose works, if only in a few scattered observations, emphasise the warning. He seems to have been the very first person in the century who definitely perceived the wanton asceticism of unvarying elision and sighed for 'the dactyl,' as he called it; he is the first, also, who laid express stress on the value of 'full' rimes and the colouring force of particular phrases. Gray, a much greater poet and not himself much of a practitioner of trisyllabics, was, on the other hand, the first to recognise the presence and the continuity of the trisyllabic foot in generally disyllabic metres from middle English downward; and he exhibits in his (unfortunately fragmentary) *Metrum* many other signs of historic knowledge and metrical vision. Johnson, in his prosodic remarks on Milton, Spenser and a few others, is, professedly, at least, of the straitest sect of believers in fixed syllabism, regular iambic arrangement and middle caesura. Yet, as is constantly the case with him in other departments of criticism, he shows, in an almost Drydenian manner, his consciousness of the other side; and, indeed, gives that side practically all it can ask by admitting that perfect 'purity,' though, as enforced above, 'the most complete harmony of which a single verse is capable,' is, if preserved continuously, not only 'very difficult' but 'tiresome and disgusting'; and that variation of the accents, though 'it always injures the harmony of the line,' compensates the loss by relieving us of this tyranny. He did not extend the same indulgence to what he calls 'elision,' that is to say, the presence of extra syllables or trisyllabic feet; or to pauses far from the centre. But the concession as to 'pure' and 'mixed' measures was itself a Trojan horse. If, the nearer you approach to purity and perfection, in one part of the

[1] Goldsmith devoted one of his essays to the subject, and some have thought it valuable. In form, it is as agreeable as everything its author wrote: to the present writer, its matter seems smatter, insufficiently veiled by motherwit.

system, the more likely your result is to be tiresome and disgusting, it will go near to be thought shortly that the system itself is rotten somewhere.

Although it would be rather dangerous to say what book of his own time Johnson had not read, there is not, to the knowledge of the present writer, any sign in his *Works* or in his *Life*, of his having come across the speculations on prose, verse and elocution of John Mason, which were published in three little tracts shortly before *The Rambler* appeared. The author was a nonconformist minister (which would not have pleased Johnson), and a careful and intelligent student of the classics (which, to some extent, might have reconciled him). He certainly, however, would have been inclined to regard Mason as a most pestilent nonconformist in prosody. Mason is somewhat inclined to musical views, but very slightly ; and he adopts what some think the illegitimate, others the sensible, plan of evading the accent *v.* quantity logomachy by laying it down that 'that which *principally* determines English quantity is the accent and emphasis.' But his great claim to notice, and, in the opinion of at least the present writer, to approval, is that he absolutely refuses the strict decasyllabic limitation and regular accentual distribution, with their consequences or corollaries of elision, forced caesura towards the centre, and so forth. He calls attention to the positively superior 'sweetness' of lines of even twelve or fourteen syllables ; and, to accommodate this excess, he not only admits feet, but feet of more than two syllables, as well as a freely movable caesura and other easements.

In the case of Mitford, also, musical considerations and musical methods[1] stand rather where they should not, assisted by some superfluous considerations of abstract phonetics ; but here, also, they do little harm. And, here (at least in the second edition of his work), there is what is not in Mason, what is not in any other prosodist of the eighteenth century except Gray, and only fragmentarily in him, a regular survey of actual English poetry from the time that its elements came together. Even now, more than a century after the second edition and nearly a century and a half

---

[1] Little room as there is here for quotations, two sentences of his book, 2nd edn, p. 111, should be given, inasmuch as they put briefly and in Mitford's clear and intelligible language the source of myriad confusions at that time and since :

'Five bars are perhaps never found forming an integral portion of an air or tune. The divisions of modern musical air run mostly in two or rather four bars, and multiplications of four.'

Nothing more should be necessary for showing to anyone acquainted with actual English poetry, that its laws, though they may, in part, coincide with, are essentially independent of, those of modern music.

after the first, this indispensable basis for prosodic enquiry has been provided in scarcely more than two other books on the subject. His is, of course, partial and not always sufficiently informed; though it is most usefully supplemented by enquiries into metre as it exists outside English in both ancient and modern languages. He dwelt too much on accent; he confused vowel and syllabic quantity; and he allowed extra-metrical syllables—a constant indication of something wrong in the system, which, in his case, was probably brought about partly by his musical ideas, and partly by the syllabic mania of the time still existing in him. But he constantly comes right in result, even when the right-coming is not quite easy to reconcile with some of his principles; and there is no doubt that this is mainly due to his study of English poetry at various times and of English poetry in comparison with ancient and modern examples in other tongues.

Last of all—for the remarks to be referred to belong, like most of his practice, and, for the same unhappy reason, in the main, to a very late period in his life—we must mention Cowper. His letters, like those of Southey afterwards, show that he might have written consecutively on prosody in a very interesting fashion; but it may be doubted whether he had cleared his mind quite enough on the subject. All know his attack on Pope ; or, at least, on the zanies of Pope, with their 'mechanic art' and rote-learnt tunes. His prose allusions to the subject are of the same gist, but show the uncleared confusion. The statement that Milton's 'elisions lengthen the line beyond its due limits' may seem to a modern reader sheer nonsense—equivalent to saying that if, in correcting a proof, you cut out a line here and a line there you lengthen the page. But, of course, by 'elisions,' he meant the syllables which the arbitrary theory of his time supposed to be elided. Yet he laid down the salutary rule that 'without attention to quantity good verse cannot possibly be written'; he declared his faith in 'shifting pause and cadence perpetually,' and he knew that, by following this practice (which, it should be remembered, Johnson had denounced as 'the methods of the declaimer'), you could make blank verse 'susceptible of a much greater diversification of manner than verse in rime' —a point which, with others in reference to 'blanks,' occupies most of his letters to Thurlow. He never completed a system to match his practice ; but, like this, his theory, such as it was, evidently looked backward to Milton, and forward to the great poets who were boys or not yet born when Cowper seriously began to write.

To some extent, of course, the impoverished state of actual prosody at the time may be taken as an excuse for the prosodic theorists, though it would be very unfair to blame the poets themselves for the sins of these others. Prosodists saw around them practically nothing but one limited side of the possibilities of English verse; and the extent to which this had to do with their errors can hardly be exaggerated. But it was perfectly open to them to look back if they chose, and a few of them did choose; while, of those who did, still fewer showed themselves able to read the open lessons which authors no more recondite than Shakespeare and Milton had for them. Moreover—and, strange as it may seem, the phenomenon has repeated itself by no means seldom since, and is fully in view at the present day—the majority of them had evidently no taste whatever for poetry as poetry. It was a machine to be taken to pieces, not a body of beauty to be appreciated.

And so, though, in any case, the calling back into fresh existence of the older and more varied poetry, and the calling into new existence of a poetry more varied still, would have antiquated their enquiries, they failed even to give due value or due explanation to what they had. For, as has been set forth already, they had something, and no small thing, in their own poets—the positive and practically indestructible establishment of definite rhythm. As Chaucer and, in regard to line-grouping, if not to line-making, Spenser, as Shakespeare and Milton, in both, once more stand irremovably as witnesses for liberty and variety in metre, so Dryden and Pope and Johnson, nay, even Collins and Gray, stand for order and regularity. We wanted both sets of influences, and we had now got them.

It will thus be seen that, from the strictly historical point of view, this period is of no small importance in regard to the particular matter treated in this chapter. It is the first in which any considerable number of persons busied themselves with the attempt to analyse and systematise the principles of English versification. It is true that, with hardly more exceptions than Gray and John Mason to whom Shenstone and Tyrwhitt, perhaps, also, Sheridan, may, to some extent, be joined, they came for the most part, to wrong conclusions; but the reason why they so came is clear. In no case, except in those of Gray partially, and Mitford more fully, did students of prosody, at this time, study English poetry as it had actually existed and base their conclusions on the results of that examination. Generally, they took the restricted prosody of their own time as the perfection of all that was possible in the subject. In some particular cases, of which Steele's is the most remarkable, they attacked the matter altogether *a priori*, and in the worst sense of that much abused term. They, then, endeavoured to construct an abstract science of prosody starting from assumed axioms and postulates, with deductions from which actual verse had to be accommodated as it best (or worst) might. No two writers may, at first sight, seem to stand farther apart than Bysshe and Steele; yet, when they are impartially examined, the faults which have been pointed out in them will be found to be equally present though differently distributed, and to be equally due to the same fundamental error of beginning with the rule, instead of with that from which the rule must be extracted. They can be convicted out of the mouth of him who, to most of them, was the greatest of poets and prophets—of Pope himself. They would not 'discover,' they would not do anything but 'devise.'

CHAPTER XII

THE GEORGIAN DRAMA

THOUGH the last forty years of the eighteenth century produced few English plays of primary importance, the period is among the most interesting in the history of the national theatre. Its study shows how complex and perishable are the conditions of dramatic excellence, and explains why one of the chief glories of the English muse sank, for at least a century, beneath the level of literature.

Paradoxical as it may sound, the decay of the drama was partly due to the advance of the actor. In the days of Betterton[1] and Barton Booth[2], the best player was, in a sense, an intermediary, and the attention of spectators could be held only if characters and situations appealed directly to their understanding. With the coming of Havard, Macklin, Garrick, Mrs Clive, Spranger Barry, Foote, Yates, Mrs Abington and King, success no longer depended on the excellence of a play. The stage began to offer a new and non-literary attraction. It was enough for the dramatist to give a 'cue for passion'; he need only serve as a collaborator, as one whose work was half finished till presented by a trained performer. O'Keeffe's success depended so largely on Edwin's interpretations that when the actor died the playwright was expected to fail. Colman the younger's Eustace de St Pierre[3] was a mere outline till Bensley gave it life, and Cumberland's O'Flaherty, in *The West Indian*, was hardly more than a hint out of which Moody, following the example of Macklin's Sir Callaghan in *Love à-la-mode*, developed the stage Irishman. When older and greater plays were being performed, the public was still chiefly attracted by the novelty of the acting. Abel Drugger was enjoyed because of Weston's by-play, and Vanbrugh's character of Lord Foppington was almost forgotten in Woodward's impersonation of it. True inspiration was still, of course, the best material on which the player could work, as Garrick found in performing Richard III or Macklin in his new interpretation of Shylock. But, even in the revival of old plays,

---

[1] 1635—1710   [2] d. 1733.   [3] In *The Siege of Paris.*

the masterpieces of the Elizabethan drama were altered to suit
the powers of the actor.   When *Hamlet* was reedited by Cibber,
and *Lear* by Nahum Tate, playwrights must have perceived that
literary talent was no longer a necessity.   It became even rarer
as the theatre rose in public estimation.   Thanks to actors, plays
had longer runs, and people paid more to see them.   Those who
contributed towards the production of these fashionable entertainments began to prosper, and the more dramatists enjoyed the
luxuries of conventional society, the less they retained touch with
the tragedy and comedy of real life.   Quin[1] was the last of the old
school, and Macklin was the first to bring his own personality into
his interpretations[2].   But the conflict between classical literature
and dramatic taste was undecided, till Garrick's genius showed that
gesture, pose and facial expression were so effective that even the
dumb-show of ballet-pantomimes could please an audience more
than old-time rhetoric[3].   An apparently trivial change in the
arrangement of the theatre drew the drama further from literature.
To give actors more space and to obviate interruptions, spectators
were removed from the stage in 1762[4], and, as the loss of these
seats would have fallen heavily on the recipient of a benefit, the
auditorium was lengthened.   Thus, although the 'apron' still projected a few feet into the auditorium, the business of the play
had no longer the advantage of taking place among onlookers.
Before 1765, Drury lane was chiefly illuminated by chandeliers,
though candle-footlights had already been introduced.   Garrick,
on returning from his continental tour[5], engaged the services of
Barthélémon, whose violin won success for many worthless pieces,
and ordered Parisian scenery and lamp-footlights from Jean
Monnet[6].   The concentration of light threw into relief the

[1] 1693—1756.

[2] 'I spoke so familiar Sir, and so little in the hoity-toity tone of the tragedy of
that day, that the manager told me that I had better go to grass for another year or
two.'   Macklin, alluding to Rich, who had dismissed him from Lincoln's Inn fields.
See Kirkman, J., *Memoirs of the Life of Charles Macklin* (1799).

[3] Noverre, in *Lettres sur les Arts*, testifies to Garrick's skill in pantomime.   Walpole,
in describing Glover's *Boadicea*, gives conclusive evidence of the importance of acting
when he says ' Then there is a scene between Lord Sussex and Lord Cathcart, two
captives, which is most incredibly absurd : but yet the parts are so well acted, the
dresses so fine, and two or three scenes pleasing enough, that it is worth seeing.'   To
George Montagu, 6 *December* 1753.

[4] See Knight, Joseph, *David Garrick* (1894), pp. 183 f.

[5] 19 September 1763—27 April 1765.

[6] Connected, at different times, with the *Opéra-Comique* and the *Théâtre de la
Foire*.   Garrick also ordered costumes from M. Boquet, *dessinateur d'habits à l'opéra*.
See Jullien, A., *L'Histoire du Costume au Théâtre* (1880).

performer's face and enabled his looks and movements to express what had formerly needed monologues and asides. When the proscenium, which had been introduced at the restoration, and footlights had completely separated the player from his audience, the performance became spectacular. Actors were now like figures in a picture, and the dramatist learnt that one of his first tasks was to manoeuvre them into poses and situations. Experience eventually taught authors how to preserve dramatic fitness amid these altered requirements ; but, for several generations, the consequence was a misuse of asides, parentheses, sudden entrances. mistaken identities and other stage effects of like nature.

Despite these temptations, authors and actors might have succeeded, as at Hamburg and Weimar, in producing art without sacrificing literature, if it had not been for the public. Georgian audiences were no longer representative of the nation. The puritan prejudice against the theatre, revived in the Bible society abolitionists and the low church evangelical party, and many thoughtful men, such as the Wesleys, John Newton, Cowper, Wilberforce and Zachary Macaulay, abstained on principle from an institution which preached a fictitious code of honour and was considered the favourite resort of the irreligious. Many more stayed away because the habits of eighteenth century England were essentially domestic. It was an age of household furniture, tea-drinking and sensibility. Men and women spent evenings at home discussing ethics, writing long, intimate letters or testing each other's gift of sentimental conversation. When the inevitable reaction came, it led people from the playhouse towards nature and the open air.

If the drama had few charms for more thoughtful and sober-minded citizens, it irresistibly attracted the *beau monde.* Lovers of social display, who were gratified by the 'jubilee-masquerade' at Ranelagh and by the Richmond fireworks[1], had begun to look for the same kind of excitement in the theatre. As performances were generally restricted to two or three houses[2], theatregoers enjoyed that sense of exclusiveness and monopoly which is dear to leaders of society. Soon, it became a social distinction to meet and be seen at these assemblies, till Hannah More admits that one of the chief pleasures was the show of the Spectators[3].'

---

[1] Walpole, letters to H. Mann, 3 and 17 May 1749.

[2] With the exception of a few unauthorised attempts (quickly suppressed) to open theatres, dramatists and actors were confined, during this period, to Drury lane and Covent garden in the season and to the Hay in the summer months.

[3] *Preface to Tragedies.*

People went early to get seats when it was known that the Gunnings would be among the audience[1], and, in the sixties, the popularity of the royal family could be gauged by the warmth of their reception at the theatre. Besides, the enterprise of the great actor-managers made these entertainments one of the principal town topics which people of fashion could not afford to ignore. Not to have judged Garrick, Macklin, Foote, Lewis, Mrs Siddons or Kemble in their latest *rôle*, not to have sat as arbiter over the contending merits of Drury lane and Covent garden[2], was a mark of provincialism. While the leisured classes bestowed their patronage, they also imposed their prejudices and traditions. The desire to cultivate selfrespect and courtesy, which is noticeable so far back as the revolution, had gradually grown, during the eighteenth century, into a meticulous observance of outward forms. Every man of breeding was expected to be a drawingroom diplomatist, who could win his way by his personality and conversation. Together with the cult of social conformity, there had gradually developed such a horror of vulgarity that any display of natural feelings was considered ungentlemanly. Lord Chesterfield reminds his son that to laugh aloud was bad manners, and that to quote an oldfashioned proverb was to betray familiarity with coachmen. The nineteenth century horror of indelicacy or coarseness now begins to appear. Johnson reproved Hannah More for reading *Tom Jones*, some of the bluestockings rejected *Tristram Shandy*, Bowdler expurgated Shakespeare and Gibbon. A class dominated by such ideals might excel in many provinces of literature, from oratory to letter-writing; but, when the glamour of social distinction drew them to the theatre, their taste proved too artificial for the appreciation of real tragedy and comedy. Good acting always won their favour; but, even Shakespeare had partially to be rewritten for them by Thompson, Garrick and Kemble. The older school still preferred comedies full of the humorous vagaries and witty conversations of their own rather trivial lives, or tragedies which flattered their sense of literary propriety by observing the unities, amidst arid rhetoric and blank verse. By the second half of the century, a more serious and emotional atmosphere began to predominate in high society. This newer phase is something more than a continuation of the ideals reflected

---

[1] Walpole to H. Mann, 23 March 1752.

[2] *E.g.*, in 1750, Barry and Mrs Cibber played in *Romeo and Juliet* at Covent garden and Garrick and Miss Bellamy at Drury lane. In 1760, Miss Brent played Polly in *The Beggars' Opera* at Covent garden and Mrs Vincent played in the same piece at Drury lane. Goldsmith, in *The British Magazine*, discussed their rival merits.

in Steele's sentimental comedies. People did not abate one jot of their respect for gentility; but they were anxious to take themselves and the theatre more seriously. They rigidly observed their father's and grandfather's cult of selfpossession ; but they also affected strong and sensitive passions. Their ideal was to repress powerful emotions beneath a refined, or even mincing, manner, till the breaking point was reached in floods of tears or in a swoon. As contact with the hard and varied realities of life was still considered to such a degree illbred that even the bailiff's scene in *The Good-Natur'd Man* was censured, people had to look to domestic incidents for pathos and passion. A look, a gesture, or a silence was, for them, charged with sentiment. They waxed tearful or melancholy over the spectacle of a woman preserving her inbred elegance under persecution and insult. They loved to contemplate the tenderness of paternal or filial instinct, and dramatists were wont to introduce sudden recognitions between a parent and a long-lost child, in order to give an emotional turn to their plays. Their dramatic ideas centred in the morality of the drawingroom or the domestic circle. Even wickedness (except when the exigencies of the plot required a melodramatic villain) was a temporary lodger in a conscience-stricken breast ; even humour was appreciated only when a rugged but domesticated character, such as a Scottish servant, almost travestied virtue by an uncouth exterior.

Such was the class which gave the theatre its tone. But the spectators who packed Drury lane and Covent garden were not entirely composed of sentimentalists. The Mohawks, whom Swift feared and Steele censured, had their descendants under George III. Bullies in the pit, like footmen in the gallery, seemed to have followed occupants of the boxes in matters of dramatic taste; but they still regarded actors as lawful victims of their arrogance and insolence. On one occasion, they demanded that Moody should beg their pardon on his knees for some imagined disrespect, and such was their tyranny that, when Sheridan put *Macbeth* on the stage, he feared a riot because Mrs Siddons omitted the candle which their favourite Mrs Pritchard always carried in the sleep-walking scene. The wouldbe playwright had other discouragements to face besides dependence on an oversensitive, narrowminded and intolerant public. Before the end of the century, plays sometimes enjoyed a run of from twenty to sixty nights, and, as there were not more than two theatres open at the same time, the unknown author had often to suffer humiliations and to descend to intrigues before his work could be accepted[1]. Yet, neither the generation of Walpole nor that of Burke lacked students of human nature possessed of creative genius, who, like Goldsmith and Sheridan, might possibly have surmounted all these difficulties if a more direct path to the heart of the nation had not already been found.

The drama's decline was the novel's opportunity. Ever since the days of Lyly and Greene, prose fiction had become a possible rival of the theatre; but the Elizabethan public was too gregarious, and had inherited too deep a love of spectacle, to care to see life through the unsociable medium of a book. After the revolution, the influence of the theatre waned; but the middle class was making its first acquaintance with culture, and, like all beginners, required its lessons in a dogmatic, unequivocal form, such as essays, satires and treatises. It was not till the middle of the century that people seemed to have mastered the principles of social ethics and began to enquire how those ideas applied to the complex tangle of character and destiny. No doubt, the drama, under favourable conditions, could have satisfied this curiosity. *Figaro* is as effective as *Roderick Random*, and *Minna von Barnhelm* shows what the stage could have made of *The History of Amelia*. But the novel was better adapted to the speculations of the time. The drama deals with crises in the lives of its chief characters and, thus, is suited to an age of action or of transition, when people are interested in the clash between old traditions and new ideas. In the novel, life is treated like a piece of complex machinery, to be pulled to pieces, carefully examined and then patiently put together again. Thus, the novel is best adapted to a generation which has already made up its mind about the framework of society, and is now puzzling over the accidents of birth and temperament which prevent many individuals from fitting into the scheme. But, though tragedy and comedy decayed, the theatre did not. During the last forty years of the eighteenth century, a long succession of talented actors, from Macklin and Foote to Kemble and Quick, revealed fresh sources of emotion and raised their calling to an honourable profession. And, if few Georgian plays can rank as literature, they yet provide an illuminating commentary on public sentiment and theatrical art.

In the sixties, amid musical entertainments such as Bickerstaff's *Padlock*, which ran for fifty-three nights, adaptations from

---

[1] See bibliography, under Theatrical Pamphlets.

Metastasio[1] and from Voltaire[2] and some fustian tragedies full of
duels and suicides, a taste for sentimental, or, as it was then called,
genteel, comedy prevailed. Even Goldsmith's *The Good-Natur'd
Man* (1767)[3] did not bring back the public taste to 'nature and
humour in whatever walks of life they were most conspicuous.'
At Drury lane, Kelly, a few days previously, had produced *False
Delicacy*, which condensed into a clear-cut situation the doubts
and heart searchings of the fashionable world. Lady Betty
Lambton refuses the hand of her beloved Lord Winworth out of a
false sense of delicacy and then finds herself pledged to further
his courtship with Miss Marchmont. Miss Marchmont is secretly
in love with Sidney, but feels bound to encourage Winworth's
advances, because she is under many obligations to his seconder
Lady Betty. Of course, there is an underplot, with two comic
characters (Cecil and Mrs Harley); but the true spirit of the
comedy is found in the scene where Lady Lambton and Miss
Marchmont are at last induced to strip off the veneer of gentility
and disclose their real sentiments. Other plays followed the
same tone, such as Mrs Griffith's *School for Rakes* (1769), in
which Lord Eustace, after abandoning the compromised Harriet
Mountfort for a marriage of convenience, is brought back by
Frampton's influence to a sense of duty ; or Kelly's *School for
Wives* (1773), in which the farcical spectacle of a man who loves
his handsome wife, and yet pays court to all other women of
his circle, is tempered by scenes of domestic emotion. But the
dramatist who most conspicuously made his mark in this decade
is Richard Cumberland.

Cumberland was the pioneer of the later sentimental comedy.
He differed from his contemporaries in untying domestic tangles
by drastic and, sometimes, almost tragic action ; and, thus,
he pointed the way to melodrama. Other dramatists of the
sixties and seventies had failed to strike this vein because they
confined the interest of the play to the correct and decorous
society in which the chief characters moved. Cumberland saw
that the leaven must come from without, and exposed the decadence of artificial civilisation by confronting it with the vigorous
and earnest lives which men were leading away from London and
county society. In *The Brothers* (1769), the scene opens on a
bleak coast lashed by a furious storm ; a privateer is wrecked,

[1] Hoole's *Cyrus* (1768), and *Timanthes* (1770).
[2] Madame Celesia's *Almida* (1771).   [3] See *ante*, vol. x, chap. ix.

whose crew of sturdy, if theatrical, pirates includes young
Belfield, who has been driven from his estate and sweetheart, and
Violetta, who has been forsaken by her husband. Both are
wronged by Belfield the elder who, now possessed of the neighbouring manorhouse, is grinding the tenants and courting Sophia,
his brother's betrothed. The sudden arrival of the dispossessed
heir and of the abandoned wife, the frustration of the villain's
designs, the reunion of the lovers after mutual misunderstandings,
the contrast between the sea-rover, with his hardy companions,
and the decadent gentry who have gathered round the manor
hall[1], supply the humour and sentiment which were then in
fashion. It is undeniable that the characters do not really live,
while the idea of a cadet turned Bohemian through a kinsman's
criminal selfishness must have been familiar to readers of Fielding
and Smollett. Yet, *The Brothers* is noteworthy. Belfield the
elder is a villain in his actions more than in his nature, and
the good side of his character is gradually evolved as the play
proceeds; his final humiliation has none of the bitterness of
revenge; and, all through the play, one feels something of the
health and freedom of the sea. *The Brothers* was produced in
December 1769 at Covent garden. In January 1771, Garrick
brought out at Drury lane *The West Indian,* in which the imagined
freedom and sincerity of the plantations come into contact with
city life. Stockwell, a prosperous business man and a member of
parliament, has summoned his illegitimate son from the West Indies
to London; but, before declaring his relationship, decides to
watch his character in the disguise of a friend. The son, under
the name Belcour, arrives among an outworn and artificial
circle, composed of the penurious captain Dudley, lodging with his
son and daughter at the house of the Fulmers (the husband a
decayed literary man, the wife a procuress), and of Lady Rusport,
his sister, an avaricious puritan, who refuses money to her brother
and tries to thwart young Charles Dudley's courtship of her step-
daughter Charlotte. The intercourse between Stockwell and the son
whom he may not own gives free play to the sentimentality which
the age enjoyed[2]; but the chief interest of the play centres in Louisa,
captain Dudley's daughter. The West Indian sees her in the street,
follows her home to the house of the Fulmers with tropical ardour
and begins an irregular courtship which brings out the emotional
elements of the play—the villainy of the Fulmers, who tell Belcour

---

[1] *E.g.*, Sir Benjamin and Lady Dove, act II, sc. 4; act III, sc. 3.
[2] Act III, sc. 1.

that Miss Dudley is only a mistress and fleece him ; the sacredness
of women's honour ; young Dudley's jealousy for his sister's good
name, leading to a challenge ; and the gradual development of
Belcour's character, impulsive and licentious on the surface, but
showing itself full of courage and chivalry as the plot thickens.
Cumberland was now rapidly making a name and a fortune. Late
in the same year, he adapted *Timon of Athens* for the modern
stage, by shortening the first four acts and rewriting the fifth, and,
early in the next year[1], Garrick produced *The Fashionable Lover*,
a purely domestic drama, reminiscent of *Clarissa*, of which the
principal figure is the elegant and rather mournful Augusta Aubrey.
Left to the care of a dishonest speculator, she is compromised by a
nobleman, courted by an ardent and honourable lover and, finally,
restored to happiness and affluence by the unexpected arrival of
her father from abroad.

Early in the seventies, public taste changed and became oldfashioned. Cradock's *Zobeide* (1771) was copied from an unfinished play by Voltaire ; the anonymous *A Hour before Marriage*
(1772) was modelled on Molière's *Mariage Forcé*. O'Brien,
indeed, kept to sentimental comedy by producing *The Duel* (1772),
founded on Sedaine's *Le Philosophe sans le Savoir* ; but, in the
same year, Mason composed *Elfrida*, with a Greek chorus.
Kenrick's *Duellist* (1773) was founded on the character of colonel
Bath in *Amelia* ; Colman the elder borrowed from Plautus and
Terence to produce *Man of Business*, and Cumberland drew
inspiration from *Adelphi* to write *Choleric Man*, both in 1774.
General Burgoyne, who, in age and associations, belonged to the
old school, now felt himself drawn to the theatre and produced
The Maid of the Oaks (1774), in which the irate parent of classical
comedy storms because his son marries without his consent, and
the witty and fashionable Lady Bab fools Dupely by disguising
herself in a *fête champêtre*. But the two authors who most
profited by, and influenced, this reversion to humour and episode
were Goldsmith and Sheridan.

She Stoops to Conquer (1773)[2] is not original in plot, but the
characters are drawn from life, and, touched, as it is, by Goldsmith's indescribable charm, the play became a revelation. It
reminded London how much instruction as well as amusement

---

[1] 20 January 1772.
[2] See *ante*, vol. x, chap. ix.

might still be found in oldfashioned situations despite their dramatic licence, provided only the morals and manners of the characters would conform to the new standard. Sheridan, meanwhile, had achieved his romantic marriage and, being faced by the problem of supporting a wife, decided to devote his literary gifts to the now profitable business of playwriting. Like Goldsmith, he reverted to classical comedy and chose, as the basis of his plot, the marriage conflict between parent and child which had come down from Terence through Italian and French theatres[1]. A father and an aunt arrange a suitable marriage for their respective son and niece, while the young people have already chosen for themselves. Out of this hackneyed situation he extracted the equally hackneyed humours of mistaken identity and of domestic discord, but with a dramatic sense which borders on genius. Miss Lydia Languish and captain Absolute are the young pair destined for each other. Unknown to their elders, they are already mutually in love; but, as Lydia has fallen a victim to the craze for sentimentality, the wealthy captain pretends to be the penniless ensign Beverley, so that their union may be to her, unquestionably, a marriage of love. This attempt at a double impersonation brings about some brilliant complications. Familiar figures in domestic and social life are thrown off their guard and betrayed, with admirable felicity, into weaknesses and absurdities generally hidden from the public eye, and the enjoyment of the spectators is all the more complete because the characters are working for the same end and frustrate their several efforts through misunderstandings.

The Rivals (1775) is a comedy of incident, the excellence of which is partly to be found in the action. Its characterisation is, in essence, conventional and shows less knowledge of human nature than does Goldsmith's work. Captain Absolute the generous, impulsive youth, Sir Anthony the testy, headstrong father, Fag and Lucy the menials who minister to their employers' intrigues, are as old as Latin comedy; Bob Acres, the blustering coward, is akin to Sir Andrew Aguecheek and had trod the stage in Jonson's learned sock; Sir Lucius O'Trigger is related to Cumberland's O'Flaherty; Mrs Malaprop has a long pedigree, including Dogberry, Lady Froth, Mrs Slipslop and Tabitha Bramble. Yet, apart from the actual business on the stage, these characters are irresistibly effective. As in the case of Goldsmith, Sheridan's importance is found in

---

[1] For the sources and text of *The Rivals*, see works by Rae, W. F., and Adams, J. Q., quoted in bibliography.

the new wine which he poured into old bottles. The Georgian
public expected in their plays a certain piquancy which should
remind them of their social or domestic life. But, whereas authors
of the sentimental school flavoured their work with emotions
pertaining to woman's affairs, Sheridan perceived that there was
another element of good breeding, quite different but equally
modern. The expansion of the British empire had called into
existence a virile and energetic governing class of soldiers and
politicians. This aristocracy felt, as deeply as any 'jessamy' or
'macaroni,' the humanising influence of polite learning and domestic
refinement, yet with a difference. As society set a value on delicate
attentions, sympathetic and discerning compliments, subtle turns
of phrase and gracefulness of manner, these arts were cultivated
as an accomplishment in order to maintain social supremacy. The
class in question, did not, like sentimentalists, affect strong passions
beneath a veneer of politeness, but, rather, a superb serenity which
rose superior to all emotion. Drawingroom diplomacy had often
appeared in letters and memoirs ; but Sheridan was the first writer
to make it the essence of a play. Despite the conventionality of the
character-drawing and of some of the situations, *The Rivals* has
an atmosphere which satisfies this ideal. As each figure moves
and speaks on the stage, the reader is conscious of a coterie whose
shibboleth was distinction—a coterie whose conversation regarded
the most commonplace topics as worthy of its wit, which abhorred
eccentricity and smiled at all those who, like Fag, Sir Anthony,
Faulkland, Mrs Malaprop and Bob Acres, fell short of the rule of
easy selfpossession.

After some initial difficulties, *The Rivals* proved a complete
success and Sheridan was launched on his career as a dramatist.
The opportunities of quick returns which the theatre now offered
had their full influence even on an author of his literary taste and
dramatic sense. His next production, *St Patrick's Day*, is a
trifle composed with no other object than to make money by
amusing the public. *The Duenna* (1775) is an adaptation of old
material to suit the fashion for operas. We meet again the stage
old man ; his name is Don Jerome, instead of Sir Anthony, but
he is just as obstinate, irascible and wellbred. Then, we have
the victim of ignorance and selfcomplacency, this time a Jew and
not a garrulous and affected old woman, but his end is dramatic-
ally the same as Mrs Malaprop's. Comic situations, as in *The
Rivals*, arise out of mistaken identities, which are admissible
only in the makebelieve of a musical farce. The plot was taken

from Wycherley's *The Country Wife*, and, though the dialogue
has much of Sheridan's brilliant phrase-making and whimsical
humour, the chief literary merit of the play must be sought in
the lyrics, with their vigorous directness and touch of classical
culture.

While Sheridan was making money, he was also perfecting his
art. He showed how much of stagecraft he had learnt when,
in 1777, he adapted Vanbrugh's *The Relapse* to the taste of the
Georgian public and brought it out as *A Trip to Scarborough*.
No more striking illustration of Sheridan's manner could be found,
and its failure on the boards is merely another of those mysteries
familiar to all who study the annals of the stage. Vanbrugh's
play has a double plot. On the one hand, there is a sort of
picaresque adventure, in which a needy gallant, by impersonating
his elder brother in a love-suit, accomplishes his revenge on an
inimitable coxcomb and wins a wife and a fortune to boot. On
the other hand, there is a complicated intrigue. Loveless, the re-
formed libertine and now the virtuous husband of Amanda, finds
that his wife has, unwittingly, invited to the house one of his
former paramours, now a blithe widow, named Berinthia. Of
course, Loveless relapses, and Berinthia encourages another of her
admirers, named Worthy, to make love to Amanda, in order that
the wife may not be inclined to spy on her husband. In the end,
Loveless accomplishes his desire with Berinthia ; but her seducer is
rejected with horror by Amanda. Sheridan showed his mastery of
construction by unifying the action. He made the first act a more
artistic exposition of the plot and economised both characters and
scenes by arranging that everything accessory should be narrated
instead of acted. Above all, he altered the motives and
actions of the characters to suit the more refined perceptions of
his own time. Berinthia is no longer a common adventuress,
nor does she urge Townley (the Worthy of *The Relapse*) to court
Amanda. She tempts Loveless in order to punish Townley for
transferring his attentions from herself to her friend. The guilty
couple are not exposed, but are shamed out of their design in a
situation of considerable tact and dramatic skill, which Sheridan
used again in *The School for Scandal*. Their assignation in a
moonlit garden is disturbed. They take cover and are forced to
overhear Amanda, against whom they are in league, scornfully
rejecting Townley. As Berinthia and Loveless emerge from their
concealment, she remarks 'Don't you think we steal forth two
contemptible creatures?' Even in the other part of the play, the

burlesque business of Miss Hoyden's courtship, a new turn is
given to the farcical stage character Lord Foppington. The final
speech which Sheridan puts into his mouth reveals his true nature
and shows a man arrogant and illbred, but of native shrewdness,
and too discerning to marry a woman in whose eyes he had been
made to appear ridiculous.

Sheridan had acquired elsewhere the matured judgment and
dramatic sense which these two ephemeral productions display.
While supporting his household and keeping his name before the
public, he had slowly and laboriously perfected his powers by con-
structing the best play of which he was capable[1]. *The School for
Scandal*, which finally appeared on 8 May 1777, is the last great
English comedy and typifies not only the excellence but the limitations of the Georgian theatre. To begin with, it is significant
that Sheridan, in the choice of his *dramatis personae*, was content
to use familiar types. Sir Peter Teazle is the traditional stage old
man who had already reappeared in *The Rivals* and *The Duenna*;
Charles Surface is the traditional young man, just as generous and
impulsive as captain Absolute, only more exposed to temptation.
As in Sheridan's earlier work, we have the professed *poseur*. This
time, he is neither a country squire who apes bravery, nor an old
woman who affects the phraseology of culture, nor yet a Hebrew
opportunist, overconfident in his own cleverness, but a character
who overreaches himself in the attempt to make a good impression,
already familiar to those acquainted with Murphy's *Know your
own Mind*. The other personages, except Lady Teazle, are not
studies of character, but occasional figures, vaguely suggestive of
the restoration comedy or of Molière[2], seen only at one angle, as
they come and go in the act of creating the background or con-
tributing to a situation. Even Sir Oliver, despite his common
sense, his pardonable vanity at finding his own picture rather than
another's spared in the portrait scene, and despite his humanity,
nurtured in a life of enterprise, is hardly more than 'an angel
entertained unawares' in an eighteenth century garb.

But, if *The School for Scandal* does not tell us anything that is
new or profound about human nature, it is a brilliant exposition
of that other superimposed character which an idle, overcivilised
society develops. It has already been shown how Sheridan, in
writing *The Rivals*, used a farcical plot to portray the peculiar

[1] On the genesis of the play, see *Shakespeare to Shaw*, Armstrong, C. F. (1913),
p. 158.
[2] *E.g.*, Wycherley's *The Plain Dealer*; Molière's *Le Misanthrope*.

graces which *élite* society admired and the peculiar ineptitudes which it despised. In *The School for Scandal*, he went further; he put on the stage, in his own pregnant way, the psychology of the overtrained world of fashion. In the first place, as conversation was a fine art in a community of drawingroom idlers, Sheridan endowed his personages with a flow of picturesque epigram, of which the studied felicity surpasses all other dialogues, including that of his own previous works. Besides this, he perceived that the intellectually unemployed turn social intercourse into a competitive struggle ; and, when he came to portray the underlying stratum of jealousy and intrigue, he brought to his task a touch of modern sentimentality from which few Georgians could escape. Behind his view of London art and artifice, there lurked the popular ideal of simple manners, and, thanks to this background of thought, he was able to show how the vices of the polite world overgrow natural instincts. Since ideas which are to succeed on the stage must be concrete, he made extravagance and scandal examples of decadence, and then worked out a crisis in the lives of characters brought under their influence. Charles Surface is the centre of a circle demoralised by extravagance till a chance episode reveals the generosity of its nature. Lady Sneerwell typifies the irreclaimable scandalmonger ; she finds so many opportunities of retaliating on the world which first slandered her that habit is now second nature. Joseph Surface, at heart, is no worse than the character whose desire for respectability exceeds his powers of compassing it; he, too, is gradually fascinated by a brilliant and corrupt society, till an unexpected event shows that he has sinned beyond forgiveness. Sir Peter is the Cato of the piece, good at heart, if selfcentred, but soured by contact with many backbiters and rendered ridiculous by the vagaries of his young wife, herself Sheridan's best creation —an example of how youth and inexperience may be blinded to the follies of fashionable life till the eyes are reopened by a sudden crisis.

Such a theme, in the hands of Cumberland, Holcroft, Mrs Inchbald, Colman or Morton would have developed into sentimental drama. The Teazle *ménage* would have provided comic relief ; Maria, a defenceless ward in their household, slandered by the scandal club and distressed by Joseph's insidious attentions, would have become the pathetic heroine of the piece. Sir Oliver, probably her father in disguise, would have appeared in the fifth act to rescue her from persecution and to restore her to her faithful Charles, who had plunged into dissipation because she was too modest to requite his love. That Sheridan was quite capable of so lachrymose a treatment is proved by his *Ode to Scandal*; but, in his comedy, he confined himself, with admirable skill and judgment, to making vice ridiculous. Of all the characters, only Sir Oliver, Rowley and Maria are colourless, because they are untouched by London frivolity. Each of the others exemplifies some vice or weakness with that consistent exaggeration which provokes laughter, because, on the stage, it seems true to life. Even more notable is Sheridan's classical sense of form and the skill with which he constructed his plot. The characters do not fall, by accident, into readymade situations, but control the plot throughout. It was part of Charles's nature to sell his family portraits and of Lady Teazle's to accept the invitation to visit Joseph. The weakness of English comedy had always been a division of interest between plot and underplot, and Sheridan's earlier work was by no means free from this defect. But, though *The School for Scandal* deals with the crisis of not less than four lives, their destinies cross one another in the culminating point. It is this intersection of interests which gives an almost unparalleled dramatic effect to the two great scenes. In the portrait scene, Joseph and the Teazles are present only by implication ; in the screen scene, all four meet at what the spectators realise at once as one of the important moments of their lives.

Yet, *The School for Scandal* is not one of the world's best comedies: it lacks inspiration. As has been shown, the English theatre had become the mirror of metropolitan wit and gentility. Its public expected polite distraction and were ready to laugh, to weep or to be amused ; but their drawingroom culture and coffeehouse experiences denied them interest in the puzzles and anomalies of human nature, out of which the greatest comedies are made. Hence, those who wrote for the stage were almost forced to revive the traditional situations and characters of old comedy, or, failing that, to give their colourless plays some topical or temporary interest. Goldsmith and Sheridan succeeded well with this dead material, because the one enlivened it with humour and the other with wit. Even in *The School for Scandal*, the lack of true insight is not hard to detect ; and, two years and a half later, *The Critic* (29 October 1779) showed that its author had nothing fresh to say concerning life.

It was now three years since Sheridan had succeeded Garrick as manager of Drury lane and had been exposed to the paper

warfare which, for over half a century, had been bickering in
the narrow theatrical world[1]. It is not surprising that, in an
atmosphere of lampoons and acrid criticisms, he should turn his
gift of dramatic caricature against his foes.   Just as Buckingham
had ridiculed actors in *The Rehearsal*, Sheridan produced on
the stage a satire against the poetasters and intriguing critics who
ranged themselves on the side of sentimental drama.   He no
longer attempted to create characters whose actions should clash
and interweave, till a situation revealed each in his true light.
He did, indeed, begin by depicting the world of theatrical vanity
and self-interest.   We have a glimpse of a married couple whose
home life is poisoned by stage-mania; two crusted literary aspirants,
full of that civilised malignity which Sheridan knew well how to
portray, and, above all, Puff, the advertising adventurer, a true
stage freak, devoid of reality, whose newly-written play the other
characters adjourn to see rehearsed.   The dialogue is as sparkling
as ever, and the characters, whether or no they are based on
contemporary[2] personalities, have just that touch of humorsome
exaggeration of which Sheridan was master.   But the second act,
instead of developing a plot, changes into a parody.   Puff's tragedy,
The Spanish Armada, is a pseudo-historical drama, and the spectators are entertained with a caricature of stage-managership and
dramatic effect.   A parody cannot rank as literature save when,
besides a certain felicity of expression, the reader is able to
recognise, not only the peculiarities, but the essence and spirit of
what is being travestied ; and it cannot be denied that the brilliant
inanities, for which this burlesque has been often praised[3], are
founded on the real practices of Georgian tragedy.   Nor is the
more personal satire of the first act relinquished.   Besides a
travesty of pedantic devices, such as exposition, peripety, climax,
conversion and stichomythia, Dangle, Sneer and Puff discuss the
performance, and their comments are an admirable caricature on
the *demi-monde* of theatrical art.

When Sheridan produced *The Critic*, he was attacking a cause
which had already won the day.   Sentimental drama had been
patronised by the most cultured circle in polite society.   Since 1750,
Mrs Montagu's *salon* had been teaching London that ladies could

---

[1] See bibliography, under Theatrical Pamphlets.
[2] *E.g.*, Sir Fretful Plagiary is generally recognised to be a caricature of Richard
Cumberland.
[3] See Sichel, *Life of Sheridan*, vol. I, pp. 602 f.

cultivate their intellect, without sacrificing their social charm, and
a series of talented bluestockings[1] were portraying drawingroom
culture in novels and plays. Mrs Cowley was already known to
the public; but the theatre did not feel the full influence of the
movement till Hannah More's *Percy* packed Covent garden at a time
when *The School for Scandal* was the attraction of Drury lane.
Hannah More was a woman of strong character, masculine intellect
and passions, which, thwarted in life, were almost bound to find
expression in literature. She had already composed *The Inflexible
Captive*, a classical drama inspired by Addison's *Cato* and Havard's
Regulus, but showing a complete ignorance of the stage, in which
the sentimental passions of son, daughter and lover are called into
play by the captive Regulus's return to Rome. Through five acts,
the hero resists the claims of state and family with dignified and
aphoristic declamation, and even the authoress herself admitted
that the play was defective in action. Three years later, Hannah
More had come into contact with the leading humorists, courtiers
and actors of London; and nothing proves more vividly the fascination of the Georgian theatre than that she should have chosen
this as a mouthpiece for her ideas. *Percy* is a manifesto, and
attempts to show how the ethics of refined society may be studied
through the ensanguined colours of tragedy. Hannah More translated into rather intense drama the discussions which interested her
own day : what duty a woman owes to her father, her husband and
her own good name; how a lover should act towards a woman in
distress and towards his own heart; the obligation of a husband
to win his wife's affection and his right to guard her fidelity,
though it cost both of them their lives; the regard for decorum
which a ' person of quality' should observe, even in moments of high
emotion. Such ideas had become too subtle for the conventional
setting of a Roman tragedy[2], and Mason's *Caractacus*, despite the
beauty of Mrs Hartley (as Evelina), had failed only the year before.
Hannah More was well in touch with the growing taste for romanticism[3] and was original enough to fill her problem play with the
chivalry and architecture of the Middle Age. *Percy* is based on a

---

[1] See *post*, chap. xv.

[2] Cf. Walpole, on a similar occasion : ' *The Siege of Aquileia*, of which you ask,
pleased less than Mr Home's other plays. In my own opinion *Douglas* far exceeds
both the other. Mr Home seems to have a beautiful talent for painting genuine
nature and the manners of his country. There was so little of nature in the manners
of both Greeks and Romans, that I do not wonder at his success being less brilliant
when he tried those subjects.' To Sir D. Dalrymple, 4 April 1760.

[3] See *ante*, vol. x, chap. x.

twelfth century story of Eudes de Faiel, which Belloy (the author of *Le Siège de Calais*) had already dramatised; but the horrible episode of Raoul de Coucy's heart was, of course, omitted. The action takes place among oldfashioned English heroes and shows how Elwina, betrothed to Percy from her childhood, has wed earl Raby at her father's behest, but cannot return his love. Just as the earl's suspicions are being aroused at this coldness, Percy returns with glory from the crusades and hastens to his lady, not knowing that she is married. The spectators watch the sentimental lover as he is gradually trapped by the jealous husband, while the heroine is torn between duty to her marriage vow and her unconquerable passion for the suitor of her youth. In the end, Elwina goes mad and drinks poison, while Raby slays Percy, and then, learning that his wife was chaste, kills himself. Artificial and insipid as the play now seems, its combination of emotion, action and theory was considered a revelation. Besides the most ample recognition in London, the drama was acted in Vienna, and the authoress was elected a member of the Paris and Rouen academies.

Percy shows what havoc a virtuous man may work, if he is passion's slave. In 1779, Hannah More produced *The Fatal Falsehood*, to prove how love, in a unscrupulous heart, may lead to even more appalling crimes. After this effort, she abandoned the theatre and devoted her pen to the propagation of religion.

Never was there an atmosphere less genial to the tragic muse. A few attempts were made at classical imitations, such as Delap's *Royal Suppliants* (1781), founded on Euripides's *Heraclidae* and *Philodamus* (1782), by Dr Bentley's son, based on a passage in Cicero's *In Verrem*. There were some Shakespearean revivals, such as Kemble's alterations of *Coriolanus* and *The Tempest*, both in 1789, and some genuine attempts at medieval tragedy, in Hannah More's manner, of which the best were Jephson's *Count of Narbonne* (1781) and Joanna Baillie's *De Montfort* (1800). These efforts, which read like academic exercises, were the more coldly received, because the age could see its own thoughts and manners reflected, almost every night, in an endless succession of new comedies.

Few comedies of this group attracted so much attention as Mrs Hannah Cowley's. In 1776, she had produced the rather sentimental *The Runaway*, in which Emily, a fugitive from a distasteful marriage, takes refuge in the Hargraves's house and is unscrupulously lured away from this retreat because her charms bid fair to seduce young Hargrave from his promised marriage with a wealthy old maid. Early in the eighties, Mrs Cowley changed to the comedy of humour and episode. In *The Belle's Stratagem* (1780), Laetitia Hardy, to be sure of winning the affections of her betrothed, first disgusts him by pretending to be a hoyden and then, while disguised at a masquerade, conquers his heart by her real charms. In *A Bold Stroke for a Husband* (1783), Olivia is plagued by her father's desire to see her married ; so, she adopts the expedient of scandalising all suitors, till Don Julio appears and she captures him by a series of complicated deceptions. Both compositions are akin to the classical school in that they give a laughable and optimistic turn to the domestic difficulties of youth ; but neither, in the true spirit of old comedy, creates humour out of the clash or eccentricity of character.

The most remarkable playwright of this decade is general Burgoyne. The author of *The Maid of the Oaks*, on returning from America, had resumed his former avocation, and, after writing an opera in 1780, produced, in 1786, *The Heiress*, which won a fortune and was preferred by some critics to *The School for Scandal*. The play, which was partly founded on Diderot's *Père de Famille* and on Mrs Lennox's *The Sister* (1769), has the unusual merit of combining the features of a comedy of manners with those of a comedy of pathos. In the first half, differences of breeding and caste are sketched with the precision of genuine comedy. The native grace and suavity of hereditary gentry are skilfully portrayed, especially in the scene where Clifford woos the charming Lady Emily, his friend Lord Gayville's sister, over a game of chess[1]; while the affectations of the vulgar rich are satirised in the scenes where old Alscrip suffers the inconveniences of fashion and his daughter expatiates insufferably on her imagined conquests in the polite world. The two households afford a pleasing study in social contrasts, which reach their climax when Lady Emily and Miss Alscrip are brought together ; and the scene shifts naturally from one side to the other, since Lord Gayville is to marry Miss Alscrip for her money. The pathetic interest centres in Miss Alton. Lord Gayville falls in love with Miss Alton in the streets, does not know who she is, traces her to her obscure lodging, like Belcour in *The West Indian*, and presses his courtship so eagerly that, to escape persecution, she enters service as Miss Alscrip's companion. It is easy to foresee what humiliations her selfrespect will suffer

[1] Act II, sc. 1.

among these purseproud plebeians, until she is unexpectedly discovered to be Clifford's long-lost sister, and the detection of a flaw in a will transfers the Alscrip fortune to her hands. Though infinitely inferior to Sheridan's masterpiece in construction and brilliance of dialogue, *The Heiress* exercised a stronger influence. It demonstrated how effectively characters could be contrasted by grouping them in two opposing parties ; it introduced a new type of snob, not only in the person of old Alscrip but in the two cleverly conceived stage characters, Mr and Mrs Blandish, who ingratiate themselves into both circles by abject flattery ; it showed what use could be made of the odious female as a foil to the virtues of the heroine whom she scorns, and it made popular an atmosphere of legal chicanery, forged wills and incriminating documents, which, henceforth, was taken over by many subsequent plays. Though Burgoyne found many imitators of his technique, *The Heiress* is one of the last productions of the eighteenth century that reflected new lights on human nature, thus retaining the spirit of comedy.

Yet another change was now coming over the British theatre. The ideas of Condorcet, William Godwin and Tom Paine[1] were in the air, and, when the public went to the playhouse, if they did not wish to be amused by operas and pantomimes, they were anxious to see these new enthusiasms on the stage. Themes were now looked for such as the rights of man, the dignity of humble life, the triumph of nature over artificial civilisation, the poetry of the country and other tenets of the growing romantic movement. Had these notions really stirred all classes, the conflict between old and new might, conceivably, have inspired a new and vigorous series of comedies. But the theatregoing public never thought of questioning the established order of the eighteenth century. These new ideas were, for them, an abstract speculation, quite distinct from their own traditions and conventionalities. Plays which now found favour necessarily ceased to be comedies and became either dramatised pamphlets or daydreams of the world set right. A public of this sort offered easy opportunities to any sentimentalist familiar with the stage ; and, during the last twenty years of the century, Holcroft, Mrs Inchbald, Colman the younger and Morton made reputations by adapting to the technique of the theatre the unsubstantial Utopias of everyday life.

---

[1] *L'Esquisse d'un tableau historique des progrès de l'esprit humain* (1793 ?) ; *Enquiry concerning Political Justice* (1793); *The Rights of Man* (1791) ; see Brailsford, H. N., *Shelley, Godwin and their Circle* (1913).

Holcroft, a dauntless fellow worker with Godwin and Paine, had begun, as early as 1778[1], to turn to account his talent for letters and his experience as prompter and strolling player; but it was not till 1792 that he produced, at Covent garden, *The Road to Ruin.* The play shows how even business men, such as the banker Mr Dornton and his head clerk Mr Sulky, conceal human hearts beneath their dry exteriors, and that even spend-thrifts, such as Dornton's son Harry, have a generous sense of duty despite their recklessness. When Harry's extravagance, at last, causes a run on his father's bank, the youth resolves to save the house by espousing the wealthy Mrs Warren, though really in love with her daughter. One half of the action takes place in the luxurious mansion of the odious widow, satirising her vicious circle, especially Goldfinch, the brainless man of fashion, with his endless tag 'that's your sort,' who is eager for the widow's wealth in order to defray his debts. In the end, the bank is saved by the staunch loyalty of Sulky; Harry, sobered by his experience, is free to marry the girl of his choice, and Mrs Warren is disinherited by the discovery of a new will. *The Road to Ruin* is Holcroft's least inartistic success; but *The Deserted Daughter* is a more striking indication of the tendency of the theatre. Taking a hint from Cumberland's *The Brothers,* he attempted to show how bad men may become good. Mordent neglects his dutiful wife, hates the world, plunges into debt and consorts with two dishonest lawyers, Item and Grime, who rob him. All this misery is due to the consciousness that he has a natural daughter, Joanna, whom he is afraid to own publicly. The play shows how Mordent passes from bad to worse, till he is on the brink of moral and financial ruin. But, just at the climax, Grime and Item are detected by means of an intercepted document; Joanna is married to the generous and wealthy young Cheveril; her relationship with Mordent is then made public; and the father, now relieved of his secret, is reconciled to his wife. *The Deserted Daughter* abounds in plagiarisms and artificialities. Mrs Sarsnet is the shadow of Mrs Malaprop; Joanna's physiognomical intuitions are copied from *Clarissa.* Item's despair at the loss of the telltale document is taken from *L'Avare* or *Aulularia*; Donald, the faithful Scottish servant, who talks unintelligible English, is the one attempt at humour. Yet, the play manages, in a melodramatic form, to portray the doctrines of the Godwin circle. Cumberland had shown, more

---

[1] *Crisis* at Drury lane. His first comedy was *Duplicity*, at Covent garden, in 1781. See, also, *post*, chap. XIII.

than twenty years earlier, how far demoralisation is due to the burden of an overgrown society. Holcroft goes further ; he champions the new belief in the perfectibility of man, and pictures how the soul springs up erect the moment that the burden is removed. Thus, in spite of its literary demerits, *The Deserted Daughter* is worth remembering, especially as Mrs Inchbald and Colman the younger had, also, chosen this doctrine as the theme of their most important work.

Elizabeth Sampson had been attracted to London by the glamour of the theatre, and, in London, she married the actor Inchbald. After she had spent several years in touring, *The Mogul Tale* was accepted for the stage, in 1784, and she established her reputation with *I'll tell you What*, at the Hay (the old Haymarket theatre), in 1785. The play is a model of construction, and, though the characters are hardly more than stage figures, the plot combines the humour of classical comedy with the moralising of the newer school. Mrs Inchbald never fulfilled the promise of this early work; but she understood the taste of the theatrical public and, in her next play, *Such Things Are* (1787), showed how successfully she could condense fashionable ideas into dramatic situations. At this time, John Howard's agitation for prison reform was a common topic of discussion, and harmonised well with popular faith in human goodness; but polite audiences at Covent garden would hardly have tolerated so inelegant a subject as gaol-life, if Mrs Inchbald had not also flattered the growing romantic taste for unreality by placing the scene in Sumatra. The central character, Haswell, as the good Samaritan among the sultan's prisoners, rouses the nobler sentiments latent within them, and discovers devotion and heroism in the deepest dungeons. The usual contrast to these grim scenes is provided by the English inhabitants of the island, especially by Sir Luke Tremor, who is always quarrelling with his wife, and by Twineall, whose attempts at social success are a satire on Lord Chesterfield's principles[1]. To put the seal on the sentimentality of the play, the sultan, in the end, proves to be a Christian, and one of the prisoners is discovered to be the wife whom he lost fifteen years before. Mrs Inchbald had a distinct gift for portraying the psychology of marriage, and, though so intricate and elusive a theme is best suited to the more leisurely treatment of the novel, she endeavoured, again and again, to compress fine-spun material

---

[1] Chesterfield's *Letters* had already been satirised with such success in *The Cozeners* at the Hay, in 1774, that two editions of the play appeared after Foote's death in 1778.

into one or other of her comedies. *Wives as they Were* (1797), a
study of a pleasure-loving girl in high society, whose nobler qualities
are gradually developed by the influence of her father in disguise,
though quite as successful as her other comedies[1], is a wholly
inadequate treatment of its theme when compared with the
powerful novel[2] into which it was afterwards elaborated. The most
typical of her domestic plays, *Every one has his Fault* (1793),
exhibits a series of ill-assorted or ill-judged marriages, from the
case of Lady Eleanor and Irwin, founded on *Amelia*, down to that
of the Placids, who quarrel incessantly, like the Dove *ménage* in
The Brothers. While showing how domestic unhappiness embitters
or even depraves each character, Mrs Inchbald rises to legitimate
comedy, and almost reaches a tragic note in the scene where Irwin
waylays and robs Lord Norland, his unforgiving father-in-law. But,
the public expected a happy issue out of all these afflictions ; so,
Mrs Inchbald invents a number of incidents which have not any
logical connection with either the plot or the characters, but which
brought tears into the eyes of her sentimental generation[3]. It
is worth noticing that the growing desire for glimpses of a less
conventional and prosaic life influenced even Mrs Inchbald. In
To Marry or not to Marry, Sir Oswin's plans to wed the
beautiful but mysterious Hester, of unknown origin, are deranged
by the appearance of his mortal foe, the exile Lavensforth. The
fugitive, attended by his faithful black servant, is lurking in the
neighbourhood, bent on murder. Yet, when it transpires that
the two enemies are father and lover of the same girl, the vendetta
evaporates in a drawingroom reconciliation.

George Colman, son of the dramatist and theatre-manager of
the same name, displayed more ingenuity in giving a romantic
atmosphere to his conventional ideas. He had already produced
two musical comedies at the Hay[4] before, in 1787, he made his name
at that theatre with *Inkle and Yarico*. Inkle, the respectable,
citybred youth, is conveying his betrothed Narcissa back to her
father, the wealthy governor of Barbadoes. On the voyage, he
and his comic attendant Trudge are accidentally left on an island
where they are saved from cannibals by two native women, with

[1] It had a run of twenty-four nights.

[2] *A Simple Story*, see *post*, chap. XIII of the present volume.

[3] *E.g.*, act v, sc. 1: Norland, while still unreconciled to his daughter, has adopted
her lost son. The small boy appears on the stage and intuitively recognises his
mother.

[4] *Two to One* (1784) and *Turk and no Turk* (1785).

whom they severally fall in love. Eventually, they reach Barbadoes, accompanied by their savage preservers. Inkle is now faced with the alternative of losing his profitable match with Narcissa or of abandoning the faithful Yarico, and, to guide him in this ethical problem, he has only the maxims of Threadneedle street[1]. Thus, the play teaches that a sound commercial training, which commands respect in London town, may lamentably fail its adept in the larger and more varied world outside, and, in the last two acts, Inkle is amply humiliated because of his signal ingratitude to his benefactress. To inculcate this lesson, Colman had worked one of Steele's *Spectators*[2] into a pleasing opera, not without touches of romantic imagination. Yarico's appeal to Inkle

> Come, come, let's go. I always feared these cities. Let's fly and seek the woods; and there we'll wander hand in hand together. No care shall vex us then. We'll let the day glide by in idleness; and you shall sit in the shade and watch the sunbeams playing on the brook, while I sing the song that pleases you

almost suggests *Paul et Virginie,* and must have sounded like music from a strange world to an English eighteenth century audience. Most of Colman's operas develop even more fanciful situations, though he softened their improbability by placing his scenes in wild and romantic periods such as the wars of the Roses[3], the Hundred Years' war[4], and the Moorish wars in Spain[5], or in an old English mansion of the time of Charles I[6]. In every case, the chief characters have the sentimental gentility which spectators admired and they are attended by servants whose uncouth manners and doglike fidelity do duty for humour. Such poverty of inspiration became only too apparent when Colman discarded picturesque settings and produced plays of modern life. *The Heir at Law* (1797) presents, indeed, in Pangloss, the stage pedant, compounded of servility, avarice and scholasticism, a character worthy of old comedy, and *John Bull*, in Job Thornberry, a sentimental type which, nevertheless, still lives. Colman's other attempts at comedy are not worth disinterring.

Thomas Morton, who was first known to the public by *Columbus* (1792), copied from Marmontel's *Les Incas,* and who first achieved success with *The Way to get Married* (1796)[7], modelled

---

[1] Act III, sc. 3.   [2] Taken by Steele from Ligon's *History of Barbadoes.*
[3] *Battle of Hexham* (1789).   [4] *Surrender of Calais* (1791).
[5] *The Mountaineers* (1793). The plot is borrowed from *Don Quixote.*
[6] *The Iron Chest* (1796). (Same theme as the novel *Caleb Williams.*)
[7] It had a run of forty-one nights.

his plays on the accepted type. But, amid all the eighteenth century sentiment and stage claptrap of incriminating documents, mistaken identities and sudden recognitions, he has flashes of whimsicality which carry the reader forward to early Victorian humour. In *The Way to get Married,* Tangent first meets Julia (his destined bride) when, in a fit of high spirits, he has girded himself with an apron and jumped behind the counter, to serve Alspice's customers. When Miss Sapless's will is read, her disappointed relatives learn that Caustic is appointed trustee of the fortune to be bestowed on any young woman about to be married who may please this misogynist. Dick Dashall is not an aristocratic debauchee but a city speculator, who takes his first clerk out hunting and arranges his business deals 'when the hounds are at fault[1]'! In *A Cure for the Heartache* (1797), the two Rapids, father and son, engaged in the tailoring business, rouse genuine laughter by their erratic attempts to play the gentleman. In *Speed the Plough* dame Ashfield's frequent allusions to Mrs Grundy[2] have made that name proverbial. Even in *The School of Reform* (1805), Lord Avondale's sordid accomplice Tyke combines, with his innate felony, eccentricity and dry humour.

Holcroft, Mrs Inchbald, Colman the younger and Morton by no means monopolised the attention of playgoers. They had to compete with innumerable farces, pantomimes and burlettas from the pens of Reynolds, O'Keeffe, Dibdin, Vaughan, Macnally, Cobb, Hoare and with many French and German adaptations, especially from Kotzebue. In 1789, Reynolds, to some extent, reverted to the examples of the classical school in *The Dramatist.* The plot is extravagantly impossible ; but the minor characters are well conceived. Lord Scratch, the newly-made peer, intoxicated by his unaccustomed position ; Ennui, who entertains the audience by boring the other characters and, incidentally, satirises the man of fashion by imitating his ways and, above all, Vapid, the dramatist, who disconcerts the company by his unforeseen and inopportune inspirations, all belong to legitimate comedy. O'Keeffe achieved the same quality of merit with *Wild Oats* (1791). The play shows how young Harry Thunder, in a passing fit of recklessness, runs away from Portsmouth academy and joins a company of strolling players. We might have expected an interesting picture of the vagrant actor's life ; but the prejudices of the public confined the chief action to genteel society. Only the character of Rover, the

---

[1] Act II, sc. 2.   [2] See, especially, act II, sc. 3.

irrepressible and impecunious comedian, is conceived in the true comic spirit. Cumberland, who had really been the first to influence the closing phase of this period of dramatic history, continued unceasingly to supply the theatre. His prolific industry produced nothing more noteworthy than *The Jew* (1794), a rehabilitation of that nation, in which Sheva, after a display of Hebrew frugality, suddenly shows Christian loving-kindness, and saves Sir Stephen Bertram's family from disunion by an unexpected act of generosity.

Bad as all these playwrights are, it is surprising that their work was no poorer. Throughout the period, the men who wrote for the theatre were gradually finding themselves enslaved to the demoralising exigencies of stage-carpentry and scenic display. This influence, at once the effect and the cause of dramatic decadence, began to appear as early as 1656 in *The Siege of Rhodes*, and, when Jeremy Collier shamed the theatre out of its chief source of amusement, managers availed themselves of 'foreign monsters,' such as French dancers and posture-makers, in order to retain the patronage of the old school. Henceforth, the stage never recovered its inspired simplicity. By the second half of the eighteenth century, spectacles were one of the chief attractions of the theatre. In 1761, Walpole describes how Garrick exhibited the coronation with a real bonfire and a real mob, while Rich was about to surpass this display by introducing a dinner for the knights of the Bath and for the barons of the Cinque ports[1]. In 1772, the English Roscius was represented on the title-page of a pamphlet treading on the works of Shakespeare, with the subjoined motto:

> Behold the Muses Roscius sue in vain,
> Tailors and carpenters usurp the reign[2];

and, in 1776, Colman, at the request of Sheridan, produced *New Brooms*, an ironical commendation of the opera's popularity. In 1789, stagemanagership was so far an attraction in itself that the same Colman was content to portray, not the manners of his age, but Hogarth's print of the Enraged Musician, under the title *Ut Pictura Poesis*. In 1791, *Cymon*, though an execrable play, was revived and had a run of thirty or forty nights, because the piece concluded with a pageant of a hundred knights and a representation of a tournay. In 1794, *Macbeth* was staged with a lake

---

[1] Letter to the Countess of Ailesbury 10 Oct. 1761. Mrs P. Toynbee's ed., vol. v, p. 133.

[2] *The Theatres. A poetical dissection. By Sir Nicholas Nipclose, Baronet.*

of real water. By the end of the century, the theatre-going public
had so far lost the dramatic sense that the audiences of Bristol
and Bath clamoured for the contemptible witches' dance which
Kemble had suppressed in his rendering of *Macbeth*[1], and London
society made a fashionable entertainment out of 'Monk' Lewis's
pantomimic melodramas[2] and a little boy's[3] ludicrous appearance
in great tragic *rôles*.

Such attractions as these had definitely degraded the scope
and province of the theatre. It has already been shown how
many tendencies hastened the perversion of the stage ; how the
thoughtful and studious turned to the novel; how the unpretentious developed a domestic culture of their own ; and how the
lovers of variety and magnificence were left to encourage in the
theatre that brilliance and sense of social distinction which have
ever since been one of its attractions. It remains to point out how
deeply realistic scenery vitiated the very spirit of dramatic representation. A play is a contrivance for revealing what goes on in
the mind, first by means of mannerisms and costumes, which are
mannerisms to be looked at, and then by words and actions. But,
as the characters of a great play move and speak on the stage, the
spectator follows these indications with something more than im-
personal interest. He is vaguely conscious of his own world of
thought and activity behind the characters, and, all through the
performance, his sympathy or imagination transforms the players
into parables of his philosophy of life[4]. Even ludicrous types, such
as Bobadill or Lord Foppington, in some sort embody his own sense
of comedy ; even the great tragedies of destiny, such as *Oedipus*
or *Lear*, in some way symbolise his unrealised daydreams of life
and death. It is in this way that players are the abstract and
brief chronicle of the time. Hence, elaborate scenery need not
hamper the true purpose of the drama, provided only that the
decorations preserve an atmosphere of unreality and leave the
imagination free to interpret the acting. But, as soon as the spirit
of make-believe is killed by realistic staging, the spectator loses

---

[1] 1802.   [2] See bibliography.

[3] W. H. W. Betty's meteoric career began at the age of twelve, at Belfast and
Dublin, in 1803. By 1804, he was established in popular favour at Covent garden and
Drury lane. In 1805, he appeared at both theatres alternately, acting, amongst other
parts, Romeo, Hamlet, Macbeth and Richard the Third. His last appearance as a
boy actor was at Bath in 1808. See bibliography, under Theatrical Pamphlets.

[4] Cf. Goethe, *Shakespeare als Theaterdichter* (1826), Genau genommen, so ist nichts
theatralisch, als was für die Augen zugleich symbolisch ist: eine wichtige Handlung,
die auf eine noch wichtigere deutet.

touch with himself.   He no longer enjoys the play as a wonderful and impossible crystallisation of his sentiments, nor can he give the characters the peculiar, imaginative setting which makes them a part of his mind.   His attention is diverted by painted canvas and welldrilled 'supers,' or, at best, he is forced to leave his own world outside and to enter into the lives and environment of the *dramatis personae.*   Innovations of costume rendered this disillusion more complete.   In the days of Quin, the characters appeared in a conventional dress, incongruous to us because unfamiliar, which raised the actors above the limitations of actual existence and made them denizens of the suggestive stage-world.   But, when Garrick played Macbeth in a scarlet and gold military uniform and dressed Hotspur in a laced frock and Ramillies wig, he was introducing realism, which destroyed the universality of the characters[1]; so that, after two generations of the new tradition, neither Lamb nor Hazlitt could endure to see Shakespeare acted; and Goethe, at a time[2] when the picture stage had firm hold of Germany, regarded Shakespeare more as a poet to be read in seclusion than as a dramatist to be appreciated in the theatre.   Nevertheless, it must not be forgotten that the genius of actors and the enterprise of managers have still kept alive the attention of scholars and poets, and this educated interest will one day succeed in effecting the reunion of literature with stagecraft.   But, in the meanwhile, authors, from the Georgian period onwards, have found that the drama of universal appeal misses fire amid realistic accessories, and they have endeavoured to give their audiences glimpses into the bypaths and artificialities of life, thus usurping the functions of the novel.

[1] Cf. Goethe, *Shakespeare als Dichter überhaupt* (n.d.), Niemand hat das materielle Kostüm mehr verachtet als er; er kennt recht gut das innere Menschenkostüm und hier gleichen sich alle.

[2] *I.e.*, *Regeln für Schauspieler* (1803), § 83, Das Theater ist als ein figurloses Tableau anzusehen, worin der Schauspieler die Staffage macht.

CHAPTER XIII

THE GROWTH OF THE LATER NOVEL

THE contents of the present chapter may seem at first sight, and that not merely to ill-informed persons, like those of a badly assorted omnibus-box. Indeed, unless the reader has at once fallen into the right point of view, the more he knows the more likely he is to see wrong. Amory, he may say, was born well within the seventeenth century. Peacock died when only the last third of the nineteenth had yet to run. Here are two centuries, or nearly so, to be covered in one chapter. Moreover, the characteristics of the various novelists to be noticed do not admit, at least in some cases, of any obvious classification of a serious and scientific kind. What has *John Buncle* to do with *Belinda*, or *St Leon* with *Gryll Grange*?

It is not necessary to be very careful in order to answer these questions. In the first place, the remarkable longevity and the peculiar circumstances of the oldest and the youngest members of the group render mere chronology singularly deceptive. It appears to be true that the author of *John Buncle* was born (though the exact year is not certain) not more than two or three years after the revolution of 1688: and it is certain that Peacock died in 1866. But Amory did not publish (though he may have written them earlier) his *Memoirs of Several Ladies* till he was nearly sixty-five, or *John Buncle* till he was nearly seventy, while *Gryll Grange*, though it appeared only six years before its author's death and has a wonderful absence of glaring Rip-van-Winkleism, is, in general conception, identical with its author's work of forty years earlier. And so we at once reduce the almost two hundred years of the first calculation to a modest sixty or seventy at most.

But there is a good deal more than this. Not only do the authors here dealt with represent the work of a manageable and definite, if immature, stage in the history of the English novel, but they also, by the very absence of their contemporaries Scott and Jane Austen, represent a transition, of the highest historical interest, between the great 'quadrilateral' of the mid-eighteenth century novel and the immense development of the kind which Scott and Jane Austen themselves were to usher in for the nineteenth century. Some of them, but by no means all, are, in a way, failures. All, or almost all, represent experiment, sometimes in partly mistaken kinds, like the terror novel of Mrs Radcliffe and Lewis, sometimes in 'sports' of individual and somewhat eccentric talent or genius, like the humour romances of Peacock. But, except in the latter case, and even there, perhaps, to some small extent, they all give evidence that the novel has not yet found its main way or ways—that it is, if not exactly in the wilderness, scarcely at home in the promised land. Hardly a single one of our company, with the possible exception of Maria Edgeworth, can be said to be purely normal: and even her normality was sorely interfered with by her father's eccentricities, by circumstances of this and that kind and, not least, perhaps, by an absence both of critical supervision and of creative audacity in herself.

Although *John Buncle*, by name at least, has a certain notoriety; although it was made the subject, by a great critic, of a criticism quite as debatable as, and only less debated than, Lamb's on Thomas Heywood; although it has been several times reprinted and has, at any rate, pleased some good wits mightily, it appears to be still very little known. And, as to its more than eccentric author scarcely any facts seem to be accessible except that he knew, or said he knew, Swift, that he was an Irishman and that, in his later years, at any rate, he lived in London. It is customary to call Amory mad; but, after repeated reading of his chief book and a fair study of his other work, the present writer has not been able to discover signs of anything more than the extremest eccentricity. He was, indeed, compact of 'crazes,' in the milder and more usual meaning of that word; and he indulged them without stint and without mercy. A passionate unitarian, or, as he preferred to call it, a 'Christian-Deist'; an eager student of several humane subjects, especially Roman antiquities, and of some sciences, especially those connected with medicine; by no means a bad critic of literature, who almost literally anticipates Macaulay in his estimate of Rymer; devoted to 'the ladies,' always in a strictly, though rather oddly, virtuous way; almost equally devoted to good food and good drink; a most imaginative describer of, and wanderer in, picturesque scenery—he composes his books by means of a succession of 'screeds,' devoted helter-skelter to all these subjects, and to a great many more.

This method, or contempt of method, Amory applies, in his two books, with the most extravagant faithfulness. In the case of the earlier, indeed, *Memoirs of Several Ladies*, it is applied in such a fashion that all but the most exceptionally equipped readers had very much better begin with the second, *John Buncle* itself. There is here enough of amusing matter, and of positive, though most eccentric, quality befitting a novel, to induce one to go back to the *Memoirs*: it is more than probable that a first introduction to the *Memoirs* might effectually prevent the reader from going on to the rest of the work, or from ever taking up anything else written by its author. Amory's announced, and, probably, quite serious, intention was to give biographies of eighteen ladies, as well as of 'the beautiful Isyphena and Judith the charming Hebrew,' with 'occasional accounts' of others. He has actually devoted a stout volume of more than five hundred pages almost wholly to one person, Mrs Marinda Benlow or Bruce, or, rather, to Mrs Marinda and all the other subjects described or adumbrated above, including a voyage to the Hebrides, continual raids on 'the destructive theology of Athanasius,' a long introduction to 'Mrs Monkhouse of Paterdale' [*sic*] 'on the banks of the river Glenkroden' [*sic*] and a large postscript of an even more miscellaneous character. The French phrase about a book 'letting itself be read' is sufficiently familiar: it is scarcely extravagant to say that these *Memoirs* absolutely refuse to submit themselves to reading, except in the fashion of the most dogged taskwork.

In *John Buncle* itself, Amory shows himself able to talk, or write, a little more like a man, if not of this, yet of his own eccentric, world. The hero becomes less nebulous: in fact, he is, at least, of the world of Dickens, when he sits down in the highest state of contentment, and, in fact, of positive carol, to a pound of steak, a quart of peas, another (or several others) of strong ale and divers cuts of fine bread. There has to be more and swifter handling to enable him to get through his allowance of more than half-a-dozen wives, all ravishingly beautiful; all strictly virtuous and rigidly Christian-Deist; most of them learned in arts and sciences, sacred and profane, and capable, sometimes, at least, of painting 'at the same time' pictures of Arcadia and of the crucifixion. They are generally discovered in some wild district of the north of England, where the hero, after perilous adventures, comes upon a perfectly civilised mansion, usually on the shore of a lake; introduces himself; is warmly received by both fathers and daughters (it is noteworthy that mothers rarely appear); argues on

points human and divine; marries; soon buries his wife; and
proceeds to console himself, after an interval more or less short, in
circumstances slightly varied in detail but generically identical.

And yet, though it is impossible to give any true description of
it which shall not make it seem preposterous, the book is not a
mere sandwich of dulness and extravagance. There is no doubt
that the quality which recommended it to Hazlitt, and made him
compare it to Rabelais, is his own favourite 'gusto.' One might
almost think that Amory had set himself to oppose, by anticipation,
not merely the school of 'sensibility' which was becoming fashionable in his own time, but the developments, nearly a century
later, which produced *Jacopo Ortis* and *Obermann*. Buncle has
his sorrows, and, despite his facility of selfconsolation, neither
mood appears to be in the least insincere, still less hypocritical.
But, sorrow is not his business in life, nor, despite his passion
for argument, introspection of any kind. It is his business to
enjoy; and he appears to enjoy everything, the peas and the antiquarian enquiries, the theological discussions and the beautiful
young ladies who join in them, the hairbreadth escapes and the
lovely prospects, nay, even the company of a scoundrel with some
character, like Curll. Hazlitt was perfectly right in selecting
the passage describing Buncle's visits with his friends the Dublin
'bloods' (some of them, apparently, greater scoundrels than Curll
himself) to an alehouse on the seashore. This display of mood is
one of the most remarkable things of its kind, and the wonder oi
it is not lessened when we remember that it was published, if not
written, by a man of seventy. That there is, practically, nothing—
either real or factitious—of the sense of regret for the past is less
surprising than that the gusto is itself not factitious in the least—
that it is perfectly fresh, spontaneous and, as it were, the utterance
of a fullblooded undergraduate. In none of the four great contemporary novelists is there this absolute spontaneity—not even
in Fielding; and Amory ought to have due credit for it.

With the final remark that this development of the eccentric
novel, towards the close of the first great harvest of the novel
itself, is, as a historical fact, worthy of no little attention, we may
pass to another single figure, and single book, also, in a way,
eccentric, but towering far above Amory in genius, and standing
alone; later than the great novelists of 1740—70; earlier than
the abundant novel-produce of the revolutionary period; exactly
contemporary with no one of much mark in the novel except

Miss Burney, and as different from her as the most ingenious imagination could devise—to Beckford and *Vathek*.

It cannot be denied that a great part of Beckford's celebrity is derived from, and has been always maintained by, sources which appeal to the more vulgar kinds of human interest. His wealth, which, even at the present day, would be reckoned great, and which, for his time, was immense and almost incredible; his lavish and fantastic expenditure of it; his pose as a misanthropic, or, at least, recluse, voluptuary; his eccentricities of all sorts; his dis. tinguished connections ; and even his long life—were powerful attractions of this kind to the vulgar. But there is no doubt that his literary powers were great: and not much doubt that, though his circumstances, possibly, circumscribed the exercise of them, they helped, to some extent, to produce the colour and character of his best work. It is a curious fact, but one attested by not a few instances, that men of narrow, or only moderately affluent, circumstances do not deal happily with imaginations of unbounded luxury. Fonthill and the means which created or supported it enabled Beckford to enlarge things still further and satisfactorily for the purposes of Samarah and Istakar.

Had he not written the unique romance which begins in one of these places and ends in (or below) the other, Beckford would still have had claims by no means insignificant to a position in literature, although his other work in the way of fiction[1] is not great, his various travels, the bibliography of which is rather complicated, are of quality high above the average[2], and his early skit in art criticism (*A History of Extraordinary Painters*) is extremely clever. Nevertheless, for all but anecdotic or very minute literary history, Beckford is *Vathek*.

This tale itself is not free from a certain overlay of deliberate eccentricity. As we read it in English, it is not Beckford's own work (though finally revised by him), but that of a certain Samuel Henley, surreptitiously published and translated from the French, which, Beckford said (if he said it)[3], he had written in

---

[1] *Modern Novel Writing or the Elegant Enthusiast* (1796), a satire not quite 'brought off'; and *Azemia* (1797), under the pseudonym 'Jenks.'

[2] The earlier parts appeared first in 1783 as *Dreams, Waking Thoughts and Incidents*, and display a rather juvenile coxcombry and jauntiness, no doubt due to the imitation of Sterne, but blended with much really fanciful writing. He suppressed most of the copies, and castigated the book severely when he reprinted it, fifty years later, with *Letters from Portugal* (1834), which are of very great merit.

[3] His interlocutor and reporter, Cyrus Redding, labours under something of the same doubt as to his 'security' which attached to Bardolph. But large and trustworthy additions have recently been made to our knowledge of Beckford and his work by Lewis

three days and two nights, thereby bringing on severe illness. Other reports say that he took something like a year over it. The matter, which will remind some readers of incidents in the life of Balzac, is of little real importance. And, perhaps, it is not too 'spoilsport' to observe that three days and two nights means about sixty-four hours and that *Vathek* does not extend beyond about eighty or ninety at most of pages like the present. Anybody who could write it at all, and had thought the lines of it out beforehand, could write three or four pages of it in an hour, have from thirty to forty left for food, sleep and the resting of his wrist—the strength of which latter would be the chief part of the wonder.

Whether, however, *Vathek* had been written in three days, or three weeks, or three months, or three years, its literary value would be affected not one jot. It is an Arabian tale of the familiar kind into which Anthony Hamilton and Voltaire had infused western sarcasm. The hero, grandson of Haroun, exaggerates the, by no means small, defects of his ancestor's character, and has very few of his merits, if any. He is what is now called a megalomaniac in everything: and, after a course of comparatively harmless luxury, devotes himself, partly under the influence of his sorceress mother, Carathis, to the direct service of Eblis. Crime now follows crime; and, though, in his journey towards the haunted ruins of Istakar (the site of the purgatory of Solomon and the inferno of Eblis himself), he conceives an at least human and natural passion for the beautiful Nouronihar, she is as much intoxicated by the prospect of supernatural power as he is himself. They are at last introduced, by a subordinate fiend, to the famous hall of Eblis, where, after a short interval, they meet with their due reward—the eternal torture of a burning heart—as they wander amid riches, splendours, opportunities of knowledge and all the other treacherous and bootless gifts of hell.

It is hardly possible to praise this conclusion too highly: it is almost Milton in arabesque, and, though Beckford has given himself insufficient space to develop the character of Nouronihar (Vathek himself, it must be confessed, has very little), there are hints and outlines which are almost Shakespearean. What opinion may be formed of the matter which leads up to this conclusion will depend almost entirely upon temperament. It has, in parts, been called, but, to some judgments, never is, dull: it

Melville, who has, also, at last rescued, from something like oblivion in the Hamilton archives, the *Episodes* to be dealt with below.

is certainly, in parts, grotesque, extravagant and even nasty. But Beckford could plead sufficient 'local colour' for it, and a contrast, again almost Shakespearean, between the flickering farce atrocities of the beginning and the sombre magnificence of the end. Beckford's claims, in fact, rest on the half-score or even half-dozen pages towards the end: but these pages are hard to parallel in the later literature of prose fiction.

There are, however, some points not directly touching the literary merit of *Vathek*, which can hardly be left quite unhandled even in the small space available here. It has been said that the tale was written in French and handed over by its author to Samuel Henley to translate. The translation, even with Beckford's own revision, is not impeccable, and sometimes fails strangely in idiom [1]. It is, however, better to read the book in the translation than in the original, which brings out too forcibly the resemblance to Hamilton and Voltaire: and eighteenth century French is not equal to the hall of Eblis. The circumstances of the actual publication are strange and not entirely comprehensible. That Henley, after much shilly-shallying on Beckford's part, should have 'forced the card' and published it without the author's permission, is not very surprising; but why he gave it out as 'translated from the Arabic' has never been satisfactorily explained. Beckford, for once reasonably enraged, published the French as soon as he could; but he did not include the *Episodes* which are referred to at the end, and which are congruous enough in *The Arabian Nights* fashion. He showed them, later, to some men of letters, including Rogers; but he never published them, and it is only recently that they have appeared, edited in French by Lewis Melville, and very well translated into English by Sir Frank Marzials. It would have been a pity if they had perished or remained unknown: but they can hardly be said to add to the greatness of *Vathek*, though they are not unworthy of their intended shrine. The first is a sort of doublet of the main story, a weaker Vathek, prince Alasi, being here actually made worse by a more malignant Nouronihar, princess Firouzkah. The heroine of the second is a peri of some charm, but her husband, Barkiarokh, is a repulsive and uninteresting

---

[1] The strangest of these errors is one which the present writer has never seen noticed. After the malodorous and murderous sacrifice to Eblis, when Vathek and his mother carouse, the French has the very ordinary phrase that Carathis *faisait raison à* the various toasts of her son. 'Do right' or 'do reason' is actually English in the same sense of pledging and counterpledging; but Henley writes: 'failed not to supply a reason for every bumper,' which, if not quite nonsense, is quite wrong sense.

scoundrel. By far the most striking is the last, the loves of the brother and sister prince Kalilah and princess Zulkais, which Beckford has left unfinished: whether from actual change of mind and taste or from one of his innumerable caprices and indolences, it is difficult to say.

The revolutionary novel of Godwin, Holcroft, Mrs Inchbald and Bage may be said to be the first instance (unless the novel of sensibility be allowed a position in the same line) of fiction proper (as distinguished from religious or other allegory) succumbing to purpose: and there may be some who would say that the inevitable evil of the connection showed itself at once. Here, of course, the French originals are obvious and incontestable. Rousseau in all the four, Diderot, to no small extent, in Bage, supply, to those who know them, commentaries or parallel texts, as it were, to be read with *Caleb Williams* and *A Simple Story*, *Anna St Ives* and *Hermsprong*. But the difference, not merely of genius, but of circumstance and atmosphere, is most remarkable.

Godwin, though he wrote three early novels of which even biographers have been able to say little or nothing, and which fail to leave the slightest effect on the most industrious searchers-out of them, produced nothing of importance in this kind till long after Holcroft, who, indeed, was a much older man. But *Caleb Williams* (1794) is the most famous and *St Leon* (1799), with all its misplanning and even unreadableness, the most original, of the group; so we may begin with Godwin.

Both the books mentioned are closely connected with *Political Justice*, to the account of which, elsewhere[1], reference must be made: their successors *Fleetwood* (1805), *Mandeville* (1817) and *Cloudesley* (1830), though they can hardly be said to be alien in temper, have far less distinction, and it is doubtful whether anyone now living has read them twice. The present writer, some years ago, found a first reading severe enough exercise to indispose him towards repetition of it, though *Fleetwood*, perhaps, is worth reading once. *Caleb Williams*, on the other hand, has been repeatedly reprinted and has, undoubtedly, exercised real fascination on a large number of wellqualified readers. It is, indeed, usual to praise it; and, in such work (for novels are meant to please, and, if they please, there is little more to be said), it is unnecessary and, indeed, idle to affect exception. The book is certainly full of ingenuity; and the doubles and checks

[1] See *ante*, chap. II.

and fresh starts of the criminal Falkland and his half unwilling servant and detective Caleb display that molelike patience and consecutiveness which distinguish Godwin's thought throughout his work. To some tastes, however, not only is the 'nervous impression' (as Flaubert called it, in a phrase of great. critical value) disagreeable, but there is an additional drawback in the total inability which they, at least, feel to sympathise with either master or man. If, at about half way in the length of the actual book, Falkland could have been made to commit a second murder on Caleb and be hanged for it, the interest would, to these tastes, have been considerably improved. Still, *Caleb Williams* has, generally, been found exciting. *St Leon*, though some have thought it 'terrible,' has more often incurred the charge of dullness. It is dull, and, yet, strangely enough, one feels, as, at least in the cases above referred to, one does not feel in respect of *Caleb Williams*, that it just misses being a masterpiece. It represents that curious element of 'occultism' which mixed itself largely with the revolutionary temper, and is associated for all time in literature with the names of Cagliostro and Mesmer. It contains the best examples of Godwin's very considerable, if rather artificial, power of ornate writing. The character of the heroine or part-heroine Marguerite (who has always been supposed to be intended for a study of the author's famous wife Mary Wollstonecraft), if, again, a little conventional, is, really, sympathetic. Had the thing been more completely brought off, one might even have pardoned, though it would have been hardly possible not to notice, the astonishing anachronisms, not merely of actual fact, but of style and diction, which distinguish almost the whole group dealt with in this chapter, and which were only done away with by Scott in the historical or quasi-historical novel. And, it is of great importance, especially in a historical survey, to remember that, when the problem of the authorship of the *Waverley Novels* presented itself, persons of very high competence did not dismiss as preposterous the notion that Godwin might be 'the Great Unknown.' In fact, he had, as these two books show, and as others do not wholly disprove, not a few of the characteristics of a novelist, and of a great one. He could make a plot; he could imagine character; and he could write. What deprived him of the position he might have reached was the constant presence of purpose, the constant absence of humour and the frequent lack, almost more fatal still, of anything like passion. The coldbloodedness of Godwin and his lack of humour were, to some extent, sources of power to him in writings like

Political Justice; they destroyed all hope of anything but abnormal success in novel-writing.

His friend and senior, Holcroft[1], possessed both humour and passion, as his plays and his possibly 'doctored' *Autobiography* show; nor is humour absent from his first novel *Alwyn* (1780), which, however, does not really belong to the class we are discussing, but is a lively semi-picaresque working up of the author's odd, youthful experiences on the stage and elsewhere. The much later *Anna St Ives* (1792) and *Hugh Trevor* (1794) are similar in general temper to *Caleb Williams* and, indeed, to *Political Justice* itself, of which some would have Holcroft to have been the real inspirer. Unfortunately, the interest, which, as was said above, must be allowed to Godwin's chief novel has never, it is believed, been discovered by any recent reader in these two long and dull vindications, by means of fiction, of the liberty, equality and fraternity claptrap; though, at the time, they undoubtedly interested and affected minds in a state of exaltation such as Coleridge's and Southey's. Holcroft's very considerable dramatic faculty, and his varied experience of life, still enable him, especially in *Anna St Ives*, to intersperse some scenes of a rather livelier character than the rest; but it is very questionable whether it is worth anyone's while to seek them out in a desert of dreary declamation and propagandist puppet-mongering.

Mrs Inchbald[2], like Holcroft, was an intimate friend of Godwin; indeed, she was one of those rather numerous persons whom that most marriage-seeking of misogamists wished to marry before he fell into the clutches of Mrs Clairmont. Pretty, clever, an accomplished actress, an industrious woman of letters, with an unblemished character in very queer society, but, very decidedly, a flirt—there was, perhaps, none of these rather heterogeneous qualities or accidents which, taken in connection with the others, was not useful to her as a novelist; and by her novels she has lived. *A Simple Story* has always been more or less popular: and the curiously 'modern' novel *Nature and Art*, in which a judge sentences to death a woman whom he has formerly seduced, from time to time receives attention. In both, her dramatic experience— for she was playwright as well as actress—enabled her to hit upon strong situations and not contemptibly constructed character; while her purely literary gift enabled her to clothe them in good

[1] See *ante*, chap. XII. [2] See *ante*, chap. XII.

form. But the criticism passed on her—that prevalent ideas on education and social convention spoil the work of a real artist— is true, except that a real artist would not have allowed the spoiling. Mrs Inchbald stands apart from Godwin and Holcroft, on the one side, and from Bage, on the other, in the fact that, as some, though not many, other people have done, she combined sincere religious belief (she was a lifelong Roman catholic) with revo- lutionary political notions; and this saved her, in books as in life, from some blemishes which appear in others of the group. But the demon of extra-literary purpose left the marks of his claws on her.

Robert Bage, the last of this quartette, is differentiated from them by the fact that he is not unfrequently amusing, while the others seldom succeed in causing amusement. Sir Walter Scott has been sometimes found fault with, first, because he included some of Bage's books in the 'Ballantyne novels,' and, secondly, because he did not include what he himself, certainly with some incon- sistency, allowed to be the best (which was also the last), *Herm- sprong* or *Man as he is not* (1796). He also omitted the earlier *Man as he is* (1792) and *The fair Syrian* (1787) but gave the three others, *Mount Henneth* (1781), *Barham Downs* (1784) and *James Wallace* (1788). There is, perhaps, some ground for approving his practice at the expense of his precept. Bage, a quaker who became a freethinker, was an active man of business, and did not take to novel-writing till he was advanced in life. As was said above, though there is much of Rousseau in him, there is almost more of Diderot, and even a good deal of Voltaire; and, it was from the latter two of the trio that he derived the free speech as well as free thinking for which even a critic and editor so wisely and honestly free from squeamishness as Scott had to apologise. As the titles of his two last novels show, and as the dates of them may explain, they are the most deeply imbued with purpose. Hermsprong himself, in fact—and one cannot but think must have been perceived to be by his author's shrewdness—is something very like a caricature. He is 'the natural man'—or, rather, the extremely unnatural one—who, somehow, sheds all tradition in religion, politics and morals; and who, as we may put it, in a combination of vernacularities, 'comes all right out of his own head.' He is, also, very dull. *Man as he is* possesses rather more liveliness; but *The fair Syrian* (of which even the British museum seems to possess only a French translation) is duller than *Hermsprong*. *James Wallace* admits a good deal of sentimentality; but

Mount Henneth and *Barham Downs*, though they have much which suggests the French substantive *fatrasie* and the French adjective *saugrenu*—though it is also quite clear, now and then, that Bage is simply following his great English predecessors, especially Fielding and Sterne—have, like *Man as he is*, and, perhaps, in greater measure, a sort of unrefined liveliness, which carries them off, and which Scott, who was almost equally as good a judge of his kind of wares as a producer of them, no doubt recognised. Bage, in fact, when he leaves revolutionary politics and ethics on one side, and indulges what Scott did not scruple to call his 'genius,' can give us people who are more of this world than the folk of almost any of his contemporaries in novel-writing, except Fanny Burney earlier, and Maria Edgeworth later. His breeding, his circumstances and, perhaps, his temper, were not such as to enable him to know quite what to do with these live personages—but they are there.

To say that Maria Edgeworth herself holds really an outlying position in the group of revolutionary novelists may seem absurd to some readers; but there are others who will take the statement as a mere matter of course. In both temper and temperament, no one could have less of the revolutionary spirit; but the influence of the time, and, still more, that of her father, coloured the whole of her earlier and middle work. There is no doubt that Richard Edgeworth—who was a sort of John Buncle revived in the flesh and with the manners of a modern gentleman—affected his daughter's work very much for the worse, by the admixture of purpose and preachment which he either induced her to make or (in some cases, pretty certainly) intruded on his own account. But it is possible that, without this influence, she would have written less or not at all.

The influence was itself derived from the earlier and less aggressive—or, at least, less anarchic—side of the French *philosophe* movement—ethical, economic, humanitarian, rather than politically or religiously revolutionary. Marmontel (not only or mainly in the actual title *Moral Tales*) was, perhaps, the most powerful single influence with the Edgeworths; there is practically nothing of Voltaire or Diderot, and not much of Rousseau, except on the educational side. If, as was admitted above, this element may have had a certain stimulating effect, it certainly affected the products of that stimulation injuriously. But, fortunately, Miss Edgeworth's native genius (we need not be afraid to use the word in regard to her, though Scott may have been too liberal in applying it to Bage) did not allow itself to be wholly suppressed either by her French models or by her father's interference. It found its way in three different directions, producing, in all, work which wants but a little, if, in some instances, it wants even that, to be of the very first class.

To mention these in what may be called hierarchical order, we ought, probably, to take first the attempts in what may be called the regular novel, ranging from *Belinda* in 1801 to *Helen* in 1834. This division, except when it allies itself with the next, has been the least popular and enduring part of her work; but, at least in *Belinda*, it deserves a much higher reputation than it has usually enjoyed. In fact, *Belinda* itself, though it does want the pro-verbial 'that!', wants only that to be a great novel. The picture of the half-decadent, half-unfledged, society of the meeting of the eighteenth and nineteenth centuries is, at times, extremely vivid, and curiously perennial. In the twentieth, at least, one has not to look far before detecting, with the most superficial changes, Lady Delacour and Mrs Lutwidge, and even Harriot Freke. The men are not so good. Clarence Harvey, the hero, is a possible, but not an actual, success, and the spendthrift Creole is mere stuff of melodrama; while the good people (in a less agreeable sense than the roly-poly pudding in *The Book of Snobs*) are 'really too good.' This does not apply to Belinda herself, who is a natural girl enough; but, in her, also, there is the little wanting which means much. *Belinda*, let it be repeated, is not a great novel; but, an acute and expert reviewer might have detected in its author some-thing not unlike a great novelist, at a time when there was nothing in fiction save the various extravagances criticised in other parts of this chapter.

The second group of Maria Edgeworth's novels with which, as has been said, the first, as in *The Absentee*, to some extent, coalesces, has had better luck, and, perhaps, deserves it. This consists of the Irish stories from which Sir Walter Scott professed to have derived at least part of the suggestion of his own national kind; these began early in 1800, with the striking, but rather too typical and chronicle-fashioned, *Castle Rackrent*; and which, later, produced its master-pieces in the already mentioned *Absentee* (1809) and in *Ormond* (1817). There is not any room here for particularising the merits of these most agreeable and still fairly wellknown books; but, from the historical point of view, there is one thing about them which deserves much study and which was probably what Scott

honoured. The utilisation of national or pseudo-national or provincial peculiarities as an attraction in fictitious treatment of
life had originated with the drama, though we find traces of it in
that rich seed-heap, the French *fabliau*. Now, the drama almost
always exaggerates ; it may drop the actual cothurnus and mask, but
it always demonstrates their reason for existence. When Smollett
borrowed the device for the novel, he kept its failing, and so did
others ; Miss Edgeworth did not. In the first division of her work,
and, even, in the third, to which we are coming, she may, sometimes,
especially in her dialogue, miss that absolute verisimilitude and
nature which the critical genius of Dryden had first detected in
the creative genius of Chaucer and Shakespeare. In her dealings
with Irish scenes and persons, she never misses it. She cannot
touch her ancestral soil (it was not exactly her native, and one might
draw fanciful consequences from the relation) without at once
acquiring that strange creative or mimetic strength which produces
in the reader of fiction—poetic, dramatic or prosaic alike—a sudden,
but quiet, undoubting conviction that these things and persons were
so and not otherwise.

Still, there are some who, whether in gratitude for benefits
bestowed upon their first childhood or because of the approach of
their second, regard the third division of Maria Edgeworth's work
not merely with most affection but with most positive and critical
admiration. The supremest 'grace of congruity' which has been
granted to the Irish books and passages must, indeed, again be
denied to this third group, at least as universally present. No
schoolboys, and certainly no Eton schoolboys, ever talked like the
personages of *Eton Montem* ; and the personal crotchets of her
father and the general crotchets of his school too frequently
appear. One is sometimes reminded of the bad, though oftener of
the good, side of Edgeworth's friend Day in dealing with similar
subjects. But, the fact remains that, in *The Parent's Assistant*
(1796—1801) and *Early Lessons* (1801), in *Moral Tales* (1801)
and *Popular Tales* (1804), *Frank* (1822) and *Harry and Lucy*
(1825), real children, save for a few touches in Shakespeare and
still fewer elsewhere, first appear—not the 'little misses' and 'little
masters' of her own earlier times, but children, authentic, independent of fashion and alive. It is not in the least necessary to
be a child-worshipper in order to see this : it is only necessary to
be, what, perhaps, is not so common, a person who has eyes.
Rosamund, whose charm may, possibly, be enhanced by the contrast
of her very detestable mamma ; Frederick, in *The Mimic* ; Frank

himself, in not a few of his appearances, both earlier and later, not to
mention many others, are examples of that strange power of fiction in
reconciling, and more than reconciling, us to what might be tedious
in fact. You might, in real life, after a short time, at any rate,
wish that their nurses would fetch them—on paper, they are a joy
for ever. While, as for strict narrative faculty, the lady who could
write both *Simple Susan* and *L'Amie Inconnue*, with the unmawkish
simplicity of the first and the unmannerised satire of the second,
had it as it has been possessed by very few indeed of her class.

Many people know that Jane Austen, in that spirited defence
of the novelist's house which appears in *Northanger Abbey*, showed
her grace as well as her wit by a special commendation of *Belinda*;
but, even those who have forgotten this are likely to remember
that the greater part of the same book turns upon satire of a
certain department of novel-writing itself to which Miss Edgeworth did not contribute. To this department—the terror novel,
novel of mystery, novel of suspense, or whatever title it may
most willingly bear—we must now come. With the revolutionary
group[1], it practically divides the space usually allotted to the novel
itself for the last decade of the eighteenth, and the first of the
nineteenth, century; though there was an immense production in
other varieties. Its own courts or precincts were populous, but
with a folk, in general, astonishingly feeble. If such a man, or
even such a boy, as Shelley could perpetrate such utter rubbish
as *Zastrozzi* and *St Irvyne*, the gutter-scribbler was not likely
to do much better. And, as a matter of fact, all those who have
made exploration of the kind will probably agree that, except
to the pure student, there is hardly a more unprofitable, as
well as undelightful, department of literature than that of the
books which harrowed and fascinated Catherine Morland and
Isabella Thorpe and the 'sweet girl' who supplied them with lists
of new performances piping hot and thrillingly horrid[2].

It is, however, not without justice that three writers—two of
the first flight of this species, and one of the second—have been
able to obtain a sort of exemption—if though of a rather curious and
precarious character—from the deserved oblivion which has fallen

---

[1] This group spread its ripples very widely, and affected some of the work of
Charlotte Smith, whose best known book, however, *The Old Manor House*, despite its
date (1793), is 'terrorist' in neither sense. Nor is the once, and long enormously,
popular *Children of the Abbey* of Regina Maria Roche (1796).

[2] It is only of late years that justice has been done to another novel-satire on these
absurd novels, *The Heroine* of Eaton Stannard Barrett (1813).

on their companions. These are Ann Radcliffe, Matthew Gregory Lewis and Charles Robert Maturin.

Something like a whole generation had passed since what was undoubtedly the first example, and, to some extent, the pattern, of the whole style, *The Castle of Otranto*, had appeared. Horace Walpole was still alive ; but it is not probable that he regarded this sudden mob of children or grandchildren with any affection. Indeed, he had just pronounced *Otranto* itself to Hannah More as 'fit only for its time'—a judgment which it is not difficult to interpret without too much allowance for his very peculiar sincerity in insincerity. At any rate, the new books were very fit for their time ; and, though the German romances which (themselves owing not a little to *Otranto*) had come between influenced Lewis, at least, very strongly, it is not certain that they were needed to produce Mrs Radcliffe. Much stronger influence on her has been assigned, and some must certainly be allowed, to Clara Reeve[1], the direct follower (again not to his delight) of Walpole, whose *Champion of Virtue* (better known by its later title *The Old English Baron*) appeared in 1777 : and, though a rather feeble thing, has held its ground in recent reprints better than either *Otranto* or *Udolpho*. Clara Reeve's really best work, though one never likely to have been, or to be, popular, is *The Progress of Romance*, a curious, stiffly oldfashioned, but by no means ill-informed or imbecile, defence of her art (1785). She also, in her *Charoba*, anticipated, though she did not originate, and it is not sure whether she directly suggested, the story of Landor's *Gebir*.

On Mrs Radcliffe herself, something of the general revolutionary fermentation, no doubt, worked ; yet, there was much else not, perhaps, entirely unconnected with that fermentation, but not directly due to it, though arising out of the taste for the picturesque, for romantic adventure, for something foreign, unfamiliar, new, as well as to the blind search and striving for the historical novel. Her own influence was extraordinary : for it was more or less directly exerted on two writers who exercised a most potent influence, not merely on the English, but on the European, literature or world in the early part of the next century. Not a few other writers in other kinds of novel or book have had bevies of Catherines and Isabellas contending for 'the next volume' at circulating library doors. It has not happened to any other to give a novelist like Scott something of his method, and a poet like Byron nearly the whole of his single hero.

[1] See *ante*, vol. x, chap. III.

Of the novels themselves, as actual works of art, or as actual procurers of pleasure, it is not easy to speak so decisively. Except in the first, *The Castles of Athlin and Dunbayne* (1789), where the author had hardly found her method, and in the posthumous *Gaston de Blondeville* (1826)[1], the general scheme is remarkably and, to some tastes, tediously uniform—repeating over and over again the trials and persecutions of a heroine who, at last, wins through them. Of the processes by which she herself, at last, achieved something beyond the stock personages who, as Scott says,

had wept or stormed through the chapters of romance, without much altera-tion in their family habits and characters, for a quarter of a century before her time,

Sir Walter's own study of her gives, perhaps, the best criticism existing or likely to exist. His title for the motive of her more accomplished books—suspense—shows the expert. But actual enjoyment and a sense of obligation, not merely for that but for help in craftsmanship, made him, perhaps, a little too favourable. It is difficult to conceive anything more childish than her first novel, which carries out the most conventional of thin plots by the aid of characters who have not any character at all, an almost entire absence of dialogue, stock descriptions, stilted and absurd language and an exaggeration of the hopeless deformation and confusion of local colour and historical verisimilitude which dis-tinguishes the age.

A Sicilian Romance (1790) is a very little better, but not much; it approaches nearer to the main theme of the persecuted heroine, the main scene of wild landscape, house or castles honeycombed with dungeons, broken stairs and secret passages, and the main method of ingenious, intricate, at first alarming, but, so far as any total result goes, almost wholly futile, incident. In the three

---

[1] This book, never united with her other novel-work, and very little known, is a curious instance of the danger of changing styles. Although published ten years after *Waverley*, it seems to have been written more than ten years before it. The author shows all the faults of the historical novel before Scott, and none of her own merits. Its hopelessness may be judged from one speech of one character, an ecclesiastic of the time of Henry III. 'I only doubt of his guilt, and that carries me no further than to *relinquishment of the prosecution*'! At the same time, with *Gaston de Blondeville* appeared a considerable body of *Poems* and *Letters*. Some of these last, describing travel, are good and connect themselves with the descriptive parts of the novels. Some of the shorter and more descriptive poems, such as *The River Dove, The Hazel Tree* and so forth are, also, mildly tolerable; but the verse romance, *St Albans Abbey*, between three and four hundred pages long, is quite insignificant in quality and insufferably tedious in quantity.

central books *The Romance of the Forest* (1791), *The Mysteries of Udolpho* (1794) and *The Italian* (1797), these motives, methods, or machineries are fully developed ; and, among Mrs Radcliffe's admirers, each has its partisans. The first is the freshest, and its heroine Adeline, perhaps, is more attractive than her successors, Emily and Ellena. The far-renowned *Mysteries* supply the fullest, the most popular and, perhaps, the most thoroughly characteristic example of the style. *The Italian* is the most varied, the least mechanical and, in the personage of the villain Schedoni (whose almost legitimate descendant the ordinary Byronic hero undoubtedly is), has, by far, the most important and, almost, powerful character— a character not, perhaps, wholly impossible in itself, and, even if so, made not wholly improbable by the presentation in the book. In fact, one may go so far as to say that, for anyone who has 'purged considerate vision' enough to behold Schedoni, unaffected by the long vista of his deplorable successors, there is power in him ; while, in all the three books, the various new motives above referred to make a strong combined appeal. In particular, though Mrs Radcliffe had never visited Italy itself, she knew the Rhine with its castles ; she knew the more picturesque parts (including the Lakes) of her own country ; and she utilised her knowledge more than cleverly.

On the other hand, there are two drawbacks (though, perhaps, one of them may be included in the other) which Scott himself perceived and admitted, and which will probably always prevent some, if not most, readers from appreciating *Udolpho* and its fellows. These are the extraordinary elaboration of means with futility of result already noted, and the 'explained supernatural,' which, perhaps, is only a subvariety of that blend. For, this latter, defence has sometimes been tried from different points of view ; some urging that surely nobody can want such nonsense as the supernatural to remain unexplained and accepted ; others, that the explanation gives room for, and, indeed, necessitates, no small possession of craftsmanship, if not of actual artistry, on the part of the novelist. Neither plea needs much critical examination. But the fact certainly remains that, to some readers, not, perhaps, the unfittest, this much ado about nothing process, in the first instance, means disappointed irritation, and, in after cases, utter boredom and lack of interest. The further prevalence of the same much ado about nothing method, even in cases where there is nothing supernatural, is, perhaps, equally tedious, if less positively irritating. It has been pointed out that pages on pages, and,

almost, chapters on chapters, of *Udolpho* are occupied by the
account of Emily wandering, or being led, about the castle for hours
by one of Montoni's ruffians, and being brought back to her room
without anything really dreadful being done to her, even in the
way of threats. Once, her aunt is, with some violence, removed
from her company ; but nobody injures her, locks the door, or
interferes with her in any way. When she is in the hall, a
wounded man is carried past; but, again, nobody even speaks to her.
She wanders about the castle and sees a track of blood (which
is not very remarkable, considering the wounded man) and concludes that her aunt has been murdered. She finds her maid in a
room. And then she goes back to her own, and—very sensibly—
goes to bed.

It is fair to say that, in *The Italian*, both hero and heroine are
exposed to much more real dangers ; and that there are situations
not by any means lacking in strength. It would certainly stand
reprinting better than the others. But it shares with them the drawback that there is no real suspense about this so-called 'novel of
suspense.' Jack is sure to have Jill ; both Jack and Jill are sure
to get out of their troubles ; and, though there is not exactly
'much ado about nothing' here, as there almost, or altogether, is
in *The Mysteries*, there is certainly rather little wool for a very
great cry.

It was one of the numerous clevernesses of Matthew Gregory
Lewis that he saw the incompatibility of a certainly happy ending
for 'a tale of terror.'   It was one result of the defects which prevented his cleverness from reaching genius that he went to the
other extreme and made *The Monk* (1796), as a whole, a mere mess
and blotch of murder, outrage, *diablerie* and indecency.   His
scheme, indeed, was much less original than Mrs Radcliffe's ; for
he had been in Germany and there is no doubt that he had
taken for his model not merely the poems of Bürger and the
other early romantics but the drama and fiction of Schiller
and of Heinse, in *The Robbers* (1781) and in *Ardinghello* (1785).
The consequence was that *The Monk* did not please people
even so little squeamish as Byron, and has never, except in a
quasi-surreptitious manner, been reprinted in its original form.
It is 'messy' enough, even in its author's revised version, being
badly constructed and extravagant in every sense. It has, however, some scenes of power. The temptress Matilda de Villanegas
(better taken as an actual woman, fiend-inspired, than as a

mere succubus) ranks next to Schedoni, in this division, as a character; and the final destruction and damnation of the villainous hero is not quite so ludicrous as it very easily might have been. Lewis, before his early death, wrote (or, rather, translated) other novels; but none of them attained, or, in the very slightest degree, deserved, the vogue of *The Monk*, or of his plays and verses. The most famous of the latter, *Alonzo the Brave and the Fair Imogene*, occurs in *The Monk* itself. Mrs Radcliffe had set the example of inserting verse, sometimes not very bad verse, but she never shows the somewhat loose, but distinctly noteworthy, novel and even influential command of rapid rhythm which was another of Lewis's oddly flawed, but by no means ordinary, gifts.

The kind itself, as has been said, flourished like a weed in the last decade of the eighteenth century, and the first two or three of the nineteenth—in fact, examples of it, such as Leitch Ritchie's *Schinderhannes*, were written in the forties, and it may be said to have left strong traces on the early, if not, also, on the later, work of Bulwer. But, in and of itself, it never produced another writer of importance, with one exception. That exception, however, Charles Robert Maturin, for the sake of at least one thing that he did, and perhaps, of a certain quality or power diffused through his other work, deserves to rank far above Lewis, and not a little above Mrs Radcliffe. In technical originality, indeed, he must give way, certainly to her, and, in a fashion, also, to Lewis; while he probably owes something to Beckford, to whose master-scene, at the close of *Vathek*, even his best things are very inferior. He borrowed his 'shudder' from the two former; but he made it much more real and much less commonplace. Probably because he was in orders, he produced his first books under the pseudonym 'Murphy,' and the title of the first, *The Fatal Vengeance* or *The Family of Montorio* (1807), may be said to be rather engaging in the frankness with which it proclaims its extraction and its character. In his next two, however (and the fact is important in connection with Maria Edgeworth's work), he came nearer home. and wrote *The Wild Irish Boy* (1808) and *The Milesian Chief* (1811). Then, he diverged to tragedy and produced the rather wellknown play *Bertram*, which was introduced (1816) to Drury lane by Scott and Byron, was very successful and was criticised with more justice than generosity by Coleridge in *Biographia Literaria*. *Women* followed, in 1818; and then, in 1820, he produced his masterpiece *Melmoth the Wanderer*.

Nothing is easier than to 'cut up' *Melmoth*; it has been done
quite recently, since the publication of a modern edition, with the
same 'facetious and rejoicing ignorance' which Lockhart pilloried
long ago, as exhibited towards Maturin's own jealous critic
Coleridge. A worse constructed book hardly exists: for it is a
perfect tangle of stories within stories. It has pathos, which,
not unfrequently, descends to the *sensiblerie* of the imitators
of Rousseau; and terror, which not unfrequently grovels to the
melodrama caricature of Lewis himself generally, and his imitators
almost always. But its central theme—the old bargain with
Satan, refreshed and individualised by the notion of that bargain
being transferable—is more than promising, and there are numerous
passages, both in the terrible and in the pathetic varieties, which
entirely escape just sarcasm. Above all, there is an idiosyncrasy
about the book which has attracted good wits both at home and
abroad—Balzac is one famous instance and Dante Rossetti another
—and which it is rather difficult to understand how any good wit,
if possessed of the power of critical winnowing, can miss. Melmoth
himself, with his famous 'piercing eyes,' touches the right nerve
not seldom, if he misses it sometimes; and the Indian-Spanish
girl Isidora or Immalee is equally successful in her different way.
Maturin followed *Bertram* with two failures in play form, and
Melmoth with a doubtfully successful novel *The Albigenses*, in
1824, the year of his death. But he stands or falls by *The Wanderer*,
with the piercing eyes, and those who can comprehend the literature of power will say that, with whatever slips and staggering, he
stands.

The allowance which ought to be made for Maturin can hardly
be extended to two sisters Jane and Anna Maria Porter, who, in
their day, enjoyed something like fame, and who seem to have
thought themselves unjustly supplanted in still greater fame by
their early friend Scott. Anna Maria Porter began at a preposterous age (she was barely thirteen) to write fiction, and
continued to do so till her death in 1832, producing, in all, some
two or three score volumes. But, even wellinformed students
of literature would be puzzled to name one of them, unless they
had chanced to be brought in contact with it, and neither such
chance contact nor deliberate research will discover much in any
of her books but amiable incompetence. On the other hand, the
elder sister Jane, who postponed her *début* till she had reached an
age double that at which her sister had begun to write, produced,

in *Thaddeus of Warsaw* (1803) and *The Scottish Chiefs* (1810), two books of which every one has heard, and which, perhaps, even now, not a very few have read. They are, however, almost utter, though virtuous and wellintentioned, rubbish; and their popularity, indeed, their existence, can only be accounted for by the irresistible *nisus* towards, and appetite for, romantic matter which characterised the time. A more complete absence of local colour and historical sense than in Mrs Radcliffe or the three sisters Lee; the tears of the sentimental, dashed, to some extent, with the terrors of the other, school; diction and conversation incredibly stilted and bombastic; adventure only exciting to the rawest palate; and a general diffusion of silliness, characterised these almost famous books. Only to a taste so crude as their own can they give any direct pleasure now; but, to the student, they may still be of some interest as an example of the days of ignorance of the historical novel, and one can excuse them something for having produced some of the most delightful exercises of Thackeray's schoolboy pencil.

It would be impossible to find a greater contrast to them than a somewhat later novel which still belongs, in one respect, to their class—that of books which lodge their name, at least, securely in literary history. This is the *Anastasius* (1819) of Thomas Hope, a man, like Beckford, of great wealth, varied taste and experience in art and travel, who established himself in literature by a single book. *Anastasius* became at once popular, and has retained respect, if not popularity, ever since; yet, some persons, not, perhaps, of very uncritical or uncatholic taste, have been known to be disappointed when they read it. It belongs, as a kind of outsider, to the old 'picaresque' class; though it has little or nothing of the low comedy which that class originally, and, in fact, generally, affected. The hero is a Greek of considerable ability and courage, but absolutely untroubled with conscience, who becomes renegade and goes through various adventures. The eastern colour which Byron had made popular, and which Hope could give with less monotony and from a more varied experience than Byron himself, may have had a good deal to do with the vogue of the book; but its author's undoubted command of satirical contemplation of life, of an ornate, if rather too elaborate, style, of descriptive power and of other good gifts, must be allowed. Its autobiographical form, though dangerous, is not fatal; but the book is, somehow, heavy reading. Even its

continual ironic persiflage, which takes up from Beckford the
manner of Anthony Hamilton and Voltaire and hands it on
to Kinglake in very similar material, becomes monotonous,
though it must be owned that a chapter of *Anastasius*, boiled
down with a whole modern novel, would supply it with ample
seasoning of a kind now much called for.   Perhaps, what casts
a greater cold over it, to some tastes, is a defect very common
in novelists, before Scott—the overdose of pure narration, unrelieved and unspirited by dialogue and dramatic action.   Nothing
happens : everything is told, and there is a fatal suggestion of
the rhetorical harangue about it, despite the variety of its scenes
and the number of its (recited) characters.   Towards the end of
the book, the author does, indeed, speak of 'getting rid of the
eternal' I 'which haunts' it.   But he does this only by interposing
another narrator, not by adopting the livelier mixture of action
and speech.   On the whole, there are few more useful exercises of
speculative criticism than to imagine the story of *Anastasius* as it
would have been told by Dumas.

We began with an eccentric and we must end with one,
though of a very different class from Amory. After a not extensive,
but, also, not inconsiderable, popularity during the period of his
earlier production, the silence which Thomas Love Peacock imposed upon himself for thirty years, and the immense development
of the novel during those same thirty, rather put him out of sight.
But, first, the appearance of *Gryll Grange*, and then his death,
followed, not long after, by a nearly complete edition of his works,
brought him back ; and, both before and after that publication, it
became rather the fashion with critics to 'discover' Peacock,
while a certain number, long before, either by their own good
fortune or their fathers' wisdom, had been instructed in him.
But he never was, is not even now, when fresh discoveries of
his work have been made, and probably never will be, popular ;
and there have sometimes been almost violent recalcitrances
against him, such as that made by Mrs Oliphant in her book on
English literature.   Nor, in more favourable estimates, has it
sometimes been difficult to discern a sort of hesitation—a 'not
knowing what to make of it.'   The compound of satire and romance
in him has puzzled many ; just as it has in Heine and in Thackeray.
There is also, it would seem, an additional difficulty in the fact
that, though he wrote, besides the admirable songs in his fiction,
and one or two estimable longer poems, criticism and miscellanea

in prose, dramas long unpublished and not of much value and some other things, the bulk of his work, and almost the whole of his possible means of popular appeal, consists of a very peculiar kind (or, rather, two kinds) of novel : one variety of which is repeated twice, and the other five times, in different material, certainly, but (in the more numerous class, especially) on an almost identical scheme and scale.

This more momentous and, perhaps, generally thought more characteristic division contains three novels, *Headlong Hall* (1816), *Melincourt* (1817) and *Nightmare Abbey* (1818), published close together, a fourth, *Crotchet Castle*, which appeared a good deal later (1831), and a fifth, already mentioned, between which and its immediate predecessor there was a gap of a generation, in more than the conventional sense of the word. Every one of these has the same skeleton plot—the assembling of a party in a country house, with more or less adventure, much more than less conviviality, no actual murders, but a liberal final allowance of marriages. Some *differentia* is, of course, provided—in *Headlong Hall*, with more than the contrasted presentation of caricatured types—optimist, pessimist, happy-mean man, professional man of letters and so forth, carried out with lively conversation, burlesque incident and a large interspersion of delightful songs, mainly convivial in character, but contenting itself with next to no plot. The next two are rather more substantial ; the long and unequal, but, in parts, admirable, *Melincourt* containing a good deal of political and personal satire on rotten boroughs, the Lake poets, political economy, perfectibilism and what not, with, for central figure, an amiable orang-outang, whom a young philosopher of wealth and position has taught to do everything but speak, and for whom he has bought a baronetcy and a rotten borough. *Nightmare Abbey*, one of the most amusing of all, turns on the unfortunate difficulty which a young man (who, in some ways, is very like Shelley) has in fixing his affections ; and contains portraits, much more remote from the original, of Byron and Coleridge. *Crotchet Castle* takes up the scheme with much less exaggeration and burlesque, with little or no personal satire, with a marked change of political and social view, in the direction, if not exactly of conservatism, of something not unlike it, and with still more remarkable advance in personal characterisation ; while *Gryll Grange* (1860) continues this still further, with adaptation to the changed circumstances of its own time.

The other two novels, *Maid Marian* (1822) and *The Misfortunes of Elphin* (1829), though they could hardly have been written by any other author, are not merely on a quite different plan, but in what may look like, though it is not, a quite different vein. Both, as, indeed, the titles show, are actually romantic in subject; and, though both (and *Elphin* almost more than anywhere else) exhibit Peacock's ironic-satirical treatment, it must be a very dull person who does not see that he is not shooting at the romance, but under cover of it. Peacock has been called a Voltairean: and, much in the form and manner of most of his tales derives, if not from Voltaire, from Voltaire's master, our own country-man, Anthony Hamilton. He is, even in his later and more mellowed condition, 'Mr Sarcastic' (the name of one of his characters) or nothing. His earlier attitude towards Anglican clergy, and his early personal lampoons on tory politicians and men of letters, are almost too extravagant to give much amusement to those who sympathise with them or any offence to those who do not. He maintained, even to the last, a purely crotchety dislike to Scott. Few people did more to spread the utterly unjust and unfounded notion of Southey and Wordsworth (he is, almost of necessity, rather more lenient to Coleridge) as profligate time-servers, who feathered their nests at the expense of their consciences. But, for all this, he was a romantic in his own despite, and his prose very commonly, his verse still oftener, betrays him.

Nor can the greatest admirer of the literature, the political views, or the ecclesiastical and academic institutions which—up to his last work, at any rate, though not there—Peacock satirises, resist, if he himself possesses any catholic love of letters and the genuine sense of humour, the heartiest and most unfailing enjoyment of Peacock's work. Except in *Melincourt*, where there are some arid passages, the whole range of his novels yields nothing but refreshment. The plot so frankly abdicates, and leaves its place to be taken by amusing, if not very closely connected, incident, that nobody but a pedant can feel the want of it; the characters, if not deeply drawn, are sketched with a *verve* not easily to be outdone; the descriptions are always sufficient and sometimes very much more; and the dialogue, in its own way, is consummate. The present chapter has been occupied with the eccentric novel in more than one or two senses of that adjective. Peacock's kind of eccentricity is certainly one of those which show the greatest idiosyncrasy, the imitation of which, though sometimes tried by persons of ability, has proved most difficult. But, in itself, it is likely to retain its faculty of pleasing perhaps as long as any kind, though never to any very large number of people. The first readers of *Gryll Grange* (even if young enough to be liable to the disease of thinking the last age obsolete) were astonished to find an almost octogenarian recluse, who had long given up writing, not in the least out of date. And the quality or gift which effected this—the quality which, fifty years later, makes the hundred year old manners and the hundred year old personages of *Nightmare Abbey* more alive than most personages of contemporary novels—is never very likely to lose its preserving or its refreshing power.

CHAPTER XIV

BOOK PRODUCTION AND DISTRIBUTION, 1625-1800

THE middle of the seventeenth century is a drab tract in the history of English book production. With the accession of Charles I, the efforts of those in power to secure control over the printing press were pursued with renewed activity, culminating, in 1637, in a Star chamber decree which reenacted the celebrated ordinance of 1586[1] with additional, and more drastic, provisions. The many troubles which were gathering round the government doubtless hindered the effective enforcement of this formidable measure. On the abolition of the Star chamber, in 1641, the decree ceased to carry any authority, and, for the moment, printers were freed from all control.

Now it was that, unhampered by restrictions, the press began to pour forth political pamphlets of every description—persuasive, polemical, abusive, scurrilous—of every shade of opinion, royalist against parliament man, puritan versus churchman, challenges and answers, newsbooks and gazettes. These, together with sermons and lectures, were printed and vended in such numbers as 'well-nigh made all other books unsaleable[2].' It seemed, indeed, as if all the efforts of the press could not keep pace with the fleeting pens of ready writers and the feverish eagerness of the public to devour their productions.

Printers were soon to discover, however, that liberty of the press was no more to the taste of the Long parliament than it had been to the hierocracy. As soon as it was able, amid the distractions of more pressing difficulties, parliament turned its attention to regulating the press in accordance with its own views. The issue of various regulations and the punishment of sundry offenders were followed, on 14 June 1643, by an order 'for the regulating of printing[3]': a brief, business-like document which aimed at the establishment of a rigorous censorship. In its main

---

[1] See *ante*, vol. IV, p. 381.   [2] Milton, *Areopagitica*.
[3] Rptd in Arber's ed. of *Areopagitica* (1868).

provisions it closely resembled the defunct decree of 1637, with the important difference that the number of printers was not limited.

It was this reactionary measure which called forth Milton's *Areopagitica*, that powerful remonstrance, which, he says, he wrote

in order to deliver the press from the restraints with which it was encumbered; that the power of determining what was true and what was false, what ought to be published and what to be suppressed, might no longer be entrusted to a few illiterate and illiberal individuals[1].

But, notwithstanding Milton's denunciation of the act and his scornful handling of the office of licenser, parliament could not afford, even for the sake of liberty, to lay aside this weapon of self defence. To what extent the censorship was effective is not very clear. The aim, no doubt, was to suppress publications inimical to the government ; and books which did not trench upon politics or religion were, probably, but little regarded ; but the newspaper press was subjected to a rigorous system of licensing[2]. Under Cromwell's rule, the censorship, reinforced by a further act in 1649, was more efficiently exercised, but was again relaxed during the unrest which followed his death.

With the restoration, we come to the final and most autocratic endeavour at state control of the press. The Licensing act of 1662, which 'asserted in the plainest terms the king's plenary prerogative in the matter of printing,' was virtually a revival of the Star chamber decree of 1637, with all its restrictive clauses, including the limitation of the number of master printers to twenty, besides the two university presses, but allowing an additional press at York. The secret of the effectiveness of the new act lay in the steps taken to secure its successful administration. The Stationers' company, to which had formerly been committed the exercise of police powers, was now superseded in that function by the appointment, in 1663, of a surveyor of the imprimery and printing presses. The new official was no less a person than Roger L'Estrange. This ardent royalist possessed very pronounced and even fantastic views upon the regulation of the press, and, in a report on the manner in which the act should be administered, he had already advised enlargement and stringent enforcement of its provisions. The extensive powers conferred upon him comprised the control of all printing offices, together with powers of search,

---

[1] Milton, *Second defence* (1654), Robert Fellowes's translation. See also Masson's *Life of Milton*, vol. III, pp. 265 ff.

[2] For some account of this see *ante*, vol. VII, chap. XV.

and also, with certain specified exceptions, the licensing of books to be printed, and the exclusive privilege of publishing news[1].

L'Estrange entered upon his duties with zest, and, under his administration, the office of licenser was a real censorship. The books which he himself licensed were conscientiously dealt with from his point of view, and he had no hesitation in deleting or altering passages which did not accord with his political creed. Under his power of search, he made midnight raids on printing houses, and at least one printer, John Twyn, suffered the extreme penalty of the law for printing seditious matter. Notwithstanding this activity, a large proportion of the books during this period were issued without imprimatur, apparently with impunity; and many publications of a questionable colour bear merely the date of publication without any indication of their source. The act, after having been in abeyance for some time, was renewed on the accession of James II; but at the revolution, L'Estrange was deprived of his office, and, with the expiry of the act in 1694, the attempt of the state to control the output of the press was finally abandoned.

The passing of the first English Copyright act in 1709 began a new period in the evolution of the law of literary property. Hitherto, the only recognised form of copyright which had existed was that which a member of the Stationers' company secured by the entry of a 'copy' in the company's register, and this was a purely trade regulation in which the author was completely ignored[2]. The monopoly of a work for a specified number of years, which was occasionally granted to the writer by royal patent, was an exceptional case and only emphasises the generally defenceless position of authors.

In the sixteenth century, the Stationers' company had virtual control of the whole trade and exercised a tolerably efficient supervision over its members. But, during the succeeding century, a number of causes tended to undermine its authority, so that, at length, it became unable either to protect its members from the piracy of outside traders or to restrain the less orderly among its own ranks. The company, at different times, sought, by various means, to regain its old power and importance, but in vain. All efforts merely served to demonstrate the impotence of the guild to

---

[1] Concerning the exercise of this privilege, see *ante*, vol. VII, chap. XV, and vol. IX, chap. I.

[2] See *ante*, vol. IV, p. 391.

control the trade in the old way, and to show that the day was past for imposing restrictive fetters upon so important a craft. The misdoings of piratical printers had long been a cause of vexation to the owners of copyrights, and when, by the final lapse of the licensing laws in 1694, all restraint was removed, booksellers were at their wits' end to know how to protect their property. Finally, the aid of parliament was evoked, and, after several abortive attempts to secure legislation on the subject, a bill, which is said to have been originally drafted by Swift, though much altered in committee, was passed in 1709, under the title 'An Act for the Encouragement of Learning.'

In this measure, the right of an author to property in his work was, for the first time, recognised, or, rather, conferred upon him, by the statute law of the country. The act provided that, in the case of old books, the owners, whether authors or booksellers, should have the exclusive right of printing them for a term of twenty-one years from 10 April 1710, and no longer. In the case of new books, authors were given the monopoly of printing them for fourteen years, and, if the author were still living, a further period of fourteen years from the end of that time. These privileges were to depend upon entry of the work, before publication, in the Stationers' register; and the interests of the public were considered in a clause which provided that, if anyone thought the published price of a book unreasonably high, the archbishop of Canterbury, or other authority, might, on appeal, fix a fair price.

At this time, the copyright of practically every book was in the hands of booksellers, and the statute was, in reality, a booksellers' act. It would appear that authors did not at once realise the advantage which the new law conferred upon them, for they continued, in most cases, to sell their work outright to booksellers, or publishers as they should perhaps be now called. Notwithstanding the definite time limit expressed in the act, publishers still clung to their belief in the existence of perpetual copyright in their properties, and continued, as of yore, to take from authors assignments of their work 'for ever.' They not only believed in their right to a monopoly in perpetuity, but backed that belief by purchasing copyrights on that basis, and by actions at law against those who, as they thought, infringed their privileges; and the cause of copyright continued to be fought by the publisher, the author counting for little or nothing in the conflict.

Two of the most important copyright cases of the eighteenth century arose out of one book. In 1729, James Thomson, for a payment of £242. 10s. 0d., assigned the copyright of *The Seasons* to Andrew Millar, his heirs and assigns for ever. In 1763, another bookseller, Robert Taylor, either relying upon the time limit of the act of 1709, or willing to take the risk of issuing a saleable book, brought out an edition of Thomson's popular poem. Millar, thereupon, began an action against Taylor, and, in 1769—Millar, in the meantime, having died—the court of king's bench delivered judgment in favour of the plaintiff. The claim to perpetual copyright was thus upheld by the court, and, at Millar's sale in the same year, Thomas Becket thought the copyright of *The Seasons* a sufficiently good property to give £505 for it. But monopoly was now being threatened from a new quarter. Cheap editions of deceased English authors were being printed in Scotland, and a shop for the sale of these books was opened in London by Alexander Donaldson, an Edinburgh bookseller. One of these reprints was *The Seasons*, and Becket, naturally wishing to protect a property upon which he had adventured so substantial a sum, applied for an injunction in Chancery against the piracy; but the case, on being carried to the House of Lords, ended, in 1774, in Donaldson's favour. Thus, the same book, which, in 1769, had, apparently, established the claim to perpetual copyright, was, also, the instrument through which the pretence to that right was finally abolished ; and the period of copyright as defined by the statute of 1709 remained unchanged until 1814.

Of the three principal agents—printer, bookseller, author—concerned in the production and distribution of books, the printer had his day in the sixteenth century. But, during the next century, a change in the balance of power took place, and the eighteenth century found the publishing-bookseller in the ascendant. The printer, ousted from his position, had then, for the most part, became the employe of the bookseller ; while the author, though rapidly gaining ground, did not come into his kingdom until the approach of the nineteenth century.

As already stated, the usual practice was for an author to sell his book outright to the publisher; but an instance of a writer retaining some control over his work is afforded by the best-known copyright transaction of the seventeenth century—the agreement for the publication of *Paradise Lost* (1667), by which Samuel Simmons covenanted to pay Milton five pounds down, with a further payment of five pounds at the end of the sale of each of the first three impressions. A little later than this, Richard

Baxter, in a vindication[1] concerning his 'covenants and dealings with booksellers,' gives interesting glimpses of the publishing arrangements of his day. Baxter was evidently not a good man of business, and when he took his famous *Saints' Everlasting Rest* (1649—50) to Thomas Underhill and Francis Tyton to publish, he made no agreement with them, but left the matter of profit 'to their ingenuity.' For the first impression of the work—a corpulent quarto of nearly a thousand pages—they gave him ten pounds, 'and ten pounds apiece, that is, twenty pounds for every after impression till 1665.' Then 'Mr Underhill dieth ; his wife is poor : Mr Tyton hath losses by the Fire, 1666' ; and, though a tenth edition was called for by 1669, Baxter got not a farthing for any further impression, but 'was fain, out of my own purse, to buy all that I gave to any friend, or poor person, that asked it.' For other works, he had the 'fifteenth book' (*i.e.* one fifteenth of the impression) for himself, with eighteen pence a ream on the rest of the impression. William Bates, author of *The Harmony of the divine attributes* (1674), must have been better at a bargain, for he managed to get over a hundred pounds for the first impression of that book, besides reserving to himself the arrangement for further editions.

In Dryden's time, the writer of plays could look to two sources of revenue. First, from the performance at the theatre, usually the proceeds of third-night representations ; and, second, from the sale of the manuscript to a publisher. A judicious dedication might, also, be a potential third source ; but it must have been an unusually good stroke when Theobald received, for his dedication of *Richard II* (1720) to Lord Orrery, a present of a banknote for one hundred pounds, enclosed in an Egyptian-pebble snuff-box of the value of twenty pounds. The sum which a successful author would get from the publisher of his play might be twenty or twenty-five pounds, and, for this, he would probably be expected to furnish a preface in order to attract readers and to swell out the size of the piece. These prefaces were often mere padding, but those of Dryden form some of the earliest essays in modern literary criticism in England. Dryden, too, was called upon to supply prologues to plays by other writers, and, finding his name was of value, he, in due course, demanded and received double the customary fee of five pounds. Later, in common with writers in other departments of literature, the more successful playwrights were able to command much larger sums for their copyrights, as in the case

---

[1] *Reliquiae Baxterianae* (1696), App. p. 117.

of *The Spartan Dame* (1712), for which Chetwood, the bookseller, paid Southerne the sum of one hundred and twenty pounds[1].

Although the Copyright act of 1709 did not seem immediately to make the position of the author stronger, yet the leaven of betterment was surely at work, and it is during the eighteenth century that the author gradually comes to the front. True, there were, as there still are, sloughs which engulfed the needy writer, and Grub street flourished. But, in the upper walks of the profession, the author was becoming a person of some importance, and one to be considered by the publisher. Literature was rising to the rank of a liberal profession, and the man of letters occupies henceforth, a recognised, and not unimportant, place in society.

A contributory cause of this improvement in the author's social and commercial position is to be found in the fact that he could now appeal to a much larger public. Reading was no longer limited to the leisured few. The active part taken by the middle classes in politics, commerce and general culture could hardly fail to engender a habit of reading; and this advance towards literature, literature, in its turn, applied itself to meet by appealing to a wider public and bringing its genius to bear more intimately on the interests and sympathies of daily life. At the same time as the rise of the professional man of letters, there may also be discerned the coming of that important person, the general reader. Buyers, as well as readers, of books became more numerous, and the large circulation of *The Tatler* and *The Spectator*[2], with their host of imitators and ephemeral successors, indicates the existence of a wide circle of readers who read for pleasure and recreation.

The patron of literature still existed, and rendered good service in its cause—of such was the earl of Oxford's generosity towards Prior, and the duke of Queensberry's care of the ' inoffensive ' Gay—and the dedication of a book might, occasionally, still be a substantial aid, though the pursuit of patrons and rewards-in-advance was not often carried to such a fine art as that to which the unscrupulous Payne Fisher had previously succeeded in bringing it. But the author whose living depended upon his pen no longer looked mainly to a patron or to a wealthy dedicatee for the concrete reward of his labours. The publisher had become the real patron. A book that was at all likely to find favour with the reading public possessed a distinct commercial value; and this pecuniary potentiality was in process of being realised by the

---

[1] See *ante*, vol. viii, p. 190.

[2] Beginning with 3000 copies, the impression rose, sometimes, as high as 30,000.

author as well as by the publisher. The author naturally endeavoured to secure his fair share of profits, and we find that not
a few writers were fully capable of looking after their own interests.

A spirit of enterprise and emulation was moving among
publishers, and men with acumen, like Tonson, Lintot, Dodsley,
Millar and others, were ready to undertake the issue of works they
deemed to be of merit on terms liberal to the author. They not
only published books offered to them by authors, but they also
planned works to meet the needs and tastes of a rapidly widening
circle of readers. Commissions for books were freely given, and,
to a large extent, the professional writer was the employe of the
bookseller. In this aspect of the literary history of the time,
picturesque anecdote has been allowed to usurp too prominent a
place, and the petty squabbles between author and publisher, which
have been held up to public view, have, undeservedly, cast a sordid
smirch upon the story of eighteenth century literature. Poets and
other 'literary creatures' might, in their more lofty moods, affect
to look down with disdain upon booksellers as much beneath
them ; but it was these upon whom they often depended to keep
body and soul from parting company, and to whom they turned in
financial difficulty. It was a common practice for publishers to
advance money upon work not yet done, and, not infrequently,
they were called on to rescue their authors from a debtor's prison.

It was during the civil war, when the art of letters was almost
submerged by the rush of political and polemical tracts with
which the country was then flooded, that the craft of printing fell
to its lowest estate, and the calling of publisher seemed, for the
time being, to retain but little connection with literature. The
chief name that stands out from this dead level is that of
Humphrey Moseley, of the Prince's Arms, in St Paul's churchyard, who devoted himself to the production of poetry and
belles lettres. His publications include the first collected edition
of Milton's poems (1645), and works by Crashaw, D'Avenant,
Shirley, Herrick, Suckling and others. There was also Andrew
Crooke, Hobbes's publisher, who, in 1642, issued two surreptitious
editions of *Religio Medici,* and was entrusted with the publication
of the authorised edition in the following year ; and it was from
Richard Marriot's shop in St Dunstan's churchyard that *The
Compleat Angler* was sent forth in 1653, whence was issued, also, the
first part of *Hudibras* ten years later. In the restoration period,
Henry Herringman, Dryden's first publisher, comes to the front as

a publisher of polite literature and may be considered successor to
Moseley in this department of letters. He acquired a wide connection with literary and scientific men of the day, and his shop,
frequently mentioned by Pepys, became the chief literary lounging
place in town. In this, the transition period of publishing,
Herringman forms a link between the old and the new order,
and was one of the earliest booksellers to give up the selling
of miscellaneous books and to devote himself entirely to the
business of his own publications.

It is with Jacob Tonson, the elder, that the modern line of
publishers may be said to begin. One of his earliest ventures
was the issue, in 1678 of Nahum Tate's tragedy, *Brutus of Alba*,
and, in the next year, he gave some indication of his ambition
to make a name as a publisher of polite literature by bringing
out Dryden's *Troilus and Cressida*, though, in order to provide the twenty pounds wherewith to pay the author, he was,
apparently, obliged to take Abel Swalle into partnership in this
publication. Henceforth, his name is associated with that of
Dryden, whose publisher he became, in succession to Herringman.
Various anecdotes have been related of occasional friction between
publisher and author; but nothing occurred sufficiently serious
to disturb permanently the harmony of their relations. The publication of Tonson's *Miscellany*, the first volume of which appeared
in 1684, under the editorship of Dryden, brought him into
prominence, and, later, earned for him Wycherley's sobriquet
'gentleman-usher to the Muses.' In the preceding year, his
instinct for a good thing had led him to purchase from Brabazon
Aylmer one half of the rights in *Paradise Lost*; but it was not
until five years later that he brought out by subscription his fine
folio edition of the poem[1]. In 1690, he bought, at an advanced
price, the other half, and thus acquired the whole rights of what
produced him more money than any other poem he published.

Hitherto, new editions of deceased dramatists and poets had
consisted almost exclusively of mere reprints of old copies, and
Shakespeare's collected works existed only in the four folios; but
Rowe's *Shakespeare*, which Tonson brought out in 1709, inaugurated a new era in the production of critical texts of the greater
writers[2]. An edition of Beaumont and Fletcher, in seven volumes,
was issued in 1711, from Tonson's new address, the 'Shakespear's
Head,' in the Strand, and it was at this shop, in the same year,

[1] In his portrait by Kneller, he is depicted with a copy of this book in his hand.
[2] See *ante*, vol. v, chap. xi.

that Swift met Addison and Steele, the last of whom, both before
and after this time, was frequently at Tonson's house. The sign
'Shakespear's Head' was well chosen, for, after Rowe's edition,
almost every important eighteenth century issue of Shakespeare—
Pope's (1723—5), Theobald's (1733), Warburton's (1747), Johnson's
(1765), Steevens's (1766), Capell's (1767—8)—carries the name of
Tonson, either by itself or in partnership with others.

Tonson's social ambitions found scope in the Kit-cat club,
of which he was, for many years, secretary. His weakness for
good society occasionally gave offence to his contemporaries ; but
he was much esteemed. Dunton, whose characterisations are
generally direct, though, perhaps, showing a happy weakness for
the best side of a man, said of Tonson that 'he speaks his mind on
all occasions and will flatter nobody' ; and even Pope, who could
not resist dubbing him 'left-legged Jacob' in *The Dunciad*, speaks
of him, also, as 'genial Jacob,' and, again, as 'old Jacob Tonson,
who is the perfect image and likeness of Bayle's *Dictionary* ; so
full of matter, secret history, and wit and spirit, at almost four-
score.' About the year 1720, Tonson retired from active part
in the business, leaving the traditions of the house to be carried on
by his nephew (Jacob II, d. 1735), and his great-nephew (Jacob
III, d. 1767). It was the third Jacob who paid Warburton five
hundred pounds for editing Shakespeare, whom Johnson eulogised,
and of whom George Steevens wrote that 'he was willing to admit
those with whom he contracted, to the just advantage of their own
labours ; and had never learned to consider the author as an
under-agent to the bookseller[1].'

As Tonson's name is associated with Dryden, so is that of
his contemporary, Bernard Lintot, closely connected with Pope.
'The enterprizing Mr Lintot, the redoubtable rival of Mr Tonson,'
began business at the sign of the Cross Keys about 1698, and he,
likewise, made plays a feature of his early publications. His connection with Pope began with the *Miscellaneous Poems and
Translations by several hands*, which he launched in 1712 as
a set-off to Tonson's *Miscellany*. Three years later, he brought out
the first instalment of Pope's translation of the *Iliad*. The terms
on which Lintot, who made the highest offer, acquired the
work, were that he should supply, at his own expense, 'all the
copies which were to be delivered to subscribers[2] or presented to

[1] Shakespeare's *Works*, vol. I (Advertisement to the Reader), 1778.
[2] There were 654 subscriptions to the work, which was issued, between 1715 and
1720, in six quarto volumes at a guinea each.

friends,' and pay the translator two hundred pounds for each volume. Under this agreement, Pope is said to have received, in all, some £5300 ; but the result was less fortunate for Lintot, who had hoped to recoup his outlay and justify the enterprise by the proceeds of a folio edition which he printed for ordinary sale. The market for this impression was, however, spoiled by a cheap duodecimo edition, printed in Holland and imported surreptitiously; and Lintot, in self defence, had to undersell the pirate by issuing a similar cheap edition. The method of publishing by subscription became a common practice in the eighteenth century, and the endeavour to secure a liberal patron for the dedication of a book was succeeded by the effort to procure a list of subscribers previous to publication. For an author who could 'command' subscriptions, this was a very helpful means of coming to terms with a publisher ; but, though this method of procedure has continued to be largely used down to the present day, authors gradually relinquished into the hands of publishers the task of canvassing.

A dispute arose over the translation of the *Odyssey* which Lintot published in 1725—6, and he, too, was splashed with mud from Pope's malicious pen. With a sensitive penchant for singling out physical defects, Pope seized upon Lintot's ungainly figure, and thus caricatured him :

> As when a dab-chick waddles thro' the copse
> On feet and wings, and flies, and wades, and hops:
> So lab'ring on, with shoulders, hands, and head,
> Wide as a wind-mill all his figure spread,
> With arms expanded Bernard rows his state,
> And left-legg'd Jacob seems to emulate.

In his dealings with authors, Lintot took an enlightened view of the dignity of letters, and the title-pages of works by many of the best writers of the day bear his imprint. A memorandum book in which he entered 'copies when purchased' has preserved a record of the sums which various authors received from him[1]. A large proportion of the entries consists of plays, and he also invested freely in law books, which seem to have been always productive property. In 1701, he purchased, for £3. 4s. 6d., a third share in Cibber's *Love's Last Shift*, and, thereafter, acquired several other plays by that writer. To Thomas Baker, a now forgotten dramatist, he gave, in 1703, £32. 5s. 0d. for *The Yeoman of Kent.* In

---

[1] Extracts from this notebook are printed in Nichols's *Literary Anecdotes*, vol. VIII, pp. 293—304.

1702, Farquhar received £15 for *The Twin Rivals*, and, four years later, just double that sum for *The Beaux' Stratagem*. For Gay's *Wife of Bath*, he paid £25, while, for *Trivia*, he gave him £43, and practically the same sum for *Three Hours after Marriage*. Mrs Centlivre had £10 each for two plays, and Steele £21. 10s. 0d. for *The Lying Lover*. Elkanah Settle, then long past his vogue, could get no more than £3. 10s. 0d. for *The City Ramble* (1711); but, for Rowe's *Lady Jane Grey* (1715), and Killigrew's *Chit-Chat* (1719), Lintot had to pay £75. 5s. 0d. and £84 respectively, while, upon Richard Fiddes's *Body of Divinity*, he expended so much as £252. 10s. 0d. His transactions with Pope amounted to upwards of four thousand pounds.

Lintot also kept translators busy. Homer seems to have had special attraction for him, and served as a kind of counterpoise to the *Shakespeare* of his rival Tonson. Besides issuing Pope's translation, he had covenanted with Theobald, in 1714, for a translation of the *Odyssey*, but this scheme was abandoned when Pope undertook his version. For a translation of the *Iliad* published in 1712, he paid John Ozell £10. 8s. 6d. for the first three books, and, in the next year, he gave the same translator £37. 12s. 6d. for his Molière. The publication of some books was undertaken on the half shares principle: in the case of Breval's *Remarks on several parts of Europe* (1726), author and bookseller each took one guinea, the latter being at the expense of producing the book and the copyright remaining his property; Jeake's *Charters of the Cinque Ports* (1728) was issued by subscription at a guinea, of which author and bookseller each had half. For Urry's *Chaucer*, eventually printed in 1721, a tripartite agreement for equal division of the proceeds was entered into, in 1715, by Urry's executor, the dean and chapter of Christ Church, Oxford, and Lintot; the dean and chapter's share to be applied to the finishing of Peckwater quadrangle, and the bookseller again paying the cost of production.

Lintot's rivalry with Tonson must have been somewhat in the nature of friendly competition, for his notebook records several agreements with Tonson, relating to the publication of various works, including a convention, in February 1718, that they should be equally concerned in all plays bought by them eighteen months from that date. He, too, in the heyday of success, retired from the turmoil of business to country quiet.

With the year 1735, there enters into the publishing lists perhaps the most attractive figure in the eighteenth century trade, Robert Dodsley, poet, playwright and quondam footman. Lintot had now some years ago resigned his business into the hands of his son Henry ; and, at the house of Tonson, the third Jacob was reigning. The substantial firm of Awnsham and John Churchill, renowned for its big undertakings, had, with the death of Awnsham in 1728, run its course ; and James Knapton, who made a feature of books of travel and works on trade and economics, was nearing the end of his career. Richard Chiswell, the 'metropolitan bookseller' of England, had long since been succeeded by Charles Rivington, who was laying the foundations of what was to become the chief theological publishing house of the next hundred years ; and Thomas Longman, successor to William Taylor, publisher of *Robinson Crusoe*, was quietly building up the business in Paternoster row where his sign, a ship in full sail, still keeps on its course. Lawton Gilliver, of the Homer's Head in Fleet street, was now Pope's publisher ; and Edward Cave had been running his *Gentleman's Magazine* since 1731. Other active names in the publishing world were John Brindley of New Bond street, Andrew Millar in the Strand, Thomas Cooper at the Globe in Paternoster row, and James Roberts in Warwick lane.

When Dodsley, with the patronage and assistance of Pope and other friends, set up his sign, Tully's Head, in Pall Mall, he was already known as a writer of poems, and his play, *The Toy-shop*, which had been published by Gilliver a few months previously, achieved the success of six editions before the year was out. In 1737, he made a great hit with Richard Glover's *Leonidas*; in the next year came Johnson's *London* ; and, soon, Dodsley was recognised as one of the leading publishers of *belles lettres*, his shop, ere long, becoming a favourite meeting place of the *literati* of the day. A sound literary taste, seconded by enterprise and business ability, brought him abundant success; and his probity of character and lovable personality endeared him to a numerous company of friends. Chesterfield, Shenstone and Spence were of this circle, and Johnson, who held 'Doddy' in especial regard, said that he looked upon him as his patron. Besides works by Pope and Johnson, it was from Tully's Head that Young's *Night Thoughts*, Shenstone's *Schoolmistress*, Akenside's *Pleasures of Imagination*, Goldsmith's *Present State of Polite Learning*, with many others of equal note were sent forth ; and, if Gray's Eton *Ode* fell flat in 1747, the failure was more than compensated for by the acclaim which greeted the *Elegy* in 1751.

But the publications by which Dodsley remains a living name in English literature are the two anthologies to which he stood in the relation of editor as well as publisher : the *Select Collection of Old Plays* (1744—5) and the *Collection of Poems by several Hands* (1748—58)[1]. When the first of these was announced in 1743, sufficient names to justify the undertaking were received in a week, and, at the time of publication, there were nearly eight hundred subscribers.

Apparently, Dodsley considered a periodical publication to be a proper adjunct to a house of standing, for he made more than one adventure in that hazardous emprise. *The Public Register*, which he launched in 1741 as a weekly rival to *The Gentleman's Magazine*, was killed at its twenty-fourth number by a boycott on the part of opposition journals. Five years later, he projected a fortnightly literary magazine, called *The Museum*, which appeared under the editorship of Mark Akenside ; and this was followed by *The World*, which Edward Moore successfully conducted from 1753 to 1756. But his greatest achievement was *The Annual Register*, which he founded in conjunction with Edmund Burke, and which still makes its yearly appearance. In March 1759, just before the first issue of the *Register* was published, Dodsley relinquished the cares of business into the hands of his younger brother, James, whom he had taken into partnership some time previously.

It is understood to have been Robert Dodsley who first suggested to Johnson the idea of the *Dictionary* ; but the chief part in the arrangements for its publication was undertaken by Andrew Millar, a man of quite different calibre. Though not possessed of great literary judgment himself, Millar had the instinct to choose capable advisers, and his hard-headed business faculty carried him into the front rank of his profession. He ventured boldly, and must have been fairly liberal in his dealings with authors, or Johnson, speaking from a writer's point of view, would scarcely have expressed respect for him on the ground that he had raised the price of literature. When Hume's *History* was in danger of falling flat, it was Millar's energy that contributed largely to securing its success ; and when, after giving Fielding a thousand pounds for *Amelia*, he feared the book would not go off, he resorted to a ruse to incite the trade to buy it.

The *Dictionary*, after the manuscript had at length been extracted from Johnson, was published jointly by several booksellers who had joined forces for the occasion. This practice of cooperation in important undertakings was a regular feature in eighteenth century publishing, and various associations for the purpose were brought into existence. One of these, called The Conger, was formed in 1719, and this was followed in 1736 by the New Conger. After these came the famous organisation which met for the transaction of business at the Chapter coffeehouse in St Paul's churchyard; hence, books brought out by the associated partners were, for a time, styled Chapter books, but, later, came to be known as Trade books. This method of publication led to many literary properties being divided into numerous shares, sometimes so many as a hundred or even more, which were bought or sold and freely passed on from one bookseller to another. In 1776, a sixteenth share of *Pamela* was sold for £18, and a thirty-second part of Hervey's *Meditations* brought £32, while, in 1805, £11 was given for a one-hundredth share in *The Lives of the Poets*. William Johnson, a London bookseller, stated, in 1774, that three-quarters of the books in the trade had his name as part proprietor. The cooperative system was attempted also on behalf of authors, and a Society for the Encouragement of Learning was founded with the object of securing to writers the whole product of their labours ; but, though some books of note were published through this channel about the middle of the century, the society can hardly be said to have flourished.

Perhaps the largest combine for the issue of a trade book, was that which brought out the edition of *English Poets* for which Johnson wrote the *Lives*. In this undertaking, some forty booksellers were concerned, and the names of the proprietors included, as Edward Dilly, one of the partners, said in a letter to Boswell, 'almost all the booksellers in London, of consequence[1].' The object was to defeat what they deemed to be an invasion of their literary property, in the shape of a comprehensive issue of *British Poets*, printed at the Apollo press in Edinburgh, in a hundred cheap and handy volumes, and sold by John Bell of the Strand. This John Bell, founder of *Bell's Weekly Messenger*, was a pioneer in the production of cheap books, and, being a man of modern ideas, he initiated, so it is said, the abolition of the long s. Another form of cheap literature which had come into vogue, was the 'Paternoster Row numbers,' so called from the Row being their chief place of issue. These publications, which came out in the form of weekly parts, consisted of standard works such as

[1] Boswell's *Life of Johnson*, ed. Hill, G. B., vol. III, p. 111.

family Bibles with notes, Foxe's *Martyrs*, the works of Josephus, the life of Christ, histories of England and the like, which, if not read, at least gave a good air to the home. One of the earliest to make a speciality of this form of publishing was Alexander Hogg, who seems to have been possessed of all the arts and wiles of the modern book canvasser ; and his assistant, John Cooke, after starting in the same line of business on his own account, made an even better thing of it. He is said to have cleared some thousands of pounds by Southwell's *Notes and Illustrations on the Bible*, and his were the little 'whity-brown' covered sixpenny numbers of the British poets on which Leigh Hunt 'doted.' This series of books, running, in all, to several hundred weekly parts, consisted of three sections : select novels, select classics and select poets—select, no doubt, meaning then, as now, those which could be reprinted with impunity.

But the booksellers did not confine their meetings at coffee-house or tavern to the business of dividing the profits on a book or of planning a new venture. They also met for social intercourse and good cheer ; and occasional gatherings at the Devil tavern by Temple bar developed into a regular club. It was at this club that Davies first conceived the idea of writing his *Life of Garrick*, and, as the work proceeded, he brought instalments of it to the club which he read to the company 'with much complacency, and not a little to their general information.' And, in their relations with authors, the festive side was not neglected by individual publishers, such as the Dillys—the big house in the Poultry—'at whose hospitable and well-covered table,' says Boswell, 'I have seen a greater number of literary men, than at any other, except that of Sir Joshua Reynolds.'

Thomas Cadell, too, the successor of Andrew Millar, celebrated the completion of Gibbon's *Decline and Fall*, in 1788, by a literary dinner at his house. Cadell, who was partner with William Strahan in many of his more important undertakings, was for nearly a quarter of a century at the head of his profession, and his name is associated with the leading historical writers of the time : Hume, Robertson, Gibbon, Blackstone, Adam Smith. This was a golden age for successful writers, and remuneration was on an unprecedented scale. For his *History of Charles V*, Robertson received £4500, and for his dull but popular history, Robert Henry was paid £3300 ; Hume's *History* is said to have brought him upwards of £5000, and Gibbon had two-thirds of the very hand-some profits on his *History* ; Cadell and Strahan paid John

XIV]   *Edmund Curll*   327

Hawkesworth £6000 for his *Account of voyages...in the Southern Hemisphere*, and gave Hugh Blair £1100 for his three volumes of *Sermons*; and Charles Elliot, the Edinburgh bookseller, was venturesome enough to give William Smellie a thousand guineas for his *Philosophy of Natural History* when, according to Lackington, only the heads of the chapters were written.

At the end of the eighteenth century, the third Thomas Longman had recently entered on his successful career ; the theological house of Rivington was in the hands of Francis and Charles Rivington, grandsons of the founder; Thomas Cadell, the younger, had succeeded his father, who was now enjoying wellearned leisure ; the firm of Edward and Charles Dilly was represented by the surviving partner, Charles ; George Robinson, the 'king of the booksellers,' had yet a year to reign over his huge business in Paternoster row ; and John Murray, lately come of age, had just assumed control of the business in Fleet street which his father, the first John Murray, had acquired in 1768.

Naturally, most of those who engaged in bookselling and publishing were primarily men of business, but there were among them not a few who knew something more of books than merely their title-pages and selling price. Many were attracted to the calling by a taste for, and appreciation of, literature, and several even aspired to enter the lists of authorship. Besides such out-standing instances as Robert Dodsley, Samuel Richardson and Thomas Davies, there was John Dunton of the *Life and Errors*, and Lackington of the *Memoirs* and *Confessions*. Thomas Evans, the humorist, who edited Shakespeare and Prior, and Andrew Jackson, the Drury lane dealer in old books, who published the first book of *Paradise Lost* in rime and cast his catalogues in similar form, are representative of another class. To the criticisms of his publisher, Joseph Johnson, William Cowper acknowledged himself to be indebted ; and Peter Elmsley, the Strand bookseller and honoured friend of Gibbon, was noted for his discriminating nicety in both the French and the English languages. To these may be added Alexander Cruden, who compiled his *Concordance* at his shop under the Royal Exchange; Arthur Collins, of the *Peerage*; the younger William Bowyer, styled 'the learned printer,' and his partner John Nichols, of the *Anecdotes*.

If Tonson, Lintot and Dodsley may be accounted among the aristocracy of the publishers of their time, the nadir of the profession is well represented in their contemporary, Edmund Curll, that shameless rascal, in whom even the writer of *The*

Dunciad found his match for scurrility. In the annals of the trade, Curll's name stands for all that is false, low, dishonest and obscene; indeed, his activity in producing books of an indecent character added a new word—Curlicism—to the language. His many misdeeds brought him varied experiences: from the trick which Pope played upon him at the Swan tavern, and the tossing he received at the hands of the Westminster scholars, up through more than one appearance at the bar of the House of Lords, down to imprisonment, fine and the pillory. But none of these things deterred 'the dauntless Curll' from his vicious course. After he had been fined for printing *The Nun in her Smock*, and had stood in the pillory for publishing *The Memoirs of John Ker of Kersland*, he continued to advertise these books in his lists, with a note appended to the latter calling attention to the fact that he had suffered fine and corporal punishment on account of it.

At the outset of his career, he put forth as a 'second edition, improv'd,' a mere reprint with new title-page—not an unknown deception, it is true; but, with Curll, literary fraud was habitual, and he had no hesitation in suggesting a wellknown writer to be the author of some worthless production by one of his hacks. Elizabeth Montagu, in a letter[1] of 12 November 1739, writes indignantly :

> I got at last this morning the poems just published under Prior's name, brought them home under my arm, locked my door, sat me down by my fireside, and opened the book with great expectation, but to my disappointment found it to be the most wretched trumpery that you can conceive, the production of the meanest of Curl's band of scribblers.

Curll's connection with the issue of *Court Poems* (1716)[2] led to his first encounter with Pope, and he afterwards made ignoble appearance in *The Dunciad*; later, these two were concerned in the talpine proceedings connected with the publication of the 1735 volume of Pope's *Correspondence*.

Curll's personal appearance, vividly sketched by Amory, was as unprepossessing as his cast of mind. 'Edmund Curll,' he says[3], 'was in person very tall and thin, an ungainly, awkward, white-faced man. His eyes were a light-grey, large, projecting, goggle, and pur-blind. He was splay-footed, and baker-kneed.' He adds, however, that 'he had a good natural understanding, and was well acquainted with more than the title pages of books.' And, since even a Curll must have his due, it should not be forgotten

[1] Climenson, Emily J., *Elizabeth Montagu* (1906), vol. I, p. 88.
[2] See *ante*, vol. IX, pp. 78 and 247.
[3] *Life of John Buncle* (1825), vol. III, p. 262.

that he published a number of books of antiquarian, topographical and biographical interest.

The name of Curll is also closely associated with Grub street, a domain which is wont to be a temptation to indulge in the picturesque—and to figure as a literary hades, inhabited by poor, but worthy, geniuses, with stony-hearted booksellers as exacting demons. Not that the existence of Grub street is to be doubted: it was, indeed, a grim actuality, and many a garreteer realised by experience

> How unhappy's the fate
> To live by one's pate
> And be forced to write hackney for bread[1].

But the iniquity was not all on the side of the bookseller, nor did the initiative come from him alone.

It was in the first half of the eighteenth century, after the expiry of the licensing laws had removed all restraint from the press, that this underworld of letters most flourished, writers and booksellers striving with avid haste to make the most out of the opportunity of the moment. Unscrupulous members of both professions were little troubled by conscience, their common concern being to produce—the one with the minimum of labour, the other at the minimum of expense—anything that would sell. Booksellers were 'out' for business, and paid as little as possible. Some of them were hard taskmasters, no doubt, but they had a sorry team to drive, and one may believe that, in general, these Grub street authors got as much as they were worth.

In his *Life of Dr John North*, Roger North speaks of the pickpocket work of demi-booksellers, who 'crack their brains to find out selling subjects, and keep hirelings in garrets at hard meat to write and correct by the groat'; and Amory, writing of Curll, says that 'his translators in pay lay three in a bed in the Pewter Platter Inn at Holborn, and he and they were for ever at work to deceive the public[2].' John Dunton, a man of many projects, who, in his time, published some six hundred books and himself was the possessor of a ready pen, had considerable experience of hackwriters. As soon as he set up in business, they began to ply him with 'specimens'; but he conceived a very poor opinion of the race, and thought their learning very often lay in as little compass as their honesty. Of William Bradshaw,

---

[1] Fielding's *The Author's Farce* (act II, sc. 3), a lively picture of a bookseller and his hirelings at work.
[2] *Life of John Buncle* (1825), vol. III, p. 263.

whom he considered to be the best accomplished hackney author he had met, and who wrote for him *The Parable of the Magpye*, of which many thousands were sold, he says,

I had once fixed him upon a very great design, and furnished him both with money and books...but my Gentleman thought fit to remove himself, and I am not sure that I have seen him since[1].

On the other hand, he represents John Shirley, who wrote for him 'Lord Jeffreys's Life,' of which six thousand were sold, as being 'true as steel to his word, and would slave off his feet to oblige a bookseller.'

One of the multifarious occupations of these literary parasites was the abridgment of successful works. Pirate booksellers, like Samuel Lee of Lombard street, 'such a pirate, such a cormorant was never before,' or Henry Hills, in Blackfriars, who regularly printed every good poem or sermon that was published, might, at their risk, reprint whole books; but the safer way was to bring out an abridgment, a method of filching against which there was no legal redress. This was the course pursued by Nathaniel Crouch, who

melted down the best of our English Histories into twelve-penny books, which are filled with wonders, rarities, and curiosities; for, you must know, his title-pages are a little swelling[2].

The 'indefatigable press-mauler,' Shirley, was an adept at this art of collection, as it was called,

his great talent lies at Collection, and he will do it for you at six shillings a sheet. He knows how to disguise an Author that you shall not know him, and yet keep the sense and the main scope entire[3].

In his daily task the Grub street denizen lost his own personality in many disguises; and Richard Savage, under the name Iscariot Hackney, thus described, with a bitter cynicism born of experience, the varied *rôle* of a hireling writer :

'Twas in his [Curll's] service that I wrote Obscenity and Profaneness, under the names of Pope and Swift. Sometimes I was Mr Joseph Gay, and at others theory Burnet, or Addison. I abridged histories and travels, translated from the French what they never wrote, and was expert at finding out new titles for old books. When a notorious thief was hanged, I was the Plutarch to preserve his memory; and when a great man died, mine were his Remains, and mine the account of his last will and testament[4].

Occasionally, an author might be an employer of his less fortunate brethren, and the Sunday dinners given by Smollett to his hacks

[1] *Life and Errors* (1818), p. 182.   [2] *Ibid.* p. 206.
[3] *Ibid.* p. 184.   [4] *The Author to be Let.*

suggest that the conditions of work in his 'literary factory' may have been less intolerable than in some other establishments.

Several of the best writers of the age—Fielding, Johnson, Goldsmith—served some apprenticeship in this lower walk, and the latter, in his *Present State of Polite Learning*, has feelingly depicted the hardships endured by the 'poor pen and ink labourer.' But, while many of those who were worthy in due time freed themselves from thraldom, others, like Samuel Boyse, sitting at his writing wrapped in a blanket with arms thrust through two holes in it, found therein a natural habitat.

The revival of literature and consequent expansion of the book trade which followed upon the return of the monarchy were accompanied by drawbacks, of which the establishment of the censorship under L'Estrange, in 1663, was only one. Two years later, business in London was almost paralysed by the effects of the visitation of the plague: a check nearly equalled the following year in the havoc which the great fire made among the stock of books, by which fresh disaster many of those stationers who had survived the plague now found themselves ruined.

By this time, Little Britain, with its artery Duck lane, had become an important centre of the retail book trade, threatening the long supremacy of the neighbourhood of St Paul's cathedral. In 1663, Sorbière, the French traveller, speaks of the vast number of booksellers' shops he had observed in London, especially in St Paul's churchyard and Little Britain, 'where there is twice as many as in the Rue St Jacque in Paris.' And Roger North, writing of the same period, says,

> Then Little Britain was a plentiful and perpetual emporium of learned authors; and men went thither as to a market. This drew to the place a mighty trade; the rather because the shops were spacious, and the learned gladly resorted to them, where they seldom failed to meet with agreeable conversation. And the booksellers themselves were knowing and conversible men, with whom, for the sake of bookish knowledge, the greatest wits were pleased to converse[1].

One of the chief of these Little Britain booksellers was Robert Scot, whom North describes as no mean scholar and a very conscientious good man. He was not only an expert bookseller, but was 'in his time the greatest librarian in Europe; for, besides his stock in England, he had warehouses at Frankfort, Paris and other places.' Here, also, was the shop of Christopher Bateman,

---

[1] *Lives of the Norths*, ed. Jessopp, A. (1890), vol. II, p. 281.

who dealt principally in old books, and from whom Swift purchased 'for our Stella' three little volumes of Lucian in French. In some shops, it was the practice to allow customers to turn over the books and, for a small payment, to read any of them on the premises. Bateman, however, would have none of this, nor would he, it is said, suffer any person to look into any book in his shop, giving as a reason :

> I suppose you may be a physician or an author, and want some recipe or quotation; and, if you buy it, I will engage it to be perfect before you leave me, but not after; as I have suffered by leaves being torn out, and the books returned, to my very great loss and prejudice[1].

Before the middle of the eighteenth century, the tide had begun to ebb from Little Britain, and, with the death of Edward Ballard, in 1796, there passed away the last of the profession who inhabited it, and the last representative of a family which, for over a century, had been famous there for its trade in divinity and school books.

John Macky, in his *Journey through England* (1724), tells us that

> The Booksellers of antient books in all languages are in Little Britain and Paternoster Row; those for Divinity and the Classics on the North side of St Paul's Cathedral; Law, History, and Plays about Temple Bar; and the French Booksellers in the Strand.

These were the chief quarters of the trade, but bookshops might be found in most quarters of the city; eastwards, along Cheapside, passing the shop of Thomas Cockerell 'at the Three-legs in the Poultry, over against the Stocks Market,' and on to the Royal exchange, where, at the Bible under the Piazza, Ralph Smith carried on his business. In Cornhill, the sign of the Three Pigeons pointed out the house of Brabazon Aylmer, from whom Tonson purchased *Paradise Lost*; and, a little to the south, London bridge was a centre of some activity, though mostly in the less distinguished branches of the trade. Holborn, too, had its booksellers, and in Gray's inn gateway dwelt Thomas Osborne[2], an expert in all the tricks and arts of his trade. In the west, John Brindley was established in New Bond street, and Pall Mall was the scene of Dodsley's operations. In Westminster hall, booksellers had plied their trade from at least 1640, and probably much earlier. Mistress Breach's portly presence was, doubtless, a familiar figure there from 1649 to 1675; Matthew Gilliflower was

---

[1] Nichols's *Literary Anecdotes* (1812), vol. I, p. 424.
[2] See, also, *ante*, vol. IX, p. 357, and vol. X, p. 166.

equally well known in it during the last quarter of the century,
and booksellers were still in occupation there at the end of the
eighteenth century.

At this time, coffeehouses were a favourite resort for social
and political gossip and the reading of the news[1]. In Guy Miege's
Present State of Great Britain, for 1707, it is remarked that

The *Coffee-houses* particularly are very commodious for a *free Conversation*, and for reading at an easie Rate all manner of *printed News*, the *Votes* of *Parliament* when sitting, and other *Prints* that come out Weekly or casually. Amongst which the *London Gazette* comes out on *Mundays* and *Thursdays*, the *Daily Courant* every day but *Sunday*, the *Postman*, *Flying-Post*, and *Post-Boy*, Tuesdays, Thursdays, and Saturdays, and the *English Post*, Mundays, Wensdays, and Fridays; besides their frequent *Postscripts*.

As being similar centres for intercommunication in the book-
world, where the *literati* met and discussed new books or learned
of projects for forthcoming works, some of the bookshops came
to be known as literary coffeehouses. One of the first to be
thus designated was a little low 'elbow-shed' at the gate of the
Lower mews, near Leicester fields. This was the bookshop of
'honest Tom Payne,' one of the most celebrated booksellers of
the day. The little L-shaped place, lighted by a skylight, was
but ill adapted for the reception of the number of people 'who
not only frequented it but during certain hours of the day were
never out of it.' The *habitués* of this nookery included Thomas
Tyrwhitt, bishop Percy, William Heberden, Bennet Langton,
George Steevens and Sir John Hawkins, and, at about one o'clock,
almost any day, would be found there a group of people
discussing literary themes or otherwise improving the art of
conversation, probably more to their own satisfaction than to
that of honest Tom, who found them much in his way. The
spacious and handsome shop which Henry Payne, a younger
brother, opened in Pall Mall with the hope of attracting some
of these literary loungers failed to detach their allegiance from
the dingy little resort, which the elder Payne occupied for nearly
fifty years and which was continued by his son till the early years
of the nineteenth century. Another of these literary howffs was
the shop in Russell street, Covent garden, kept by Thomas Davies,
the actor, whom Johnson befriended and whose *Life of Garrick*
brought him more fame and probably more money than all his
bookselling. It was when taking tea in Davies's back parlour,
which looked into the shop through a glass door, that Boswell,

[1] Concerning coffeehouses as literary resorts, see *ante*, vol. IX, pp. 31—37.

in 1763, at length had the gratification of being introduced to Johnson.

The book-collector in search of fine editions, and the reader with literary tastes enquiring for the latest hit in *belles lettres*, would, naturally, go to Tonson's, Payne's, Dodsley's, or one of the other leading shops, such as that of Samuel Smith, bookseller to the Royal society, who spoke with fluency both French and Latin, and specialised in foreign literature. But, among the wider and less cultivated class of readers, there was a large demand for small and cheap books in what is commonly known as practical divinity, and this literature formed an important feature in the stock-in-trade of the smaller booksellers. In the seventeenth century, James Crump, who had his shop in Little Bartholomew's Well-yard, was one of the publishers who made a speciality of providing this class of book, and Richard Young, of Roxwell in Essex, a voluminous writer of such matter, furnished him with *A short and sure way to Grace and Salvation, The Seduced Soul reduced, and rescued from the Subtilty and Slavery of Satan,* together with some thirty other tracts with similar compelling titles; and these, consisting severally of eight or a dozen pages, were sold at a penny each. More substantial examples of this class of popular literature are the 'practical' works of Richard Baxter and *The Pilgrim's Progress*, of which eleven editions appeared within ten years of its first publication. John Dunton, who, with wide experience in catering for the popular taste, had great faith in the commercial value of such books, printed ten thousand copies of Lukin's *Practice of Godliness*, and, concerning Keach's *War with the Devil* and *Travels of True Godliness*, of which the same number were printed, he ventured the opinion that they would sell to the end of time.

But practical divinity, though immensely popular, was not the whole of the literature which the lower reading classes affected. Cheap quarto 'histories'—*Reynard the Fox, Tom a Lincoln, or the Red Rose Knight, The Life and Death of Mother Shipton, Scogin's Jests*, with many others of that genus—had a ready sale at sixpence or a shilling, while the smaller chapbooks—the 'Penny Merriments' and 'Penny Godlinesses' which Pepys, with an eye ever alert for the broad humours of the populace, found amusement in collecting—were printed vilely and sold in thousands. These latter consisted of old popular favourites, such as *The Friar and the Boy, The King and the Cobbler, Jack of Newbery*, with *Cupid's Court of Salutations*, garlands of songs,

books of riddles, cookery recipes, dream interpreters and
fortune tellers. While the Licensing act was still in force, many
of these trifles were solemnly submitted to the censor, who, apparently, did not consider it part of his office to refine the coarse
crudities which appealed to the taste and wit of the democracy,
since they bear his imprimatur on their title-pages. Besides being
exposed for sale in the smaller shops, they were hawked about
the streets by 'flying stationers,' or 'running booksellers,' and
carried further afield by country chapmen or hawkers, who got
their supplies from the shop of William Thackeray, at the Angel
in Duck lane, or John Back, at the Black Boy on London bridge,
or from one of the several other stationers who specialised in this
literature and sometimes combined with it the sale of pills or of
'Daffy's Elixir Salutis' at half-a-crown the half-pint bottle.

The business of a retail bookseller was carried on mainly by
direct transactions in his shop. In the eighteenth century, the
rubric posts, referred to by Ben Jonson in his oft-quoted lines 'To
my Bookseller,' were still in use as a means of advertising new
publications, and Pope makes mention of them as a conspicuous
feature of bookshops in his day. Upon these posts were stuck up
the title-pages of works to which the bookseller desired to call
attention. Lintot made extensive use of them, and it was near the
end of the century before they disappeared, John Sewell in Cornhill, according to Nichols[1], being, perhaps, the last who exhibited
the leading authors in this way. It seems that, about the middle
of the century, the custom of displaying new books upon the
counter was an innovation recently adopted from Oxford and
Cambridge booksellers[2]. For the extension of his business, a
pushing tradesman would also be active in the circulation of
'proposals' (prospectuses) for subscriptions to forthcoming books ;
and there were yet other devices at the command of an enterprising man, such as that adopted by Payne, who, in 1768, sent out
copies of Richard Gough's *Anecdotes of British Topography*, to
such as were likely to buy them, with the result, as Gough records,
that, when William Brown, the other bookseller, had sold but five,
Payne had disposed of forty or fifty.

The 'sale of books by way of auction, or who will give most for
them' had already been in practice on the continent for three
quarters of a century when William Cooper, a bookseller who
carried on business at the Pelican in Little Britain, introduced it

---

[1] Nichols, *Literary Anecdotes*, vol. III, p. 405.
[2] *Ibid.* vol. IV, p. 440.

into England. The first sale was that of the library of the late
Lazarus Seaman; it began on 31 October 1676, and occupied
eight days. The success of this experiment soon caused the innovation to become popular, and, before the end of the century,
considerably over one hundred auctions had taken place. The
majority of these sales were held by Cooper and Edward Millington,
the latter a born auctioneer, whose quick wit and wonderful fluency
of speech contributed in no small degree to his success in this *rôle*.
He may have professed that his object was to afford 'diversion
and entertainment' without any sinister regard to profit or advantage; but, by his ready fund of professional patter, he could
often enhance the values of his wares, 'and sell 'em by his Art for
twice their worth[1].'

Booksellers were not long in perceiving that this method of
disposing of private libraries might, with similar advantage, be
applied to relieving their own shelves of overweighted stock,
and quite a number of sales consisted of books from this source.
Prominent among the many who conducted book auctions in the
eighteenth century are Christopher Bateman, the Ballards, Lockyer
Davis and his son-in-law, John Egerton. Samuel Paterson, too,
who gave up bookselling for auctioneering, was, in his day, a noted
cataloguer, with a wide and curious knowledge of the contents of
books; but he had an invincible weakness for dipping into any
volume that might excite his curiosity during cataloguing, so it
not infrequently happened that catalogues were ready only a few
hours before the time of the sale. The *domus auctionaria* which
Samuel Baker set up in York street, Covent garden, in 1744, was
the earliest establishment devoted entirely to book auctions. On
Baker's death, in 1788, his partner George Leigh, of the famous
crumple-horn-shaped snuff-box, associated with himself Samuel
Sotheby, and thus brought into the firm a name which has survived
to the present day.

The chief rules under which sales were conducted were much
akin to those still customary; but the sums by which bids advanced
were curiously small, a penny being a common bid. Tricks of the
trade developed on both sides with the progress of the business.
Cases of an auctioneer raising the prices by phantom bids were
not unknown; and already, in 1721, we find suggestion of the
fraudulent 'knock-out' in practice among booksellers. Concerning
a certain auction in that year, Humfrey Wanley, in his journal
as Harleian librarian, records 'for the information of posterity ...

---

[1] Brown, Thomas, *Elegy on Mr Edward Millington* (in *Familiar Letters*, 1718).

that the books in general went at low, or rather at vile rates : through a combination of the booksellers against the sale[1]; and he observes, also, that the current prices of books had much advanced during late years.

It is possible that the success of the 'auctionary' method of disposing of superfluous stock may have suggested the catalogue of books at marked prices as a means of facilitating communication between bookseller and buyer and of placing additional temptation in the way of the latter. At all events, by the middle of the eighteenth century the practice of issuing such catalogues was widely in use, and many booksellers sent out their priced catalogues annually or even twice a year. Conspicuous among these was Thomas Osborne, insolent and ignorant, but with enough business wit to amass a considerable fortune, the Ballards, noted for their divinity catalogues, the Paynes and James Lackington. Lackington, whose *Memoirs* contain a lively account of his remarkable business career, with a strange variety of other matters, including the state of the bookmarket of his day, began life as a shoemaker, but soon abandoned that calling for the more congenial occupation of trafficking in books. From his initial experiment in bookselling, the purchase of a sackful of old theology for a guinea, he progressed steadily, in spite of lack of education. His first catalogue, issued in 1779, caused mirth and derision by its many blunders, but he got rid of twenty pounds' worth of books within a week. He sold for ready money only, and made a practice of selling everything cheap with the object of retaining the customers he had and of attracting others. The success of these principles, which he was not above proclaiming in his carriage motto, 'Small gains do great things,' brought him an enormous increase of business. His shop, known as 'The Temple of the Muses,' occupied a large corner block in Finsbury square, and has been described as one of the sights of London[2]. In the centre stood a huge circular counter, and a broad staircase led to the 'lounging rooms' and to a series of galleries where the volumes arranged on the shelves grew shabbier and cheaper as one ascended. Every one of these thousands of books was marked with its lowest price and numbered according to a printed catalogue. In 1792, Lackington estimated his profits for the year to be about £5000; at that period, he was issuing every year two catalogues, of which he

---

[1] Nichols, *Literary Anecdotes*, vol. I, p. 91 (where is printed a series of interesting extracts from Wanley's journal).

[2] Knight, C., *Shadows of the Old Booksellers* (1865), pp. 282—3.

printed more than three thousand copies, and he calculated that he was selling upwards of 100,000 volumes annually.

In his *Memoirs*, written about 1791, Lackington observes that

the sale of books in general has increased prodigiously within the last twenty years. According to the best estimation I have been able to make, I suppose that more than four times the number of books are sold now than were sold twenty years since.

He also remarked that the recent general introduction of histories, romances, stories and poems into schools had been a great means of diffusing a taste for reading among all ranks of people. The extensive increase in the habit of reading naturally brought with it the need of an ampler supply of literature, and, though books had become cheaper and more plentiful, it is hardly to be supposed that the demands of the large body of general readers could be satisfied by the limited number of books they were able to buy or borrow, and the medium of circulating libraries was an obvious method of augmenting supplies.

The earliest recorded date of the establishment of a circulating library in London seems to be 1740; but, for some fifteen years before this, Allan Ramsay, the poet bookseller, had been lending out to the citizens of Edinburgh English novels and romances at a penny a night, possibly to the scandal of the unco guid, but thereby letting a breath of wider air into the particularism of the Scottish literary taste of the time. The movement soon spread, both in the metropolis and in the provinces: in 1751, the enterprising William Hutton of Birmingham added a library to his bookshop; and, in the same decade, a subscription library was established in Liverpool. John Nicholson, familiarly known as 'Maps,' had his library in Cambridge; and, by the end of the century, others were to be found in most towns of any importance. The numerous private bookclubs which existed in every part of the country also formed a considerable channel for the distribution of books. In these clubs, members contributed a certain sum periodically for the purchase of books, which were circulated in rotation among subscribers, much in the same fashion that still obtains.

The chief lists of current English books in the middle of the seventeenth century are the catalogues issued by John Rothwell and William London. It was in 1657 that the latter, a Newcastle bookseller, brought out his *Catalogue of the most vendible Books in England*, prefaced by an 'Introduction to the use of books' from his own pen. It is significant of the prevailing taste of the time that more than two-thirds of the books in this list come under the heading divinity. Various other catalogues appeared; but there was no organised attempt to publish a regular list of new books until 1668, in which year John Starkey, a Fleet street bookseller, issued, under the title *Mercurius Librarius*, the first number of what are known as Term catalogues[1]. Starkey was soon joined by Robert Clavell, of the Peacock, in St Paul's churchyard, and, from 1670 to 1709, the list was issued quarterly under the title *A Catalogue of Books continued, printed and published at London*. Clavell also brought out, in 1672, *A catalogue of all the Books printed in England since the Dreadful Fire*, a fourth edition of which, continued to date, appeared in 1696; and publications relating to the popish plot were so numerous that he thought it worth while to issue, in 1680, a special catalogue of them. In 1714, Bernard Lintot essayed to take up the work of recording new books; but his *Monthly Catalogue* came to an end after eight numbers, and, again, there was a lapse, until John Wilford, in 1723, began another *Monthly Catalogue*, which ran for six years. From about this point, the gap is partially filled by lists of new books in the monthlies, such as *The Gentleman's Magazine, The London Magazine, The Monthly Review* and *The Critical Review*. Advertisements of new books, especially those issued by subscription, are also to be found in newspapers, and critical notices of books begin to appear in reviews. In 1766, there was published, for the use of booksellers, *A complete catalogue of modern books, published from the beginning of this century to the present time*, and this was followed by several similar compilations, the most active in this field being William Bent of Paternoster row, who continued his work into the nineteenth century.

A considerable proportion of the business of distributing books from the publisher to the retail bookseller was effected through the medium of sales, and trade sales were as much an institution of the eighteenth century as were trade books. These sales, to which only booksellers were admitted, and often only such as were invited by having a catalogue sent to them, consisted either of new books, which were offered to 'the trade' on special terms before publication, or of the stock of a bookseller retiring from business, or, again, of the remaining stock of certain books which had not 'gone off' to the publisher's expectations. It was customary for purchasers of these 'remainders' to destroy a large proportion of them and charge

---

[1] Reprinted by Arber, E., 3 vols., 1903—6. For an account and bibliography of these and other catalogues, see Growoll, A., *Three centuries of English booktrade bibliography*, New York, 1903.

full price for the rest ; and there was an understanding that, if anyone was known to sell such books under publication price, he should be excluded from future sales. James Lackington, the cheap bookseller, who always took a strong line of his own, after a time broke through this custom, and sold off his purchases at a half or even a quarter of the regular price.

In the provinces, the expansion of the booktrade after the restoration was not less marked than in the metropolis, though the volume of business still remained insignificant compared with that of London. From early times, stationers had been established in certain important centres, but, between 1640 and 1647, there were bookshops in about forty different towns, and, in 1704, John Dunton speaks of three hundred booksellers now trading in country towns. Some of these enlarged their sphere of operations by itinerant visits to neighbouring places ; in this way, the needs of Uttoxeter and Ashby-de-la-Zouch were supplied by the Lichfield bookseller, Michael Johnson—father of Samuel Johnson—who, also, on market days, made the journey to Birmingham and opened a shop there. In the middle of the eighteenth century, William Hutton, the historian of Birmingham, made similar visits from Birmingham to Bromsgrove market. In 1692, Nevill Simmons, bookseller, of Sheffield, held the first book-auction in Leeds, on which occasion, as related by Ralph Thoresby, who was a buyer at the sale, the room was so overcrowded that the floor gave way. A few years previous to this, the enterprising Edward Millington had introduced to the bookbuyers of Cambridge and other towns this attractive method of selling books ; and Dunton, in 1698, startled Dublin booksellers by taking across a large quantity of books and selling them by auction there. Other supplies were carried into the country by certain London booksellers, who attended regularly the chief provincial fairs, such as Sturbridge and Bristol, which were still important centres of book-distribution ; and a considerable number of books found their way direct from London to country customers, many of the clergy and other buyers of better-class literature having a bookseller in town from whom they ordered such books as they wanted. It might very well be expected that books to be found on the shelves of provincial shops would be chiefly of a popular nature, and this Lackington discovered to be the case when, towards the end of the eighteenth century, he made his progress through the principal towns in the north. He was struck by the scarcity of books of the better class in the shops he

visited: in York and Leeds, it is true, there were a few good books
to be seen, but in all the other towns between London and Edinburgh, he declares that nothing but trash was to be found.

Owing to legislative restrictions which permitted no presses to
be set up outside London, except at Oxford, Cambridge and
York, hardly any printing was done in other parts of the country
before the end of the seventeenth century.   By 1724, however,
presses had been started in nearly thirty other places ; but Oxford
and Cambridge continued to be the chief provincial centres of book
production.

At Oxford, the university press, which, in 1669, was installed
in the new Sheldonian theatre, made great progress under the
vigorous direction of John Fell, and the excellent work which it did
during this period is seen in books like Wood's *Historia* (1674),
and Hudson's *Dionysius* (1704).   Clarendon's gift of the copyright
of his *History of the Rebellion* provided for it, in 1713, a new
habitation and the title Clarendon press.   At Cambridge, it was
owing to the zeal of Richard Bentley that, at the end of the
seventeenth century, the university press there experienced a
corresponding revival and the real foundations of the modern
institution were laid.

With the exception of John Baskerville's work at Birmingham,
the book printing done in other provincial towns in the eighteenth
century is not of much account.   At York, Thomas Gent combined
topographical authorship with the art of printing, but excelled in
neither ; and, in the same city, John Hinxman, in 1760, published
the first two volumes of *Tristram Shandy*.   The booksellers of
Newcastle were numerous enough to have a Stationers' company of
their own about the same date.   At Bristol, there was William
Pine, the printer, also Joseph Cottle, the bookseller who published
poems by Coleridge, Southey and Wordsworth ; while Eton's
bookseller, Joseph Pote, was well known for half a century.   Of
private presses, the most noteworthy was that which Horace
Walpole maintained at Strawberry hill from 1757 to 1789[1].
Unsatisfactory workmen were not his only trouble, for, in a letter
of 1764, to Sir David Dalrymple, he complained that

the London booksellers play me all manner of tricks.   If I do not allow them
ridiculous profit they will do nothing to promote the sale; and when I do,
they buy up the impression, and sell it at an advanced price before my face.

North of the border, some respectable printing by Robert Urie
in Glasgow was followed by the establishment of the classic press

[1] See, also, *ante*, vol. x, p. 245.

of the brothers Robert and Andrew Foulis; and it was John Wilson of Kilmarnock who printed the first edition of Burns's poems in 1786. But Edinburgh was the headquarters of the Scottish book-trade, and the business of printing books for the English market, which afterwards became a great industry, had already begun, though the earlier manifestation of its development—the printing of the cheap books imported into England by Alexander Donaldson and John Bell—did not meet with appreciation from the London trade. In the earlier part of the eighteenth century, the admirable printing done by James Watson and the scholarly press of Thomas Ruddiman foreshadowed the excellence that was to become characteristic of Edinburgh printing; and, when James Beattie was making arrangements for the issue of a subscription edition of his essays in 1776, he was advised to have it printed in Edinburgh, as 'it would be more elegantly and correctly done than in London.' In the latter half of the century, William Creech was the leading figure in the Edinburgh trade, and his principal contemporaries were John Balfour, John Bell and Charles Elliot. Archibald Constable entered on his initial venture in publishing just four years before James Ballantyne, of Kelso, made, in 1799, his first experiment in book-printing, which led to the establishment of the famous Ballantyne press.

The dominant names in the Dublin trade during the eighteenth century were those of George Faulkner and Stephen Powell. But, Irish booksellers displayed their activity chiefly in reprinting all the best new English books, both for home use and for export. Since Ireland was outside the scope of the Copyright act, and produced nothing to tempt reprisals, this practice could be pursued with impunity, and the story of eighteenth century literature abounds in complaints against the misdeeds of these pirates.

CHAPTER XV

THE BLUESTOCKINGS

DURING the first half of the eighteenth century, Englishwomen had little education and still less intellectual status. It was considered 'unbecoming' for them to know Greek or Latin, almost immodest for them to be authors, and certainly indiscreet to own the fact. Mrs Barbauld was merely the echo of popular sentiment when she protested that women did not want colleges. 'The best way for a woman to acquire knowledge,' she wrote, 'is from conversation with a father, or brother, or friend.' It was not till the beginning of the next century—after the pioneer work of the bluestockings, be it observed—that Sydney Smith, aided, doubtless, by his extraordinary sense of humour, discovered the absurdity of the fact that a woman of forty should be more ignorant than a boy of twelve.

In society, at routs or assemblies, cards or dancing were the main diversions. Women were approached with flattering respect, with exaggerated compliment, but they were never accorded the greater compliment of being credited with sufficient intelligence to appreciate the subjects that interested men. What dean Swift wrote in 1734 to Mrs Delany from Ireland applied equally well to general opinion in England : 'A pernicious error prevails here among the men that it is the duty of your sex to be fools in every article except what is merely domestic.'

There were then, as there always had been, exceptions. There were women who, by some unusual fortune of circumstance, or by their own persistent efforts, had secured a share of the education that was given to their brothers as a matter of course. One such woman, Elizabeth Carter, a learned linguist and prominent bluestocking, wrote to Mrs Montagu concerning a social evening :

As if the two sexes had been in a state of war the gentlemen ranged themselves on one side of the room where they talked their own talk and left us poor ladies to twirl our shuttles and amuse each other by conversing as we could. By what little I could overhear our opposites were discoursing on the old English Poets, and this did not seem so much beyond a female capacity but that we might have been indulged with a share in it.

The faint resentment underlying this gentle complaint indicates how a few women with a natural and cultivated taste for literature began to regard the limitations imposed by traditional prejudice on their mental activities. As an unconscious protest against this intellectual stifling, as well as against 'the tyranny of cards,' it began to be

much the fashion for several ladies to have evening assemblies, where the fair sex might participate in conversation with literary and ingenious men, animated by a desire to please[1].

The first 'conversation,' however, had been given in the early fifties, many years before Boswell wrote this. It was held at the house of Mrs Vesey, wife of Agmondesham Vesey, a member of the Irish parliament, and daughter of Sir Thomas Vesey, bishop of Ossory. She was a witty Irishwoman with a taste for literature, who determined to unite the literary and the fashionable society of her acquaintance—worlds that had hitherto been kept apart.

Much perverse ingenuity was wasted by the writers of the first quarter of the nineteenth century in trying to account for the term 'bluestocking.' Abraham Hayward, de Quincey, Mrs Opie, all sought for an obscure origin in France, in Italy, anywhere, in fact, save where it lay embedded in the writings of the bluestocking circle. The point is still disputed, but critical authorities lean to the Stillingfleet origin, supported by Boswell, and corroborated by Madame d'Arblay. During the annual migration of the great world to Bath, Mrs Vesey, meeting Benjamin Stillingfleet, invited him to one of her 'conversations.' Stillingfleet, the disinherited grandson of the bishop of Worcester, was a botanist and a poet, a philosopher and a failure. He had given up society and was obliged to decline the invitation on the score of not having clothes suitable for an evening assembly. The Irishwoman, a singularly inconsequent person, giving a swift glance at his every-day attire, which included small-clothes and worsted stockings, exclaimed gaily: 'Don't mind dress. Come in your blue stockings.' Stillingfleet obeyed her to the letter; and, when he entered the brilliant assembly where ladies in 'night gowns' of brocade and lutestring were scarcely more splendid in plumage than men in garments of satin and paduasoy, the shabby recluse claimed

---

[1] Boswell's *Life of Johnson*, ed. Hill, G. B. (1887), vol. iv, p. 108.

permission to join them by whimsically murmuring: 'Don't mind dress. Come in your blue stockings.'

Stillingfleet was so popular at these conversation parties, that 'blew stockings,' as he was called, was in great request.

'Such was the excellence of his conversation,' wrote Boswell, 'that it came to be said, we can do nothing without the blue stockings, and thus, by degrees, the title was established.'

By one of the ironic subtleties of nomenclature, a term originally applied to a man was gradually transferred in deepened tint to the women of these assemblies. It was a name, 'fixed in playful stigma,' as one of the circle happily phrased it. For, though bluestockings were estimable women, individually held in high honour, the epithet 'blue,' if not a designation of scorn like *les femmes savantes*, held at least a grain of goodhumoured malice ; possibly, because few of them were free from what their 'queen,' with frank selfcriticism, called, 'the female frailty of displaying more learning than is necessary or graceful.'

But it is only just to say that Mrs Vesey[1], 'the first queen' of the bluestockings, was free from this particular female frailty. Though she delighted in literary conversation, she had neither literary ambition, nor desire to pose as a learned woman. She was ethereal and imaginative, and, said her friends, even in old age, combined the simplicity of a child with the eager vivacity of eighteen. Her intimates called her the sylph, and, of the bluestocking hostesses, without question, she was the best-beloved. By nature unconventional, Mrs Vesey was noted for her amusing horror of the paralysing effect of the conventional circle. Her large reception rooms in Bolton row—and, later, in Clarges street— appropriately upholstered in blue, were crowded with guests, who, by her deft arrangement of chairs and sofas 'naturally broke up into little groups' that were 'perpetually varying and changing.' There was 'no ceremony, no cards, and no supper,' and Mrs Vesey, we are told, had the almost magic art of putting all her company at their ease without the least appearance of design. And, what was possibly even more conducive to the success of her assemblies, 'it was not absolutely necessary to talk sense.'

Vesey, though not a model husband, was an excellent host, with sufficient interest in literature to help Lord Lyttelton with his *Life of Henry II*, and to be delighted when he was elected a member of Johnson's Literary club. Husbands were not much in evidence in the bluestocking circle—by a curious coincidence,

[1] See, also, *ante*, vol. x, chap. xi, p. 261.

they were rarely seen in Parisian salons—but Vesey, undoubtedly, contributed to the success of his wife's literary parties. To the Veseys belongs the credit of being among the first to welcome authors and people with an interest in literature to social intercourse with the great. Even of Johnson, Croker remarks in a footnote that, 'except by a few visits in his latter years at the *basbleux* assemblies of Mrs Montagu, Mrs Vesey, and Mrs Ord, we do not trace him in anything like fashionable society.' In the bluestocking coteries, however, he was regarded as a literary lion of the first rank, 'whose roar was deeper in its tone when he meant to be civil.' We get a bluestocking picture of the literary autocrat from Bennet Langton, one of the best talkers among the 'blues,' who, knowing Boswell's amiable hero-worship, sent him an account of an evening at Vesey's. Here, surrounded by duchesses, lords, knights, and ladies, 'four if not five deep,' Johnson held converse with Barnard, provost of Eton, while the company listened with respectful attention. The evenings were probably pleasanter, however, when there was less monopoly, and the various groups conversed among themselves. Hannah More, whose critical judgment was equal to that of any of the bluestockings, not only gave precedence to 'Vesey, of verse the judge and friend' in her poem *Bas Bleu*, but she also wrote 'I know of no house where there is such good rational society, and a conversation so general, so easy and so pleasant.'

For more than thirty years, Mrs Vesey's house was a notable centre of the most cultivated society in London. After her husband's death, however, her mind became clouded, and, for a few years before she died in 1791, she was unable to recognise her friends, who, nevertheless, visited her with a loyal devotion, lest at any time she should regain her faculties, and miss their society. In 1787, Hannah More wrote:

> Mr Walpole seldomer presents himself to my mind as the man of wit, than as the tender-hearted and humane friend of my dear infirm, broken-spirited Mrs Vesey.

Though Mrs Vesey was indirectly responsible for the title of the bluestocking coteries, it was Mrs Montagu[1], who, by her dominant character, by her husband's wealth and by the almost unique position she made for herself in London society, was speedily recognised as what Johnson in a moment of wrath satirically called her, 'the Queen of the Blues.' Elizabeth

[1] See, also, *ante*, vol. x, chap. xi, pp. 261 ff.

Robinson was born at York in 1720, one of a family of twelve children. Much of her childhood was spent in Cambridgeshire, with her maternal grandmother, the wife of Conyers Middleton, librarian of Cambridge university. At Cambridge, the pretty precocious child was looked on as something of an infant prodigy. Middleton not only allowed her to come to his academic parties, but he would afterwards, with educational intent, require from her an account of the learned conversations at which she had been present. At the time of her marriage, he somewhat pompously reminded her: 'This University had the honour of Mr Montagu's education, and claims some share in yours.' Her father, an accomplished amateur artist, delighted in cultivating the gift of swift repartee that she had evidently inherited from himself. Her mother, from whom, perhaps, she inherited her taste for literature, was related to Sterne. At home, she disputed and argued goodnaturedly with her brothers, till their emulation produced in their sister 'a diligence of application unusual at the time'—a diligence that resulted in a knowledge of French, Italian and some Latin, though, influenced by fashion, she was sometimes ashamed to own to the latter accomplishment.

While staying with her grandmother in Cambridge, she was taken to call at Wimpole, the seat of the second earl of Oxford. Here, she made acquaintance with the earl's only daughter, Prior's 'Noble lovely little Peggy,' who, in 1734, married the second duke of Portland. Though Elizabeth Robinson was only thirteen at the time of this marriage, the young duchess of eighteen found a good deal of pleasure in the child's witty letters, and, as she grew older, frequently invited her to Bulstrode. This friendship introduced her to a cultivated circle, among whom were Lord Lyttelton, Mrs Delany—then Mrs Pendarves—and many more, who, besides helping to form her literary tastes, became her lifelong friends and good bluestockings. She was early 'brought out' by her father, who, proud of his vivacious daughter, took her into society at Bath and Tunbridge when she was only thirteen. At the age when girls of today are enjoying their first balls, Elizabeth, satiated with years of recurring gaieties, wrote concerning Bath: '"How d'ye do," is all one hears in the morning, and "What's trumps?" in the afternoon.' Scarcely a year later, she writes to her mother, 'there is nothing so much wanted in this country as the art of making the same people chase new topics without change of persons.' And, through its slightly involved expression, one may detect, even at that early age, a foreshadowing of her bluestocking parties.

This 'art' she made a point of cultivating after her marriage in 1742, with the wealthy Edward Montagu, grandson of the first earl of Sandwich. She was twenty-two, and her husband twenty-nine years older; but, as her cold practical nature had already decided that 'gold is the chief ingredient in worldly happiness,' the discrepancy in their ages was not considered a drawback to the solid advantages of wealth and position. When, in 1744, their only child died in infancy, she sought happiness in social and intellectual pleasures with even greater avidity than before.

Mrs Montagu had not long been married before she discovered that her husband's town house in Dover street was too small for her magnificent projects of entertaining. Mr Montagu, therefore, built a fine house in Hill street, into which they were able to move in 1748. Here, in her famous Chinese room, she began to give a series of receptions, and, in 1753, she writes to Mrs Boscawen that her 'Chinese Room was filled by a succession of people from eleven in the morning till eleven at night.' There is not any precise information as to when she began to give her bluestocking parties, but it was probably after she became acquainted with Mrs Vesey. Though Hannah More gives Mrs Vesey preeminence in her poem *Bas Bleu*, it is generally conceded that Mrs Montagu was the undoubted 'queen' of these assemblies. Lady Louisa Stuart, granddaughter of Lady Mary Wortley Montagu, and daughter of the third earl of Bute, gives a detailed and not too flattering account of Mrs Montagu's 'attempt at an English salon':

'The only blue stocking meetings which I myself ever attended,' she wrote, 'were those at Mrs Walsingham's and Mrs Montagu's. To frequent the latter, however, was to drink at the fountain-head ... Mrs Montagu eclipsed them all[1].'

She then gives a somewhat sarcastic portrait of the hostess, and, while allowing that she had quick parts, great vivacity, no small share of wit, and competent learning, she credits her, also, with a superabundance of vanity, and concludes with the insinuation that her 'excellent cook is probably the only one of the powers that could carry on the war single-handed.'

'Thus endowed,' she writes, 'Mrs Montagu was acquainted with almost all persons of note or distinction. She paid successful court to all authors, critics, artists, orators, lawyers, and clergy of high reputation ... she attracted all tourists and travellers; she made entertainment for all ambassadors, sought out all remarkable foreigners, especially if men of letters[2].'

[1] *Gleanings from an Old Portfolio* (Correspondence of Lady Louisa Stuart), ed. Clark, Mrs Godfrey (privately printed, 1898), vol. III, p. 61.
[2] *Ibid.* p. 62.

Lady Louisa was not a bluestocking—she had, indeed, 'a horror of appearing in print lest she should lose caste'—and her evidence, though seasoned with a dash of malicious humour, is probably less biassed than that of the bluestockings whose pens were too often tipped with the honey of mutual admiration. She flings the fine scorn of a *grande dame* on the bluestocking habit of opening the gates of society to those who had not been born within the sacred ringfence; she ridicules, with the prejudice of her class and period, the 'college geniuses with nothing but a book in their pockets.' She stigmatises Mrs Montagu's company as a 'heterogeneous medley,' which, with all her sparkling wit and manifold attractions, she was never able to fuse into a harmonious mass. 'As they went in, so they went out, single, isolated'; a result, partly owing, no doubt, to Mrs Montagu's habit of arranging her guests in one large, disconcerting half-circle. Madame d'Arblay also mentions this peculiar formation, at the head of which sat the lady of the house, and, on her right, the guest of highest rank, or the person of the moment whom she most delighted to honour. Lady Louisa, not restrained by bluestocking loyalty, frankly holds the custom up to ridicule. 'Everything at that house, as if under a spell, was sure to form itself into a circle or semi-circle.' And she tells, further, of 'a vast half-moon' of twenty-five ladies of whom she was one, seated round the fire, and of the vain efforts of the men, when they solemnly filed in from dinner, to break through it.

Lady Louisa's facts are probably as correct as they are amusing; but, as facts invariably take the colour of the medium through which they are presented, be it sympathy or antipathy, it is only just to dilute her sarcasms with some of the admiration and high regard expressed by the bluestocking coteries. If not an ideal hostess, Mrs Montagu had many of the qualities that go to the ruling of a salon. Lord Lyttelton, one of her intimate court of Platonic admirers, was amazed, he once told her, that those 'dangerous things...beauty, wit, wisdom, learning and virtue (to say nothing about wealth)' had not, long before, driven her from society. Her wit, from childhood to age, was indisputable. By the alchemy of her dexterous mind she could transmute her wide reading, her swift impressions, her varied experience into what she aptly called 'the sal volatile of lively discourse.' Living, as she did, in the limelight of a critical society, it was inevitable that her character should be freely discussed. But, though her complacent vanity might, occasionally, be censured, her affectations deplored, her flattery derided, yet we are told that even those who were most diverted with her foibles would express a high opinion of her abilities. 'In her conversation she had more *wit* than any other person, male or female, whom I have known,' wrote Beattie. Dr Johnson, whom, said Mrs Thrale, 'she flattered till he was ready to faint,' paid her back in the same seductive coin. When she showed him some plates that had belonged to queen Elizabeth, he assured her that 'their present possessor was in no tittle inferior to the first.' At another time, he said of her,

Sir, that lady exerts more mind in conversation than any person I ever met with. Sir, she displays such powers of ratiocination, such radiations of intellectual excellence as are amazing.

And Lord Bath once told Sir Joshua Reynolds that 'he did not believe that there ever was a more perfect human being created, or ever would be created, than Mrs Montagu.' Even Lord Macartney, much given to 'elegant pleasantries,' who 'piqued himself upon carrying compliments beyond the moon,' having flattered Mrs Montagu to the furthest limit of credulity, would confess to his intimates: 'After all, she is the cleverest woman I know. Meet her where you will, she says the best thing in the company.' Horace Walpole might occasionally wing his sly shafts of malicious wit in her direction, but there are few greater tributes to the interest of her assemblies and of the bluestocking coteries generally than his, and Soame Jenyns's and Owen Cambridge's—the old wits as a younger generation irreverently called them—frequent attendance.

Even her enemies allowed that she had a sincere love of literature. She 'makes each rising wit her care,' said a contemporary poem, and her kindly discriminating help to struggling authors, and authors who were past struggling, earned for her the high-sounding title, the 'female Maecenas of Hill Street,' bestowed on her by Hannah More. When Anna Williams, the blind poetess, was left with a precarious income, Mrs Montagu gave her an annual allowance of £10, a kindness greatly appreciated by Johnson, who, in his 'wild benevolence,' had given Mrs Williams, in company with other derelicts of humanity, a home under the shelter of his roof. After Edward Montagu's death, when she became sole mistress of his wealth, she gave an annuity of £100 to Mrs Carter; and, when there was a question of a government pension for Beattie, she assured him with the utmost delicacy that, should the project fail, she herself would supply the necessary funds. These are only a few instances out of many; her correspondence is full of allusions to the needy and distressed. **Nor** were her gifts all in the sordid coin of commerce. Not only did she give generously to her literary friends the encouragement and sympathy that, in dark moments, are of more value than gold, but she would promote their interests in every way possible, after the manner of the ladies of the Parisian salons. It was Mrs Montagu's wide-reaching influence that materially helped to spread the fame of Beattie's *Essay on Truth*, as a counterblast to Hume's 'infidel writings.' Later, it was she who suggested its reissue by subscription; and, though she was indefatigable in her efforts to enlist subscribers, she was much disappointed because it only produced about four hundred guineas profit for the author. She gave him introductions to Lord Kinnoul and his brother, the archbishop of York, who both made plans for his advancement. In 1772, she writes: 'I was in hopes to have something done among the Great that might forward my hope for you'; and, when *The Minstrel* appeared, not only did she send copies to Lord Lyttelton, Lord Chatham and others of her personal friends, but she told Beattie, 'I wrote immediately to a person who serves many gentlemen and ladies with new books, to recommend it to all people of taste. ... I have recommended it to many of our bishops and others.'

Having so active an interest in authors and their works, it was not surprising that she should one day appear as author herself. In 1760, when Lord Lyttelton published his *Dialogues of the Dead*, the last three were advertised as 'composed by a different hand,' the hand of Mrs Montagu: though, in deference to the prejudice of her day, she preferred to shield herself behind a veil of anonymity, which she was not sorry that most of her friends were able to penetrate. The *Dialogues* met with much criticism, favourable and otherwise. Johnson called them a 'nugatory performance,' and Walpole, by nature unable to resist an opportunity for epigram, wrote of them as the dead dialogues, a prophecy that time has almost fulfilled. Those by Mrs Montagu were between Cadmus and Hercules; Mercury and a modern fine lady; Plutarch, Charon and a modern bookseller. The first is full of solid good sense—too solid, indeed, for satire—but every phrase is trite and obvious, without a glimmer of the wit that Mrs Montagu scattered freely in her talk and letters. Mrs Carter gave it fatal, discerning praise when she assured its author that it 'has all the elegance of polite literature.' The dialogue between Plutarch and the bookseller is severe on the popular taste of the day, and suggests that popular taste, like human nature, never changes.

'I unadvisedly bought an edition of your *Lives*,' the bookseller says to Plutarch; 'a pack of old Greeks and Romans... and the work which repaired the loss I sustained... was the *Lives of the Highwaymen.*' The second dialogue, between Mercury and Mrs Modish, is in Mrs Montagu's happiest vein of light sarcasm. It is by far the wittiest of the whole collection, and met with unqualified success. It is a lively satire on the fashionable woman of the period, who, when Mercury summons her to 'pass the Styx,' is 'engaged, absolutely engaged... to the Play on Mondays, balls on Tuesdays, the Opera on Saturdays, and to card assemblies the rest of the week.' She suggests, however, that he should wait till the end of the season, when she might like to go to the Elysian fields for a change. 'Have you a Vauxhall and Ranelagh?' she asks. 'I think I should not dislike drinking the Lethe waters when you have a full season.' Compliments flowed in from the bluestocking circle who were inclined to preen themselves on their 'queen's' literary success; and Mrs Montagu, exhilarated with the heady wine of public applause, wrote to Mrs Carter, 'I do not know but at last I may become an author in form.... The Dialogues, I mean the three worst, have had a more favourable reception than I expected.'

It was not, however, till nine years later, that the great literary effort of her life appeared, an *Essay on the Writings and Genius of Shakespeare*, carrying the sub-title 'with some remarks upon the misrepresentations of Mons. de Voltaire.' In her letters, one may trace its germ at an early stage, with here and there evidences of its gradual growth. In a letter to Lord Bath, in 1761, she writes a long criticism of Voltaire's *Tancred*, in which she compares the 'natural sallies of passion in our Shakspear' with 'the pompous declamation' of Voltaire in *Tancred.* Three years later, Mrs Carter mentions Mrs Montagu's 'criticism on Macbeth' and, when Johnson's preface to the 1765 edition of Shakespeare with all the other prefaces appeared, she writes of Johnson's as the ablest of them all. Mrs Montagu's *Essay* was, in great measure, a protest against the strictures that Voltaire had for years hurled at Shakespeare, from whom he had freely borrowed. As many English readers knew, he had taken whole scenes from *Macbeth* for his *Mahomet*; the plot of his *Zaïre* was only *Othello* slightly disguised; but indignation in England deepened to disgust at Voltaire's introduction to *Sémiramis*. Miss Talbot, a bluestocking, wrote to Mrs Carter in 1745, 'Voltaire has just published with his *Semiramis*, the foolishest, idlest, coarsest critique that ever was[1].'

---

[1] For criticism of Shakespeare in the eighteenth century see vol. v, chaps. XI, XII.

In her introduction, Mrs Montagu says, 'I was incited to this undertaking by great admiration of his genius, and still greater indignation at the treatment he has received from a French wit.' The whole gist of the *Essay*, however, so far as Shakespeare is concerned, is summed up in the trite conclusion of the introduction, 'Nature and sentiment will pronounce our Shakespear a mighty genius; judgment and taste will confess that, as a writer, he is far from faultless.' Her vindication of Shakespeare, it may at once be admitted, was what a contemporary called it, 'a work of supererogation'; but the attack on the literary dictator of Europe, even though, in its daring, it may suggest the proverb concerning fools and angels, was at least, well-merited. In Paris, particularly, when, five years later, the *Essay* was translated into French, Voltaire's credit as an authority on Shakespeare was felt to be seriously damaged. He had boasted that his translation of *Julius Caesar* was 'the most faithful translation that can be, and the only faithful one in the French language of any author, ancient or modern.' Such confidence invited attack, and Mrs Montagu fell on his errors with a pitiless enjoyment that gives life and vigour to this part of her destructive criticism. She points out that, in this only faithful translation, Voltaire has utterly misread the meaning of several words and phrases, and, with a relish sharpened by indignation, her unsparing pen points out 'the miserable mistakes and galimathias of this dictionary work.' After an attack on Corneille, with whom Voltaire had compared Shakespeare, to the disadvantage of the latter, she finally hopes that 'the many gross blunders in this work will deter other *beaux esprits* from attempting to hurt works of genius by the masked battery of an unfair translation.'

The essay, though published anonymously, met with a flattering reception. *The Critical Review* wrote of the author as 'almost the only critic who has yet appeared worthy of Shakespeare,' and most of the other reviews—save *The Monthly Review*, which condemned the language of the *Essay* as affected—were, on the whole, favourable. From the bluestocking circle, she received reams of eulogy, and perhaps Johnson was the only dissentient in the chorus of praise when he remarked to Sir Joshua Reynolds, 'Sir, it does *her* honour, but it would do nobody else honour.' Modern criticism agrees with Johnson, and the *Essay* is condemned as 'well-intentioned,... but feeble[1],' and quite without value in the enormous bulk of Shakespeare criticism.

[1] *History of Criticism*, by Saintsbury, G., vol. III, p. 173.

It brought her, however, a considerable measure of contemporary fame in England, and her bluestocking adherents were proud of their 'queen's' achievement in the world of letters. 'She is the first woman for literary knowledge in England,' said Mrs Thrale, while Fanny Burney wrote that the general plaudits given to the book 'mounted her... to the Parnassian heights of female British literature.' When, in 1776, she visited Paris she had the satisfaction of finding her *Essay* well known, and herself a celebrity. She was a welcome guest at many of the Parisian salons, she adopted Parisian rouge, criticised French plays and French acting with severity and, by a singular chance, her visit coincided with the opening of the French academy on the occasion when Voltaire's famous abusive *Letter to the Academy* was read by d'Alembert. Shakespeare was again denounced in language so unrestrained that even some of the forty, wrote Mrs Montagu, 'shrugged their shoulders' and showed other strong signs of disapprobation. At its conclusion, Suard said to her, *Je crois, Madame, que vous êtes un peu fâchée de ce que vous venez d'entendre. Moi, Monsieur!* she replied, with her ever ready wit, *point du tout! Je ne suis pas amie de Monsieur Voltaire*[1] Her bluestocking friends rather feared that her Parisian success would unduly inflate her selfesteem Mrs Delany wrote to Mrs Boscawen a witty little sketch of her as Madame *de* Montagu, to which Mrs Boscawen replied, 'Much I fear that she will never be Mrs Montagu, an Englishwoman again!' However, their fears were not realised. She came back to England and was soon her former English self, something of a *poseuse* perhaps, a good deal of an egotist, but always possessing such brilliant qualities of mind and intellect, such a gift for steady friendship, that she remained as firmly fixed as hitherto on her bluestocking throne, on which she had still more than twenty years to reign.

But, of the members of the bluestocking circle none was more 'darkly, deeply, beautifully blue' than Mrs Elizabeth Carter, who, though unmarried, took brevet rank as matron after the custom of her day. She was the daughter of Nicholas Carter, perpetual curate of a chapel at Deal, and one of the six preachers at Canterbury. As a first step in her education, she was sent to Canterbury for a year to learn French in the house of a Huguenot refugee. On her return home, she took lessons with her brothers in Latin, Greek and Hebrew, but she acquired knowledge with such difficulty

[1] *Letters* of Horace Walpole (1904), vol. IX, p. 444.

that her father advised her to give up attempting the classical languages. She continued, however, with dogged persistence. She rose early, and, to keep her attention from flagging at night, she took snuff, bound wet towels round her head and chewed green tea and coffee. As a result of this undaunted plodding, she gained so solid a knowledge of Greek that Johnson spoke of her later as one of the best Greek scholars he had ever known. By degrees, she added Italian, German, Portuguese and Arabic to her languages. She was, at the same time, educating her young step-brothers, one of whom was sent to Cambridge.

As a linguist, who spoke fluent French, who could write pure, literary Italian, who, at need, could talk in Latin, who 'delighted' in German, who knew something of Hebrew, Portuguese and Arabic and who was among the best Greek scholars of her time, her views on the study of languages are worth considering, particularly as they accord with some of the most modern and intelligent methods of teaching in vogue today. She knew practically nothing of Greek and Latin grammar, and used to speak of them, says her biographer, 'with some degree of unmerited contempt.' He hastens to explain that, as a science, she understood grammar, but, he adds significantly, *not as taught in schools.* Her fine intellect quickly discovered that the commonsense method of acquiring a foreign language is identical with that of learning one's own. A preliminary store of words and phrases must be assimilated before grammar can be of use, and she regarded it 'rather as a consequence of understanding the language, than as a handmaid....'

Though grammar was not, for her, an obstructive fetish in the acquirement of a new language, she yet had a cultivated eye for grammatical errors, and a fault that she had detected in a line of Homer 'kept her awake at night.' At another time, she disputed with archbishop Secker over the translation of two verses in *Corinthians,* and, after consulting the original, the archbishop was compelled to admit that 'Madam Carter' was in the right.

She was introduced to Cave, of *The Gentleman's Magazine,* by her father, and contributed verse to his magazine so early as her seventeenth year. In 1738, he published for her a thin quarto of twenty-four pages; poems that had been written before she was twenty. Johnson, who was then doing hackwork for Cave, wrote Greek and Latin epigrams on the author, to whom he had been introduced by the publisher. At another time, he said that 'Eliza' ought to be celebrated in as many languages as *Louis le Grand,*

and, in proof of his high opinion of her abilities he asked her to contribute to his *Rambler*. Numbers 44 and 100 are hers ; four 'billets' in no. 10 are by Hester Mulso, afterwards Mrs Chapone, and no. 30 is by Catherine Talbot, all accomplished ladies of the bluestocking circle. Richardson the novelist, seeing Elizabeth Carter's *Ode to Wisdom* in manuscript, printed it without permission in *Clarissa*. Her remonstrance was the prelude to an acquaintance with him, and she sometimes joined his 'flower-garden of ladies' at North End, his *petticoaterie*, according to the scoffing Walpole. It is said that he gravely consulted her on the qualities that should distinguish the perfect man before he created Sir Charles Grandison.

Her first serious effort in literature was *Examination of Mr Pope's Essay on Man*, which she translated from the French of Jean Pierre de Crousaz. It was thought that this might lead to an acquaintance with Pope, and Sir George Oxenden warned her father

that there is hardly an instance of a woman of letters entering into an intimacy of acquaintance with men of wit and parts, particularly poets, who were not thoroughly abused and maltreated by them in print ... Mr Pope has done it more than once[1].

Shortly afterwards, she translated Algarotti's *Newtonianismo per le Dame* into English, under the title, *Sir Isaac Newton's Philosophy explained for the use of the Ladies, in Six Dialogues on Light and Colours*. She was then twenty-two, and Thomas Birch wrote of her as, 'a very extraordinary phenomenon in the republic of letters.' Elizabeth Carter was not, by temperament, a literary woman; her pleasure was in acquiring knowledge rather than in giving it out. In all her studies—save that of German, perhaps, which she began with the view of preparing herself for a place at court—she had not, apparently, any ambition beyond her passion for study. Even the great literary achievement of her life, the translation of *Epictetus*, was made to oblige her friend Miss Talbot, and was not, at first, intended for publication.

Catherine Talbot, with her mother, lived in the household of bishop Secker and his wife. She was an accomplished woman, but she did not read Greek, and, in 1743, she wrote to Mrs Carter that she was 'vastly curious' to read those precepts of Epictetus that had not been translated. It was not till 1749, however, that Elizabeth Carter, to please her friend, began a rough translation of the work that was to be the foundation of her modest fortune, as well as to

[1] *Memoirs of the Life of Mrs Elizabeth Carter*, by Pennington, M., vol. 1, p. 44.

add enormously to the fame she already enjoyed as the learned
Mrs Carter. These few pages were submitted to the bishop of
Oxford, who found the translation good. Its only fault, he said,
was its elegance of diction, that block of stumbling to many
eighteenth century writers. Epictetus, the bishop reminded her,
was a plain man, who spoke plainly, and the translation ought
to be less smooth to preserve the spirit of the original. When
Mrs Carter wrote back that she had 'some defence of her passion
for ornament,' the bishop replied grimly, 'Why would you change
a plain, home-awakening preacher into a fine, smooth, polite writer
of what nobody will mind?' But Mrs Carter was not easily
persuaded to renounce the 'elegance of polite literature' into
which she was transforming the Greek slave's trenchant exhorta-
tions. It was only after Miss Talbot added the weight of her
opinion, and wrote 'I am much of my Lord's mind... for energy,
shortness and plainness,' that she was induced to put her translation into a more direct form. The bishop wrote a few pages as a
model of the rough almost literal translation which he advocated,
but perhaps he was a little chagrined at her obstinacy, for, a few
months later, she laments that 'Epictetus and I are miserable that
... my Lord had so inhumanly given us up to our own devices.'
Bishop Secker, however, gave her valuable help in correcting it,
devoting a whole month, when he was laid up with gout, to its
revision. It was he, probably, who, in 1753, suggested its publication, for, from that time, it was prepared for the press. When it
was at length finished, Miss Talbot urged her friend to collect
materials for the life of Epictetus, to be published with it, to
which Elizabeth replied: 'Whoever that somebody or other is, who
is to write the life of Epictetus, seeing I have *a dozen shirts to
make*, I do opine, dear Miss Talbot, that it cannot be I.' She,
however, added the *Enchiridion* and notes, at the bishop's suggestion, and the whole was finished in 1756, just seven years after
it was begun.

In the work of correcting sheets for the press, bishop Secker
again gave ungrudging assistance; and, in one letter, we find her
thus whimsically adjured:

Do, dear Madam Carter, get yourself whipt, get yourself whipt... I know
you mean to be careful; but you cannot without this help... The first thing
I have cast my eyes upon is Epictetus for Epicurus...

Epictetus appeared before the public in 1758, and its success and
sale make it one of the minor romances of publishing. It was in
one volume, large quarto, and 1018 copies were struck off at first;

but, as these were insufficient, 250 more were printed a few months later. It was issued by subscription, and the price was a guinea in sheets. In her own copy were the names of no fewer than 1031 subscribers, and, since many copies were not claimed 'by way of compliment,' Mrs Carter gained nearly a thousand pounds profit. Richardson's bill for printing the first impression amounted to £67. 7s. Two further editions were printed in her life-time, and, for many years, it remained a good selling book at a high price. *Epictetus* gained for its author a European reputation. So far afield as Russia, where, said Elizabeth Carter, 'they were only just beginning to walk on their hind legs,' there appeared a notice of the learned Englishwoman, and she was told that the Tsarina had read it through with high approbation. After its publication, she was regarded by the bluestocking circle with something akin to awe, and it is almost a relief to find her intimates, Mrs Montagu and Miss Talbot, jestingly referring to her 'uncle Epictetus,' or writing of her as 'cousin-german to Xenophon,' while Walpole, with his facile talent for bestowing unchristian names, frequently calls her Mrs Epictetus Carter.

After *Epictetus*, Mrs Carter did not write anything more for publication, though, in 1762, Lord Bath persuaded her to publish a small volume of poems that had been written at various times. She gave such reluctant consent to this that Miss Talbot accused her of thinking it 'no small degradation from a quarto of Greek Philosophy to dwindle into an eighteenpenny pamphlet of English verse.' The dedication was to the earl of Bath, and, writes her biographer, 'is wholly unsullied by that flattery which is too often a disgrace both to the author and the patron.' But this praise is somewhat discounted, when, on the next page, he quotes a letter from Mrs Carter, indicating that Lord Bath wrote the dedication himself!

For the remainder of her long life, Elizabeth Carter settled down to the comfortable enjoyment of her fame on the modest competence of which the profits from *Epictetus* were the foundation. Her influential friends invested this money profitably; and, some years later, when Mrs Montagu inherited her husband's fortune, she allowed her friend £100 a year. Lord Bath did not leave her an annuity, according to the expectation of many of the blue-stockings; but his heirs generously made good this deficiency by a grant of £100 a year. During the summer months, she lived with her father at Deal, or went on visits to her friends among the great at their country houses. The winter she invariably spent in

London in handsome and comfortable apartments in Clarges street, within easy distance of several of the bluestocking hostesses. 'She kept no table,' and never dined at home, except when ill, or unable to go out. In the wide bluestocking circle, she was always a welcome guest, and, not only did they invite her to their houses, but they invariably sent for her their sedan chairs or carriages, which again carried her back to Clarges street by ten o'clock at the latest. She was, apparently, a sympathetic listener rather than a talker, but she was always, to the end of her long life, a notability in the inner circle of the bluestockings.

The bluestocking, however, whose fame reached to the furthest ends of the earth—though as a philanthropist rather than as a blue—is Hannah More[1]. When she first appeared in the bluestocking coteries, she had not yet become a passionate reformer, a stern moralist, 'the eminent divine,' as she was called in later years. Her connection with the blues represents the 'gay and worldly' side of her serious life. During her first winter among them she was still in the twenties, and her hasty impressionist descriptions of the literary society of London scintillate with the fresh enthusiasm of a girl whose eyes and mind are slightly dazzled by unaccustomed experiences. She was not unworthy to be admitted to the society of those learned ladies and ingenious gentlemen. She spoke fluent French, polished by conversation with some French officers on parole, who often visited her home. Her father taught her Latin, and some mathematics, though, frightened by her precocity, he did not take her far in the latter science. Her elder sisters, not having any fortune in prospect, opened a boarding-school at Bristol to which she was sent, at the age of twelve. Later, like her four sisters, she taught in the school, assiduously carrying on her own education at the same time. She studied Latin, Italian and Spanish, improving her style by translations and imitations of the *Odes* of Horace, and some of the dramatic compositions of Metastasio.

Hannah More was a precocious child—a child who, indisputably, was the mother of the woman. In youthful days, she would treasure any stray scrap of paper on which she scribbled verses or essays that were always adorned with 'a well directed moral.' When her ardent wish took form in the shape of 'a whole quire of paper to herself,' it was soon filled by the budding moralist with supposititious letters to depraved characters, intended to reclaim them from their errors. The one romance of her life began when she was twenty-two, and came to naught, though, indirectly, it paved the way for her literary career. She was engaged to a wealthy man of good position, the cousin of two of her pupils. This gentleman named Turner is said to have had every good quality to make marriage a success, save 'a cheerful and composed temper,' and—still more important lack—the initial courage to marry. Twice was the wedding-day fixed and postponed, when Hannah, on the advice of her friends, determined not to be trifled with any longer. Turner was repentant, but Hannah was inexorable. Finally, however, he insisted on settling on her an annuity of £200, to compensate her for her great expense in preparing to be the wife of a man of large fortune. This income permitted her to devote her time to literary pursuits, though, when she first visited London in 1774, she had not published anything except a small play for schools, *The Search after Happiness*. She was introduced to London society by one of those fortunate events that suggest the guiding hand of destiny. She, with two of her sisters, had not been in London a week when she wrote to a friend describing her emotions at seeing Garrick as king Lear. Her friend, who knew Garrick, showed him the letter, and, as the actor was curious to see the young enthusiast, an introduction was arranged. The day after this she was invited to the Garricks' house to meet Mrs Montagu, and, as her biographer succinctly puts it, 'her introduction to the great, and the greatly endowed, was sudden and general.' Her portrait, painted some years later by Opie, suggests a strong and pleasant personality, and one finds that, wherever she was taken by the Garricks, she gravitated towards people of high rank in intellect by a species of mental elective affinity. She had long desired to see Johnson, but Sir Joshua Reynolds, at whose house she met him, prepared her, as he 'handed her up the stairs,' for a mood of possible sadness and silence in the great man. She was, however, fortunate enough to find him advancing to meet her 'with good humour in his countenance, and a macaw of Sir Joshua's in his hand,' while he gallantly greeted her with a verse from a morning hymn of her own composition. Other introductions speedily followed: to Edmund Burke, to bishop Percy, the collector of the *Reliques*, who was 'quite a sprightly modern, instead of a rusty antique,' and to other distinguished members of the bluestocking coteries.

In the following year, 1775, Hannah again visited London in February. This time, she dined at Mrs Montagu's, where she met

Elizabeth Carter and Mrs Boscawen, the widow of the admiral. The bluestocking parties were now at their zenith, and the clearcut thumbnail sketches Hannah gives of the chief *dramatis personae* are always vivid and lifelike. Of Mrs Montagu, she says,

> She is not only the finest genius, but the finest lady I ever saw ... she lives in the highest style of magnificence ... her form is delicate even to fragility ... she has the sprightly vivacity of fifteen, with the judgment and experience of a Nestor.

The young provincial, though not 'violently modish,' kept at least one eye on the fashion, and permitted her hair to be dressed in the extravagant mode that, as moralist, she was compelled to censure, even while she adopted it. She quickly noted Elizabeth Carter's indifference to dress, which, with tactful euphuism, she thus describes. 'Mrs Carter has in her person a great deal of what the gentlemen mean when they say such a one is a "poetical lady"... however, I like her much.' She was, perhaps, most attracted by Mrs Boscawen, who, she said, was polite, learned, judicious and humble. This first impression was strengthened as she knew her more intimately, and there was not one of the bluestocking ladies of whom Hannah wrote with more admiration, though, perhaps because but few of her letters—that were thought not inferior to those of Mrs Montagu—have been published, she is less well-known to the general reader.

In 1775, after her return to Bristol, Hannah More told her sisters that she had been 'so fed with praise and flattering attentions' that she would find out her real value by writing a poem, and offering it to Cadell. In a fortnight, she had finished *Sir Eldred of the Bower*, to which she added the poem entitled *The Bleeding Rock*, written some years before Cadell had probably heard something of her, as he not only offered for it a sum beyond her expectation, but 'very handsomely' said that, if she could discover what Goldsmith had received for his *Deserted Village*, he would allow her the same price. A unique fashion surely of receiving a young writer, even in the eighteenth century! The two poems, which scarcely filled thirty small pages, were welcomed with acclaim by the bluestockings. Garrick recited them, Johnson added a stanza, Richard Burke called the book 'a truly elegant and tender performance,' and the writer's head, said her sisters, needed to be unusually steady to withstand the flood of adulation —and it was!

In the following year, the Garricks hospitably offered Hannah a suite of rooms in their house, and, from that time onwards, for more than twenty years, whenever she came to London, she invariably stayed with them at the Adelphi, or at their Thames-side retreat at Hampton. Under Garrick's influence, her next literary venture was the play *Percy*, which launched her in London society as a celebrity. The bluestockings congratulated her and themselves on its extraordinary success, and if they did not 'crown her, cover her, hide her with laurels,' as Richard Berenger, one of them suggested, Mrs Boscawen, on its twelfth performance, sent her a laurel wreath with the 'stems confined within an elegant ring,' for which she returned thanks in 'an elegant copy of verses.'

She had almost finished *The Fatal Falsehood*, when, in 1779, David Garrick died, and, greatly affected by his death, she determined to write no more plays. From this time, her thoughts followed their natural trend towards serious subjects, and, in her letters, she gradually reveals herself as philanthropist and reformer. She even attempted, said Cowper, 'to reform the unreformable Great,' and her *Thoughts on the importance of the Manners of the Great* went into many large editions[1]. Her grief at Garrick's death found some vent in *Sensibility*, a poem addressed to Mrs Boscawen, in which several bluestockings are mentioned. The poem, however, that made the greatest stir in the bluestocking coteries, was *Bas Bleu, or Conversation*. It is illustrative of the fact that Hannah More, with her strong sense of dramatic values, had the faculty of mentally visualising the significance of the various movements with which she was connected. This poem, as she explained in the preface, owed its name to the mistake of a foreigner of distinction, who gave the literal name *Bas-bleu* to a small party of friends that had often been called by way of pleasantry *Blue Stockings*. She says further that these little societies—sometimes misrepresented—were composed of persons distinguished in general for their rank, talent, or respectable character, who met frequently at Mrs Vesey's and at a few other houses for the sole purpose of conversation. She adds a brief tribute to the charm of these gatherings, where, she says, learning was not disfigured by pedantry, good taste was not marred by affectation and conversation was as little disgraced by calumny, levity and other censurable errors as has, perhaps, been known in any society. The poem is not of permanent value, though Johnson told her that 'there was no name in poetry that might

[1] The tracts with which she tried to reform the poor, *Village Politics* and the *Repository Tracts*, had an amazing success, and were found so well-suited to the purpose that the Religious Tract society was formed to continue the work.

not be glad to own it.' Naturally, this *poème à clef* had a great vogue among the bluestockings, as most of them were mentioned either by their own names, or under some classical appellation. It was written to amuse Mrs Vesey, and, after circulating some years in manuscript, was eventually printed in 1786.

Perhaps the most curious friendship in the *bas-bleu* coteries, was that between Hannah More and Horace Walpole. She was not long in discovering that 'Horace liked nonsense talk better than Greeks or Romans,' but, apparently, she could do her own share of such conversation. When she spent evenings among the bluestockings, she frequently mentions that she and Horace Walpole, with another friend or two, 'make up a pleasant little coterie of their own.' Friendly correspondence passed between them, when they were away from London ; and, when Hannah More went to live at her cottage, Cowslip green—cousin in name, declared Walpole, to Strawberry hill—he collected all his own works, printed at the Strawberry hill press, to give her 'for remembrance. As a mark of great distinction, he printed her *Bishop Bonner's Ghost* at the famous press, for distribution among their common friends—in other words, the bluestockings. He gave her a beautifully bound Bible, which she wished he would read; but, in spite of the amazing differences of character between the cynic and the reformer, they remained good friends till his death. He was on intimate terms with Mrs Carter, too, and both the famous bluestocking ladies were amazed when his *Letters* were published. The Horace Walpole there revealed was an entirely different person from the bluestocking they had known. When he talked with them, there were not any traces of 'that truly French, light and frivolous way of thinking which is so evident in his printed letters.' Indeed, it was something of a shock to them to find that he had actually selected his letters for publication.

Hannah More was the chief chronicler as well as the poet laureate of the blues. It is from the hasty impressionist sketches in her letters that we gather the significance of the movement. Of a bluestocking evening at William Pepys's, she says

> There was all the pride of London, every wit and every wit-ess...but the spirit of the evening was kept up on the strength of a little lemonade till past eleven, without cards, scandal or politics.

A terse description that might serve as a type of most of the bluestocking meetings. This cult of 'conversation—the pursuit of ideas,' as it has been defined—acted as a subtle leaven to the hard brilliant materialism of the eighteenth century. The social refinement introduced by the bluestocking interest in literature can be better appreciated by a glimpse at the glaring foil made by ordinary society.

'On Monday,' writes Hannah More, 'I was at a very great assembly at the Bishop of St Asaph's. Conceive to yourself one hundred and fifty or two hundred people met together... painted as red as bacchanals; poisoning the air with perfumes; treading on each other's gowns; not one in ten able to get a chair... ten or a dozen card tables crammed with dowagers of quality, grave ecclesiastics and yellow admirals.'

It was another advantage of the *bas-bleu* societies, that 'common or genteel swearing' was not countenanced: and, as tea, coffee, orgeat and lemonade were the only beverages offered, intoxication —then a general vice of society—seldom brought its embarrassments into their midst.

From the somewhat elusive references to the bluestocking parties, we gather that—unlike the Parisian salons—there was not a fixed day or date for any of the meetings. A dinner might be given by Mrs Montagu, after which there would be 'a strong reinforcement of the Blues'; or, Mrs Vesey would hold an assembly of rank, fashion and *literati*: 'so blue it was Mazarin blue,' as Horace Walpole once described 'a Vesey.' Or, Mrs Boscawen might 'receive,' though parties at her house were usually more exclusive, and thirty or forty was there considered quite a large meeting. These were the principal bluestocking hostesses, to whom came 'the elite of London both for talent and fashion.' Since the first conversation had been given by Mrs Vesey, these societies had multiplied, and, from the seventies to the end of the century, bluestocking meetings were held in many other London houses. Sir Joshua Reynolds, 'the idol of every company,' and his sister had most interesting evenings at their house in Leicester fields and, later, at Richmond. Here, even Johnson was 'as brilliant as himself, and as good-humoured as anyone else,' and there was 'scarce an expletive man or woman' among the company. Mrs Thrale, of the 'little silver tongue,' welcomed rank and talent to her home at Streatham, and much good talk was heard in the famous library. Miss Mary Monckton, afterwards the witty countess of Cork and Orrery, had, said Boswell, the finest *bit of blue* at her parties. Dressed in fine thin muslin in the coldest weather, she would nonchalantly receive her distinguished guests with 'a nod and a smile and a short "How do do"'; and then, without moving from her seat in the middle of the room, would continue her conversation, lounging on one chair while she leaned on the back of another. At this house, the guest of honour was Johnson, of whom dean Marlay once remarked, 'the ladies might well be proud when they could turn a wolf-dog into a lap-dog!'

Mrs Chapone, born Hester Mulso, occasionally gave blue-stocking receptions that were 'rational, instructive and social,' and, also, unfortunately, somewhat spiritless and dull. Though Johnson thought sufficiently well of her literary talent to include her among the few contributors to his *Rambler*, the promise of her youth never ripened to any noteworthy performance, if we except *Letters on the Improvement of the Mind*, which, in its day, was considered an educational work of the first importance. The author was, by temperament, argumentative, impulsive, emotional; and, perhaps because of her experience, such qualities are condemned in her *Letters*. These are only interesting now as embodying an acclaimed ideal of eighteenth century feminine manners. Mrs Chapone was frequently a guest at North End, where she would earnestly discuss with Richardson his female characters. Mrs Delany, that 'fairest model of female excellence,' asserted that Mrs Chapone was the prototype of some of his principal heroines, which, she said, 'is the reason they are not really so polished as he takes them to be.'

Perhaps the most charming description of a bluestocking evening is from the vivid and sprightly pen of Fanny Burney[1]. She was a blue, but not of what Hannah More called the old set. She had not long visited among them—where *Evelina* and her own amiable personality secured her a warm welcome—before her appointment to a post at court. She snatched an evening from her wearisome duties, however, to visit Mrs Ord, a later but hardly less distinguished hostess than the original three, and there found practically all the members of the circle: Mrs Montagu, Mrs Boscawen, Owen Cambridge, Horace Walpole, Sir Lucas Pepys, Leonard Smelt, Bennet Langton and Lady Rothes, his wife, Mrs Carter, Mrs Chapone, William Pepys and others. The talk was of *The Streatham Letters*, the correspondence between Mrs Thrale and Dr Johnson which had just been published, and many of the blues feared the indiscretions of her too fluent pen. It is a lively and graceful picture of eighteenth century society, and an excellent representation of the friendly charm of the *bas-bleu* meetings.

---

[1] See Hill, Constance, *Fanny Burney at the Court of Queen Charlotte* (1912), chap. XIII.

CHAPTER XVI

CHILDREN'S BOOKS

CHILDREN'S books, throughout the history of English literature, have been in that literature, but not of it. Phrases and persons from nursery lore have passed irrevocably into the national arsenal of metaphor and allusion, while the sources of them may not have had any claim to serious literary consideration. Children, too, have annexed the books of their elders—*Robinson Crusoe* is the standard example—and have almost established a prescriptive right to the conquered territory. But not many books written specially for children have also been enduring literature, in any real sense, though the exceptions are notable. The nursery library, in fact, has been a separate thing; developed differently, furnished from a different standpoint, with works written in a different vein of inspiration and produced, commercially, with different limitations and standards. Nor is the criterion of judgment upon it, whether the reader or the historian be the judge, the same as upon more solemn or artistic performances.

Its history really opens in the eighteenth century. Yet, in the beginnings, the 'grown-up' and the child coincide, in a way. The writers who, in the first volume of this work[1], treated of the riddles of Cynewulf, Aelfric and Aldhelm, and of the scholastic labours of Alcuin at York, were chronicling the very earliest books for children in the language. Those who, in the same volume[2], discussed the metrical romances of 1200—1500 set forth at large the adult works whose *disjecta membra* were still the framework of the cheapest books for children in the eighteenth century; while Aesop, and bestiaries, and such a collection as *Gesta Romanorum* were certainly, to some extent, read by children as well as by the older flock at whom the monkish editors aimed.

---

[1] Chaps. IV and V.　　　　　[2] Chaps. XIII and XIV.

But these early productions are hardly what would be meant today by the term 'children's books,' which, perhaps, is best and most conveniently interpreted as 'books read or meant to be read by children for pleasure or for profit, or for both, in their leisure hours.' Children read medieval riddles and schoolbooks, certainly; but they read them perforce, as part of their education. So far as the social life of these early periods is clear, it is probable that children read little out of school, for the simple reason that, outside learned establishments, there was nothing to read. The fables and anecdotes of which they acquired a knowledge must usually, from the same cause, have been communicated to them either orally or by the chances of tuition. Apart from purposes of education, children had no books of their own before the seventeenth century, and very few then.

Educational books deserve brief mention. They are only literature by accident, but they are, sometimes, not wholly scholastic. Aelfric's *Colloquy* and the numerous successors to it have this feature of artistic composition in them, that they are not merely tabular; the dialogue form could be given a certain fictitious vivacity. It long survived the renascence[1]. Erasmus endued it with fresh popularity and authority, and it persisted until the eighteenth century. *Sententiae Pueriles*, a work of this kind which, in form, goes back to Aelfric, appears in various editions over a long period, the last being 1728. *Pueriles Confabulationculae* —there were two works of the same name, one by Cordier, the other by Evaldus Gallus—appears in 1693—with a preface dated 1548.

Such works as these—the powder of learning with the jam of amusement thinly spread—stand midway between the only two other kinds of written or printed books for children in the Norman, Plantagenet and Tudor centuries. The pure lessonbook—powder and no jam—was, of course, a necessity. It is not of great interest or value here to pursue its history in detail, and its position has already been discussed[2]. Alphabets were printed in numbers

---

[1] Of one curious instance of longevity no preliminary stages seem to exist. In 1745—6, John Newbery published *The Circle of the Sciences*, a dialogue manual in seven volumes. It went into several editions, and other publishers reissued it between 1780 and 1800. The seven volumes comprise seven subjects almost identical with those of the *trivium* and *quadrivium* of scholasticism. Newbery said that he himself compiled it at great pains; but the choice of subjects implies some pedigree for his selection. No ancestors for the little books, however, have been discovered. The facts are an example of the way in which children's books at once preserve and mutilate very ancient material.

[2] See vol. III, chap. XIX; vol. VII, chaps. XIII and XIV; vol. IX, chap. XV; and the corresponding bibliographies.

from the sixteenth century onwards; the stationers' records give many entries. In the same century, the hornbook appeared—an alphabet, a short syllabary, and, usually, the Lord's prayer, printed on a little sheet of paper, nailed on a piece of board of the shape of a spade's head and covered with transparent horn. It conferred two words on the language—'criss-cross-row' and 'ampersand.' This invention was succeeded, late in the eighteenth century, by the battledore, a folded card containing, as well as the literary elements, a few woodblock illustrations; battledores were still being manufactured in 1840, so sluggish and yet so long is the stream of elementary instruction. Alphabetical rimes began to appear under Elizabeth, though familiar verses or jingles like 'A was an Apple-pie' did not get into print (they may have been in oral existence) till at least a century later.

Another early species (of the fifteenth and sixteenth centuries) was neither a schoolbook nor a book of mere recreation: the succession of 'books of courtesy,' which became current soon after the invention of printing. For historical purposes, they have been admirably grouped (and as admirably edited) in two publications of the Early English Text Society, *The Babees' Boke*[1], and *Queene Elizabethe's Achademy*. They provide the antithesis to monkish or literary education. The pamphlets in them were written to fit the young gentleman for this world, not for the next; and for the active life of this world rather than for the contemplative. They describe manners, not culture: their ideal is anticipated in Chaucer's squire. They were not for the poor of Langland:

> Now may each cobbler send his son to school,
> And every beggar's brat learn from his book,
> Turn to a writer and get into a lord's house.

To that end, you must enter a monastic or cathedral school: there, you could get learning. Here, in these treatises, you got, instead, virtue and knowledge of the world. Incidentally, it may be noted, readers were warned against adult works: 'Keep them from reading of feigned fables, vain fantasies, and wanton stories, and songs of love, which bring much mischief to youth[2].' The alternative was 'good Godly books.' But there was not any special provision of such works.

These educational and semi-educational books have been mentioned because, in early periods, they possessed the importance

[1] See vol. III, p. 341.
[2] Rhodes's *Boke of Nurture* (1577); printed before 1554.

conferred by isolation. The effect of that isolation is seen when, in more authentic beginnings of children's literature, 'good Godly books' first emerge. The new feature is a natural by-product of the national life. The end of religious persecution in its more virulent forms, the Elizabethan diffusion of knowledge and enthusiasm, the Jacobean growth of style, the puritan fierce flame of morality, the vast increase in the activity of the press—all helped to make the child-mind, not, perhaps, a centre of intensive cultivation, but, at least, not a fallow field. But, since all previous efforts (except the decayed and, so to speak, illegally acquired romances, which will be dealt with when chapbooks are considered) had been, more or less, more rather than less, didactic, the new product was, also, didactic. Its novelty lay in the fact that it was not a text-book. It was purely moral, not forensic nor technical. It was a grim affair, with few literary merits. Hell-fire was its chief theme; anything might turn out to be a faggot for the conflagration of wicked little souls. More than a century later, Mrs Sherwood was influenced by the same obsession. The kingdom of heaven might be of children; but children were always dreadfully in jeopardy of another fate.

The best vision of these grisly performances is to be seen in one of them. Thomas White, minister of the gospel, in *A Little Book for Little Children* (1702)—a volume of brief moral addresses—recommends his audience to read

no Ballads or foolish Books, but the Bible, and the *Plain-mans path way to Heaven,* a very plain holy book for you; get the *Practice of Piety*; Mr Baxter's *Call to the Unconverted*; Allen's *Allarum to the Unconverted*; read the Histories of the Martyrs that dyed for Christ; and in the *Book of Martyrs....* Read also often Treatises of Death, and Hell, and Judgement, and of the Love and Passion of Christ.

Some perfectly horrible stories of martyrdom ensue. Foxe's *Book of Martyrs*, as it is colloquially called, was and long continued to be, perhaps still is in some strata of society, a great incentive to piety and gateway to religious adventure; and it must be admitted that many children like such horrors, and do not suffer any harm from them. Still, White's love of tortured saints (young ones, for choice) and his readiness to describe their torments in detail pass the limits of innocuous ferocity.

The religious works catalogued by White as suited to the young were adult or semi-adult in purpose. More definitely juvenile was the anonymous *Young Man's Calling...a Serious and Compassionate Address to all Young Persons to remember*

their Creator in the days of their Youth (1685). The author of a
great part of it was, probably, Samuel Crossman, whose initials
are at the end of the preface. 'Richard Burton' (*i.e.* Nathaniel
Crouch) wrote the residue. An eighth edition appeared in 1725,
so the book was clearly in demand. Crossman outdoes White in
his examples of martyrdom; his homilies, also, are longer, but not
at all more valuable or enduring. Like White, he was vigorously
protestant. Some *Divine Poems*—passably good hymns—were
included in the final pages. Among the advertisements at the
end is one of *Winter Evening Entertainments*[1]. This, perhaps—
one work alone excepted—is the nearest approach, before the
eighteenth century, to a child's book in the modern sense.

> Here's Milk for Children, Wisdom for Young Men,
> To teach them that they turn not Babes again,

says a prefatory poem. The 'wisdom' was, presumably, the ten
coarse stories of the jest-book type ('ten pleasant and delightful
relations') which form the first part; the 'milk,' no doubt, the fifty
riddles of the second part, each of which is adorned with an
explanation, an observation and a moral, to say nothing of dupli-
cated woodcuts. A somewhat similar work was *The Father's
Blessing Penn'd for the Instruction of his Children* (by W. J.,
M.A.), the date of which may be roughly conjectured from one of
the 'riddles in rhyme' which (in addition to thirteen 'lessons')
it contains:

> Q. What rare Outlandish Fruit was that of late
> Which Heaven sent us to restore our State?

> A. Our Statesmen had the *Scurvy* deeply, sure
> The Princely *Orange* was a sovereign cure.

It is accompanied by a woodcut of an orange. This cut and
its fellows did duty elsewhere, in another *Little Book for Little
Children*, also by Thomas White (not dated; the frontispiece,
however, is a portrait of queen Anne). Here, too, is a mixture of
education and amusement—a cut of a hornbook, some spelling
lessons, alphabetical rimes and riddles. The volume is notable
for the first appearance in print of *A was an Archer*, and the
lines displaying the errors of misplaced punctuation, beginning
'I saw a Peacock with a fiery Tail.' Practically contemporary

---

[1] No copy earlier than 1737 ('Sixth Edition') is available to the writer. But the
description in the advertisement of 1685 exactly coincides with the contents of the
1737 edition, in which the author is given as Richard Burton—Nathaniel Crouch.
Crouch died, probably, before 1725. *Winter Evenings*, and variants upon it, is a
perpetually recurrent title among children's books.

with this was *The Child's Week's-Work*, by William Ronksley
(1712). It is the best of all these early attempts to purvey
'pleasure with profit duly mixt,' though there is more profit than
pleasure in it. Its simplicity of method and absence of dogmatic
frenzy are remarkable. In four successive series of lessons, each
calculated to occupy a week, it runs up to words of four syllables.
A monosyllabic verse may be quoted:

> Hear you a Lark?
> Tell me what Clerk
>   Can match her. He that beats
> The next Thorn-bush
> May raise a Thrush
>   Would put down all our lays.

Finally, perhaps the most popular—or, at any rate, most widely
read—of all these oppressive compilations was James Janeway's
*Token for Children: being an Exact Account of the Conversion,
Holy and Exemplary Lives, and Joyful Deaths of several young
Children* (? 1720): a supreme example of morbid and gloating
piety. The title conveys its scope. It was not alone; three or
four works like it can be discovered; but it was the most highly
coloured.

A more polished type—indeed, pietists might have said a politely
immoral type—is the Chesterfield of the seventeenth century, *A
Lady's Gift* (1688, published without authorisation, often reprinted). Halifax—the trimmer—could write admirable English,
and, if his *Advice to a Daughter* (the sub-title) is worldly, it
is, also, honest and sensible. It had other counterparts in the
next century besides Chesterfield's *Letters*. *Advice to a Young
Nobleman, Letters from a Tutor to his Pupils* and similar works
carried out the gentlemanly ideal of making the best of this world
without either despising or making too much of the next.

Works of these types were, if not common, at any rate not
unique. They are not, perhaps, in the direct succession of pure
children's literature: they are but the unennobled ancestors.
But they deserve not to be forgotten by the historian. The more
authentic pedigree follows a line of less unmixed descent—lines,
rather, for the family has, at first, three branches. The older
branches are among the oldest forms of literature preserved to us:
the cadet branch is fathered by two eminent men.

To take the youngest first. The parent work in it has, naturally,
been overshadowed by greater works in the chapter on its author
in a previous volume[1]. All through the eighteenth century, a

---

[1] Vol. VII, chap. VII.

work called *Divine Emblems; or Temporal Things Spiritualized*, by John Bunyan, was recurrent in little rough editions. It was not until 1889 that this was identified as a curtailed version of a longer book—*A Book for Boys & Girls: or, Country Rhimes for Children. By J.B.* The first edition contained seventy-four 'meditations'; in 1701, an editor revised it ruthlessly, and cut the number of emblems down to forty-nine. It consists of short poems —exceedingly bad poetry, but plain rugged morality—on such subjects as the frog, the hen, and other common objects, each with a rimed moral. Bunyan declares his object:

> I do't to show them how each fingle-fangle,
> On which they doting are, their souls entangle,
> As with a web, a trap, a gin, or snare,
> And will destroy them, have they not a care.

His 'morals are as recondite and laborious as those of *Gesta Romanorum*. The importance of the book lies in its authorship, its intention and its method. It reveals not a little of the inspired tinker's mind. It shows a real desire to provide something special for children, not merely the old clothes of adult literature cut down. And it is a deliberate use of a responsible artistic form and of material not traditional but original.

By Bunyan stands a lesser man but a more skilled artificer— Isaac Watts. His *Divine Songs* have already been treated[1]. They are quoted every day, and usually misquoted. Some of them—three or four, at most, it may be; but that is an honourable percentage—will resound through nurseries for generations yet to come: the rest are dead, slain by time. For their epoch, they were not far from perfection, as publishers saw. They were reprinted endlessly for far more than a century. Mrs Trimmer, in 1789, gave them renewed vogue by a *Comment* setting forth their virtues and elaborating their doctrinal teaching. Another writer adapted their theology to unitarian beliefs. They were at once carried off into the literary Alsatia of the chapbook. A kind of imitation appeared in 1751, *Puerilia*, by John Marchant, 'Songs for Little Misses, Songs for Little Masters, Songs on Divine, Moral and other Subjects.' They had a certain spirit, but did not strike the imagination of the day: only two editions were issued.

It was the chapbook, that last poor refuge of Middle Age enchantments, which provided children with what they wanted in the reign of queen Anne and the first three Georges. They had to learn the alphabet, they had to read the guides to goodness, the

[1] Vol. IX, p. 178.

Ollendorfs of petty culture, the anecdotal or poetic allurements to superior virtue, which, as a matter of fact, young persons are often quite ready enough to acquire without force. But they were not less ready to enjoy other fare. A famous passage in *The Tatler* (No. 95), in which Mr Bickerstaff describes his little godson as absorbed in the stories of Bevis and Don Belianis and other great and famous heroes, sums up the charm of forbidden romance with the nicest perfection. The chapbook was what the poor and the young could read familiarly. In these little penny, two-penny and sixpenny productions—octavo in form, with sixteen pages, at first, but, after 1726, usually duodecimo, with twenty-four pages—the last fragments of the old romances were enshrined. They existed before 1700—certainly early in the eighteenth century, at least; but few early copies have survived, and it was not until the Georgian era that they were profusely manufactured.

Who wrote these versions is not known. They may have been abbreviations of the manuscript texts of the thirteenth or four-teenth centuries; but the discrepancies are so marked that, more probably, they were oral versions committed to print independently in some obscure way. They were issued all over the king-dom, the centres with the greatest output being, apparently, London (Aldermary churchyard in particular), Dublin, York, Glasgow, Newcastle, Stirling and Banbury. The books were not, in the first instance, meant for children, though, in the latter half of the eighteenth century, whole series expressly juvenile appeared (the Banbury set was the best known and, perhaps, best produced); but children possessed themselves of them. Wood-blocks were used almost haphazard: Guy slaying a boar in one booklet was George slaying a dragon in another. The indigenous heroes of Britain—Tom Thumb, certain Jacks, Hickathrift, Friar Bacon—were here preserved in a vernacular epic cycle, with such additions as fashion, fact, or sheer literary piracy from time to time provided. In some volumes, indecency was the sole point; others were merely coarse in a natural way; in all, the English was vile. After 1800, they fell into a decline: better production ousted them from favour; 'the blocks and types were getting worn out....Catnach buried them in a dishonoured grave[1].'

The chief addition to the common stock of chapbook material made in the eighteenth century were the adventures of Robinson Crusoe and Gulliver, Watts's poems, the adventures of Philip Quarll (a pseudo-Crusoe), anecdotes decked out with names invented

[1] Ashton, J., *Chapbooks of the Eighteenth Century* (1882).

by John Newbery for his own much better productions, collections of nursery rimes (after about 1760) and various versions of Perrault's fairy tales ; towards the end of the century, eastern and Arabian tales were added.

It was the chapbook, also, which preserved to us our scant native fairy lore. Andrew Lang once said that England had but one authentic fairy-hero—Jack the slayer of Blunderbore and other giants. But, wherever the stories originated in the long history of man's mind, many were current, and England once was 'al fulfild of fayerye.' Popular taste ascribed the decay of Titania's kingdom to monks : where monks were, 'farewell, rewards and fairies.' But the stories remained ; and a curious allusion in bishop Corbet's rough but charming seventeenth century poem shows that they were respected and treasured :

> To William Churne of Staffordshire,
> Give laud and praises due,
> Who every meal can mend your cheer
> With tales both old and true:
> To William all give audience,
> And pray ye for his noddle:
> For all the fairies' evidence
> Were lost if it were addle.

William Churne, whoever he was, perished, and his tales with him ; and the sad friends of fairy truth must go up and down with careful search for such relics as they may find in the byways of folklore. It was from France that the revival of magic came. Fairy tales reached the French court about 1676, and set a fashion of simplicity, sometimes real, more often affected. In 1696, Charles Perrault began to publish (in Moetjen's *Recueil de pièces curieuses et nouvelles*) the famous stories alleged to be written by his little boy ; they came out in a separate volume in 1697, as *Histoires ou Contes du Tems Passé, avec de Moralités* ; the frontispiece contained the immortal legend, *Contes de ma mère l'Oie.*

This is not the place to go into the anthropology of fairy tales in general, or of these fairy tales in particular. It is quite probable that Perrault's son did actually tell the tales himself to his father, much as he heard them from his nurse. Their delightful simplicity made them instantly popular. An English translation appeared, apparently, in 1729[1], by Robert Samber. The stories

---

[1] Advertised in *The Monthly Chronicle*, March 1729 (Andrew Lang, on the authority of Austin Dobson, in *Perrault's Popular Tales, with Introduction, etc.*, 1888). The earliest surviving copy is the sixth edition, 1764, giving both French and English. Mrs Trimmer, born in 1741, was familiar with the tales in her childhood.

passed speedily into chapbooks, as did those of Madame d'Aulnoy
about the same time. It should be added that they were provided
with 'morals': *Red Riding Hood* proved that

> Wolves for sure there are
> Of every sort, and every character;

while *Bluebeard* exemplified 'curiosity, thou mortal bane.'

So, the fairy tale attained print, and tradition became literature. About the same period, the other strain of traditional lore,
also, was glorified into printed matter. Nursery rimes have all
manner of origins, and may be detected in allusions long before
they appear whole and unadorned. But, there was, apparently, no
Corpus Poetarum Infantilium till, in 1744, Cooper published
Tommy Thumb's Pretty Song Book, in two volumes. Here, for
the first time, some unknown hand established a classic. Here
was the nucleus upon which, in all probability, all later collections—and there was not much to be added to it—were founded.
The rimes, in themselves, do not call for comment. Except for a
few which would offend modern taste, they are the same—verbally,
for all practical purposes—as nurses use today.

No earlier collection, if one was made, survives; and it is
sixteen years before another is recorded—*The Top Book of All*[1];
the date, 1760, is determined by a little woodblock at the end.
This is not entirely a nursery rime book; it contains nine familiar
rimes, Watts's *Sluggard,* some riddles and three wellknown short
tales. To the same date—but not with any certainty—is ascribed
the famous *Gammer Gurton's Garland,* published at Stockport:
it is described on the title-page as 'a new edition, with additions.'
In or about the same year—here, too, there is not any certainty,
for not one copy of the first edition is known—was born the chief
rival of the alleged Gurton as a rimer, mother Goose[2]. Newbery's
surviving copyrights in 1780 included *Mother Goose's Melody.*
There is reason to believe the book had been in existence for
some time before, though there is no evidence whatever for a
statement sometimes made that the publisher Fleet first issued it
in 1719.

Such is the archaeology of children's books, before the first
great *diaskeuast* arrived. There were lessonbooks of several
kinds, there were moral treatises in prose and verse, there was a

---

[1] The instructive full title is given in the bibliography of this chapter.
[2] The name is, of course, a translation of *Mère de l'Oie,* who presided over Perrault's
fairy tales. But it is much older. Gammer Gurton and Tom Thumb have a similar
oral antiquity.

mass of oral tradition just creeping into type, there were decayed
adult works. But, all was without form and void. The appearance
of the books that were produced was mean. The trade in them
was spasmodic and unorganised. No one took them seriously or
thought of them as a necessary branch of the commerce in printed
matter. It was a typical eighteenth century business man, John
Newbery, farmer's son, accountant, merchant's assistant, patent-
medicine dealer, printer and publisher, who saw the possibilities
and the openings. He began to publish books at Reading in
1740, but removed to London in 1744 (first to Devereux court
and then to the address long associated with children's books,
St Paul's churchyard). The first year in the metropolis saw his
first child's book—*The Little Pretty Pocket Book.* It was a neat,
well-printed volume, with very fair woodcuts. It contains a
dedication 'to the Parents, Guardians and Nurses in Great Britain
and Ireland,' and incitements to games, with moral applications
dragged in. It was designed to 'make *Tommy* a good Boy and
Polly a good Girl.' No doubt it did so; and the process must
have been far from disagreeable. It was followed the next year
by three volumes of *The Circle of the Sciences. The Lilliputian
Magazine* (1751–2), *The Governess or Little Female Academy*
(by Sarah Fielding, the novelist's sister), *The Twelfth Day Gift,
Mother Goose's Melody,* her *Tales* and, most celebrated of all,
Goody Two Shoes[1], were among his early publications.

The characteristics of Newbery's books were very marked.
They were strongly and yet attractively produced, with good print
and paper. They contained a great variety of matter, and were
thoroughly alive in every way. There is a real personality behind
them, even though they are now as utterly obsolete as their contemporary, the dodo (which is illustrated in a Newbery natural
history of 1775). The English is plain and respectable; the
coarseness of earlier, and even some coeval and later, productions
is almost entirely absent. There is a strong vein of honest
vigour running through them—*The Twelfth Day Gift* has a
frontispiece labelled 'Trade and Plumb Cake for ever, Huzza!'—
and the commercial success of the industrious apprentice is frequently insisted upon. The author—it is not unlikely that

[1] There is much evidence, amounting almost to certainty, that Goldsmith wrote
Goody Two Shoes, or, at least, had a hand in it. See Welsh's, C., introduction to his
facsimile reprint of the earliest extant edition (1881). It is also said that Goldsmith
edited *Mother Goose's Melody.* The evidence is hardly strong enough to make this
more than a pleasant and credible hypothesis.

Newbery himself is the single individual behind such feigned
benignities as Mrs Lovechild, Tommy Trip and Giles Gingerbread—
is really trying to please children as well as to improve them.
'He called himself their friend, but he was the friend of all mankind': Goldsmith spoke from experience.

John Newbery died in 1767, having definitely created a new
branch of literature. His business split into two—one under
Francis Newbery (a nephew) and the other under a second Francis
Newbery (a son) and Thomas Carnan (a stepson). The firms were
not amicable rivals, and Carnan and Francis the younger also
quarrelled and separated, apparently in 1782. Ultimately, 'all the
old publications of Newbery passed into the hands of Elizabeth [the
nephew Francis's widow] and to Harris and his successors[1].' The
final legatees of this ancient firm, Messrs Griffith and Farran, survived into the twentieth century, still publishing children's books.

The trade side of these works is an important one, and it may
be convenient to deal with it at this point. The publisher—in the
eighteenth century still more than half retailer as well as producer—had, for obvious reasons, greater power over juvenile books
than over serious adult works. Indeed, he was often the author
himself; the later Newbery's most formidable rivals, Darton and
Harvey, were even artists and engravers (very bad ones) as well.
The publisher determined that momentous detail, the format of
the volume ; and it might, with some reason, be contended that his
taste in this direction, from 1750 to 1760 and from 1800 to 1810,
has not been equalled since. Certainly, the gilt and brightly
coloured covers made of Dutch paper—copies so bound are now
rare, and the paper is no longer made—the entire decency and
fitness, as of an Adam house, in margin, type and spacing, the
enduring ink and clean impressions of the best specimens, show a
standard of production at least as well suited to a domestic
interior of Georgian England as more ambitious binding and
typography to more lavish periods. The publisher, too, decided
on the quantity and quality of the illustrations : Bewick, Stothard
and some of the producers of colour-work early in the nineteenth
century reached a very high level of quality, and the quantity was
seldom stinted. He decided, also, as is the custom today, the size
of an edition ; and the numbers, where they can be discovered,
are surprisingly large. One firm, at least, usually printed 2000 for
a first edition, and such works as Roscoe's *Butterfly's Ball* had
an immediate circulation literally as great as that of a really

[1] Welsh, C., *A Bookseller of the Last Century* (1885).

successful novel of today. Moreover, the sales were steady and longlived. Berquin's *Ami des Enfans* ran to 20,000 copies in ten years. A dozen of Priscilla Wakefield's books went into not less than sixty editions (apart from piracies) in twenty years. Mrs Trimmer's *Robins* sold to the extent of two editions every three years for a whole generation at least. The prices were low, as expressed in our values; from sixpence to three shillings and sixpence, with one and sixpence as a very general average, for volumes with copperplates; woodblock editions (which tended to disappear after about 1790, except in chapbooks) were even cheaper, and coloured plates did not cause any great increase, mainly, no doubt, because the colouring was done by hand, by regiments of children, who dabbed on each one colour in one place[1]. The colours have a gay grace not always achieved by more perfect mechanical means. Authors were not highly paid; but their relations with publishers seem to have been intimate and pleasant, on the whole : the publisher was a tradesman, but a man of some dignity as well. After Newbery, many firms specialised in children's books. The value of 'juvenile' copyrights was often considerable ; some works were even worthy of being turned into 'trade' books—issued, that is, by syndicates of publishers. The story of copyright sales is very suggestive[2]. Piracy abounded.

These business details largely explain the activity that ensued upon Newbery's death. He and the next generation of his family made it perfectly clear that there was a chance of supplying children's books in an adequate format. Commerce was alive to opportunities, and the creation of a good supply was inevitable and immediate. And, as for the demand, the epoch which produced the bluestocking was not likely to omit from its programme of orderly omniscience the very foundations of taste and learning. The age of the revolution was an age of education, which was viewed, on the one hand, as a prophylactic against, and, on the other, as the most active stimulant of, a new era. But, in some circles, it was still thought unworthy to write for children. Nearly every author from 1780 onwards apologises for his or her work in a preface. One of the best and most popular writers, S. S., never revealed that her name was Dorothy Kilner, even though she lived into a less dignified age. Her *Adventures of a Pincushion, Memoirs of*

---

[1] This method was still being used by the present writer's grandfather between 1850 and 1860, though, at the same time, Baxter was doing oil-process prints for him.
[2] See Shaylor, J., *The Fascination of Books* (1912), for many examples of sale catalogues and prices.

a Peg-top and *Jemima Placid* (to name no other works) were all
published either anonymously or under a pseudonym ; many pirates
did not even print the pseudonym. They are very unaffected
little tales : ordinary and natural and delightful. Her sister, as
M. P., wrote no less popular books. Lady Fenn, author of
Cobwebs to Catch Flies, was another secret purveyor to the
nursery : she wrote as Mrs Lovechild and Mrs Teachwell.

To pursue the history of every individual who followed in the
way which Newbery had opened would be endless. Publishers
were eager to publish, the public—full of generous projects and
prolific of new philanthropic societies—not less eager to buy. The
period which ended in 1825 may best be described as one of strife
between two principles. The 'moral tale,' in those years, reached
its highest development and perished, while the enemy it attacked—
the fairy tale, the element of fantasy and fun—emerged triumphant.

Whatever the drawbacks of the moral tale, it had one conspicuous merit, never so fully displayed at other times in the
history of children's books. All its exponents wrote admirable
English and could tell a story. They were the unadvertised lower
ranks of the bluestockings (Hannah More herself wrote treatises
and *Sacred Dramas* for children, and Mrs Chapone's *Letters* were
a classic of orthodox educational opinion). They respected themselves, their language and their subject, and, at the same time,
though Miss Pinkerton indubitably existed in many quarters, they
seldom (except in prefaces) mistook grandiloquence for ease of
style. They fall, naturally, into groups on the lines of current
thought : religious beliefs and educational theories being the influential factors.

The established church takes an important, though, from a
literary standpoint, not the foremost, place. Its protagonist in
the nursery was the redoubtable Sarah Trimmer, to whom Cal-
verley applied the only possible adjective—'good Mrs Trimmer.'
Mrs Trimmer wrote only one really notable child's book, apart from
tracts and educational works ; but that book, first published in
1786, is still being printed, published and read. Probably, it
would not be recognised by its original title : *Fabulous Histories :
Designed for the Instruction of Children, respecting their Treatment of Animals.* Here are to be met those excellent little robins
—*The History of the Robins* was the later title—Pecksy, Flapsy
Robin and Dick ; here, too, the learned pig is gravely discussed.
Even though the story is unflinchingly didactic, it has everywhere
naturalness and charm. Its earnestness is so simple, and the

author's own interest in the narrative so clear, that age has not destroyed its individuality. It contains, incidentally, a footnote which lights up, as by a flash, the whole conception of moral tales. A mockingbird is introduced into an English scene, and the author, always careful of truth, warns the reader that 'the mock-bird is properly a native of America, but is introduced here for the sake of the moral.' Volumes could not say more.

The Robins is Mrs Trimmer's main claim upon the memory of children; but, in writing about children, rather than directly for them, she wielded, at the time, even more power. As a staunch churchwoman, she was desperately afraid of Jacobinical tendencies; she believed a vast French conspiracy existed to destroy Christianity in England, and she kept a very wary eye upon both books and education. Her zeal went into details too minute for mention here. Its most relevant excursion was a very surprising adventure into fairyland. In *The Guardian of Education* (a polemical magazine she conducted from 1802 to 1804), she mentioned children's books current half a century before, among them some of Perrault's tales. A correspondent at once complained and asked for greater severity of judgment because *Cinderella* was

perhaps one of the most exceptionable books that was ever written for children... It paints the worst passions that can enter into the human heart, and of which little children should, if possible, be totally ignorant; such as envy, jealousy, a dislike to mothers-in-law (*sic*) and half-sisters, vanity, a love of dress, etc., etc.

Mrs Trimmer, who, by her own confession, had been brought up on Perrault, agreed that this lady was right. She was supported, a little later, by a tremendous manifesto of the Society for the Suppression of Vice, expressly denouncing such stories. It is difficult, indeed, to find any toleration of fairyland in these stern moralists.

The other wing of church activity was represented by Mrs Sherwood, and she, too, bore witness against fairies. In 1820, she edited Sarah Fielding's *Governess*. This, probably, is the fiercest example of editorial recension in the whole of literature; it far surpasses Bentley's revision of Milton. The changes are purely arbitrary; the book was virtually rewritten. Mrs Teachum's 'Little Female Academy' was moved from the north to the south of England, and every single story told in the course of the narrative was changed. In the original, there had been two fairy tales: these were cut out because such stories 'can scarcely ever be rendered profitable... You are, I know, strongly impressed with the doctrine of the depravity of human nature,' and it would be quite impossible to introduce that doctrine as a 'motive of action in such tales.'

Mrs Sherwood, however, is better known for her original work. There can be few persons born before about 1870 who were not brought up on *The Fairchild Family* (written in India in 1813, but not published till 1818: other parts were added to 1847). Like *The Robins*, it is still published—usually with much pietistic matter left out—and read. Of all the moral fabulists, except Maria Edgeworth, Mrs Sherwood was the best story-teller. Her English is of an extraordinary simplicity and lucidity, and, though she accumulates an immense wealth of detail in her scenes, they are invariably as clearcut and finely moulded as a good silhouette. The tremendous visit to the gallows in *The Fairchild Family* is a masterpiece of horror: it has won praise from the most unsympathetic critics. And who, reading that still vivid book, has not hungered to eat the meals generously and often described in it? No incidents in books for children, except, perhaps, a few in Grimm, and in one or two isolated stories, cleave to, and inhere in, the brain through life as do Mrs Sherwood's.

She wrote other very popular books. *Little Henry and his Bearer* (1815) is a classic of missionary work; it echoed and reinforced the efforts made by its author in India with the help of Henry Martyn. It was translated into many tongues, including Chinese. *Susan Grey* (1802) was written for the elder girls in a Sunday-school. *Henry Milner* (1822—7) was the story of a model boy and a tutor whose complacent virtues make even the egregious Mr Barlow, of *Sandford and Merton*, seem unenlightened. *The Infant's Progress from the Valley of Destruction to Everlasting Glory* was one of the numerous adaptations of Bunyan to particular beliefs and circumstances. Mrs Sherwood, in spite of a prodigiously active life of benevolence and domesticity, wrote almost to her dying day; and, with the little stories 'written up' to stock illustrations for various publishers, she has well over three hundred books to her credit. Practically, all of them of any importance introduce her strongly marked religious views.

Enthusiasts are the best mirror of tendencies; and Mrs Trimmer and Mrs Sherwood were both enthusiasts. The moral tendency is much less explicit in other writers. Least of all is it intrusive in the best of them; the best, perhaps, of all writers for children— Maria Edgeworth[1]—as her novels prove, was, also, an inspired

---

[1] See *ante*, chap. XIII.

story-teller. In sheer skill of construction alone, her *Parent's Assistant* (1796 ; enlarged in later editions), *Moral Tales* (1801), *Harry and Lucy* and *Frank* are masterpieces of the inevitable. The moral, it is true, is always perfectly clear, but it is a sympathetic moral—it is a part of universal justice and human nature. The grace and tender humour of these little tales has never been surpassed ; Scott's often quoted eulogy of *Simple Susan*—'when the boy brings back the lamb to the little girl, there is nothing for it but to put down the book and cry'—is hardly a hyperbole.

The tales were written chiefly to illustrate and work out Maria Edgeworth's father's system of education, which, in turn, was an offshoot of Rousseau's doctrine. So, also, was *Sandford and Merton*[1], in which the eccentric personality of Thomas Day found a restrained expression. It is a work now in manner and form quite obsolete, and its lack of humour, often parodied, will probably prevent its ever being seriously considered again by appraisers of children's books. But, if the character of Mr Barlow can be got over, the story—or its string of stories—is full of interest. It has a good deal of social criticism implicit in many of its details. And the episode in which Harry Sandford is called a blackguard, and fights, touches an unusual stratum of human nature for the moral tale. Day also wrote *The History of Little Jack* (1790).

French influence—as Mrs Trimmer cried in alarmed accents—was rife in the nursery. As early as 1740, a *Spectacle de la Nature* had been translated successfully. Arnaud Berquin, 'surnommé à juste titre l'Ami des Enfants,' published the work from which his 'just title' comes—*L'Ami des Enfans*—in 1782 (translated in 1783). It was successful alike in France, in French in England and in English. He wrote, also, *Le Petit Grandisson*, a sentimental tale which was translated into English, and himself (by a pleasant irony) turned Mrs Trimmer's *Familiar Introduction to the Knowledge of Nature* into French. The very popular *Looking Glass for the Mind* was a compilation from his works. By him stands another Rousseauist, Mme de Genlis ; her treatise on education, *Adèle et Théodore* (1782), was translated (1783) and her *Tales of the Castle* (1784) were very popular in an English version (1785). Miss Edgeworth, Barbauld and Aikin, and others were given a French dress, and many of the quaker tales of Mary Elliott (afterwards Mrs Belson) were produced in both tongues

[1] Vol. i, 1783; vol. ii, 1786; vol. iii, 1789; translated into French—probably by Berquin—in *an VI de la République*, 1798.

simultaneously. There was clearly, in spite of the revolution, much commerce of juvenile ideals.

Quakers were very active during this period, though most of their works have stood the test of time very ill. Mary Elliott produced a number of short tales (*Aunt Mary's Tales, Tales for Boys, The Rambles of a Butterfly* and others) between 1810 and 1820, all of which sold largely. Priscilla Wakefield has already been mentioned : she wrote some sixteen works between 1791 and 1810, the best-known being *Mental Improvement, Juvenile Anecdotes, Leisure Hours, An Introduction to Botany* and *Instinct Displayed.* She was a remarkable woman, largely responsible for the character of her grandson, Edward Gibbon Wakefield. She has fallen into oblivion ; yet, admirers from America made special pilgrimages to see her in her old age. Lancaster 'backed' her as against Mrs Trimmer. Minor fabulists include Mary Mister (*The Adventures of a Doll*, 1816), Miss Sandham, Maria Crabbe, Esther Hewlett, I. Day, Arabella Argus (*The Juvenile Spectator* and *Adventures of a Donkey*), and many others.

To another branch of nonconformity we owe poems that have become proverbial. It has been alleged that Ann Taylor's *My Mother* is the most often parodied poem ever written; but *Twinkle, Twinkle, Little Star* must run it very close; while the splendidly martial beat of

> The dog will come when it is called,
> The cat will walk away,

not merely stirs recollections of infancy in numerous breasts, but offers some shrewd facts about natural history. It is by Adelaide O'Keeffe (daughter of the minor dramatist of that name), who collaborated with Anne and Jane Taylor in *Original Poems* (1804—5); her name was dropped in later editions for unknown reasons. She wrote other and inferior volumes independently. The joint collection is the first instance of the moral tale in verse. It is modelled, avowedly, on Isaac Watts, but with the addition of dramatic interest. It contains awful warnings, poems of crime and punishment, in which a fault is proved to be a fault by some terrible lesson: a boy who fishes is caught on a meathook, a girl plays with matches and is burnt to death, and so on. The poems, in their day, were a new idea, well carried out and enormously successful. *Hymns for Infant Minds* (1808) and *Rhymes for the Nursery* (1806) are less minatory; they have a gentle piety which can never be valueless, especially when conveyed with aptness of language and metrical skill. The Taylors' poems simply say themselves; the metre is as sure and inevitable as the moral.

The gifted family of Taylor was, also, responsible for a good many other works. The father—a man of great originality and character—was an engraver and a writer. Mrs Taylor wrote didactic works: Jefferys wrote; Isaac wrote; Anne and Jane wrote, apart from their poems; their descendants wrote. 'It was almost impossible to be a Taylor and not write.'

Imitations of such a success were at once forthcoming; they have not ceased to this day. The best are Miss Turner's. Her *Cautionary Stories* are contained in the volumes prettily named *The Daisy* (1807) and *The Cowslip.*

Miss Turner alone of the Taylors' rivals has a facility equal to theirs; her metrical skill is unfailing; her language may be the merest prose, but it goes with an infectious swing. Charles and Mary Lamb, in *Poetry for Children* (1808), essayed the same kind of performance, not without success; but they hardly succeeded in going beyond prettiness and gentleness. The Taylors and Miss Turner were more resolute moralists and less unfaltering craftsmen.

One other poet may be mentioned here. William Blake's *Songs of Innocence* (1789) were produced by their creator in so peculiar a way that they had not any part in the real history of children's books. It required a later generation to rescue them, as, in other ways, Herrick and Traherne were rescued, from an accidental obscurity.

Apart from propagandists and retributory moralists, much good work of a plain kind appeared in various ways. The most eminent of these less pronounced philanthropists were Dr Aikin and his sister Mrs Barbauld, whose *Evenings at Home* is a companionable and homely miscellany. *Hymns in Prose* is a series of nature-studies in really fine prose; extracts taken out of their context might easily today be mistaken for simple passages from Maeterlinck. *Easy Lessons* are what the title claims. Mrs Hofland—*The Son of a Genius* (1816), *The Clergyman's Widow* (1812) and *Theodore* were among her best-known books— was more stagey and pompous, without the clearness of equally determined but less heavy moralists. Maria Hack, another quaker, wrote very successful *Fireside Stories* (1825), a good little moral tale, *Harry Beaufoy* (1821) and several pleasant semi-educational works. Agnes Strickland's early work—*The Moss House* (1822), for instance—was in the form of instructive fiction. Mrs Pilkington, who took to writing because of her straitened circumstances, concocted some *Biography for Boys* (1808) and *for Girls* (1809), an abridged translation of Marmontel's *Moral Tales* and, among other works, the portentously named *Marvellous Adventures: or, the Vicissitudes of a Cat* (1802).

The most illustrious author who ever wrote for children (and yet Goldsmith and Dickens and Thackeray might dispute the title, though they did not write so much) has been reserved till the end of the moralists. Charles and Mary Lamb's *Mrs Leicester's School* (1807) was certainly a moral tale; rather a dull one in itself, but interesting because of its author and its style. Equally certainly *Prince Dorus* (1811) and *The King and Queen of Hearts* (1805) were not moral tales; nor were they, for that matter, either a commercial success or a literary production in any way worthy of Lamb. They belong to the reaction against morality, and would not attract much attention but for the names of Lamb and Godwin. The *Poems* have already been mentioned. *Tales from Shakespeare* (mainly Mary's)—written for Godwin's neat little *Juvenile Library*—have a curious charm: it would be possible to read them in ignorance and be sure that they were the work of a competent writer. On the other hand, for their particular purpose, they have strong defects. The language is very long-winded for children, and the train of thought too often adult; while they frequently give a very incomplete version of the plays[1].

But though, in the eyes of reviewers and the chroniclers of the serious, the moral tale occupied the larger part of the nursery, the 'objectionable' fairy tale and its offshoots still persisted. Indeed, like the fabled camomile, the harder you trod it, the faster it grew. In the chapbooks, it and non-moral rimes—about Jack and Jill and the Babes in the Wood and their peers—had an inglorious popularity. But, in the editions with coloured illustrations which poured from the press between 1800 and about 1830, it endued fine and honourable raiment. The best extant collection of these works contains about 400 volumes, which it is obviously impossible to examine in detail. *Ex pede Herculem.* They have a strong family likeness, for the excellent reason that they were produced imitatively to suit a fashion. That fashion was set, or, at any rate, rendered dominant, by the best of all these picture books—William Roscoe's *Butterfly's Ball* (1806—7), written for his little son Robert. There is not any moral here; the book is nothing but fancifulness and graceful frivolity. There were hosts

---

[1] Lee, Sidney, preface to *The Shakespeare Story Book*, by Mary Macleod (1902).

of imitations, the best and the best-known being Mrs Dorset's *Peacock at Home* and *Lion's Masquerade*. They nearly all appeared in the same year, 1807, which reveals the imitative vigilance of the publishing trade. Of *The Butterfly's Ball* and *The Peacock at Home*, 40,000 copies were sold that year.

Akin in pictorial appeal, but of more pedestrian execution, were many facetious jingles and storybooks, for the most part derivatives of the nursery rime. *The Life and History of A Apple Pie, The Dame and her Donkey's Five* (1823), *The Gaping Wide-mouthed Waddling Frog* (1823; a version of an ancient cumulative rime that appears in *The Top Book of All*, in 1760) were among the most noteworthy. *Dame Wiggins of Lee* (1823), of this numerous fellowship, attracted the attention and eulogy of Ruskin. *The History of the Sixteen Wonderful Old Women* (1821) contains the first instance of the metrical form commonly called the limerick, and usually ascribed to Edward Lear; it is here used, with skill and finish, for some preposterous adventures.

The importance of these works lies not in their individual merits but in their collective mass. Public opinion was changing. The 'renascence of wonder' had spread to the nursery, and a new age was at hand. It is hardly possible to treat of later books within the limits of this work; their numbers and variety defy compression. The reign of Victoria, almost from its inception, saw children's books much as they are now, in their *morale* and ideals. Fresh ideas came, and new methods of production changed the outward appearance of the nursery library. But, in essentials, it was full-grown; it was emancipated from the tyranny of dogma, and the seeds of all its developments had taken root.

The modern era can be dated almost by one book—George Cruikshank's edition of the *German Popular Stories* of the brothers Grimm (1824—6). Once again, English childhood re-entered fairyland by foreign aid. The immediate popularity of the book was evidence of the change in taste. A further step towards freedom and aesthetic attractiveness was made by Sir Henry Cole ('Felix Summerly') and the enlightened publisher, Joseph Cundall, with *The Home Treasury*; while Catherine Sinclair's delightful *Holiday House* (1839) showed that not only was amusement harmless, but naughtiness itself might be venial and even pleasant. The moral tale was killed, and the crudities of the rival 'pretty gilt toys for girls and boys' were reborn and regenerated in the work of greater artists and more ambitious publishers. Morality turned itself to usefulness: the Howitts (Mary first introduced Hans Christian Andersen to English readers), 'Peter Parley' (S. G. Goodrich was the most active claimant to the pseudonym) and similar writers composed their excellent books and poems from a plain, serious point of view—they furnished matter of fact, cheerfully phrased, not matter of doctrine, aggressively insisted upon. Harriet Martineau and others wrote stories which were nothing but stories, and in which the wider range of human knowledge enormously increased the narrative interest.

The logical coincided with the historical development. Modern fairy tales began to be written, and the higher kind of levity produced nonsense. Lewis Carroll's two *Alice* books (1866 and 1872) and *Sylvie and Bruno* (1889) were works of genius; but they could not have won a hearing and undying applause if the minds of the audience had not been prepared by what had gone before. The fairy tales of Andersen, Kingsley, Jean Ingelow, George MacDonald, Ruskin, Thackeray, Mark Lemon and other writers still living were not glorified folklore; but they could not have been published—perhaps not even written—but for the glory that had come to folklore after repression. Only an age ready to be childish after having learnt the hopelessness of tacking morals on to fairy tales could have welcomed Lear's *Book of Nonsense* (1846). Magazines of wide scope came with the 'sixties. Education was utterly divorced from pleasure—in books. Concurrently with the rapid increase of the adult novel, and, as the natural consequence of the relief from insistence upon 'instruction,' stories pure and simple grew in favour and numbers—stories either of real life, like Miss Yonge's or Mrs Ewing's, or of genuinely romantic adventure, like the tales of Ballantyne, Marryat, 'Percy St John' and many others; nor were the adult works of Marryat, Kingsley, Lytton, Stevenson and others forbidden. They culminated in the modern school of juvenile fiction, adult in form and young only in style and psychology. Henceforward, indeed, children's books demand not history, but criticism.